SHADES OF RIGHT
Nativist and Fascist Politics in Canada, 1920–1940

Between the two world wars a range of extreme right-wing groups sprang up across Canada. In this study Martin Robin explores the roots and development of these groups in the 1920s and 1930s.

He begins with the Ku Klux Klan, discussing their origins, rise, and decline, and then considers other right-wing extremist political groups. Some were nativist, most notably Adrien Arcand's National Social Christian Party. Robin provides a detailed account of Arcand's organization, its origins, and ideology. He then turns his attention to Fascist influence and organization in Canada's Italian and German communities during the depression decade. He concludes with a discussion of the decline and suppression of Fascist groups following Canada's entry into the Second World War.

MARTIN ROBIN is Professor of Political Science, Simon Fraser University. Among his other books are *The Saga of Red Ryan, The Bad and the Lonely,* and *Pillars of Profit.*

To my parents
Leo and Freda Robin

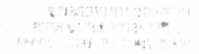

MARTIN ROBIN

Shades of Right
Nativist and Fascist Politics in Canada, 1920–1940

UNIVERSITY OF TORONTO PRESS
Toronto Buffalo London

© University of Toronto Press 1992
Toronto Buffalo London
Printed in Canada

ISBN 0-8020-5962-7 (cloth)
ISBN 0-8020-6892-8 (paper)

Printed on acid-free paper

Canadian Cataloguing in Publication Data

Robin, Martin
Shades of right : nativist and fascist politics
in Canada, 1920–1940

includes index
ISBN 0-8020-5962-7 (bound)
ISBN 0-8020-6892-8 (pbk.)

1. Canada – Politics and government – 1921–1930.*
2. Canada – Politics and government – 1930–1935.*
3. Canada – Politics and government – 1935–1948.*
 4. Ku Klux Klan (1915–   ) – Canada – History.
  5. Fascism – Canada – History.   I. Title.

FC549.R6 1991   320'.0971   C91-094962-X
            F1034.R6 1991

Cover photo: Stuart Thompson, City of Vancouver Archives,
CVA 99-1496

This book has been published with assistance from the Canada Council
under its block grant program.

Contents

Preface

This study peers into some dark corners of the Canadian political edifice between the two world wars. While Canada was beset by a variety of nativist organizations during the tribal decade of the 1920s, the focus here is on the meanest, and most notorious of the groups – the Ku Klux Klan, a toxic American transplant that enjoyed, since its inception during the Reconstruction years and rebirth during the First World War, a well-earned reputation as a purveyor of hate and violence. The Klan's peculiar intrusion into Canada, with due emphasis on the remarkable – albeit brief – craze phase in Saskatchewan, is the subject of the early chapters of this book.

The remainder deals with the politics of hate, and Fascism, during the troubled depression decade. When Canada's economic system faltered, eruptions followed and strange political organisms squirmed into the light of day. Among them were anti-Semitic Goglus, hateful National Social Christians, and brown-shirted members of the Nationalist Party of Canada who, in consort – or otherwise – with comrades in English Canada and Quebec, drilled and dreamed of a new national or world order based on the steel creed of Fascism. Sharing their infatuations, though not all of their antipathies, were small but active minorities within Canada's German and Italian communities, taken with the glories of Mussolini's Italy and Hitler's New Germany. An account of Canada's native and ethnic Fascism, its sources, and its rise and decline with the onset of the Second World War completes this study of elements of the right extreme in Canada between the wars.

Grants from Simon Fraser University's President's Research Grants

Committee and the Social Sciences and Humanities Research Council aided my research. Help was forthcoming, in various ways, from Professor Laurent Dobuzinskis, Professor John Zucchi, and Pierrette Winter, and I thank them. I am grateful, as well, to Anita Mahoney, who typed a final draft of the manuscript, and to the numerous librarians, at Simon Fraser University and elsewhere, who facilitated the research. Any deficiencies that remain are, of course, my own responsibility. I thank my family – my wife, Grace, and children, Freda, Sarah, and Mira – for their patience and understanding throughout.

Imperial Klouncil, Kanadian Knights of Ku Klux Klan
Vancouver Public Library, 8956-D

Celebration

MAY 24TH

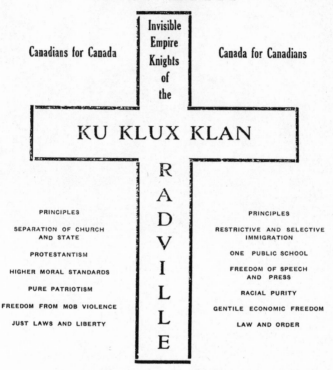

Canadians for Canada

Invisible
Empire
Knights
of
the

Canada for Canadians

KU KLUX KLAN

R
A
D
V
I
L
L
E

PRINCIPLES

SEPARATION OF CHURCH
AND STATE

PROTESTANTISM

HIGHER MORAL STANDARDS

PURE PATRIOTISM

FREEDOM FROM MOB VIOLENCE

JUST LAWS AND LIBERTY

PRINCIPLES

RESTRICTIVE AND SELECTIVE
IMMIGRATION

ONE PUBLIC SCHOOL

FREEDOM OF SPEECH
AND PRESS

RACIAL PURITY

GENTILE ECONOMIC FREEDOM

LAW AND ORDER

Speakers will include:

Rev. S. P. Rondeau   Rev. J. T. Hinds
Rev. Madill   Dr. Cowan
Rev. H. J. Kinley, B.A., and other local speakers.

RADVILLE, Sask.

Announcement of Klan meeting in Radville, Saskatchewan
South Saskatchewan Star, 15 May 1929

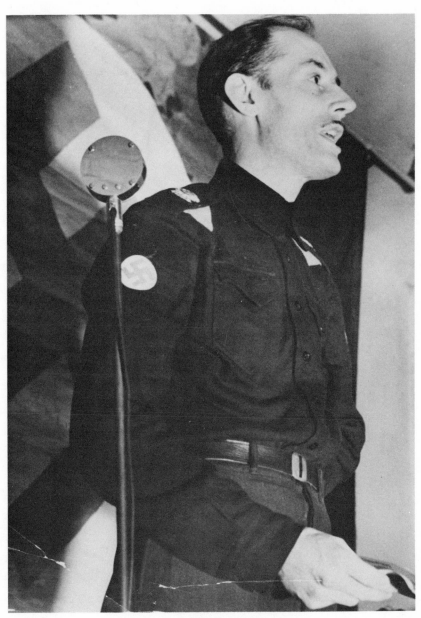

Adrien Arcand addressing a meeting
Montreal Gazette

Meeting of the National Social Christian Party, May 1938

Le magazine Maclean/L'actualité

Members of the Caboto Committee and prominent leaders of Toronto's *fascio*
Ontario Archives, AO 197

National Unity Party salute
City of Toronto Archives, GM 52654

1

Northern Knights

Men, mysteriously summoned from their homes and responding without question, are holding midnight enclaves on lonely mountain tops, in deep woodlands. The picturesqueness of history is being re-enacted before our eyes – the history of fifty years ago, the history of those dark days of reconstruction that followed the Civil War. The Ku Klux Klan is in the saddle again.

And, most strange of all, the Klansmen are riding northward. They are laughing at the claims that they will not be allowed on Northern soil. They are already there.

Victoria Daily Times,
21 Feb. 1921

On 1 January 1925, Reverend Dr C. Lewis Fowler, a former Baptist minister and ex-president of a dubious institution of lower learning known as Lanier University in Atlanta, Georgia, arrived in Toronto, Canada, on a saving mission.[1] The purpose of Fowler's visit was to enlighten his northern neighbours about threats to their national and racial purity posed by a variety of dangerous interlopers – Jews, blacks, Catholics, Central and East Europeans – all of whom, Fowler sup-

posed, were intent on undermining the supremacy of the white race and British Protestant Canada. The Reverend Dr Fowler's proposed instrument of deliverance, installed in an office on the fifth floor of the Excelsior Life building, was an organization known as the Ku Klux Klan of Kanada.[2]

In promoting and chartering his new organization, Fowler joined a host of like-minded crusaders, strung out from New Brunswick to British Columbia, who, in the mid-1920s, discovered personal salvation – and sporadic profits – in a fraternal order dedicated to the practice of the politics of hate. The incipient Canadian Klan was the visible northern extension of an organization called the Invisible Empire of the Knights of the Ku Klux Klan, a society of vigilance and regulation born in the reconstruction days following the Civil War and reborn during the patriotic frenzy of the First World War. Although the Klan appeared in the 1920s in countries as diverse as New Zealand, Lithuania, Cuba, and Mexico, only in Canada, according to the authoritative Klan historian David Chalmers, did the Ku Klux Klan evoke 'a substantial answering response.'[3]

The early Reconstruction Klan was a white-supremacist sectional organization, mainly restricted to the South and dedicated to securing the 'political impotence and social subordination' of the newly emancipated blacks.[4] The half-dozen ex–Confederate officers who gathered one day in December 1865 in the town of Pulaski, Tennessee, to pass the time, relieve their boredom, and form a social club had no other purpose, according to most accounts, than fraternal fun. The Pulaski Six barbarized and alliterated the Greek word for circle (kuklos), dabbled in secret oaths, clothed themselves in weird masks and flowing cotton robes, and dashed around town and countryside on horseback, amusing whites and scaring blacks. But the good fun turned into an awesome nightmare for blacks and their sympathetic friends at a time when the South was, in the words of an early Klan historian, 'rotten ripe' for the emergence of a potent instrument of vigilance, social regulation, and political restoration.[5]

The Civil War traumatized the South and brought to power in its aftermath political and social groups that threatened the restoration of the livelihood, status, and political power of traditional elements of white society. The carpet-baggers and the scallywags ensconced in positions of power, the Union and Loyal leagues, the emerging black vote, the dangerous militias, the state regimes imposed during the years of congressional reconstruction, together represented, according to Alabama editor Ryland Randolph, an Exalted Cyclops of the Tuscaloosa Klan, a 'galling despotism' that brooded 'like a nightmare over these southern states ... a persistent prostitution of all government, all resources, and all powers, to degrade the White Man by the establishment of Negro supremacy.'[6] The emergent Ku Klux Klan was, for a variety of Southerners – from well-bred plantation gentlemen and ex–Confederate officers to the 'pore, no-count white trash' – an instrument of deliverance from the perceived new despotism. Soon after its creation, the Pulaski den expanded into a regional organization, and its pranks gave way to ugly displays of intimidation and terror. At the Nashville convention in the summer of 1867, attended by delegates from Tennessee, Alabama, Georgia, and neighbouring southern states, the Klan was reorganized and a statement of principles adopted. What came to be known as the 'Invisible Empire' that 'sees all and hears all' was headed by a Grand Wizard. Realms, dominions, provinces – peopled by Ghouls – were presided over by an array of Grand Dragons, Giants, and Cyclops.[7] The statement of principles emphasized chivalric conduct, noble sentiment, generous manhood, and patriotism, while the organization's professed goals included commitments to protect the weak and defenceless from the lawless and violent, defend the constitution, and 'aid and assist the execution of all constitutional laws and ... protect the people from unlawful seizure and from trial except by their peers in conformity with the laws of the land.'[8]

All of this seemed as innocent as the odd ritual and diverting theatre adopted by the expanded Pulaski social club: the pointed hoods with red-trimmed apertures for the eyes, nose, and mouth; the ankle-length gowns with loose, flowing sleeves; the secret oaths and nightly torchlight parades conducted in funereal silence, single file, through the main streets of southern towns. But the Klan had its other gruesome side, with which ordinary blacks, Radical, Union and Loyal leaguers, and Republican candidates became all too familiar. A secret society 'of the nature of a vigilance committee or patrol, designed to correct such civil abuses as did not come within the purview of the law, or were neglected by the officers of the law,'[9] the Klan resorted to intimidation and violence – whippings, kidnappings, beatings, murder, and hangings – to accomplish its goals of protecting the weak and restoring law and order. There was no contradiction; it was merely a matter of definition. The weak were the classes of vulnerable and formerly dominant whites threatened by the invasion of Northerners, the betrayal of scallywags, the social sass and political activation of blacks, who in the words of General Nathan B. Forrest, Imperial Wizard, were 'holding night meetings ... going about ... becoming very insolent.'[10] The law and order the Klan sought to restore were the old ways, rules, and hierarchies menaced and undermined by 'Negro lecherousness, Negro violence, Negro insurrection, and Negro dominance.'[11]

Though professedly a non-political body, the Reconstruction Klan was, in fact, a highly political organization employing violent means to accomplish restorative ends. Throughout the years of radical reconstruction (1865–72), the Klan rode in nine states, from Tennessee and the Carolinas to Mississippi, Arkansas, and Texas, where it practised an effective politics of hate and force. 'The method of the Klan was violence,' David Chalmers wrote. 'It threatened, exiled, flogged, mutilated, shot, stabbed and hanged. It disposed of Negroes who were not respectful, or committed crimes, or belonged to military or political organizations such as the Loyal and Union Leagues. It drove out Northern school teachers and Yankee storekeepers and politicians, and "took care of" Negroes who gained land and prospered, or made inflammatory speeches, or talked about equal rights. It assaulted carpetbag judges, intimidated juries, and spirited away prisoners. It attacked officials who registered Negroes, who did not give whites priority, or who foreclosed property.'[12] As self-appointed defenders of southern honour, and progenitors of a war of terror in select wide expanses of the occupied South, the Klan ranged freely during the early years of Reconstruction rule and enjoyed considerable success in terrorizing blacks, intimidating their white sympathizers, 'normalizing' relations between the races, and blunting the 'revolutionary, social and political drives' of radical activists.[13] By January 1869, however, when Imperial Wizard Forrest instigated the Order's formal dissolution and the destruction of its records and vraiments, the Klan was a spent force. Its very success in 'normalizing' the South; the inability of Wizards and Dragons to control the anarchic forays of individual dens; the growth of an opinion opposed to its increasingly random violence; and the mass arrests, confessions, and convictions following the imposition of martial law resulted in its virtual disappearance by 1872.

Although the Klan came to be known in the present century as an institution dedicated to the protection and advancement of 100 per cent Americanism, its Reconstruction predecessor was a mainly sectional organization restricted to particular areas of the nine southern states, where it flourished during its peak years from 1866 to 1869. Within the South itself, the Klan infected some areas and avoided others. As a rule, the Klan rode best in the Piedmont, upland areas of the South where the blacks formed a smaller percentage of the population, where economic distinctions between the races were less pronounced, and where, as Chalmers noted, 'society had been less hierarchical before the war' and 'the Negro ... less respectful of the Whites ("the Pore, no count white trash") whose status was less differentiated from his own.'[14] In the North, among the states counted in the vast territories stretching to the Canadian borders and beyond, where British institutions, and law and order – British-style – held sway, the Ku Klux Klan barely existed, except as evidence, widely broadcast in the press – from Philadelphia, Pennsylvania, to Toronto, Canada – of an incorrigible, southern American predilection for violence and disorder.

Not so its successor. Where the Reconstruction Klan was white-supremicist and southern-based, its successor targeted a variety of groups – Jews, Catholics, and foreigners, as well as blacks – and extended its empire across the entire nation, and beyond. The old Klan defended southern honour; the new, comprehensive 100 per cent Americanism. Created by an itinerant Alabama preacher, travelling salesman, and professional fraternalist, who designated himself 'Colonel' after serving as a private in the first Alabama volunteers in the Spanish-American War,[15] the reconstructed Klan raged like a fever during the early and mid-years of a decade designated by historian John Higham as the 'tribal twenties.'[16]

The new Klan reflected, at the outset, the peculiar illusions and romantic predilections of its founder, a gentleman 'whose heart exuded southern sentiment as a plum does juice.' Son of a former Alabama Klan officer who earned an uncertain living as a doctor, farmer, and mill owner, Colonel William J. Simmons turned his considerable oratorical talents to preaching religion and selling garters before settling into the satisfying world of fraternal organization. The Masons, the Knights Templar, the Spanish-American War Veterans, and a host of other organizations were favoured by Simmons who, one day, consecrated himself to the task of resurrecting the white-robed night riders that 'had redeemed the Honor of the Old South.' 'I was always fascinated by Klan stories,' Simmons later recounted. 'My old Negro Mammy, Aunt Viney, and her husband, used to tell us children about how the old Reconstruction Klansmen used to frighten the darkies.'[17]

Though segregated and disfranchised in vast areas of the South, 'the darkies' were still around in large and threatening numbers when Colonel Simmons met with a group of lily-white colleagues at Atlanta's Piedmont Hotel in the autumn of 1915 to call from the dead a modernized version of the Invisible Empire of the Knights of the Ku Klux Klan. The colonel's goals, initially, were modest: to create a new, patriotic 'purely benevolent' organization, 'restricted, like many others, to White, Caucasian, native-born Americans.' The timing was excellent. Barely a week after Colonel Simmons and his colleagues lit the skies above Atlanta's neighbouring Stone mountain with the flames of a burning cross, calling the Invisible Empire from its 'slumbers of half a century to take up a new task and fulfill a new mission for humanity's good,'[18] D.W. Griffith's film *The Birth of a Nation* opened in a variety of theatres across the country. A stirring national epic based on T. Dixon's best-selling *The Klansmen*, which romanticized and eulogized the Reconstruction Klan, Griffith's film played before vast audiences and provided the colonel's revival scheme with a publicity jolt potent enough to launch the new organization.

Although Colonel Simmons energetically recruited members throughout the war years, the Invisible Empire remained, until the early 1920s, an organization more 'invisible than imperial.'[19] Simmons invented a ritual outlined in the Kloran, sold insurance and regalia to new recruits, appropriated initiation and membership fees, established a fetish of secrecy, and directed a patriotic campaign of vigilance and espionage against spies, aliens, slackers, strikers, and idlers. But the colonel was a better dreamer than organizer, and it was not until a pair of key lieutenants arrived in the early 1920s that the Klan rode anew in earnest. Edward Young Clarke and Elizabeth Tylor were perfectly suited to the task of spreading the gospel of Klannishness. Specialists in public relations and fraternal organization who handled the accounts of organizations like the Harvest Home Festivals and Better Babies Parades, as well as fund drives for the Anti-Saloon League and the Theodore Roosevelt Memorial Fund, Clarke and Tylor were joined together in an organization called the Southern Publicity Association when Colonel Simmons arrived with an offer they could not refuse.[20]

The result was a remarkable expansion of the Klan and its rapid diffusion among wide sections of American society. Clarke and Tylor were quick to convert Colonel Simmons's primitive assemblies into an effective sales organization. 'The salesmen of memberships were given the entrancing title of Kleagles,' Frederick Lewis Allen wrote. 'The country was divided into Realms headed by King Kleagles, and the Realms into Domains headed by Grand Goblins; Clarke himself, as chief organizer, became Imperial Kleagle, and the art of nomenclature reached its fantastic pinnacle in the title bestowed upon Colonel Simmons; he became the Imperial Wizard. A membership cost ten dollars; and as four of this went into the pocket of the Kleagle who made the sale, it was soon apparent that a diligent Kleagle need not fear the wolf at the door. Kleagling became one of the profitable industries of the decade. The King Kleagle of the Realm and Grand Goblin of the Domain took a small rake-off from the remaining six dollars of the membership fee, and the balance poured into the Imperial Treasury of Atlanta.'[21]

As a business, racket, and fraternal order, the Klan did marvellously well. Its growing real-estate interests were handled by a separate company, while manufacture of Klan regalia was consigned to the Klan-owned Gate City Manufacturer Company of Atlanta. Insurance schemes were hatched in a multitude of Klaverns. Searchlight Publishing Company, based in Atlanta, took care of the printing, publication, and distribution of literature. Kleagles and Kludds, recruited from Masonic and Orange lodges and from the ministry of local Protestant churches – mainly fundamentalist – presided over Lodges and Klaverns filled with the good and honest citizens of rural small-town America.[22] The secret rituals outlined in the Kloran, the initiation ceremonies, the kneeling before altars and the solemn pledges, the silent torchlight parades, the barbecues and picnics, the mumbo-jumbo that rivalled P.T. Barnum's, all tickled the fancy and relieved the boredom of a growing membership recruited from Protestant fundamentalist denominations – the United Babbitts of Small-Town America seeking diversion, fraternity, and protection from the array of evil groups and forces inhabiting post-war America. 'Its white robe and hood,' Allen wrote, 'its flaming cross, its secrecy, and the preposterous vocabulary of its ritual could be made the vehicle for all the infantile love of hocus-pocus and mummery, that lust for secret adventure, which survives in the adult whose lot is cast in drab places. Here was a chance to dress up the village bigot and let him be Knight of the Invisible Empire.'[23]

The bigots, from villages, towns, and cities, flocked to Klan Lodges not merely for reasons of fraternity and adventure. They enlisted because it vented the hates and deflected the fears of besieged Protestants of post-war America. The black was the main target of the Reconstruction Klan, a white-supremacist society feeding on traditional southern race prejudice. The reconstructed Klan took broader aim against a bundle of social threats: blacks, in the North and South, including an unsettling number of uppity 'new Negroes'; Jews from Eastern and Central Europe and urban America, singled out by Henry Ford, among others, as parasites feeding off the tender carcass of gentile America; the flood of garlic-scented, intoxicated, unassimilable, Central and Eastern Europeans competing for scarce jobs against good and honest native-born citizens; armies of Catholics collected in a supranational subversive organization centred in Rome and headed by an Italian megalomaniac. The post-war years were times of stress, social dislocation, and economic recession. The blunted reform urge, the turn inward following the European crusade, was reflected in a surge of conformity to the precept of 100 per cent Americanism and the rise to eminence of nativist organizations resembling the Know-Nothings and American Protective Association in the nineteenth century. Like its nativist predecessors, the reconstructed Klan was both a social and political organization. More than a secret society offering services and succour to the like-minded, the Klan penetrated the larger community, where it located myriad immoralities undermining the folkways of Protestant, small-town America. The revived Klan was a vigilance society and espionage system, an enforcer of Protestant folk morality neglected by the laws, legislators, and police. 'In its outlaw methods of expressing the sentiments of the community,' Siegfried wrote, 'the Klan is Fascist in inspiration. As a secret society it has made itself the rallying point of the movement, a sort of Vigilance Committee, whose duty it is to administer punishment and make examples. It is almost mob rule in favour of order, under the control of the purists of Protestant nationalism.'[24] The Klan did, extra-legally and informally, according to one writer, what the churches talked about. The result was the spread of intimidation and violence on a broad scale and the entry, out of necessity, of the Klan into the political process. Across the country, from Portland, Maine, to Portland, Oregon, errant citizens were dealt with by hooded interveners: Jews and Catholics were delivered boycotts, threatening notices, and letters of intimidation; blacks were whipped and tarred and feathered; foreigners were told to go home or were run out of town; bootleggers and gamblers were pushed off Main Street. According to Higham, 'hardly any infraction of the village code seemed too petty for intervention. An undertaker refused the use of his hearse to a bereaved family unable to pay cash in advance; Klansmen drove him out of town. A businessman failed to pay a debt or practiced petty extortions; Klansmen tarred and feathered him. A husband deserted his family, or failed to support it, or maintained illicit relations with women, or gambled too much; Klansmen paid him a minatory call. A widow of doubtful virtue scandalized the neighbors, Klansmen flogged her and cut off her hair.'[25]

As self-appointed enforcers of Protestant village morality[26] and practitioners of 'Americanization by intimidation,' the Klan entered willingly into the political process in a variety of states from Arkansas to Oregon, where governors were elected or overthrown, senators dispatched to Congress, state legislators held hostages to Klaverns and

Wizards.[27] At the 1924 Democratic National Convention, numerous state delegations were controlled by the Klan, whose participation became as big an issue as the party's choice of presidential candidate.[28]

The Klan's large presence at a national political convention signalled its remarkable advance beyond the original southern enclave. Born, and born again, in the South, the Klan had become, by the early 1920s, a national, and international, organization. 'The Invisible Empire has no fixed boundaries,' Siegfried observed, 'but moves like a storm across the country, with the center of depression changing every moment.'[29] There were, it is true, regions immune to the opportunistic infection: immigrant-laden eastern cities like New York and Boston; the black-belt areas of Georgia, Alabama, and the Carolinas; the gulf coast of Alabama and Mississippi; the mining towns of western Pennsylvania and mill towns of Ohio. The Invisible Empire tended to steer clear of the enemy, where it was powerfully concentrated.[30] But in vast other regions of 'highly fragmented disorganized Protestant America,' filled with old-stock Americans threatened by change, influx, and recession,[31] the reception was often enthusiastic: in broad areas of the southeast and southwest; in the western states of California, Washington, and Oregon; in the Rocky Mountain state of Colorado; and in pockets of the Midwest, including Ohio and Indiana, where the Indianapolis organization, headed by Wizard David Stephenson, assumed the title of 'Queen of Northern Klandum.'[32]

It was the Klan's northern surge and booster urge that carried its message of comprehensive Americanism beyond the international border into the neighbouring territory of the Dominion of Canada. Hierarchical and authoritarian at the top, the Klan was afflicted at the outset with a surfeit of anarchic local autonomy, with a multitude of Kludds, Kligrapps, Giants, and Wizards – boosters all – ready to defy headquarters, abscond with funds, and carry the message of Klandum into new and inviting territories, whether county, state, or nation. Borders mattered little, as Siegfried observed, as the Klan moved like 'a storm across the country.'[33] Drawn by the prospects of gain and thrill of conquest, itinerant Wizards and Kludds – some outcasts and renegades from state or national organizations – were ready to go anywhere, including stodgy British North America, in search of converts and dollars.

The weakest prospect of all, of course, was the province of Quebec, where Catholics comprised 80 per cent of the population. Though anti-Catholicism bulked large in the Klan's galaxy of hates, the Klan sensibly shied away from predominantly Catholic towns, cities, provinces, or nations. The Klan's entry into Quebec was brief, and invited ready exposure by an attentive press. The first reference to Klan activity in Quebec, or Canada for that matter, was an article in the *Montreal Daily Star* on 1 October 1921, announcing the organization of a branch of 'the famous Ku Klux Klan' in the city of Montreal.[34] 'A band of masked, hooded and silent men gathered recently in the northwest part of the city behind the Mountain, to discuss business,' the *Star* reported; 'of all sorts and sizes and gowned and hooded in various colors and fashions, they presented a motley appearance.'[35] The branch stumbled along for a while, applied unsuccessfully to Atlanta for regalia and organizational aid, then disappeared from sight and was barely heard from again. In late 1922, however, a series of incendiary fires in a variety of Catholic institutions, including the Quebec Cathedral and the rest-house of the Gentlemen of Saint Sulpice at Oka, Quebec – resulting in an estimated $100,000 damage and destruction of early records of New France – brought the Klan again into prominence. Allegations that Klansmen had set the blazes and were contemplating a large recruiting drive invited a spate of warnings and editorials in the Quebec press, including *La Presse*, which featured an editorial cartoon of a hooded Klansman pointing to a map of Canada and saying, 'That's where I'll establish my field of action.'[36] Despite disclaimers by Atlanta authorities, including Imperial Wizard William J. Simmons, who insisted the Klan was in no way 'responsible for incendiary fires in Canada or elsewhere,' suspicions lingered, but Quebec's incipient Klan quickly passed from the public's attention.

Maritime Klaverns enjoyed a similar oblivion. There were a few cross-burnings at Fredericton, Saint John, and Marysville, New Brunswick; rumours of stirrings in Prince Edward Island; and an offer made to an organizer of the territory of New Brunswick, where James (Dirty Jim) Lord of Saint Stephen, the representative for Charlotte County in the provincial legislature, was rumoured to be a key recruit.[37] A former insurance agent and compulsive joiner of fraternal organizations, Lord was, according to *Saturday Night* Klan prober P.M. Richards, a member of the Klan's Koncilium and successful salesman, in his home province as well as neighbouring Ontario, of Klan membership and regalia.[38]

Compared to the barren territory of Quebec, Ontario yielded improved results for Lord and fellow Klan salesmen. Home of a vibrant and extensive Orange Order, and former base of D'Alton McCarthy's Equal Rights Association, as well as the militant, if evanescent, Protestant Protection Association – a Canadian version of the nativist American Protective Association – Ontario was visited, in the early 1920s, by several itinerant organizers. As early as December 1922, the attention of Prime Minister W.L. Mackenzie King was drawn, by a Welland Catholic priest, to the activities of a Mr Marten, Imperial Kleagle of the Invisible Empire, who visited Welland and other border cities 'with the avowed purpose of starting a Ku Klux Klan in Canada.'[39] According to a Welland *Tribune-Telegraph* reader, the Klan's sole purpose in entering Canada was 'to make Canadians and Canada 100 per cent American and to spread Anti-British propaganda ... The Klan wants the whole American continent to be 100 per cent American but as long as there is any Canadian blood left to defend it Canada will remain 100 per cent British and true to British Liberty and the good old Union Jack.'[40]

The Welland probe was followed by other sorties, by an accelerating circulation of Klan literature, and by a rash of unsavoury incidents that drew the attention of authorities in Toronto, Hamilton, Ottawa, and numerous smaller towns. The Toronto tour of American organizer W.L. Higgit in 1923, during which he advocated a Canadian-American confederacy to 'establish a mandate over Mexico' and 'prohibit the dumping of European emigrants on this continent,'[41] was followed by R. Eugene Farnsworth's declaration before a Toronto audience that the Klan proposed 'not to punish with tar and feather, but to avenge wrongs ... not to indulge in law breaking but in distributing retribution. We call upon all good, native-born Protestants to join us in our work.'[42] Almond Charles Monteith of Niagara took Farnsworth's admonitions seriously enough to sign up thirty-two members before the provincial police visited and dispossessed him, in an Orange Lodge Hall, in December 1923, of a pistol, a membership list, and an expense statement of two hundred dollars covering the cost of a cross-burning.[43] Two years later, in February 1925, the *New York Times* reported the 'first official appearance' of the Klan in Ontario when provincial secretary Lincoln Goldie announced that representatives of the Invisible Empire, Knights of the Ku Klux Klan of the Dominion of Canada, and a companion organization – the Hidden Knights of the Midnight Sun of the Dominion of Canada – had applied for incorporation.[44]

It was not until December 1925, however, that several Yankee heavies, led by C. Lewis Fowler, launched a campaign so extensive that *Saturday Night* Klan watcher P.M. Richards was moved to describe the Klan as 'the most active and fast growing organization that this country contains.'[45] The source of the new thrust was a Torontonian, R. Cowan, who, in December 1925, in New York City, joined with a pair of outcast organizers in an attempt to penetrate the lucrative Canadian sales territory. Both of Cowan's partners – J.H. Hawkins and C. Lewis Fowler – had extensive American Klan experience: Hawkins, in Maryland, where he served as Grand Dragon, [46] and Fowler in New Jersey, Tennessee, Georgia, and elsewhere, where he held a variety of titles, including King Kleagle of the Realm of New Jersey.[47] The upshot of the New York rendezvous was the formation of the Knights of the Ku Klux Klan of Canada, installed, in the new year, in Toronto's Excelsior Life building with Cowan as Imperial Wizard (president), J.H. Hawkins as Imperial Klailiff (vice-president and chief of staff), and Fowler as Imperial Kligrapp (secretary). Together, the three of them formed the provincial Koncilium, or official governing body of the order.[48]

Newly constituted and chartered, the Klan penetrated in succeeding months a number of small towns and cities, including Exeter, London, Hamilton, Barrie, Sault Ste Marie, Welland, Ottawa, and Niagara Falls. For the most part, Ontario Klansmen restricted themselves to practising queer rituals, burning an occasional cross, staging an odd meeting in odd dress, and spreading, through the spoken and written word, the gospel of a white, Protestant, gentile, Canada. Speakers, and publications like the *Kourier* and *American Standard,* both American-based, warned of the take-over by Jews of 'all the industries of the continent,' including the silk business and radio industry 'established and invented by gentiles.'[49] Readers of the *American Standard*, a semi-monthly of a 'particular latrine sort,' edited by Fowler, enlightened its Ontario readership about 'Jew Monies Urging Sex Vice' and 'Jewish Corruption in "Jazz," ' while the *Kourier*, alert to the dangers of cannibalism, red menaces, and black lechery, wrote about 'Human Corpses Eaten by Reds' and 'Negro Bucks Hugging and Violating Young White Girls.'[50] Catholics received special attention. Papal plots and Columbus Day frauds, the subversion of civil government by 'Romanists,' the antithesis of 'Monarchical' Romanism and free 'Republican American,' were favoured subjects of pamphlets widely circulated by the *American Standard*, which prescribed a variety of remedies for the ills of society, including 'the exclusion from America of the Jews who work against Christianity,' revision of citizenship laws to wipe out 'the alien vote,' and 'return of the negroes to their homeland of Africa.'[51]

However strident and bizarre their printed propaganda, the Ontario Klansmen remained, for the most part, mundane fraternalists eager to disassociate themselves from the reputation of violence and lawlessness, tar and feathers, that plagued their American relatives. They were not entirely successful. Despite protestations of commitment to law and order, honest-to-goodness Canadianism, British fair play, and full autonomy from their American brethren, scattered incidents here and there provided ample fuel for press and authorities to tar the local Klan with the brush of American disorder. There was the episode in Sarnia, where George Garner, an American anti-Catholic evangelist, and a side-kick named King, who wore the insignia of an American Orange Order and publicly blessed the Ku Klux Klan in Sarnia, desecrated the St James Roman Catholic Church by the forced removal from its tabernacle of 'a gold ciborum, twelve consecrated hosts, one benediction host, and the pyx in which it was contained.'[52] A fiery cross, ten feet by five feet and constructed of saplings, provided an eerie entertainment for residents of the mountain hamlet of Ancaster, where, according to the local police commissioner, a Chicago-based organization known as the African Brotherhood of America was considering the erection of a home for 'colored children and aged colored folk.'[53] In the Belleville fairgrounds, a cross was burned to intimidate supporters attending a public meeting sponsored by the

South Hastings Liberal candidate Charles Hannah.[54] S.B. Dawson, president and manager of the *Belleville Intelligencer*, was visited by a Klan delegation, headed by a Reverend George Marshall and Cannif Ruttan, both claiming to be high officers of the Klan, who suggested that he dismiss a Catholic printer in his employ; the visit moved Dawson to denounce 'the ugly-headed bigotry and intolerance ... raised in Belleville.'[55] George Devlin was shot at during a wedding reception at Sault Ste Marie 'by a person or persons who left a fiery cross as evidence of authorship.'[56] According to *Saturday Night*, Klansmen in Sault Ste Marie launched a campaign to drive Italians from employment in the big steel mills and other local industries and fill their places with native Canadians and British-born.[57] In Barrie, William Skelly and two officers of the local Klan branch were implicated, in June 1926, in an attempt to blow up St Mary's Roman Catholic Church. Several years later, the cohabitation and impending marriage in Oakville of a 'colored man,'[58] Ira Johnson, to a young Oakville white girl, Isabelle Jones, inspired several Hamilton Klan members to 'uphold British justice and to further promote good citizenship' by lighting a cross outside Johnson's aunt's home before entering and removing Miss Jones to the care of her 'heartbroken and frantic mother.'[59] For his part in the rescue operation, William E. Phillips, a Hamilton chiropractor, was convicted, fined fifty dollars, and later imprisoned for three months under a law prohibiting the wearing of masks publicly at night.[60]

The Klan's desultory attempts at intimidation and skirmishes with the law, duly reported by a press seeking sensational linkages with their American cousins, seriously hampered the Ontario organizational campaign. According to A.D. Monk, the Klan attracted the attention of the RCMP. 'With the greatest law force in the world – the Royal Canadian Mounted Police – interested in their meetings,' Monk wrote, 'their conclaves will, if they continue at all, be as peaceful as a church social without even the thrill of ice cream.'[61] From the moment of the Klan's appearance in Ontario, the local police were alerted to Klan mischief and tracked its affairs. 'Men can organize for fraternal purposes,' Ontario commissioner of police, General V.A.S. Williams, noted in February 1925, 'and if they keep within the law they're not likely to be interfered with. The moment, however, that the Ku Klux

Klan breaks the law we will drop on them just as sure as anything.'[62] Deputy police commissioner A.J. Cuddy, noting that the Klan was organizing in Niagara Falls, Hamilton, Toronto, and Montreal, stated: 'It does not matter how much they call themselves British. We know who they are, have their names, and they are an American crowd from across the line who are doing the organizing. We know how long they have been organizing.'[63] Newspapers and journals as diverse as the *Belleville Intelligencer, Montreal Gazette,* Toronto *Globe, Saturday Night,* and *Canadian Forum* never failed to heap scorn and ridicule; to condemn the 'offensive buffoonery,' dismiss the Klan as a 'scheme to sell cotton nightgowns to boobs,'[64] or warn, as *Canadian Forum* did, that a Klan revival 'begins with mumbo-jumbo and ends with bloody murder.'[65]

Like their tame Ontario counterparts, the bulk of western Klansmen did not advance much beyond the mumbo-jumbo phase. The attention of Manitobans was first drawn to the Klan in 1922 when St Boniface College was burned to the ground and ten students lost their lives.[66] The fire, like others at Catholic institutions across the country, was preceded, in the last two months of 1922, by a notice of warning, signed by the Klan, and followed by a denial, from Imperial Wizard William J. Simmons of Atlanta, that 'the Ku Klux Klan is any way responsible for incendiary fires in Canada or elsewhere.'[67] Two years later, during the summer of 1924, an Oklahoma Klansman, J.R. Bellamy, visited Winnipeg and informed his local audience that Canada was 'being overrun with undesirable sects and beliefs' and that 'we to the south have decided that you will welcome our aid in freeing you from these sinister influences.'[68] Bellamy vowed that, in two months' time, 'the sheeted figures of the local subjects of the Invisible Empire will ride at night.' Despite Bellamy's claims, the Klan barely stirred in Manitoba until the summer of 1928 when Daniel Carlyle Grant, a former street-railway operator and Moose Jaw Klan organizer, who claimed Brandon citizenship and American Klan experience, announced that several thousand Manitobans had recently enrolled[69] at an inaugural meeting in the Norman Dance Hall, on Winnipeg's Sherbrooke Street, attended by 150 Klansmen and Klanswomen – without robes, hoods, or burning crosses – and an eager *Free Press* reporter. Grant launched a campaign to clean up, purify, and 'disembowel' Manitoba's capital city of 'vice, wantonness, graft and corruption.'[70] He condemned 'the scum of papist Europe,' hailed 'Gentile Economic Freedom,' attacked the Jews as 'slavemasters ... throttling the throats of white persons to enrich themselves,' and warned against the 'intermarrying of Negroes and whites, japs and whites, chinese and whites. This intermarriage is a menace to the world,' he concluded, 'if I'm walking down the street and a Negro doesn't give me half the sidewalk I know what to do.'[71]

For all of Grant's bombast and bigotry, the Manitoba campaign of the Imperial Knights of the Ku Klux Klan fizzled. 'Despite the fact that the K.K.K. styled themselves as the "Invisible Empire," ' a *Regina Leader* reporter wrote of the Normal Hall Klan meeting, 'no invisibility was noted at the meeting tonight. None was attired in the white robes and hood so commonly associated with the Klan, nor was the conspicuous cross of the K.K.K. in the hall.'[72] When the *Winnipeg Free Press* published the next day an elaborate front-page account of the Norman Hall meeting, featuring an eight-column headline reading, 'Ku Klux Klan Plans To Clean Up Winnipeg,' Grant was horrified and apologetic, claimed he was misquoted, denied criticizing Winnipeg police officials or demanding their dismissals, and returned to Saskatchewan where, following the election of Conservative J.T.M. Anderson as premier, he was awarded a provincial government job, in Weyburn. When the Liberals returned to power in Saskatchewan in 1934, D.C. Grant was fired, and assisted, in 1935, in Tommy Douglas's successful federal campaign. Grant eventually joined the Social Credit Party.[73]

West-coast Klansmen fared marginally better than their Manitoba counterparts. Before the real push came, in the autumn of 1925, there were two brief attempts to penetrate the British Columbia market. A first notice of the Klan's arrival appeared in the 17 November 1922 edition of the *Cranbrook Courier* in which H. Moncroft, 'Chief Klansmen, Canadian Division,' invited applications for membership in Cranbrook Klan No. 229. Moncroft required that all applications be in writing and stipulated that 'all applicants must be British subjects between the ages of twenty-one and forty and must be qualified horsemen possessing the necessary skill and daring to uphold the law and order at all costs.'[74] The equestrian announcement fell, apparently, on deaf ears, since nothing was heard, in succeeding weeks and

months, of Cranbrook Klan No. 229. It did invite, however, a response
– from N.A. Wallinger, the MLA for Cranbrook, who 'was unable to get
any evidence or information';[75] from Attorney General Manson, who,
in a fit of dark humour, threatened to turn the Klan 'loose on the
enforcement of the Liquor Act'; and from the *Victoria Daily Times*,
which wrote, 'the police plan to keep an eye on all mystic rites performed according to the rules of the order at night around some
burning brands in lonely woods. They say they will have something
to say as soon as members of the Klan, garbed in white shirts, begin
to dash around on horseback at night and attempt to interfere with
the rights or seek to dictate terrorism how persons should conduct
themselves or their business in any community.'[76]

The Klan's second sortie, in Vancouver, in October 1924, invited
further public indifference and official derision. The fault, in this
instance, may have lain with the organization's obliviousness to the
forty-ninth parallel. Applications circulated by Klan organizers
pledged allegiance to the constitution of the United States, defended states' rights, and listed a Lincoln, Nebraska, mailing address.[77]

A more serious invasion was launched in the autumn of 1925, by
a band of renegades from the neighbouring states of Washington and
Oregon, where the Klan had gained a considerable membership,
political clout, and notoriety in past years. Chief of the northwest
invaders, who appointed himself Imperial Klazik of the Canadian
Knights of the Ku Klux Klan of the Realm of British Columbia soon
after passing the customs booth at Blaine, Washington, was Luther
Ivan Powell, former resident of Shreveport, Louisiana, and the chief
architect of the Klan's thrust into the Pacific Northwest, from California, in 1921.[78] By the time Major Powell deserted Oregon for the
greener Washington and British Columbia pastures, the Klan had expanded in Portland and environs to twenty-five thousand members;
created the Skyline Corporation, charged with the task of building a
huge skyscraper in downtown Portland; helped defeat an incumbent
Republican governor; and aided in the passage of a compulsory public-school initiative that undermined state support for parochial
schools, mainly Catholic.[79] The president of the state senate, and
speaker of the House, K.K. Kublai – a Harvard graduate and business-

man whose initials earned him a free membership in Klan local No. 1 – owed his position, in part, to Klan support.[80]

Major Luther Powell's enthusiasm and good works were felt in Washington and, briefly, in British Columbia, in succeeding months. After falling out with Oregon Grand Dragon Fred Gifford over funds, power, and Atlantic control, Powell set up business headquarters in the Securities Building in downtown Seattle and appointed himself King Kleagle of Washington and Idaho. By most accounts, the energetic major did a real good job on the Washingtonians. Moose and Odd Fellows' halls, Masonic temples, and lodges of the Knights of Pythias in Walla Walla, Spokane, Olympia, Tacoma, Seattle, and numerous small towns throughout the state were filled with hooded convocants who agitated, paraded, socialized, and sometimes supped in restaurants, like the Klansmen's Roost on Seattle's Westlake Avenue, 'where kozy komfort and komrade kare kill the Grouch with Viands Rare.'[81] A demon organizer, Powell established a hundred-man Klavern aboard the battleship U.S.S. *Tennessee*, anchored in Puget Sound, and ran, from his sixth-floor offices, the Women's Klan, the State Command for the Realm of Washington and Idaho, Seattle Klan No. 4, and the Junior Order of the Ku Klux Klan.[82] Of particular interest to emigrant Canadians was the Royal Riders of the Red Robe, a Klan affiliate that later merged with the National American Krusaders.[83] Run by a naturalized Canadian, Dr M. Rose, the crimson-robed Royal Riders was home to foreign-born, naturalized Americans of the right sort: 'a real patriotic organization to Canadians, Englishmen, and other White, gentile, Protestants.' Greeks, Italians, Balkans, and other undesirables were barred.[84]

Luther Powell's Washington stint ended, as usual, with recriminations, secessions, protests against Atlanta's 'despotism and autocracy,' and a migration northward into British Columbia. Joined by a Reverend Keith K. Allen, a former chief of detectives of Oregon Grand Dragon Gifford's Klan machine, the Major visited Vancouver during the autumn of 1925 and set up shop at 'Glen Brae,' a Matthews Street Shaughnessy mansion, built in 1910 by lumber tycoon William Lamon Tait and containing seventeen rooms, six bathrooms, a ballroom, and an elevator.[85] In the following months, and years, British Columbians were treated to an energetic campaign, with uncertain results. Klaverns were set up in Vancouver and New Westminster, and an island push was made by Captain W.D. Laycock, DSO, who claimed, from his headquarters in Victoria's Dominion Hotel, support in Nanaimo, Ladysmith, and Duncan.[86] Meetings and parades were held, now and then; an occasional cross burned; bonfires lit at Kitsilano Point and elsewhere; regalia displayed; and an assortment of officers appointed, including Exalted Cyclops, Klockards, Kludds, Kligrapps, and Klaziks. Among its active members, the Klan counted a few stray clergymen, including Reverend C.E. Batzold, later arrested for fraud, and the prominent Reverend Duncan McDougall, pastor of Point Grey's Highland Church and a confirmed opponent of booze, political corruption, Catholics, Jews, and Orientals.[87]

The Klan's program was a modest and modified sort calculated to win the hearts of loyal, law-abiding British Columbians. 'We don't go in for lynching or taking the law into our own hands,' Kleagle Laycock informed a gaggle of inquisitive reporters. 'We are bound by oath to conform to the lawful and constitutional authorities. We stand for the supremacy of the White race, the exclusion of the Orientals, the elimination of dope, and are after the political grafters. The Klan is built on the principles laid down in the twelfth chapter of Romans.'[88]

Among the variety of available target groups, the B.C. Klansmen favoured the Orientals. Coast Jews were a mere ethnic speck, blacks virtually non-existent, Central Europeans diffused, and Catholics hardly numerous in a province where separate schools and French-language education were minor or absent issues. There was, however, a vibrant tradition of anti-Orientalism, which the Klan gladly tapped. Defined, during succeeding waves of hostility preceding the Klan's arrival, as 'rice-eating animals unclean in habit and leprous in blood,'[89] Chinese, Japanese, and East Indians had been attacked, barred, intimidated, segregated, and deprived of basic civil, economic, and political rights by a succession of provincial regimes catering to prejudiced and aroused constituents of all classes and political parties. 'Vancouver, B.C.?' a New York *Evening Post* editorial queried, following British Columbia's 1907 anti-Oriental riots. The response, in the same editorial: 'Yes, ten thousand B.C.'[90] There was, indeed, little new the Klan could add to the abuse heaped on the heads of the beleaguered

Orientals, who, in 1921, comprised a mere 7.5 per cent of the provincial population.[91] But the Kludds and Klaziks contributed as best they could, in their own small way. Scarcely a meeting, demonstration, or utterance passed without reference to yellow perils and necessary prescriptions, including 'the complete prohibition of Asiatic immigration into Canada, repatriation of Asiatic immigration ... repatriation of all Asiatics at present domiciled in this country and expropriation of their property here.'[92]

While the majority of British Columbia politicians shared the Klan's views on Orientals, few, if any, were ready to welcome its arrival or encourage its growth in a province in which the 'Oriental Question' had been satisfactorily resolved politically by a succession of effective discriminatory and exclusionist policies. The official policy in British Columbia, as elsewhere, was to monitor the Klan and tolerate its activities as long as there is no breach of the law or attempt to usurp the enforcement of 'law and order.'[93] Not all politicians, however, were content with a laisser-faire approach. Soon after hooded congregants began flitting among the salons of Glen Brae mansion, a local labour MLA from Burnaby, F.A. Browne, dragged the Klaverns into the House by moving an amendment to the address in reply to the speech from the throne, condemning the Klan as 'a fraudulent, alien, terrorist organization' bent on promoting 'religious hatred among our citizens' and substituting 'lynch law for duly constituted authority.'[94] Browne's resolution, which urged the government 'to take the necessary steps to restrain this insidious movement and bar its membership from all elected or official positions under the Crown,'[95] sparked a lively debate and invited heated intervention from both Attorney General Manson and Premier John Oliver, who cited 'outrages' in the United States 'attributed to the Klan' and noted it was 'not for the good of Canada that we should have a self-constituted voluntary organization which claims to be superior to the law of the land.' While the premier opposed Browne's resolution – which was eventually withdrawn – he did agree to press the federal immigration authorities to bar the entry of Klan organizers, a strategy endorsed by an attorney general troubled by the Klan's insistence on changing 'the good word Canadian to Kanadian.' Manson asked, rhetorically, about the need for 'alien literature to urge our people to be ordinary, decent, law-abiding citizens'; voiced his suspicion that Klan literature, preaching 'true Britishness,' had been written by an American; and marvelled at 'Americans coming here to tell Canadians how to preserve British ideals.'[96] In support of his patriotic diatribe, the attorney general read to the House choice extracts of letters from an unidentified American correspondent, outlining the schemes and scams of Luther Powell and his associates who 'worked Oregon out and when the field became too tame for them now seek work of destruction in British Columbia.'[97]

As it turned out, Luther Powell's Canadian venture proved brief and unrewarding. After he returned south on business, Powell's reentry into Canada was barred by the immigration authorities, who, following an appeal, allowed him a thirty-day visit. Powell's subsequent communication, by telegram, to the premier, requesting leave to appear before the House to answer charges made against the Klan, was dismissed as 'too preposterous to be considered,'[98] a response endorsed by the mass of British Columbians who pursued their lives, loves, and hates, in subsequent years without the aid of the Ku Klux Klan. There is no evidence that Major Luther Powell stayed his appointed thirty days in British Columbia, before pursuing possibilities elsewhere; or that the few Klaverns that servived after him into the 1930s counted more than a handful of members.[99]

As in British Columbia, the Alberta Klan's limited success was not attributable to any absence of organizational zeal, or the unavailability of easy target groups. When Klan emissaries first crossed the Rockies from British Columbia in 1924, they discovered a surfeit of visible and vulnerable groups sifted and shunted, during previous decades, to the base of the social pecking order. Perched at the pinnacle were Anglo-Saxon Protestants from eastern Canada, Britain, and the United States – the true Alberta natives well-represented among the economic and political élites of the province. Relegated to the lower social rungs were a collection of garlic-addicted undesirables, subject in varying degrees to the extensive and persistent prejudices and discrimination of a frontier province: blacks, limited to a mere 1,524 in the entire province in 1911 by a restrictive Department of Immigration catering to local groups who wanted 'no dark spots in Alberta';[100] Chinese, segregated, boycotted, unfairly taxed, and designated dangerous competitors of native white labourers; Jews, concentrated in urban merchandising and other trading activities, including cattle-buying, and perceived by some fellow Albertans as Shylocks, robbing the Salt of the Earth; Central and Eastern Europeans, including Doukhobors and Mennonites, rated a notch or two above the Orientals and blacks and thought by local élites, and reformers, to possess a bundle of moral and social defects.[101]

With such a feast of targets, it is little wonder that the itinerant Klansmen expected wonderful results from their Alberta campaign. The first Alberta Klan rumblings were heard in Calgary in April 1923, when the local police and Roman Catholic authorities received letters signed by the Klan, threatening to burn down Catholic-owned buildings in the city.[102] In the next few years, several British Columbia–based organizers began soliciting memberships and collected several thousand dollars from approximately a thousand Albertans, who paid ten dollars each for the pleasure of contemplating masks, hoods, bedsheets, and burning crosses – then left the province.[103] The abortive British Columbia invasion, based, as the *Vermilion Standard* noted, on the 'cupidity of its promoters and the gullibility of the public,'[104] was followed by a more sustained effort, launched in late 1929 by a pair of nativist agitators drawn to the foothills from neighbouring Saskatchewan. A former brakeman employed by Canadian National Railways, the secretary of the Railway Trainmen's Brotherhood, member of the Dominion Council of the Great War Veterans' Association, and a First World War Canadian Expeditionary Force veteran, R.C. Snelgrove toured the province for five months, between October 1929 and February 1930, establishing several Klaverns in small centres of southern Alberta before departing for places unknown. His colleague, John James Moloney, a professional anti-Catholic agitator from Ontario, stayed around several years and managed to convince several thousand Albertans that the Ku Klux Klan had a role to play in the emergent West. Like their prairie cohorts to the east, the Alberta Klansmen were pro-British, 100 per cent Canadian, anti-immigrant, and, above all, anti-Catholic. Their allegiance to the British Crown was 'unquestionable.' Only 'white Protestants' could join the provincially chartered organization committed to the principle of 'Protestantism, separation of Church and State, pure patriotism, restrictive and selective immigration, one national public school, one flag and one language – English.'[105] Immigrants from Central and Eastern Europe, who arrived in the tens of thousands following conclusion of the railways agreements of 1925, were designated as diseased and crime-ridden, likely candidates for prisons and insane asylums, job robbers, unassimilable, and ignorant of 'the ideals of Canadianism.'[106]

To ease the anxieties of Protestant Albertans, competing with immigrants for jobs, space, and status, and with eastern Canadians for a share of the national wealth and power, J.J. Moloney's Alberta Klan offered the comforting old Ontario nostrum of anti-Catholicism. The evils inflicted on native Albertans, the threats to civil society, morality, and the national polity, were traceable to an all-encompassing conspiracy of a Catholic minority against the Protestant majority, a conspiracy trumpeted in Moloney's *Liberator*, an anti-Catholic rag that replaced his Saskatchewan-based *Western Freedman*.[107] It was the Klan's view that the Pope in Italy, and the Quebec-based Catholic church, sought total domination of the Dominion of Canada, nationally and regionally, East and West.[108] The threat was both demographic and political. A high birth rate, a high rate of mixed marriages resulting in assimilation to the Catholic spouse's religion, and the increasing flow of immigration from Catholic countries threatened the demographic and social dominance of the Protestant majority, just as Quebec's inordinate political power and the infiltration of Catholics into key positions in the federal Parliament, Cabinet, and public service menaced the Protestants' political hegemony. The problem was especially acute in the western provinces, in danger of losing their British and Protestant character, their status as young Ontarios, because of federally sponsored increased immigration, separate-school, and minority-language impositions, and eastern political economic preponderance, which enabled Ottawa to dictate inimical language and religious policies to subject provinces.[109]

Moloney's frontier crusade began in the Vermilion district, an Orange Order centre, then spread to the far corners of the province. Within months, Klan locals appeared in disparate villages and small towns in the Vermilion district, in Hanna and Stettler, in Camrose,

Wetaskiwin, Red Deer, Ponoka, Irma, Rosebud, and sundry other places. In all, according to Palmer, Klaverns were organized in more than fifty villages and towns, and membership counted between five thousand and seven thousand persons.[110] The Alberta Klan drew mainly, though not exclusively, from the lower-middle class and took hold in areas where Catholics were in a distinct minority. A key supporting role in the spread of the Moloney Klan was played by the Orange Order. Alberta Orangemen shared the Klan's anti-Catholic phobias, and their leaders, lodge halls, and membership lists became key organizational aids.[111]

Alberta's major cities, Calgary and Edmonton, were not immune from the brief Klan infection. Calgary was invaded in the fall of 1930, and several Klaverns were established during a five-month organizational drive.[112] Edmonton – Rome of the West – received special attention, since it dominated the largely Catholic north country and served as the seat of the host of tax-free institutions – convents, monasteries, seminaries, colleges, churches, and hospitals – feeding, according to Moloney, off the labour and taxes of native Protestant Albertans.[113] Moloney worked the Edmonton crowds for several years, delivered hundreds of speeches, organized a handful of local Klaverns, distributed thousands of copies of his *Liberator*, and succeeded, according to his own testimony, in saving 'over seven hundred boys and girls from the dangers of mixed marriages.'[114] On the eve of the 1931 Edmonton municipal election, local Klansmen launched a virulent slander campaign against incumbent Major Jim Douglas, the son of a Protestant minister and formal Liberal MP who, it was alleged, had capitulated 'to the magic of Rome' and condoned 'a plot … on foot of a Jesuitic nature to bring our city under the police leadership of a R.C. Colonel Bryan.'[115] The Klan's intervention was instrumental in Douglas's loss to Labour candidate Daniel K. Knott.[116]

The Edmonton municipal intervention was not typical of the Alberta Klan's political role. For the most part, the Alberta Klan stayed clear of municipal and provincial politics, and politicians, at all levels, avoided identification with the militant Protestant organization. Unlike neighbouring Saskatchewan, where the governing Liberals were tied to a federal party linked to 'Catholic power,' Alberta was governed provincially by the independent United Farmers of Alberta (UFA). Nor did readily exploitable sectarian or religious issues present themselves during the brief time of the Klan's Alberta growth. In Alberta, unlike Saskatchewan, both the separate-school and French-language questions were muted, while the immigration flood of the late 1920s, which the UFA itself came to be wary of, was linked to the federal Liberal party. Limited in size and mum in politics, the Alberta Klan was dismissed as an inconsequential organization by Premier J.E. Brownlee, who insisted 'the government had not given any instructions to the police, or any other agency or body, to make any investigation in the matter, for no need of such action has arisen.'[117] The premier's views were shared by agriculture minister George Hoadley, who noted that the Klan did not dispute the government's position on sectarian schools, and queried 'What else could the Klan have against our government?'[118] Hoadley felt that any 'political action the Ku Klux Klan may take in Alberta is likely to be along Dominion lines.'[119] Beyond submitting questionnaires to candidates, and burning a cross or two to celebrate the election of the Conservatives to the House of Commons in the 1930 general election, the Klan stayed clear of Alberta federal politics.[120]

Despite its minuscule size, import, and political participation, the Alberta Klan, like its fraternal brothers elsewhere, received considerable and often sensational press coverage. Whatever respectability the Klan sought was confounded by a press cognizant of its sensational legacy and newsworthiness. Lit crosses, petty incidents of intimidation, and court wrangles all received due attention and contributed to the Moloney Klan's rapid slide into oblivion. When cartoonist Archie Keyes caricatured the Drumheller Klansmen, who counted as members approximately forty businessmen, including prominent coal-mine owners, the Klan responded with a burning cross on his front lawn.[121] Fred Doberstein, a Lacombe blacksmith prone to amorous escapades, was kidnapped, tarred and feathered, and threatened with death by a group of local robed citizens who claimed Klan membership. When C.B. Halpin, editor and publisher of Lacombe's weekly, the *Western Globe*, editorialized against the Klan, he received a note signed by the local Klan secretary, threatening severe punishment, including the burning of his house and business to the ground. Members of the Communist-controlled Mine Workers Union of Canada, locked in a bitter dispute in the Crow's Nest Pass district in 1932, were greeted with burning crosses, threatening 'Beware Reds' signs, and a stray bullet by opponents identified as Klan members.[122]

Perhaps the Klan's most adverse publicity arose from the legal scrapes of Imperial Wizard J.J. Moloney with opponents, fellow Klansmen, and the Crown. No stranger to the courts in Saskatchewan and Ontario, where he pursued his early anti-Catholic career, Moloney left an Alberta trail dogged with a succession of widely broadcast suits, countersuits, convictions, and brief incarceration, for libel, slander, and theft.[123] Demoralized and exhausted by court fights involving, so he maintained, 'pure frame-ups activated by forces whose wrath I have incurred through fighting for principle and right,'[124] Moloney abandoned Alberta, and the moribund Klan, in the mid-1930s, before returning in 1938 to fight William Aberhart, the secular provincial pope, who resided in the 'Palatial Macdonald Hotel,' drove around in a 'high-priced Buick car,' and proved his 'Nazi love of the spectacular ... decking his chauffeur in an elaborate uniform.'[125] Moloney's Alberta sojourn proved inconsequential, and his return to fringe hate politics was interrupted by further court fights in Saskatchewan, Manitoba, and Ontario. During the early war years, he dropped entirely from public sight. Legend had it that the former Imperial Wizard expired sometime around the war's end, after summoning a priest and reconciling himself to the church he had so vehemently abandoned in his youth.[126]

2

The Sasklan

It seems ... almost unbelievable that, in the great British Dominion of Canada, a gang of adventurers can come here and do what they have done, take thousands of dollars out of the pockets of innocent men ... They have had the audacity to tell us what the Union Jack stands for. Imagine a few Canadians going over to the United States and starting in on a campaign to tell the people what their flag stands for and what the Constitution of the United States means. They would be tarred and feathered and railed out of town.

Magistrate J.H. Heffernan, Regina Morning Leader,
8 May 1928

One wintry day in November 1926, in the city of South Bend, Indiana, an ex–Exalted Cyclops accepted an offer to help launch a Christian benevolent association in the distant Canadian province of Saskatchewan.[1] The offer was made by a fellow Indianan, Lewis A. Scott, who had just returned from a visit to Toronto, Canada, where he had obtained from Wizard C. Lewis Fowler the exclusive right to organize the Saskatchewan Realm of the Invisible Empire of the Knights of the Ku Klux Klan.[2] Though a seasoned organizer, Scott, and his son Harold, who joined the enterprise, lacked the gab and blarney needed to mesmerize the hordes of yawning rubes. For that reason Hugh Finley (Pat) Emmons – alias Pat Emory – was enlisted. Formerly Exalted Cyclops of Valley Klan No. 53 of South Bend and St Joseph County, 'Pop' or 'Dad' Emmons, as he was sometimes known, had been at or near the centre of Klandom in a state where David Curtis Stephenson, the ex–socialist stump orator turned Grand Dragon, had grown so powerful that judges and senators, congressmen and governors, fell over one another, seeking, or avoiding, his support.

As the Scotts knew, Emmons was no piker. He was a Klan pro, there and active during the brief dark age of Stephenson's ascension; a witness, during the years 1923 to 1925, to the roadhouse orgies, the boycotts of Jewish and Catholic businesses, the parades of robed rubes in Winamac and Kokomo, the tarring and feathering, the ballot-box stuffing, the vigilantism of the Horse-Thief Detective Association, the antics of Muncie's Chicken Blood Gang, and the weird machinations in Stephenson's Indianapolis Klan Castle, an elaborate suite of rooms in the Kresge building where the Grand Dragon feigned consultations, on a fake telephone line, with President Warren Harding.[3] All of this Pat Emmons, the multi-chinned, jolly, ex–saloon keeper, gambler, horse-race addict, and evangelist, knew and talked about to a senatorial committee following his removal from the Klan in 1926. When the Scott boys arrived at Pat Emmons's door with a Saskatchewan offer, they found the ex-Cyclops dog-tired of hate and politics and ready for a clean Klan geared to spread the message of Christian benevolence in territories distant from Winamac and Kokomo. So, Pat Emmons took up the Scott boys' offer, travelled with his companions in the dead of winter to Regina, Saskatchewan, and, in late December 1926, set himself up at the local Empress Hotel.

Business, it turned out, was brisk. Within a fortnight, the message was out, Klan literature delivered to hundreds of households, and numerous contacts made with potential consumers. In return for a ten-dollar membership fee plus three dollars covering the first quarterly dues, recruits received, with a delivered receipt carefully marked 'donation,' application forms, secret passwords, and distress signals to warn insiders of the presence nearby of dangerous outsiders. At

large, well-attended gatherings, advertised as revival meetings of the
Ku Klux Klan, the audience was treated to a real feast: ushers in full
regalia flitting among the aisles; occasional crosses, burning or fitted
with electric light bulbs; solemn renderings of the national anthem
and 'Onward Christian Soldiers'; and feisty speeches from Emmons
– sometimes introduced as a Canadian, from south of Toronto – outlining the values, purpose, and prospects of the 'greatest Christian,
Benevolent Fraternal Organization ... in the world today.'[4] Emmons
accentuated the positive, informing his audience, as he did at a
Grand Theatre meeting in late May 1927, that the American Klan
had enrolled 8.5 million members and controlled 42 of 48 states,
while its Canadian affiliate, at a recent conference in Toronto, counted as members 'some of the greatest men in the Dominion.'[5] He
mentioned the good things that the Klan stood for: pure manhood
and pure womanhood, Protestantism, white supremacy, law and order, 'a close relationship between pure Canadians,' separation of
Church and State, and 'one language – English, from coast to coast.'
And he warned the 'Jap,' Negro, and 'Chinaman' who threatened to
drive 'white Canadians ... out of business' that, unless proper respect
was shown for the laws of the country and the Union Jack, they would
be forced to leave Canada, 'and leave it forever.' While obedience to
the law was enough, apparently, to secure freedom from deportation,
it was not sufficient to gain membership in Regina's newest fraternal
association. 'If you want to go into the Israelites,' Emmons noted, to
loud applause, 'you have got to be a Jew. If you want to join the
Knights of Columbus, you've got to be a Roman Catholic. If you want
to join the Ku Klux Klan, you have to be a white Protestant.'[6]

Many did join, and the Klan local in Regina, where the provincial
headquarters was established, counted at its peak nearly a thousand
members. Not content with pickings in the Queen City, the Scott-
Emmons gang, or their representatives, slipped into the countryside,
to the villages of Ceylon and Radville in the south and along the road
to Moosamin, then east to Indian Head, Grenfell, Whitewood, Kip-
ling, South Qu'appelle and Fort Qu'appelle.[7] Southwest of Regina,
stretching to the Alberta border, Klan locals sprouted in succeeding
months in wondrous profusion: in Mossbank, Limerick, Lafleche,
Kincaid, Hazenmore, Swift Current, Shaunavon, Assiniboia, and

other centres, including the tiny village of Woodrow, which counted 153 Ku Klux Klan members – including 31 women – of the total population of 218.[8]

The Klan's major southern operation was directed at a community, located at the juncture of the Moose Jaw River and Thunder Creek, first charted by Captain John Palliser in 1857 and named, according to one account, after the Cree settlement of Moosichapishanissippi.[9] A railway centre forty miles away from Regina, nestled in a quiet valley at the end of the CPR 'Cinderella' run, Moose Jaw was known among the local board of traders as Saskatchewan's 'Friendly City.' 'It will quickly raise money for a girl who loses her legs beneath a freight train,' wrote one observer, 'or a baseball player who loses an eye in a game.'[10]

When jolly Pat Emmons first showed his bulbous face in Moose Jaw's Empress Hotel in the early weeks of 1927, he found the local residents both friendly and ready. Recently promoted from Klan Klockard to Kleagle by King Kleagle Lewis Scott, Emmons worked the Moose Jaw territory on a commission basis. Out of every thirteen dollars raised – ten dollars initiation fee and three dollars for the first quarterly dues – he could keep eight, out of which local expenses were to be paid. After complaining of insufficient remuneration and returning briefly to South Bend in protest, Emmons was awarded the full thirteen dollars, pending issuance of a charter from Toronto. For every new member enrolled in the surrounding sales territories, he was entitled to a further two dollars.

Emmons employed tried and trusted techniques in enrolling the locals, some of whom had been solicited earlier, with uncertain results, by Klan organizer J.S. Lord and Captain Monger. Emmons had better luck. As membership expanded, an office was leased and staff hired, including Charles Puckering and J. Van Dyck, a Melville policeman.[11] Potential customers were sent mysterious postcards, with the inscription: 'Your fondest aspiration after this old world is Heaven, but before you go we need you in Henman Building three eleven.'[12] Ministers of the church, including Reverend T.J. Hind of the First Baptist Church, were offered 'deadhead' honorary memberships and a fee to speak at Klan rallies. Several accepted. 'Here is how he won a minister in Moose Jaw,' a curious rabbi later wrote. 'He made him an honorary member in the Klan. A few days later, he offered him $25 to deliver a lecture on Christian ideals to a Klavern (the Klan meeting). He increased his lectures, and continued the fees, till the Minister was doubling or tripling his income by Klan lectures. Within a few months, as Pat put it ...the minister who had made his calls on a bicycle began to make them on a "Big Six" while smoking fat cigars, and the Minister had become an enthusiastic Klansman.'[13]

The Klan's appeal in Moose Jaw was not restricted to needy ministers of the gospel. Emmons's salesmanship, his blarney, his references to large contributions and the imminent arrival in southern Saskatchewan of Henry Ford and Thomas Edison – both reputed Klan supporters – his announcement that the large-hearted Scott boys themselves had kicked fifty thousand dollars into the Klan kitty, pleased the locals and eased the entry of hundreds of labourers, clerks, professionals, and housewives into the Klavern, which eventually counted two thousand members.[14] Local businessmen were favourite targets, and many joined the ministers of the gospel as deadhead members. A lavish banquet, paid for out of membership fees, resulted in a raft of new members.

In soliciting support, Emmons fed the locals a mixed diet of pros and cons. On the positive side were glowing statistics about American Klan growth; the Canadian expansion; the warming prospects of developing indigenous Klan institutions, including a home and restaurant; the principled commitment to 'one flag, one school, one race and one language.' 'He came into my office,' a local businessman recalled, 'and told me he was organizing a Christian foundation which would ... help business. I don't remember whether he once mentioned the Klan but he talked and talked. I told him I was busy. He beamed and went right on. Finally, I offered him five dollars.'[15]

When it came to antis, Emmons was flexible, and tailored his hates to suit local preferences. 'We sent people antis,' he later recalled. 'Whatever we found that they could be taught to hate and fear, we fed them. We were out to get the dollars and we got them.'[16] While blacks, Jews, Catholics, Japanese, and Chinese received their due swipes, Emmons saved his major ammunition for the sinners – the bootleggers and dopesters, prostitutes, pimps, and gangsters, congregating in and around Moose Jaw's renowned red-light district.

Among the several streets and avenues of vice in western Canada
– Annabella Street in Winnipeg, Third Street in Lethbridge, Sixth
Avenue in Calgary, Avenue C in Saskatoon, and Kinistino Street in
Edmonton – Moose Jaw's River Street ranked near the very top, or
bottom. Adjacent to the retail-business district and running smack
into the CPR station, River Street hosted the trainloads of harvesters,
homesteaders, railwaymen, and commercial travellers eager to forsake the stale tedium of CPR day coaches for evening couches warmed
by the ample bosoms and rumps of waiting madames. In post-war
Moose Jaw, it has been noted, moose, live or stuffed, were outnum-
bered by the boozeries, gambling dens, and whorehouses of River
Street, and by thieves, dope pedlars, and gangsters, some of whom
travelled the Soo line northwest, from Chicago and Minneapolis, to
hide in the distant haven of small-town Saskatchewan.[17]

River Street thrived, in part, because the police winked, and here-
in lay the Klan's opportunity. Although waves of reformers took aim
at River Street, the local police, headed by Chief of Police Walter
Johnson, took their tithes and looked the other way. The Johnson
administration was both lax and stable, so entrenched that the wholesale arrest, in 1924, of the force's entire night shift on charges of
breaking and entering failed to disturb the chief's serene hold on
power.[18] Emmons's clean-up campaign, in defence of 'pure manhood and pure womanhood,' apparently changed all this. Chief
Johnson and his deputy were fired by the police commission, which
granted the retiring chief, who had served twenty years, a month's
severance pay.[19] In subsequent months, and years, Klansmen and ex-
Klansmen were elected to the Moose Jaw city council, which maintained a stern moral vigilance, banning, among other things, the
employment of white girls in Chinese restaurants.[20] Evidence of the
Klan's glory days in Moose Jaw could be found in subsequent years
on the wall of a ward of the Moose Jaw hospital, which displayed a
Klan plaque, thusly inscribed: 'Confederation ... Law and Order,
Separation of Church and State, Freedom of Speech and Press,
White supremacy.'[21]

The culmination of the River Street campaign was the great Kon-
klave of 7 June 1927, held on Moose Jaw's south hill, where reporters counted between eight thousand and ten thousand attendees

from towns as disparate as North Battleford, Indian Head, Yorkton, and Saskatoon. The four hundred Klansmen from Regina who arrived on a special CPR train were chauffeured to the rally site in a cavalcade of cars. White-robed volunteers collected memberships and donations, while the crowd was treated to prayers, hymns, a fiery sixty-foot cross, and harangues from an assortment of Klockards and Kleagles, including the Reverend David Nygren of Chicago who, on the golden wheat fields of rural Saskatchewan, warned of the danger of intermarriage with blacks.[22] The featured speaker was Emmons, who announced a plot to rub him out. 'The River Street gang have threatened to murder me,' he disclosed. 'Let them do it. Then I ask you, brothers and sisters, to skin my body and make it into a drum. Then beat the drum in River Street to the glory of God and the Ku Klux Klan.'[23] The Reverend T.J. Hind pleaded that Pat Emmons was too valuable to lose, and volunteered his own body and skin, in place of his revered colleague's.[24]

Whatever momentary thrills the promised sacrifices and fiery crosses provided, they were not enough to quell, in succeeding weeks, a growing uneasiness among Moose Jaw fraternalists that the Ku Klux Klan of Saskatchewan somehow lacked a sound, honest, and democratic foundation. While the Scott boys and Emmons persisted, throughout the summer and early autumn of 1927, with their missionary work, they found local members increasingly impatient and sceptical about the Klan's benefits and direction. Questions were asked: whether they were selling the real Klan, where the money was going, when charters would arrive from Toronto, and when representative committees would be struck to look after local affairs. Evasive answers prompted further inquiries, complaints, banishment of dissidents, and representations to the provincial authorities, including Premier James Gardiner, who corresponded with Ontario authorities about the Klan's antics, then dispatched an investigator to Toronto and Indiana in pursuit of relevant background information.[25] As the Gardiner file grew, so did the trepidations of the Scott boys and Pat Emmons, who announced a deadline of 15 September for prospective Klan members, beyond which fees and dues would rise to twenty-five dollars per person – a ploy that provoked a mild run on memberships.[26]

In early October, the Scott-Emmons gang, possessed of the remains of an estimated 169,000 hard-earned prairie dollars, quietly
left town for Toronto, where a tall tale of deficits and sacrifices was
related to the Imperial palace officers.[27] Of the Scott boys' activities
following their Toronto visit, little was known. Several accounts had
them in Australia, burning crosses and peddling regalia.[28]As for Pat
Emmons, he visited Florida, for sun and rest, then returned home,
to face public exposure and extradition attempts, in South Bend, Indiana.

The prairie troubles may have disheartened Toronto's Imperial officers, but not enough to cause them to abandon the Saskatchewan
territory. Following the disengagement of the Scott boys and Emmons, the Saskatchewan charter reverted to Lewis Fowler and
friends, who quickly dispatched a new emissary to the waiting wheat
fields, an agitator with considerable Klan experience, both north and
south of the border.[29] 'We have had Mr. Emory [Emmons] with us
and he went from us,' the Reverend T.J. Hind intoned in a biblical
cadenza, 'but there has come another – a noble gentleman – and so
far as we know, he is a true man.'[30]

The object of the Reverend Hind's transferred adulation was J.H.
Hawkins, who arrived in Saskatchewan in early October following
hurried consultation with Imperial officers. Dispatched as a trouble-
shooter, Hawkins was an old Klan hand who took aim at trouble spots
then, more often than not, shot himself in the foot. Formerly a
schoolteacher, Hawkins was, by his own account, a member of the
bars of Alabama and Virginia, and an optometrist who served as
president of the Virginia Optometrical Society.[31] Among his several
philanthropic ventures was a stint as head of something called 'the
Mecca of America organization' that 'cared for orphans and dependent children in Alabama.'[32] Preferring burning crosses to social work,
or fitting spectacles, Hawkins embroiled himself in Klan politics in
Maryland as Grand Dragon; in Solebury, Pennsylvania, as Exalted
Cyclops; and finally, in Toronto, Canada, where he briefly served as
Lewis Fowler's Imperial Klailiff following the Klan's entry across the
border in the winter of 1925.[33] After falling out with Fowler, flirting
with the rival Ku Klux Klan of the British Empire, and visiting Virginia to tend a sick wife, Hawkins returned to Toronto in 1927 and rec-

onciled himself with Fowler in time to earn the Saskatchewan assignment.

With Hawkins in the field, residents of Moose Jaw and Regina – and their country cousins – quickly forgot about Pat Emmons and his transgressions. A mellifluous speaker and grand entertainer, Hawkins drew crowds and converts at numerous meetings in villages, towns, and cities across the province. The message was old Yankee gruel – white womanhood, racial purity, gentile economic freedom, threatening hordes of Jews, blacks, Orientals, and immigrants – modified for Canadian prairie consumption. 'I am loyal to Canada and the British Crown,' he informed a rapt Saskatoon audience,

> a Canada composed of those strong virile men of the North, the Nordic or Anglo Saxon race ... men whose forefathers fought for this country by expenditure of British blood and treasure, whose sons died in Flanders field that it might continue ... men who eat meat once a day and who require a bath once a week, but I am not loyal to a Canada composed of men who jabber all the tongues that destroyed the effort to build the Tower of Babel, men who tighten their belly-band for breakfast, eat spaghetti and hot dog and rye bread for lunch and suck in his limburger cheese for supper – men who crowd our own people out as the example at Yorkton by offering to work for ten cents an hour, men who come to Canada with tags on them telling you their destination. God deliver Canada from men of this character ... let us see that the slag and scum that refuse to assimilate and become 100 percent Canadians is skimmed off and thrown away.[34]

The Virginian's robust Canadianism sold well at meetings, from Estevan to Omega, adorned with huge crosses lit with electric light bulbs set on platforms draped with Union Jacks. When critics challenged his nationality, Hawkins responded with lame statements of adherence to Canadian laws and the constitution, patriotic fulminations, references to his Canadian-born wife, and, on occasion, unfurlings of a full-sized Union Jack that he kept, neatly folded, in the pocket of his coat.[35] 'An alleged optometrist,' recalled journalist C.H. Higginbotham, 'he looked like every southern gentleman is supposed to look, but whether he was a gentleman from anywhere is questionable. I remember him best at a meeting in the Moose Jaw skating rink, where there was standing room only with about three hundred present. He was a tall man with a mane of white hair. His frock coat and striped trousers seemed as appropriate on him as a peak cap and overalls on a Saskatchewan farmer. His features were good, voice unctuous. I was sitting at the press table wearing the look of intense boredom young reporters are supposed to wear. I was writing nothing because at that time we were instructed to write nothing unless all hell broke loose. Doctor Hawkins glanced down at the press table. "Look at him," he roared, "he's not taking down anything. He's in the pay of the Jews and Roman Catholics." '[36]

The Hawkins road show was a key factor in the Klan's recovery following the widely publicized Scott-Emmons débâcle; a revival enhanced, in 1927–8, by the hustings forays of a stump orator who complemented the Yankee's oratorical bluster with a good dose of old Ontario ultra-Protestant anti-Catholicism.[37] John James Moloney, it appeared, knew his enemy well, though whether he spoke truthfully about what he knew was another matter. Born on Friday the thirteenth, of Irish-Catholic parents, in Hamilton's north end, 'where men were men and police went in pairs,'[38] Moloney was raised in St Mary's Catholic parish and attended as a youth St Mary's Separate School, run by the sisters of St Joseph. After serving as an altar and sanctuary boy under Father Thomas Coughlin – who later became Detroit's infamous, bigoted, radio priest – he continued his studies at St James College in Berlin, Ontario, and later, at a seminary in Montreal, where he undertook the 'last lap' in studies for the priesthood.[39] Sadly, it was never completed. Felled by a bout of flu, Moloney was removed to the Hotel Dieu and placed under the care of the Sisters of Petite Soeur de St Joseph.[40] 'One in particular, a very pretty maiden, took a liking to me,' he later wrote. 'Poor Petit, as she called me and pretty soon I found that the iron bars and the cold grey walls of a Convent did not securely encase the ideas of popery.'[41]

The Hotel Dieu temptation began a deep slide, culminating in Moloney's heretic conversion to militant Protestantism. After joining the Catholic Extension Missionary Canvassers' Band in Toronto, and working as subscription agent for the *Catholic Register,* Moloney soon ran afoul of a Father O'Donnell, the *Register* editor whose alleged anti-British and pro–Sinn Fein views he found repugnant. Matters quickly came to a head. Moloney was dismissed, and sued for libel and lost wages while O'Donnell responded with criminal charges, alleging the theft of one hundred dollars in retained subscription monies. After a bitter court trial, Moloney was acquitted, 'fell into irreligion,' converted to Protestantism in August 1922 – after consulting Dr William Patterson of Toronto's Cook's Presbyterian Church – and consecrated what remained of his erratic career to denouncing 'the errors of Romanism.'[42] A fiery orator, cognizant, or so he insisted, of 'the secrets of Romanism,' he spent the following three years touring Protestant and Orange Ontario – from Woodstock to Grimsby, Holstein to Orangeville, Seaforth to Exeter – exposing Papal plots and Catholic conspiracies. 'It was the crusade of the word of God,' he wrote, 'against what I believed to be the Scarlet Woman – Rome.'[43]

It was not until early February 1926 that J.J. Moloney took his crusade beyond Ontario's borders to distant Saskatchewan in pursuit of an old nemesis betrothed, in Moloney's view, to the Scarlet Woman. A violently anti-Liberal participant in the general election of 1925, Moloney trailed W.L. Mackenzie King to Prince Albert, where he supported an independent Conservative candidate in a federal by-election that returned King to the House of Commons.[44] After entertaining assorted Gyros, Round Table Knights, and Orangemen in Victoria, Moloney returned to Saskatchewan in May 1927, in time to attend a post-mortem meeting of a militant, Protestant organization recently deserted, and publicly embarrassed, by a trio of Yankee hucksters.[45]

J.J. Moloney's discovery of the Ku Klux Klan – and the Klan of Moloney – was a matter of mutual benefit. Lacking a true, blue, Canadian mesmerizer to balance the gab of Hawkins – and vocation of Emmons – the Klan discovered in Moloney's fiery eloquence a tonic for the vapid back-sliding of Saskatchewan's Protestants. As for Moloney, one anti-Catholic platform – with or without burning crosses – was as good as another – and the more, the better. 'In Canada,' he later wrote, 'we have the Klan, the L.O.L., R.B.P., Orange Young Britains, True Blue, Irish Protestant Benevolent Society, etc., all doing splendid work in their own way to cope with Rome political.'[46]

In the weeks and months following Moloney's entry into the Klan wars, Saskatchewanians turned out, and took note. A tireless orator ready to harangue three meetings a day, Moloney combed the province for both audiences and readers of his *Western Freedman*, a weekly hate sheet, 'uncompromisingly opposed to the Catholic Church as a system,' with a circulation claimed to exceed twelve thousand.[47] While Hawkins targeted a wide range of Yankee Klan demons – including blacks, Jews, and Orientals – Moloney concentrated mainly on the Catholics. Sometimes advertised as 'the Canadian Orator' or an 'ex-cleric,' he exposed at tens of meetings across the breadth of Protestant Saskatchewan a vast Catholic conspiracy to enslave ordinary, decent Canadians. Embattled, according to Moloney, throughout the world, including Italy, where Mussolini threatened the hegemony of 'the Wolf of the Vatican,' the Catholic church had sinister designs on Canada, 'looked upon as the strongest and fastest growing Roman Catholic country in the world.'[48] Within Canada, the church's prime base was Quebec, which 'true to its ultra conservative church has fought all reforms, refusing their women the vote, denying the widow her dowry rights, insisting on their own church controlling the labour unions, jailing bible sellers, torturing exponents of free speech ... and exempting church-owned property from taxation.'[49] Church-inspired iniquities were the legitimate concerns of fellow Canadians, not merely because Quebec was part of Canada. Vigilance was needed because, outside of Quebec, the church was 'enacting a form of gradual aggression which, if permitted to continue, will envelope the whole of Canada.'[50] The cradle war, growing intermarriage, privileged wealth, and governmental access secured and enhanced both Catholic power and the favoured position of the French language, which appeared on postal money orders, train tickets, paper money, corn-flake boxes, drug-store supplies, and national airwaves, 'much to the disgust of the West and Ontario.'[51] Most threatening of all was the insinuation of the church's message into the minds of the young through Catholic penetration and control of the educational system. As the Klan meetings heated and multiplied during 1927 and 1928, so did J.J. Moloney's fables – of governmental aid favouring Catholic orphanages; of the withholding of jurisdiction over natural resources from western provinces by the federal government until Catholics could be guaranteed privileged separate schools; of nuns teaching in public schools; of crucifixes replacing Union Jacks in classrooms; of Protestant children kneeling after hours before crucifixes and idols in basements of rural churches serving as public schools.[52]

The great Catholic conspiracy was not restricted to a growing demographic and institutional penetration of Saskatchewan life. So pervasive was the threat that it entered the very oratorical arenas, halls, skating rinks, and hotels frequented by 'the Canadian Orator' whose speeches and writings were filled with revelations of plots, against both Protestantism and the person of J.J. Moloney. Few people, J.H. Hawkins informed a Prince Albert audience, 'knew the dangers which faced Mr. Moloney and others who went about the country rousing Protestants to do their duty.'[53] The inquisition began in Ontario, where, according to Moloney, he was wrongfully dismissed from gainful employment, criminally prosecuted, spied upon at meetings, burnt by acid added to his shaving water, and, at Rothesay, the target of an attempt by 'some wild ones' to blow up the local Presbyterian church.[54] The prairies, it appeared, were no safer, and Moloney's trail through Protestant, Catholic, and mixed Saskatchewan was strewn with incidents: a sheet thrown over him on the stairway of a Catholic-owned hotel in Macklin; 'letters galore' to Ontario asking whether he had stolen money or seduced women; a shower of overripe eggs at Meota; a priest-inspired petition at Macklin; vandalized posters in Luseland; a shooting threat and blow on the head with an iron bar in Melville; a plot to heave rocks and sabotage the lighting system of a hall in Mazenod; a stand-off with a gang of '40 semi-intoxicated half-breeds led by two heelers.'

Moloney's altercations sometimes reached the courts, or reverberated over the air waves. When he delivered a pair of guest lectures over Saskatoon's radio station CHVC, in January 1928, slandering the Catholic church, the station's director, responding to critics, banned future broadcasts. Soon after, an application for renewal by the International Bible Students' Association, which held the station's broadcast licence, was refused on grounds that several of their programs had featured 'religious matter of a controversial nature.'[55] A quarrel with a heckler at a public meeting in Radville became so heated that it led to a court trial, to hear charges that Moloney had struck his opponent. The judge, who heard the case in a local movie theatre that served as a court of law, thought otherwise, and dismissed the charges. When Gerald Dealtry, the feisty editor and publisher of the Saskatoon weekly *The Reporter*, described Moloney in the October 1927 edition as a 'spreader of a putrid kind of propaganda,' a 'last chance ballahoo artist for the Ku Klux Klan,' a 'coward who obtained tonsure' for the purpose of escaping conscription – noting, in conclusion, that 'even the Pope in Rome could not make a silk purse out of a sow's ear'[56] – Moloney sued for libel, and won. Dealtry was fined two hundred dollars.

Moloney's antics and oratory, like Hawkins's, were big news in Saskatchewan in the months following the departure of the Indianans for greener fields. Sent westward by God, or by some omniscient Imperial Wizard, Moloney and his miraculous appearances and frenetic touring among wheat-field Protestants contributed to the Klan's revival following its dark moment of humiliation, a revival secured by an array of local leaders enrolled by Emmons who remained committed to Klan principles, which, in the words of a local Imperial Wizard, 'of themselves made an appeal to many people in Saskatchewan.'[57] Though the alien mesmerizers commanded star billings at numerous Klan meetings, the mundane organizational work fell to the diligent locals who, in late October 1927, revived and reconstituted the abandoned organization. 'Here, then, was a fine, ready-made organization of 40,000 or 50,000 men and women,' a *New York Times* correspondent wrote, following the flight of the Hoosiers, 'waiting for new owners, and even though it was conspicuously lacking funds, the opportunity was too good to be passed by.'[58]

The site of the Saskatchewan Klan's resurrection – as an indigenous organization – was Moose Jaw's Bijou Theatre where, on 26 October, delegates met at a convention to create 'an organization covering the whole province to arrange for the carrying on of the work of the Klan.'[59] According to the official statement of a newly constituted publicity committee, 'a complete organization was affected and officers elected, everyone of whom must be Canadian born.' A financial statement, audited by a leading firm of chartered accountants, was submitted for the consideration of the delegates who, after a lengthy debate, rejected affiliation with the eastern Canadian organization and 'finally decided to continue as a Saskatchewan Klan.'[60] Organizational work was to be directed solely by the local Imperial Executive, with organizers and lecturers placed 'on a straight salary basis plus expenses,' and no one connected with the organization was entitled 'to receive any commission.' Robes, hoods, tar and feathers, it seems, had no place in the prairie Canadian organization. 'The Klan in Saskatchewan did not pattern its work after that of the United States,' the Imperial Wizard later announced, 'and its members do not wear the long robe and helmet of the Klansmen to the South ... and what is reported to have happened in the United States has no more connection with the organization here than the flood of Bible days with the high water of the Mississippi in 1927.'[61] According to a prominent Conservative lawyer and Klan sympathizer, the renewed Klan was 'not an alien organization at all. There were a few alien organizers to start it but they have all been driven out with the exception of Hawkins, who is hired on a salary. It is an entirely Saskatchewan organization with no affiliation with any organization in Canada or the United States.'[62]

Saskatchewan's born-again Klansmen did not waste time in lighting crosses and spreading the word to the far corners of the prairie realm. Where the Scott-Emmons gang focused mainly on the south, the reborn Klan enlisted thousands more in the central and northern regions of the province. Southeast of Saskatoon, locals sprouted in Melville, whose chief of police joined the order, and Yorkton – the Flower Town of Saskatchewan – whose flower children, boys and girls, were threatened, according to a Klan correspondent to the local newspaper, by a variety of noxious weeds, including 'a Chinese den, a so-called Club, and a pool room.'[63] 'Gentlemen, it is near time to weed the garden,' Mayor A.C. Stewart and fellow aldermen were exhorted, 'and don't have mercy on the weeds.'[64] Between Saskatoon and Yorkton, meetings were held and members enrolled in an assortment of towns, including Qu'Appelle, Kenaston, Nokomis, Wadena, Watrous, and Esterhazy. A similar thrust occurred west of Saskatoon in the tiny villages of Alsask, Luseland, and Unity, as well as the larger towns of Biggar and Kerrobert, where Local 91 became an active Klan centre.[65] North of Saskatoon, between Hudson's Bay Junction in the east and Unity in the west, at least fifteen Klan locals appeared overnight, while southeast of Prince Albert, the towns and villages of Melfort, Tisdale, Kinistino, and Star City – where one-third of the entire adult population enrolled – boasted large and active locals. Home to a politically active Catholic population and a militant Orange Lodge, Prince Albert was a favourite meeting place of Klansmen like Moloney whose activities were closely monitored by the wary local member of Parliament, W.L. Mackenzie King.

Nor did the spreading infection escape Saskatchewan's northern metropolis, Saskatoon, where the Klan became an active force following the first attempts at organization, by Pat Emmons, in June or July 1927. According to Emmons, credit for the Klan Saskatoon surge was due to Dr J.T.M. Anderson, the provincial Conservative party leader who first approached the Indianan in the foyer of his two-room suite in Moose Jaw's Empress Hotel, in May 1927, with a proposition to accept a 'Dr. Smith of Moose Jaw who was then a candidate for the Provincial Legislature as a member of the Klan and use the Klan organization in the city of Moose Jaw to secure his election.'[66] During subsequent meetings, Emmons insisted, Anderson urged the Indianan to organize a Klan in Saskatoon and furnished him, and organizer Charles Puckering, 'with the names of a number of persons in this city of Saskatoon ... in order to lay the foundation for the organization of the Klan at Saskatoon.'[67] At Regina's Champs Hotel, and at the Western and Flanagan hotels in Saskatoon, further alleged meetings took place at which Emmons received a list of names of potential Klan members, including 'a number of Liberals who ... had served the Liberal Party in the province of Saskatchewan for many years and had been entitled to certain favours from the said party which they had not received.'[68] According to Emmons, Anderson felt 'these Liberals were in a state of mind where he thought they could easily be influenced to join the Klan and work against the government.' It was Emmons's job to get them into the Klan, Anderson reportedly explained, after which he 'would do the rest himself.'[69]

Pat Emmons, and his successors, did draw Liberals and Conservatives into the growing Klan, which, by 1929 counted 129 locals, spread across the length and breadth or rural, and urban, Saskatchewan. The provocative oratory of Hawkins and Moloney; the sermonizing of the deadhead ministry; the banquets, parades, and lit crosses; the revival meetings from Esterhazy to Climax – charged with prayers, patriotism, fraternity, and hate – and the circulating literature and wide press publicity pushed the Ku Klux Klan into the homes and hearts of an estimated twenty-five thousand Saskatchewanians, a membership that compared favourably in size with the two pre-eminent cooperative organizations: the Saskatchewan Grain Grower's Association, which counted approximately thirty-five thousand members at its peak, and the United Farmers of Canada (Saskatchewan Section), numbering barely thirty thousand during the late 1920s.[70] 'That high-pressure American organizers, activated by the prospect of obtaining money from the credulous,' a *Queen's Quarterly* correspondent wrote at the peak of the Klan craze, 'could enroll tens of thousands of ordinary decent citizens in an organization with a record such as that of the Klan in the United States is an illuminating sidelight on a people's mentality. Still more illuminating is it when one realizes that a large proportion of the people of the province who have not joined the Klan have taken the movement so seriously as to cause it almost to be regarded as part and parcel of the social and political scheme of things.'[71]

3

Glory Days

That the Ku Klux Klan had entered, however tenuously, into the 'scheme of things' in Saskatchewan in the waning years of the 1920s is beyond doubt. Among the queer collection of Sons of England, Odd Fellows, Masons, Knights of Columbus, Orangemen, Wheat Poolers, B'nai B'rithers, and more, that composed the province's quilt of fraternities, the Klan came to occupy, albeit briefly, an accepted, and not inconsequential, place. Formed, then abandoned, by a trio of Hoosier hucksters, the Klan drew to its Klonvocations and cross-burnings, during the months following its 'curious and fantastic' renaissance, converts from diverse walks, strata, and genders of Saskatchewan life. Klanswomen, like Moose Jaw's Margaret Wilkinson, were drawn by the example of their husbands' membership, by discounted initiation fees and dues, and by opportunities to sponsor and attend Klan bakes, whist drives, luncheons, theatricals, and musicals.[1] Among the smitten menfolk, there was a sampling of small businessmen, clerks, and salespersons; manual workers, including mechanics, truck drivers, railwaymen, carpenters, plumbers, and labourers; and a few farmers, including employees of the wheat pool and feed and grain-elevator companies. 'The majority of those responding to the initial call of the Klan in Regina,' Calderwood concluded from a study of directories of membership lists, 'were of the social level of artisans and clerks, with a few entrepreneurs, mostly petty, and a few unskilled workers thrown in.'[2]

Though the Saskatchewan constituency was drawn mainly from

the lower-middle strata, the Klan was not devoid of members of local prominence. Several doctors, lawyers, teachers, and justices of the
peace became members, joining the twenty-odd clergymen and ten
politicians noted by Calderwood in his study. Among the many
municipal officials who joined, there were, according to Calderwood,
eight mayors, eleven village overseers, seven reeves, twelve secretary-
treasurers, and thirty-seven councillors.[3]

The Klan's officialdom did not differ substantially from the rank
and file in social composition. They were predominantly lower-middle class with a healthy additional mix of professionals and tradesmen. With the notable exceptions of Moloney and Hawkins, they
were almost exclusively native Saskatchewanians. The Imperial Wiz-
ardship fell to J.W. Rosborough, the Ontario-born Orangeman and
United Church member who resided in Buffalo, New York, before
immigrating, during the First World War, to Saskatchewan, where he
was employed with the provincial government, and in the private
sector as an accountant.[4] Rosborough's underlings had similar pet-
ty-bourgeois credentials. Scattered among the Cyclops and Kligrapps
were salesmen, opticians, clerks, carpenters, railway employees, doctors, mayors, reeves, teachers, and farmers. The Klan's secretary,
Imperial Kligrapp Charles H. Ellis, was a Canadian National Tele-
graphs operator and, later, a provincial government clerk.[5] Leading
organizers included Moose Jaw's street-railwayman D.C. Grant;
Melville's ex–police chief Thomas Pakenham; and Charles H. Puckering who, following a Klan career as secretary, organizer, lecturer,
and director of extension, served in an executive capacity with several milling companies, including in the positions of manager, accountant, and secretary-treasurer of Western Grist and National
Mills. Well into the Depression, Puckering sat on the Moose Jaw City
Council.[6]

For lecturers, the Rosborough Klan recruited a willing corps of
ministers, men like the Reverend Dr Keeton, the Qu'Appelle United Church minister who addressed a Klan banquet on 'the example
of the life of Christ';[7] Reverend L.B. Henn of Macrorie, who announced, at a public meeting, that the 'primary aim of the Klan is
to render service to one and all'; or the Reverend W. Titley, of Imperial, who urged 'every true Protestant to support the Klan ... an

old organization that had been revived to defend Protestant rights and truths.'[8] While as many as twenty-six ministers from a variety of denominations were bona fide Klan members, or close sympathizers,[9] there were several who played pivotal roles in the Klan expansion. The Reverend William Surman, minister of Regina's Cameron Memorial Baptist Church, served as an itinerant lecturer and as exalted Cyclops of the Regina Klan, while the Reverend T.J. Hind, of the First Baptist Church, was a local power in Moose Jaw, where he addressed numerous meetings following the transfer of his loyalties from the Emmons to the Rosborough Klan.[10] The United Church's principal contributor was the Reverend S.P. Rondeau, minister of the Woodrow United Church and former moderator of the Saskatchewan Synod of the Presbyterian Church, who, after admitting to a twenty-year American residency, noted that 'about thirty thousand ministers ... some of the most notable professors, some of the wealthiest men by the thousands, belonged to the Klan at the United States.'[11]

Though Klansmen entertained, and were entertained, by tens of devoted ministers, the Saskatchewan organization was by no means an exclusively religious body. Klan life did offer, it is true, some elaborate ceremonial fare for ritually starved local white Protestant gentiles. The official Klud was filled with biblical references and ceremonies infused with occult religious rites and symbolism.[12] Sacred altars, vessels of dedication fluid, holy sprinklings, dedicatory prayers and Klodes, led by Kludds, all figured in the elaborate scheme of ritual. But the Klan in Saskatchewan, as elsewhere, was as much a social and educational, as religious organization. It was an excuse for ordinary people – gentile, white, and Protestant – to get together, to socialize and attend meetings small and big, where crosses were burnt, speeches heard, and patriotic anthems or hymns sung, like 'The Maple Leaf Forever,' 'The Old Rugged Cross,' 'Onward Christian Soldiers,' and 'God Save the King.' From Kerrobert to Moose Jaw, Klanspersons attended whist drives, luncheons, barbecues, musicals, and Klan plays, like *Wives on Strike*, centred on a plot of domestic rebellion, which 'afforded real humour' to an audience of five hundred in Moose Jaw.[13] To keep the membership abreast of public events and issues, and organizational events, a monthly newspaper, *The Klans-*

man, published by the publicity department of the Ku Klux Klan, appeared beginning November 1928, edited by Imperial Kligrapp Charles H. Ellis.[14] *The Klansman* featured sermonettes by the Reverend Messrs Hinds and Rondeau; reprints of anti-Catholic diatribes from *The Sentinel*; expositions by men like George Exton Lloyd of the National Association of Canada, on the immigration menace; an occasional quote from *Pravda* calling Pope Pius a 'heavenly liar and Godly thief';[15] and reports from the editor on Klonvocations and other organization events. Wheezy Klansmen with respiratory disorders read in advertisements of the healing powers of the asthma pills of Mrs E. North, of Indian Head, Saskatchewan, while Klansmen with skin disorders were offered the certain palliative of Mrs North's equally promising 'Nightingale Eczema and Skin Disease Remedy.'[16] Prominent advertisements were run by the Protestant Book House, of Saskatoon, which featured an assortment of titles, including *The Secret Confessions of a Priest Exposed, Why Priests Should Wed* by ex-priest Dr Fulton, and *Black Convent Slaves* by a Mr Hendrikson. An order of five books entitled the subscriber to complementary copies of two hot favourites: *Life of Ex-Nun Minnie Morrison* and *Awful Disclosures of Maria Monk.*[17]

Not all *The Klansman*'s revenues, it appeared, were collected from advertisers. Soon after the first monthly issue, *The Klansman* launched a vigorous subscription drive offering valuable prizes to leading participants. Contestants who topped the monthly subscription sales list received fiery-cross ties or scarf pins, made of red stones set in platinum, which 'when worn at night gave the effect of an illuminated cross.'[18] Ten subscriptions or better brought a Klan button for the coat lapel.

The tie pins, buttons, and burning crosses were in hot demand throughout 1928 to 1929 as Saskatchewanians streamed by the thousands to growing locals in search of ritual, social companionship, diverting messages, and ready relief from boredom and social stress. The Klan grew – albeit briefly – because it was aggressively marketed and answered certain social needs. Without the initial Hoosier salesmanship and boosterism, the subsequent inflammatory oratory of skilled demagogues, or the mundane organizational talents of men like Rosborough, the Klan might have enjoyed nothing more than instant oblivion. Nor should its plain offerings of fraternity and novelty to the bored prelates and plain folk of insular Saskatchewan be underestimated. 'Their orthodox Protestantism,' Siegfried wrote of small-town America, '... has persisted unchanged beneath an impenetrable veneer of boredom. Nothing can exceed the mediocrity of these small communities, where local public opinion aggressively spies on anyone suspected of being different. The Klan was never entirely successful in the big cities with their mixture of races and groups, nor yet in the isolation of the open country, but ... an intellectual aristocracy scarcely exists in ... shut-in communities, where even the school teacher is held on a tight leash. Society is run by a narrow-minded middle class and inspired by a Protestant clergy to whom the Invisible Empire is not without its attraction.'[19]

From Kokomo, Indiana, to Kinistino, Saskatchewan, the Ku Klux Klan offered a sufficient bucket of fraternal fun and packaged gimmicks to tickle the collective fancies of hordes of rubes and Babbitts. But the appeal did not stop there. Complementing the loyalty and love of Klansmen, for Klode and crosses, flag and country, religion and race, was a corresponding basket of hates that fed on, magnified, and exploited the prejudices – latent and manifest – of host communities. Saskatchewan, in the 1920s, like Indiana or Oregon, was a mixed place, ethnically and attitudinally. It may not have been, as James Gray noted, 'a wasteland of bigots' in which everybody went around 'making nasty gestures at the object of their bigotry'; a community devoid of 'ordinarily tolerant, decent, people who minded their own business and were usually willing to take people at their face value,'[20] but neither was it the Eden of tolerance devoutly wished for by cosmopolitan liberals or besieged minorities. When Pat Emmons, and the Scott boys, first set up shop in Saskatchewan, they found hundreds and thousands of local 'ordinary, decent' residents programmed, ready, and willing to pocket the 'antis' peddled. 'No American adventurers could come in and get the people to pay $13 of their hard-earned money in the country districts where money is very scarce,' a prominent conservative lawyer and Klan supporter wrote R.B. Bennett, 'if the public mind was not every much alive to things as they are.'[21] As David Smith observed, 'to interpret the racial and religious hostility that accompanied the Klan's growth as originating with that growth ignored similar sentiments evident in Saskatchewan before the Klan's appearance,'[22] sentiments Patrick Kyba had in mind when he wrote: 'The Ku Klux Klan was alien to Saskatchewan in the sense that it had never made an appearance here before, but in a sense it was also autochthonous, for it was nurtured on sentiments and prejudices that had been present in Saskatchewan society for years.'[23]

What livened the public mind in Saskatchewan, in the late 1920s, to 'things as they were' was an accumulation of fears and prejudices assiduously cultivated during previous decades by assorted self-appointed guardians of public morality. The Ku Klux Klan did not invent prejudice in Saskatchewan. It was already there in abundance, rooted in groups and processes – economic, social, and political – perceived as threatening to the status and power of native, Anglo-Saxon, Protestant Saskatchewanians.

Not the least of the demons were immigrants, mainly from Central and Eastern Europe, whose arrival and settlement during the mid-1920s were greeted with concern, sometimes consternation, by an aroused Anglo-Saxon element. Though the Central and Eastern European immigration flow had halted during the war, and slowed to a trickle in the early post-war years, a renewed influx in the 1920s stoked the fires of a languishing nativism. Impetus to the flow, and the reaction, was provided by the Railway Agreements of 1925, between the federal government and the CNR and CPR, authorizing the railways to encourage immigrants from 'non-preferred' Eastern and Central European countries to immigrate and settle in Canada as 'agriculturalists, agricultural workers and domestic servants.' The agreement lasted two years, was renewed in 1927 for another three, and contributed to a substantial increased flow of 'alien' settlers into rural and urban Saskatchewan. Where Saskatchewan in 1921 counted 47.1 per cent of the population as non–Anglo-Saxon, by the decade's end the situation was reversed: the Anglo-Saxons became a minority. The bulk of the new immigrants settled in rural Saskatchewan blocs, resisted absorption and 'Canadianization,' clung to habitual ways, pressed for foreign-language provision in public schools, supported the governing Liberal party, and reproduced at a faster rate than the Anglo-Saxons.[24]

The threatening demographics did not go unnoticed by nativist groups ready to flush out hordes of enemy aliens and foreign radicals hidden among the haystacks and hamlets of rural Saskatchewan. The trouble with immigrants from Central and Eastern Europe was their imperviousness and stubbornness, quaint folkways, economic greed, clustering tendencies, and habitual resistance to assimilation to the Canadian and British ways of life. 'If we leave our new Canadians undisturbed in their own customs and ways ... deny them the ability to assimilate to our culture,' wrote Robert England in 1929, 'it will result one day in a vastly increased electorate, incapable of understanding our needs, hammering at the door of our civilization, demanding freedoms and rights coloured by their memories, traditions and restricted lives.'[25] Canadianization and restriction of entry – until those already here had been properly assimilated – were imperative if Canada – or Saskatchewan – was to survive as an orderly, integrated community. To alleviate the threat of social and political upheaval, crash programs of acculturation and immigration restriction were needed. Until the immigrants could be properly melted into true Canadians, quotas and restrictions were needed to slow the tide. 'Anglo-Saxon insularity, racial prejudice, and economic advantage have alike pleaded for restriction of Central European Immigration,' England observed, 'on the score that we have failed to assimilate those who have already settled in Canada.'[26]

Proponents of Canadianization, quotas, and restrictions were common among a spectrum of groups and organizations wary of the dangers posed to the hegemony – economic, social, and political – of the settled British element. Trade unionists heard from their leaders – and J.H. Hawkins – about the evils of contract labour, Oriental wage competition, scabrous Central Europeans, and the drift of ethnic agriculturists into the slums and crime wards of the cities. 'With regard to our own boys working in railway gangs and other jobs in Canada,' Premier James G. Gardiner wrote to W.L. Mackenzie King, 'they say that where a foreign-speaking foreman is in charge, a foreign-speaking cook is preparing the meal and ninety percent of the employees are foreign-speaking, it is impossible for Canadians, used to different conditions, to remain in the same camp.'[27] Veterans in the Great War Veterans' Association – later the Royal Canadian Legion – called for rigid restriction of immigration 'to such races as are so related to the British or French peoples by blood or tradition as to be readily assimilated and amenable to our traditions, customs and laws.'[28] Agriculturalists, in the Saskatchewan Grain Growers' Association and the United Farmers of Canada (Saskatchewan Section), responded in the mid-1920s to soft prices, economic crowding, and foreign-import restrictions, with calls for quotas on immigration and moratoriums on grand colonization schemes.[29] Conservative and Progressive politicians joined with municipalists and spokesmen for patriotic societies like the Orange Order, the Sons of England, and the Women's British Immigration League, in campaigns to halt the tide of 'non-preferreds.' Pre-eminent among the exclusionists was the fervent Right Reverend George Exton Lloyd, bishop of the Diocese of Saskatchewan, who, in 1928, formed the National Association of Canada, to press, in consort with the Sons of England, the Orange Order, the Royal Canadian Legion, and other patriotic organizations, for restrictive immigration policies.[30] A London-born, Toronto-educated 'muscular Christian,' Lloyd dedicated his noisy public career to the service of Christ, the Anglican church, the British Empire, and, not least, the sacred cause of keeping the Canadian West British.[31]

In the years following his assumption of the bishopric, George Exton Lloyd spared no effort in rousing his fellow Saskatchewanians, and Canadians, to the defence of an Anglo-Saxon, British West, a crusade that Klansmen joined in the dying years of the decade. 'He has two pet aversions,' T.C. Davis wrote to Mackenzie King, 'the Roman Catholic Church, and the people who are not British-born. He does very little church work as a Bishop and, in fact, is not fitted for this kind of work but was cut out to be an agitating politician. His natural bent, therefore, drives him to an active part in politics.'[32] Government officials, newspapers, the Empire Club, interested organizations of every sort, including the Social Service Council of the Church of England and the parliamentary committee investigating immigration matters, were flooded with representations from the tireless cleric who campaigned against the 'dirty, ignorant, garlic-smelling, non-preferred continentals.'[33] It was the bishop's considered view that the great railway companies were party to a conspiracy to 'denationalize and mongrelize' the country by preferring the non-preferred, choking the flow of British immigration, and selling the 'nation's blood, character and future to make a railway dividend.'[34]

The problem with foreigners, according to Lloyd and his nativist allies, was not merely their unkempt personages, economic greed, ignorance of British ways, and weakness for garlic. What mattered as much, or more, was the fact that they were predominantly Catholic. When the Klansmen first rode into Moose Jaw and Kinistino, they were pleased to discover vibrant and readily exploitable currents of anti-Catholicism and ultra-Protestantism, traceable, in some instances, to the days of the territorial government. At the forefront of the anti-Catholic agitation were Orangemen who established Lodges in the territories soon after securing a western beachhead in neighbouring Manitoba in the early 1870s.[35] Following the attainment of provincial status by Manitoba's western neighbours, in 1905, the prairie Lodges filled with so many Orangemen that Saskatchewan was second only to Ontario in membership.[36]

Like their fraternalists elsewhere, the Saskatchewan Orangemen were ferociously anti-Catholic and not adverse to spreading their views among diverse constituencies of the province. Orange Lodges and settlements served as garrisons, 'protected fortresses' from which was fired 'the red hot gospel truth' of One Canada, British and Protestant.[37] Colouring the Orange universe, in Saskatchewan as elsewhere, was a Catholic conspiracy, centred in Rome, and Quebec, to colonize the country through political penetration – at the federal and provincial levels – immigrant inundation, and the expansion of the rights, power, and number of the Catholic population. 'The whole country and the Departments of the Government are flooded with Catholics, who are absolutely in control and do as they like,' wrote prominent Saskatchewan Orangeman J.F. Bryant. 'There is no question whatever that the present situation is to make Canada Catholic through the control of Quebec and Saskatchewan.'[38] 'In Canada there should be, and could be, only one nationality and language,' an Ontario Grand Master proclaimed, ' and that is English and not French. This is a British Country and a French Republic should have no future on this continent. Let us be determined that this Dominion both in sentiment and language shall be British from ocean to ocean.'[39]

Orange agitation in Saskatchewan in favour of 'Equal Rights for All, Special Privileges to none'[40] predated the autonomy bills of 1905 and continued unabated into the 1920s when the Ku Klux Klan received a warm reception among Orangemen for its virulent anti-Catholicism. Saskatchewan Orangemen were avid publicists and lobbyists who pressed before a succession of governments and public forums a bundle of issues – which the Klan readily appropriated – relating to separate schools, sectarian influence in public schools, French language rights, and non-preferred immigration.[41] 'At the same time that this organization made its appearance,' Premier James Gardiner wrote to Mackenzie King, announcing the Klan's arrival in Saskatchewan, 'there developed a great deal of activity in all localities where an Orange Lodge is located.'[42] Not only did Orange and Klan opinion on the French and Catholic menace overlap; their membership was often the same. The *Sentinel* gave the Klan extensive and favourable attention, and its editorials and articles were reproduced in *The Klansman.* Orange meeting halls and membership lists were readily used by Klan organizers. 'In Saskatchewan the Klan managed to forge cordial links with the Orange Order,' Houston and Smyth noted in their study of the historical geography of the Order. 'The *Sentinel* provided sympathetic accounts of its presence, Orangemen were prominent in its ranks, and in many ways the two were interdependent. They were also to a large extent geographically coterminous. The Klan drew support from communities of the same British and Ontario character that supported the Orange Order.'[43]

Though the Klan fed off the historical ultra-Protestantism of the Orange Order, nourishment was forthcoming, as well, from a range of established Protestant churches in a province where, in 1927, 233,000 out of a population of 850,000 were Catholics. As early as the days of the territorial government, Saskatchewan became a zone of contest between churches – Protestant and Catholic – as well as political parties.[44] Early Catholic church political interventions, in the final decades of the nineteenth century, in defence of separate

schools and minority-language educational rights were followed by
the pronouncement during the 1905 election campaign of Archbishop Langevin urging the faithful of his archdiocese to withdraw support for the Provincial Rights Party, which opposed the constitutional
guarantees for denominational schools embodied in the automony
bills of 1905.[45] Separate-school and language-rights issues perked and
bubbled in the years preceding and following the war when clergymen and congregants from several Protestant denominations actively
combated the entrenchment and extension of Catholic education
and French language rights, a crusade subsequently joined by Klansmen who enjoyed active and tacit support from sectors of the devout.
Allegations of a Catholic conspiracy and pronouncements favouring
the reduction of immigration of non-preferreds – mainly Catholic –
the imposition of quotas, and French-language educational restrictions were common during the post-war years at church meetings
and conventions. At their 1927 convention in Saskatoon, Baptist
ministers sounded the alien alarm, warned of the dire consequences of an expanded Catholic electorate, and attacked the federal government for bowing to 'monied Catholic interests.'[46] Anglicans and
United Churchmen were equally vigilant. 'The Church of Rome with
her great political influence and effective machinery,' the bishop of
Qu'Appelle noted, in a charge to the thirtieth session of the Synod
the the Anglican Diocese of Qu'Appelle, 'appears to find it easy to
avail itself of any opportunity for colonizing and peopling vast areas with a Roman Catholic population chiefly of European extraction.
This cannot be to our advantage ... Great vigilance is required if we
are to preserve Anglo-Saxon traditions and high national ideals.'[47]
At a meeting, in November 1926, of Anglican clergymen of the Diocese of North Saskatchewan, a resolution was passed, demanding
return to the provinces of Saskatchewan and Alberta of control over
natural resources 'unwarrantedly and unlawfully retained by the
Federal Government at the request ... of the Roman Catholic Clergy of Quebec.' Retention of resource control, the resolution noted,
was a means of coercing 'and fostering separate schools on the above
named provinces.'[48] Among the most active of the anti-Catholic and
exclusionist Anglicans were Cannons Burd of Prince Albert and
Armitage of Saskatoon who, with Bishops G. Exton Lloyd and McAd-

am Harding of Qu'Appelle, drew up a memorial for presentation to the General Synod of the Anglican Church, condemning, among other things, the inordinate and iniquitous representation of Catholic priests among immigration agents employed by the federal government.[49] At the fourth conference of the United Church of Saskatchewan, meeting in June 1928, overtures were heard from the Assiniboia Presbytery, a hot-bed of anti-Catholic sentiment, complaining of the use of 'objectionable' French textbooks in the public-school system, the presence of crucifixes and religious emblems in select public schools, and the use of convents and other church buildings as public schools.[50]

The ministerial allegations of unwarranted Catholic and French-language incursions were shared and exploited during the dying years of the decade of the 1920s by the Klan, which enjoyed limited, but not insignificant support within diverse Protest denominations. The vast majority of Saskatchewan clergy, it is true, stayed clear of the Klan, and no organic links were ever established between the Klan and church groups. And there was no shortage of prominent clergymen, or congregants, willing to condemn the Klan publicity – men like Dr Charles Endicott, who announced his opposition before the Saskatchewan Conference of the United Church 'from the word go';[51] the Reverend E.R.M. Brechen of Young, who described the Klan as 'unpatriotic, unChristian, mischievous in its methods';[52] or a majority of the Saskatoon Presbytery of the United Church who, in October 1927, recorded their opposition to the Order.[53] But there developed as well, as the Klan's popularity spread, a countervailing sympathy among groups – ministers and congregants – drawn to a novel non-denominational vehicle selling prejudices long entertained. As Calderwood concluded in his excellent survey of the Klan's religious support, 'at least twenty-six Protestant Ministers were either bona fide members of the Ku Klux Klan or directly involved in it,'[54] including thirteen from the United Church, four Baptists, four Anglicans, three Presbyterians, a Lutheran, and a Pentecostal. Except for Baptists like Surman and Hind, who served in the large population centres of Regina and Moose Jaw, the great majority of ministerial Klansmen were drawn from small towns where fundamentalist currents of religious opinion fed the growing stream of opposition to liberal theology. While the United Church contributed the greatest number of ministerial supporters, 'the more conservative and fundamental the Church,' Calderwood concluded, 'the greater was the tendency of clergy to endorse the Klan openly.'[55] The Klan's reaction in Saskatchewan – as elsewhere in North America – to the uncertainties of social change, the strains of urbanization, the liberalization of mores – was paralleled and reinforced by a religious revolt of fundamentalists against the liberal and modernist tendencies of the established denominations. 'In reaction against the widespread acceptance within the Church of Darwinism, biblical criticism and political involvement,' a Canadian church historian wrote of the fundamentalist surge, 'it added the vigour and intolerance of crusading counter-revolution.'[56]

While some fundamentalists, like Hind and Surman, crusaded for Christ and the Klan, many of their compatriots were prepared merely to stand by and let the Klan have its day. There was, among both main- and side-stream ministers and their congregants, a disquieting unwillingness to condemn or combat the Klan, whose leaders often boasted of substantial support among the faithful. Irked by the Klan's embrace of a number of their denominational brethren, liberals in the Saskatoon Presbytery of the United Church of Canada forwarded the following resolution to the committee on references and overtures of the Saskatchewan Conference of the United Church, meeting in Regina's Knox Church in June 1928: 'Whereas it is being stated that the United Church is backing the Ku Klux Klan, and that the people are being asked to join the organization because of that fact, therefore this presbytery of Saskatoon desires to place on record: first that the United Church is not supporting the Ku Klux Klan in any way; second – that this presbytery believes that the principles of the Ku Klux Klan are in opposition to the teaching of Jesus and therefore cannot be supported by the United Church of Canada. Further, that a copy of this resolution be sent to the conference for further action, if they see fit, also to the press.'[57]

When the committee on references and overtures recommended that the conference refrain from making 'any deliverance on the question,' a majority of delegates concurred, despite the pleas of Liberal Charles Endicott, who argued that 'it ought to be clearly understood that the United Church is not behind the Klan.'[58] While Dr Endicott had his supporters, others applauded the contrary response of a fellow delegate, who insisted 'it also ought to be understood that the Church is not fighting the Klan.'[59]

However divided the six hundred delegates may have been on the Klan question, there was, it appears, virtual unanimity among pro- and anti-Klan ministers on the merits of the guest address delivered to the conference by Toronto's Rabbi Ferdinand M. Isserman, who had been extended a 'unanimous invitation' to appear before the delegates.[60] Following the guest speech, a most unusual confrontation occurred, between a Rabbi and a Wizard. 'As I emerged from the doors of the Church,' Rabbi Isserman later wrote,

I noticed an individual rapidly endeavoring to reach me. He accosted me and to my utter astonishment and amazement he said: 'I am Rosborough, Imperial Wizard of the Klan in Saskatchewan. I want to congratulate you on your address. Fully one-half of your audience were Klansmen and they applauded you so generously because when you voiced the hope for unity and brotherhood, you were voicing Klan ideals.' I couldn't collect my breath quickly enough to say Sholom Aleichem to my Imperial friend. I pointed out that if brotherhood was a Klan ideal, it had pursued most unfraternal tactics in the States to obtain them. He then hastened to dissociate his organization from those in the States. He claimed that the Saskatchewan Klan was different, despite the fact that its organizers were American, who when the America field had been played out, came to Canada for fresh territories and more of those about whom Barnum said that one was born every minute ... the Wizard claimed that the Klan was not anti-Jewish, but that it only admitted Protestant Christians as the Bnai Brith only admitted Jews. A half hour of conversation failed to convince me that the Klan was not an organization inimical to Canada's highest interest.[61]

Fortunately, for the Wizard, the Rabbi's scepticism about the Klan's true purposes was not shared by the faithful of Kinistino, Climax, Melville, and Moose Jaw, who, throughout the year 1928, flocked to widely attended meetings of the militant, pan-Protestant

Association. Though the Hoosier hucksters brought with them a handy range of proven targets, their native successors adapted the agitation to local conditions, focusing on and exploiting issues – education, language rights, and immigration – long sensitive in the polyglot province. In the Rosborough Klan's nativist firmament, blacks, Orientals, and Jews figured as bit players, their places as ogres taken by immigrants and Catholics eager to foist alien ways on a vulnerable, Anglo-Saxon population.

To Saskatchewan's nativists, old and new, the major institution guaranteeing the integrity and cultural survival of the precarious Protestant majority was the uncontaminated public school, and Klansmen, throughout 1928 and 1929, pressed the education issue with an enthusiasm – and venom – seldom witnessed before in the province. When it came to education, Klansmen – like Orangemen – had their strong likes and dislikes. Dear to their patriotic hearts was the public school, free of sinister sectarian or foreign-language influences, an institution mandated to preserve Protestant Anglo-Saxon culture and to Americanize, or Canadianize, the uninvited alien who had slipped by the immigration sentries. Among Klansmen's favourite dislikes were separate Catholic schools, sectarian influences in public schools, and, in the case of Canada, subversive French-language provisions thrust on the public schools by a conniving Catholic minority.

The bare facts of the matter did not trouble Klansmen greatly. They were unconcerned that of the 4,776 school districts in existence in Saskatchewan in 1928, only 31 had separate or minority schools, with 8 of these Protestant, in districts where the majority of the population were Catholic.[62] They cared little that only 153 of the approximately 8,500 teachers in the province were nuns, who taught a mere 7,081 of the province's estimated 225,000 pupils;[63] or that in only 133 schools in a province with 4,776 public school districts in 1926, was French taught up to grade 7 or 8.[64] Nor were Klansmen troubled that, in only a handful of schools, in predominantly Catholic districts, did an occasional crucifix appear in the classroom, emblems usually removed following interventions by local boards and by the Department of Education.[65]

Facts, to Klansmen, mattered less than emotions, which were readily heated by a frenzied agitation exploiting phobias, against Catholics and French, entertained by organizations as diverse as the established Protestant churches, the Saskatchewan School Trustees Association, and the Orange Order. The Klan did not invent the phobias. They merely magnified them into live and large issues in the communities, primarily in southern Saskatchewan, where educational conflicts were usually contained, if not eliminated, by customary compromises and interventions. Long-simmering educational issues were brought to a full boil with the aid of the Klan, which added a novel demagogic ingredient to traditional religious and cultural wars.

The provincial Department of Education, and the affected school districts, felt the heat soon after the Klan entered the fray.[66] When l'Association Catholique Franco-Canadienne de la Saskatchewan petitioned the government to aid in the training of bilingual teachers, a shower of protest letters from the Klan and the Orange Order descended on the besieged department.[67] A rendering of 'O Canada,' in French, at a Normal School convocation, brought howls of denunciation. A campaign of complaints, by the Protestant rate payers of Bégin, against excess French-language instruction invited a hurried departmental investigation, which concluded the charges were unfounded. Inflamed Protestant militants in the Poirier school district did not bother complaining. They simply broke into and removed offensive crucifixes from the wall of a local school.[68] In the Moose Pond district, a Klan-inspired action was taken against several French-speaking trustees, charging them with permitting the use of French as a language of instruction beyond the first grade.[69] The justice of the peace who heard the Moose Pond case was himself a Klansman and the subject of a writ of prohibition, sponsored by the besieged trustees who sought to disqualify him.[70] At Gravelbourg, where Catholics heavily dominated the school district, the rental of several rooms in a convent by the school-board for use as a public school, the appearance of crucifixes on the walls, the employment of nuns as teachers, and the alleged excess French instruction engaged the Klan and Protestant rate payers in a protracted acrimonious battle with Catholic residents and the provincial government.[71] A similar conflict developed in the Gouverneur district, where Klansmen urged Protestant rate payers to withdraw their children from the school in protest against the teaching of French, the alleged replacement of the Union Jack at the front of the school by a crucifix, and the display of religious emblems. When truancy charges were pressed by Catholic trustees against the offending rate payers, the Klan retained the prominent conservative lawyer, Orangeman, and former head – for seven years – of the Saskatchewan School Trustees' Association, J.F. Bryant, to fight the case.[72] Bryant's argument, that the school was no longer public because it engaged in illegal French instruction and displayed religious emblems, was bought by the two presiding justices of the peace, both Klansmen, who dismissed the charges.[73]

Up front as a publicist in the school wars was the Reverend S.P. Rondeau, who delivered numerous public lectures under Klan auspices, pressed the schools issue before the Assiniboia Presbytery and annual conferences of the United Church in Saskatchewan, and wrote a spate of articles – in the *Orange Sentinel* and *The Klansman* – exposing a sinister Catholic conspiracy to subvert Protestant and public education in the province. 'We affirm that the object of these peculiar majorities,' Rondeau wrote in a pamphlet on the Gravelbourg dispute, 'is to wipe out the identity of the Common School. When the "trek" is sufficiently strong from Quebec, New England and Belgium; when farm-buying and centralization are sufficiently accentuated, the 150 French centers in Saskatchewan will duplicate Gravelbourg one hundred times; for Gravelbourg is only one of similar conditions in other parts of the province.'[74] The emblems and nuns of Gravelbourg were not the sole concerns of Reverend Rondeau, a Klan brother of French-Canadian origin, who vehemently objected to the continued use in French-language courses, pending the issuance of new materials, of a textbook containing passages considered offensive to Protestants. When the controversial *Magnum Reader* was finally replaced in September 1928, following years of agitation, Rondeau, and the Klan, celebrated.[75]

The Klan's school assault was a major headache, not only for Catholic educators, but for a provincial Liberal government long committed to maintaining an effective compromise among competing educational and cultural interests. Since its inception as a province in 1905, Saskatchewan had been ruled by a succession of Liberal re-

gimes, led by Premiers Scott, Martin, and Dunning, who constructed and maintained effective governing coalitions of Catholics, immigrants, and moderate Protestants. The Liberals were placators. Farmers were delivered useful goods and beneficent programs,
immigrants patronized and settled in cosy clusters, and Catholics
granted educational concessions sufficient to move George Weir to
conclude, in his 1934 study, *The Separate School Question in Canada,*
that 'Roman Catholic influences, as discernible in amendments to
school legislation during the last twenty years, had been more vigilant and far-reaching in Saskatchewan ... than corresponding influences in Ontario.'[76] In 1926, when James Gardiner succeeded
Charles Dunning as premier, following an election in June 1925, in
which the Liberals won fifty of the legislature's sixty-one seats, the
coalition seemed as solid as ever.[77] Two years later, however, in the
midst of a ferocious campaign of opposition focusing on education
and immigration issues – in which the Klan played a key role – the
Liberals faced an erosion of support so serious that it threatened
their long-standing hegemony. 'There seems to be a wave passing
over the West, just now,' a Liberal organizer noted in June 1928, 'that
is making the people panicky.'[78]

Premier James Gardiner was not unaware of the Klan's capacity for
making waves and, from the first days of its arrival, kept a wary eye
on its misdoings. 'There has been organized in the Province of Saskatchewan a Ku Klux Klan,' Gardiner wrote to King in August 1927,
'some of the organizers have come to the West from Ontario. It
would appear, from their general activities in the Province, that the
main object of the organization is to spread propaganda which will
be of benefit to the opponents of the Government, both Provincial
and Federal, at the time of the next election. At the same time that
this new organization made its appearance, there developed a great
deal of activity in all locations where an Orange Lodge is located.
From each of these localities has come information to the effect that
all the leading Orange Conservatives are spreading propaganda to
the effect that the Catholic Church is controlling the activities of
both the Federal and Provincial Governments.'[79] Throughout the
Scott-Emmons campaign, Gardiner kept a close watch, gathered
reports from informants and complainants, built a file, correspond-

ed with Ontario officials about Klan activities there, and, in pursuit of hard evidence on the misdoings of its imported leaders, dispatched a detective to Ontario, Michigan, and Indiana.[80] When distraught Klansmen sought the premier's aid in recovering monies taken by Scott and Emmons – who left town several days after the return of the dispatched detective – Gardiner was able to boast that he knew more about their organization, and its unsavoury background, than they did. 'In a country of this kind more than one can play the secret service game,' Gardiner informed the legislature, 'and we know just about as much as to what is going on in the Ku Klux Klan as they do themselves.'[81]

Whatever Gardiner did know of the Klan, he kept pretty quiet about, until the throne-speech debate in late January 1928, which heard the leader of the Conservative opposition, J.T.M. Anderson, call on 'all the forces of the province opposed to the present government to fight the Liberal Government and endeavor to defeat it.'[82] The premier, it seems, included the Klan among Anderson's opponents, and responded before an astonished opposition and excited press – which headlined the speech across the province the next day – with a bitter broadside against 'an organization that is thriving upon prejudice and hatred.'[83] Gardiner, in the parlance of the times, took his gloves off. The Klan's American legacy of lawlessness and bloodshed; its hatred of Negroes, Jews, and Catholics; the Scott-Emmons migration and scam; the tribulations of local duped Klansmen – all were dealt with in a wide-ranging root-and-branch condemnation of an organization 'whose main object' was 'to play upon the prejudices of the people in other parts of the Dominion and the North American continent in order that someone would have an easy living[84] ... We in Canada have never found it necessary to get proper enforcement of Law and Order by having an organization parading about the country wearing hoods over their heads so that people do not know who they are. Any man who has not backbone and courage to stand in the open has no place in British institutions of government.'[85]

The premier's stand on the Klan surprised few people, friends or foes, familiar with his background, temperament, and political ideology. An Ontario-born Laurier Liberal who studied briefly in Lincoln, Nebraska, before graduating from the Normal School in Regina in 1905, and the University of Manitoba in 1911, Gardiner was first elected to the legislature as the member for North Qu'Appelle in a by-election in 1914, following a three-year stint as principal of Lemberg Public School. In subsequent years, he was repeatedly returned to the House, rose in eminence in the legislative caucus, assumed control of the party machine, and, under Dunning, was appointed to Cabinet as minister of highways.[86]

The Ku Klux Klan was anathema to everything Gardiner believed in, and practised. As a Laurier Liberal, he abhorred the Klan's anti-Catholicism. As a pluralist, he opposed its monomaniacal nativism. As an educator in an ethnically and religiously diverse province, he rejected the Klan's demagogic intolerance of minority rights. As a prime builder, and manager, of a political machine that enrolled and bought ethnic voters, he appreciated the Klan's capacity to foment prejudice, draw away Liberal Protestant voters, and destroy carefully nurtured accommodations and coalitions.

Gardiner might have kept his views and opinions about the Klan to himself, had the Order died quickly after the Scott-Emmons fiasco. But the Rosborough Klan thrived and, worst of all, was fostering divisions and alignments threatening the survival of the Liberal party and government. When Mackenzie King first heard from Gardiner about the early Klan growth and heightening anti-Catholic sentiment in Saskatchewan, he warned: 'What you are face to face with is, I think, only the spreading to Western Canada of the influence of the Orange Order as the electioneering nucleus of the Tory Party. You cannot, I think, do a better thing than to expose as quickly and as completely as possible tactics such as those which your letter describes.'[87] When Gardiner finally decided to follow King's suggested course and publicly expose and condemn the Klan, his intention was not merely to weaken the tenuous hold among duped Saskatchewanians – including many Liberals – of a phantom organization he found abhorrent. He had a larger purpose: to link the Klan with political enemies who, in the preceding months, were disposed to draw together in opposition to the government. 'This is one of the groups in Saskatchewan,' Gardiner announced in his Great Klan speech, 'apart from the two groups of my honourable friends opposite who are opposed to this government and if my honourable friends want any cooperation that is the only place I know they can get it ... and when they are appealing to all the forces of this province opposing the government to get together in Saskatchewan to fight the forces of the Liberal party, well, all I can say, is that they will find those Liberal forces pretty much alive.'[88]

The opponents targeted by Gardiner's campaign of association were the Progressives, with six members in the legislature, and the Tories, who counted a mere three. No friend of the Progressives, who entertained strange notions of group government, fiddled with the farm interest, diverted Liberal votes, and fostered dangerous three-way constituency fights, Gardiner was prepared to smear his anti-Klan brush wide enough to include them in the growing conspiracy of cooperation among regime opponents. While support for the federal Progressive wing declined steeply from 1921, when sixty-five members were returned to the House of Commons, the provincial counterparts held their representation, of six, in the election of 1925. The Progressives' status as official opposition, and their increasing inclination to seek alliances with other opposition groups, invited the continuing acrimony of the premier, who, in a speech following the July 1927 Liberal provincial convention, linked the Klan and Progressives to venal American antecedents. According to Gardiner, the Non-Partisan League in 1917 'went into the southern part of the province and collected $70,000 in hard cash and notes from the farmers of some dozen constituencies and they did not elect a single member of the Legislature.'[89] Four years later, he continued, farmers in the northeastern part of the province were canvassed by itinerant salesmen of protest, with similar results. The Klan, Gardiner insisted, was merely the most recent scam and vehicle of the same pseudo reformers and 'get-rich-easy' politicians – 'some of whom are not even citizens of the Dominion of Canada, and who are collecting money from citizens of our cities with the ostensible purpose of doing some good to the people of this country.'[90] Gardiner returned to the same scam theme in his January 1928 great Klan speech, when he reminded the Progressive MLA Dr Reginald Stipe that the day of the get-rich-quick politician in Canada 'was rapidly passing away ... and it cannot pass too quickly for me.'[91]

The premier's associations and innuendoes were poorly received by Progressives like E.S. Whatley, the MLA for Kindersley, who bitterly opposed the Klan and asked – in the midst of the Klan debate – whether Gardiner was 'trying to connect the K.K.K. with the Progressive Party.'[92] Whatley later announced to the House that 'any organization that attempted ... stirring up of religious and racial hatred and animosity had no place in Saskatchewan,'[93] a sentiment shared by Progressive leaders like M.J. Coldwell and many rank-and-filers who were opposed to alliances with Klansmen or, for that matter, Conservatives fighting the Gardiner government. But there were other Progressives, leaders and rank and file, who willingly bought the Klan's conspiracy theories and joined the organization. While the Klan had something to offer a wide range of Saskatchewanians – including Liberals – it proved especially attractive to Progressives who, Calderwood concluded from an examination of Klan membership lists available in the Gardiner papers, 'probably ran a close second to the Conservatives, in supplying the Klan with members.'[94] Klan membership lists included the names of prominent Progressives like the Reverend A.J. Lewis, an ex-MP defeated in the 1925 election; John MacLoy, a former Progressive candidate and member of the board of directors of the United Farmers of Canada (Saskatchewan Section); and E. Jones, secretary-treasurer of the Rosetown Progressive Party Association.[95] Social and demographic factors, as well as ideological and policy affinities, facilitated the acceptance, or tolerance, of Klan doctrine among Progressive supporters, many of whom were American, Anglo-Saxon, or Scandinavian Protestant immigrants who brought with them into Saskatchewan during the pre-war years conspiracy sentiments nurtured south of the border. The Klan enjoyed strong support in the many towns located along railway divisional points filled with Protestant American settlers, and it appealed, in some instances, to the moral sentiments of small businessmen fearful of the conspiracies of big interests against the common people.[96] 'The K.K.K. is similar ... to other organizations which have sprung up when people have lost confidence in constituted authority,' a correspondent of the Progressive *Western Producer* noted, 'when they feel that justice too often miscarries; that politics and patronage figure too largely in our courts; that the welfare of the state is made subservient to the interest of party, permitting privileges to influential minorities – privileges detrimental to the best interests of society as a whole.'[97] Among the privileged minorities targeted by Saskatchewan Progressives, whether native-born, or from Britain, Ontario, or the United States, was the Quebec-based Catholic church. Klan and Progressive views on Quebec and Catholicism's alleged excess power, on the need for immigration quotas, on insidious sectarian influences on public education, overlapped. David Smith noted that most observers of Saskatchewan politics in the mid-1920s 'defined an important feature of the Progressive movement in provincial politics – its hostility to non–Anglo-Saxons.'[98] 'There is the certain feeling of need to keep the country English-speaking,' a *Manitoba Free Press* correspondent wrote of the Klan surge in Saskatchewan. 'There is the feeling that the Saskatchewan government is combining with the Federal government and the Catholic church to make Saskatchewan Catholic in complexion. They will tell you that where in the states you see a sign "Mac's Garage," that does not mean that the owner is a Scotsman. Not at all. Mac means "Make America Catholic." None of that for Saskatchewan.'[99]

The Conservatives, it appeared, were even better disposed towards the Klan than the Progressives. Heirs to the Provincial Rights Party, defeated in the 1905 election, the Saskatchewan Tories had been, for over two decades, a party in the wilderness, overwhelmed in a succession of elections by a powerful Liberal machine and devoid of significant support from continental immigrants, French Catholics, the farm establishment, and moderate Protestants. But the heightening of religious and ethnic tensions following the disastrous 1925 election, the arrival in office of a new fractious premier inimical to the Progressives, and the emergence of a new pan-Protestant oppositionist opinion triggered and kindled by the growing Klan, created for some prominent party leaders alluring possibilities for growth and cooperation.

The Tories were hardly unanimous on the subject of the Klan. There was, among them, a minority of Catholics who abhorred divisive religious politics and Klan affiliations and warned that any dealings with Klansmen would be both immoral and disastrous for the party, provincially and federally. Saskatoon's J.J. Leddy and Regina barrister A.G. MacKinnon, for example, were prominent Conservative and Catholic provincial politicians convinced that the fomenting of religious strife was 'false to the true principles of Conservatism and of Canadian citizenship.'[100] They were joined by a moderate 'better element' within the Protestant majority, men like Colonel E.C. Gregory who asked in an open letter why the 'probability of religious warfare' seemed more attractive to some party members than 'the peace of religious tolerance.'[101]

Gregory's views notwithstanding, tolerance of the Klan and religious intolerance of Catholics became fashionable among a number of Conservatives in the months preceding and following Premier James Gardiner's first anti-Klan tirade. Klaverns and Klonvocations were clogged with Tories whose party, assailed by a premier in league with Papists, became the favoured vehicle of ultra-Protestant militants eager to free the province from the hold of the Gardiner-Papist axis. Klan membership lists were filled with the names of Tory supporters, and their meetings attended and harangued by party activists. According to Dr Walter D. Cowan, the Klan treasurer, former Unionist MP, Regina Conservative elected for Long Lake to the House of Commons in the general election of 1930, and columnist for the *Regina Standard*, the Klan was 'the most complete political organization ever known' in the West.[102] 'Every organizer in it is a Tory,' he wrote R.B. Bennett. 'It cost over a thousand dollars a week to pay them. I know it for I pay them. And I never pay a Grit. Smile when you hear anything about this organization and keep silent.'[103]

Cowan's admonition to silence was heeded by prominent Conservative colleagues who welcomed the Klan's arrival, appreciated its ignition potentials, gloated over prospects of a political windfall, yet resisted identifying publicly with Saskatchewan's hoodless day-riders. Cowan himself was a noisy, uninhibited, up-front, Klansman, a prominent Conservative who turned down an offer of Klan leadership but never denied his membership. But he was an exception. Other prominent Conservatives who found the Klan friendly and useful were more circumspect, though not quite enough, it turned out, to avoid identifications that became public and political issues. J.F. Bryant, the Tory lawyer and Orangeman, was a key player in the Tory-Klan game. President of the Regina Conservative Association, vice-president of the provincial association, and future minister of public works in Saskatchewan's first Conservative-dominated provincial government, Bryant shared with the Klan some vital conspiratorial assumptions about the desperate state of affairs in Saskatchewan, which he entered in the year 1901. The Catholic church, in Bryant's view, sought total domination of Saskatchewan – and Canada – and its effective instrument was the Liberal party. 'The whole country and the departments of the government,' he wrote R.B. Bennett, 'are flooded with Catholics who are absolutely in control and do as they like ... There is no question whatever that the present intention is to make Canada Catholic through the control of Quebec and Saskatchewan ... I can prove this by documentary evidence from their own records which I have in my possession.'[104] Proof, to Bryant, mattered less than faith – the faith of an Orangeman and Klan fellow traveller that sustained him through Saskatchewan's religious wars of the late 1920s. Though Bryant denied he was ever a Klan member, he welcomed the Order's arrival, cheered its growth, and acted as the Klan's solicitor in several widely publicized sectarian educational cases that hit the courts. It was J.F. Bryant's view that the Catholic vote was hopelessly Liberal and forever lost to the Conservative party, who could win power only if its political base was broadened to include a grand majority of Protestants – Liberal, Progressive, and Conservative – awakened through a religiously and racially divisive campaign to the Catholic conspiracy. The Klan could serve as a key ingredient of the campaign, ready and willing, as it was, to do the dirty work necessary to excite and direct Protestant opinion towards the Conservative party. For this, Bryant insisted, the Klan deserved the tolerance, if not hidden support, of the Conservatives, who hoped to win the vote of the tens of thousands of hitherto apathetic Protestants. The Klan was 'going very strong,' Bryant wrote R.B. Bennett, 'and will be of great assistance in defeating the present Government and I do not think that we should throw any stones at them any more than we should expect that the Liberals should throw stones at the Knights of Columbus or any other similar organization that is strongly supporting them.'[105] Bryant's position was echoed by prominent Tory Francis Reilly, who wrote R.B. Bennett: 'We would be foolish not to profit by the Klan movement as the Conservative party does not owe any thanks to the Church for by it we have been kept in the opposition. On the other hand, the Klan will be a short-lived movement and is not conservative in principle and we have to keep clear of entanglements. It would be fatal to condemn the Klan and it might be as dangerous for the future to commend it.'[106]

It is not unlikely that the leader of the provincial Conservative party, J.T. Anderson, shared the views of J.F. Bryant – and Reilly – about the electoral utility of the Ku Klux Klan. Anderson's true relationship with the Klan remains shrouded by mystery and controversy, and with good reason: he was anxious to keep whatever contact he may have had with the Ku Klux Klan, as much as possible, from public view. The election of Anderson to the leadership of the Conservative party in 1924, and his return, following a brief resignation in 1926, were critical events in the developing Tory-Klan game, which Premier James Gardiner monitored, with some interest. A transplanted Ontario Orangeman and professional 'educationist,' as he liked to say, cognizant of the nuances and exploitive potential of the sectarian schools, immigration, and Canadianization issues plaguing the Liberal government, Anderson served as inspector of schools in Yorkton (1911–18) and Saskatoon (1922–4) and as director of education of new Canadians prior to his resignation from the government in 1924.[107]

In the emergent cultural politics of the mid-1920s, Anderson was no bit player. A confirmed proponent of Canadianization through the Boy Scout movement, the uncontaminated public school, the exercise of large discretionary powers – including deportation – by immigration bureaucrats, and the application of selective immigration quotas, Anderson played a major role in shifting the locus of public debate in Saskatchewan towards the social and cultural issues of immigration and education, issues the Ku Klux Klan sniffed soon after landing in Moose Jaw and Regina.[108] In the changed political arena of the late 1920s, there was no shortage of claims, by Liberals and disaffected Klan members, that Anderson had established direct, and useful contacts with the Klan. An article by a former Klansman, in the rural weekly *The Reporter*, placed the Conservative leader and future premier on several occasions 'in the K.K.K. rooms in 405 Connaught Block, in Saskatoon.'[109] Affidavits of Pat Emmons and his secretary, Charles Puckering, presented at a public meeting in Regina in May 1928, and reproduced in the leading newspapers, were equally suggestive. Anderson, according to Emmons and Puckering, first approached Emmons in May 1927, at the Klan office in Moose Jaw's Empress Hotel, seeking Klan aid in support of the Conservative candidate, a Dr Smith, in an approaching Moose Jaw by-election.[110] At subsequent meetings in Regina's Champs Hotel, and in the Western and Flanagan hotels in Saskatoon, Anderson according to the affidavits encouraged Emmons to organize a Klan local in Saskatoon and offered him a list of names of persons he 'was to approach in order to lay the foundation' for the organization of the Klan there.[111] Included in the list were several Liberals out of favour with the Gardiner government. 'The said Dr. J.T.M. Anderson ... furnished me with the names of a number of Liberals,' Emmon's affidavit read, 'who he said had served the Liberal party in the province of Saskatchewan for many years and had been entitled to certain favors from the said party which they had not received. That those Liberals were in a state of mind where he thought they could easily be influenced to join the Klan and work against the government, and pointed out if I got them into the Klan he would do the rest himself.'[112] Earlier, before a Regina court, Emmons testified that Anderson and several Conservative colleagues, including Dr W.D. Cowan, had 'snatched the organization' from him and constantly bothered him with political matters in attempts 'to get the Klan behind politics.'[113]

The extent of Dr J.T.M. Anderson's success in rallying disaffected Protestants and Klansmen to the cause of a revitalized Conservative party was evident at the party convention of mid-March in Regina, a meeting attended by a contingent of Klansmen who shuffled back and forth between the Tory meeting and a Klonvocation conveniently scheduled nearby at the same time.[114] Klan literature was distributed at the convention door and adjoining ante-room without interference, while inside, as J.F. Bryant informed R.B. Bennett, 'the K.K.K. were very active ... as were also the Orangemen ... the head officers of both organizations were present and the organizers of the Klan being very evident throughout the hall. We had some difficulty in keeping them in the background but succeeded in doing so without incident whatsoever.'[115]

The convention proceedings reflected the prevailing ultra-Protestant mood and attendance. In areas of public finance and economic policy – relating to issues like power production and distribution, agricultural aid, or government retrenchment – party pronouncements were liberal, reflecting a sober commitment to win support among farmers and Progressives, a commitment embodied in a resolution inviting 'the support and cooperation of all parties, groups and individuals opposed to the present Liberal administration.'[116] On the schools and immigration issues, however, and on the matter of representation in the party organization, no similar cooperative disposition – towards Catholics – was evident. The party opted for the 'promotion of empire settlement,' immigration 'on the selective principle,' and the encouragement of settlement of 'native Canadians' on 'Saskatchewan's vacant lands.'[117] The schools resolution, formulated by Bryant – who chaired the Resolutions Committee – and agreed to by 'the Protestant organizations,' trotted out the worn demons of the use of textbooks with 'denominational or unpatriotic bias,' the use of religious emblems in public schools, as well as 'the holding of public schools in buildings devoted to religious purposes.'[118] As to representation on the party's governing councils and committees, Catholics were denied even token membership by the more than three hundred delegates in attendance, only three of whom – Joseph Foley of North Battleford, J.J. Leddy of Saskatoon, and A.G. MacKinnon of Regina – were Catholic.[119] When Leddy appeared on the list of nominees to the party's advisory committee, he was approached by the chairman of the nominations committee and asked to withdraw. He refused and was defeated by a candidate nominated from the floor. A.J. MacKinnon's bid for the presidency of the Regina zone of constituencies similarly failed when his name mysteriously disappeared from the list the nominations committee presented to the convention on the final day.[120]

The absence of Catholics, and menacing presence of Klansmen, at the Conservative convention met with a mixed response among leading party officials, provincial and federal. Anderson, like Bryant, was satisfied with the convention results, including the absence of Catholic representation since, according to one prominent observer, he considered it 'inexpedient that any Catholic should hold office' in the organization.[121] That Klansmen attended in abundance, flitted among the delegates, were consulted on policy matters, and distributed their hate literature without interference, Anderson apparently considered entirely acceptable, despite complaints from the excluded Catholic minority, Protestant moderates, or, it seems, federal Conservative party leader R.B. Bennett. In the weeks following the convention, R.B. Bennett was inundated with letters from distressed Tories such as Gregory who concluded, 'some of the leaders of the Conservative party had endeavored to make an alliance with the Klan for the purpose of defeating the present local government';[122] or Yorkton barrister Patrick Doherty, who maintained that 'a large wing of the Convention in some manner had made up its mind to hitch itself to the K.K.K.'[123] With an eye on Quebec and an approaching federal election, Bennett felt it would be nothing short of 'a national calamity if a religious quarrel' were to develop in the province of Saskatchewan.[124] 'At the recent Convention held in Saskatoon,' Bennett wrote Anderson, 'no single Roman Catholic was permitted to be elected to any official position. Surely this was not inadvertent. This cannot but be injurious to the Conservative party throughout Canada, and I cannot think it will be of assistance to you in Saskatchewan. Apparently the Ku Klux Klan circulated literature at the door of the Convention. Should this have been permitted? I am bound to say the whole situation is giving me very, very great concern.'[125]

If the Tory-Klan tryst was, for R.B. Bennett, a matter of great concern, for provincial Liberal premier Jimmy Gardiner it was a glad opportunity to press the fight against the unholy alliance denounced in his January legislative speech. Whether Gardiner's Klan was made of straw, as John Diefenbaker suggested,[126] or of iron, the premier wasted little time, during the weeks and months following the Conservative convention, in exposing its lineages and linkages, a task considerably enhanced, in the eyes of the premier, by the return and subsequent widely publicized trials in May 1928, in Regina and Moose Jaw, of Hoosier scoundrel Pat Emmons.

The premier and his attorney general were probably not terribly concerned about the strength of their case against Emmons, who returned to face charges of misappropriation of funds, based on an information laid by his former Moose Jaw secretary Melville police chief J. Van Dyck. In the absence of the Scott boys, the Crown's case, as J.F. Bryant insisted,[127] was as weak as the subsequent charge, heard in Moose Jaw before Magistrate L.F. Sifton, that Emmons had dispossessed an ingenuous Klanswomen, Mrs Margaret Wilkinson, of $6.50 under false pretences. For the Gardiner government, the contemplated political results of a publicized show trial were far more attractive than the legal ones. The Liberals obviously wanted Emmons to sing, as C.H. Higginbotham, who covered the Klan story as a young journalist, noted, 'and he did.'[128] In place of a conviction, a madrigal was heard, a song as clear and beautiful – to Liberal leaders – as Emmons's earlier efforts in Indiana, where he appeared as a prize pigeon to expose the misdoings of the notorious Stephenson Klan. To ensure that not a single note was missed, 'Gee' Johnson, the government's former *Hansard* reporter, attended to record events. Maintaining a 'watching brief' in the public gallery was Big Jim Cameron, chief organizer of the Saskatchewan Liberal party. J.F. Bryant attended the event for the Conservatives, as did Dr J.T.M. Anderson 'in view of information ... that Emmons intended making an attack on him.'[129]

The Regina and Moose Jaw trials, as Higginbotham observed, were identical farces peopled by collections of hucksters and dupes, relating bizarre stories of Klan doings and misdoings. Van Dyck complained of confusions and pressures by unnamed government officials to enlist his aid in getting Emmons back. A sad letter asking 'Pop' Emmons to intervene, on Van Dyck's behalf, with Indiana Governor Jackson to find him a job as motorcycle policeman was read to the court.[130] Rosborough appeared following a bout of flu, disclaimed international affiliations, and tooted the horn of a new clean Klan. Petty officials J.H. Riddell and C. Ellis informed the court about deposits, drafts, transfers, and petty cash. Moose Jaw Exalted Cyclops and optometrist Dr F.S. Ivay recalled selling spectacles to Emmons, while C.H. Puckering elaborated on deadheads and first-, second-, and third-degree Klansmen. As the spokesperson for duped Klanswomen, Mrs Wilkinson condemned the phony Canadianism of Dr Hawkins, recalled being informed that Henry Ford and Thomas Edison were Klan members, and claimed the 'donation of the sum of $6.50 to the propagation fund of the Invisible Empire of the Ku Klux Klan,' entitled her 'to have and to hold all rights, titles, honors and protection as a citizen of the Invisible Empire Fold at Moose Jaw, Realm of Saskatchewan.'[131]

What pleased 'Gee,' Big Jim Cameron – and Wee Jimmy Gardiner – most of all were the choice utterances of the defendant H.F. Pat Emmons, who told a good long story – about Klan craft, Klan lore, and Klan lineage; Lewis Fowler and the Scott boys; the Indiana connection; the enlistment of dupes and deadheads; the entitlements to a share of the proceeds from the corny sale of hate to willing rubes. But the political stuff, chronicling the Hooded Adventures of Dr J.T.M. Anderson, was what really grabbed Big Jim and Wee Jimmy, and the asides and broadsides about Tory-Klan connections. 'I was good and sick,' Emmons complained within earshot of J.F. Bryant. 'My heart was broken. We built this organization up as a Christian fraternal organization and then Dr. J.T.M. Anderson, of Saskatoon; Dr. Smith of Moose Jaw; Dr. Cowan of Regina; these men snatched it out of my hands ... Every time I went into one of those hotels there was a group of politicians trying to get at me to come and fix the Klan to turn it over to them for some men to vote. Dr. Anderson, of Saskatoon, every time I would land into town, he would ... come to my hotel to talk political conference, and when I went to Moose Jaw to speak, my secretary let him slip in on me.'[132]

Pat Emmons told a good enough story to earn acquittal from Magistrate Heffernan in Regina, who volunteered: 'We have a very poor manhood when we allow this gang from the United States to come here and collect money and have the audacity to tell the people of this Province what the principles of British nationhood are'; and from Magistrate Sifton of Moose Jaw, who thought 'there was a sacred duty imposed on the men of this province and of this city, and that duty was to protect their women, whether it be their wives, sisters and relatives, from perpetration upon them of fraud ... the surprising feature of the disclosures made at this trial is that men who were members of the organization made dupes not only of themselves but also allowed their wives and even their mothers to fall into the same deceptive net.'[133]

Though free to return to home to Indiana, Emmons lingered long enough in Saskatchewan to perform a further duty thought useful by the Gardiner government. He presented, at a public meeting in Regina's City Hall – attended by hundreds of incensed Klansmen who came to hear 'the K.K.K. exposed' by the 'Ex–Grand Klazik of the U.S.A.' (as a *Regina Leader* ad ran)[134] – affidavits, sworn by himself and Puckering, outlining the Anderson-Klan hotel rendezvous in Moose Jaw, Regina, and Saskatoon.[135] Soon after, according to Dr Anderson, Emmons was quietly advised 'to leave the country, and forthwith he was taken over to a little town' near a CPR station where 'in fear and trembling he hid behind a tombstone in a village graveyard until the train came along.'[136]

Emmons's performances evoked howls of complaints from Conservatives and Klansmen, and nods of affirmation from the Liberals. The response of Imperial Wizard Rosborough, challenging the Emmons testimony and affidavits, reproduced in leading local newspapers, was filled with so many disclaimers – of robes, helmets, gowns, prejudices, violence, or affiliation – national, international, or Conservative, that a *New York Times* correspondent, in describing 'the diverting tale of the Ku Klux Klan in Saskatchewan,' concluded the local variety was 'innocuous' and 'platitudinous.'[137] Both Dr W.D. Cowan and J.F. Bryant responded to the Emmons performance with indignant letters to the *Leader.* Without disclaiming membership in the Klan, Cowan denied ever knowing Emmons or of efforts to get the Klan into politics. Bryant protested the use of irregular court procedures for 'political purposes,' disavowed membership in the Klan, denied Tory-Klan linkages, and dismissed the entire Emmons affair as a Liberal caper. As for Dr Anderson, he issued a lengthy statement of his own, claiming that Emmons 'was brought back ... with the knowledge and consent of the Gardiner Government the sole idea being not to fulfill the demands of justice but to attempt to injure the Conservative party' and himself.[138] Anderson alluded to contacts between Liberals and Emmons, in South Bend, Regina's parliament buildings, and, yes, hotels, where plots were hatched to ensnare Tories. He complained of Liberal cowardice, degrading political methods, and attempts to malign him with 'false statements.' But nowhere in his lengthy retort was there a denial that he had ever attended Klan meetings, or met with Emmons in the places cited, to discuss matters of mutual concern. When J.F. Bryant passed along copies of the Emmons-Puckering affidavits to a concerned R.B. Bennett, who faced questions from C.A. Dunning about Saskatchewan Tory-Klan connections, Bennett confessed: 'I do not like the look of these affidavits. I had no idea Dr. Anderson had so little discretion.'[139] Bennett advised Anderson to take legal proceedings to clear his name. 'In connection with the affidavit executed by Mr. Puckering,' Bennett wrote, 'may I direct your attention to the provisions of ... the Criminal code ... for clearly the lawyer who signed the document ... is liable to have proceedings taken against him, and I think it would have a salutary effect if such proceedings were taken, providing of course that such case was supported by satisfactory evidence.'[140] Dr Anderson never did take the future prime minister's advice, or deny that he had ever met and strategized with Emmons in hotels, or wherever.

The Tory consternation following the Emmons affair was reassuring to the premier, who remained convinced, throughout the spring and summer of 1928, that a flat-out attack on the Klan and its unholy linkages would yield reasonable political dividends. Gardiner's satisfaction with the Emmons trial results was evident in a pair of letters to Liberal stalwarts. To a Rosetown supporter, he commented that the trials 'proved every remark' he made 'in the legislature last session' and that the Tories' 'little plan to involve the province in a religious political war, will be detrimental to them.'[141] To a second Liberal he wrote: 'By the time we are through with [Anderson], I do not think he will be able to squirm out of the position he has got himself into.[142] There were Liberals, however, who thought otherwise, and counselled prudence; men like organizer W.C. Barrie who noted that 'Gardiner attacked a problem, when he attacked the Klan,' and that Emmons's arrival had merely 'added more coal to the fire'; or Senator Andrew Haydon who complained to the prime minister that 'the Premier out there has been too rigid and too fierce and that he made a real mistake when he went into the field against the Ku Klux Klan ... His going out publicly has aroused the protestant interest in the Province, which is exceedingly strong.'[143] When James Gardiner went public against the Klan, he was aware that Liberals, as well as Conservatives and Progressives 'with rather strong views in opposition to Catholics and foreign-speaking people,' had gone over to the Klan.[144] But he thought their number small and insignificant, compared to the 'great deal of support from reasonable people' the party stood to gain 'across the province.'[145]

With the reasonable electorate in mind, James Gardiner took to the wheat fields in a ferocious campaign to expose, smoke out, exorcise, and expel the Klan from the collective psyche of Saskatchewanians. At widely attended public meetings in Dysart, Lemberg, Hanley, and other towns along the way, the premier featured the Klan, fought the Klan, linked the Klan to Conservatives, and defended the government's record on educational and immigration issues against the crazed assaults of Moloney and Hawkins, Hind and Rondeau, Pickering and Snelgrove. The premier's speeches were no mere tirades; they were laced with details, documents, disclosures, and statistics, martialled to establish the Klan's violent American lineage, its seditious predilections and linkages with Conservatives, as well as firm up the government's own reputation as tolerant, decent, efficient, and beholden to no special interest, least of all the Catholics. Gardiner waved and quoted incriminating letters and documents, from Fowler, Hawkins, Emmons, and Lord, proving the Klan's eastern and southern connections; he repeated new and old stories about scams, misappropriated funds, and get-rich-quick artists; and he warned of the infiltration of the government service, police forces, churches, and business organizations by a seditious organization of bigots, practising weird rituals, seeking to 'undermine the discipline of every national organization.'[146] The Tory tryst, Anderson's foreplay with Emmons, the consummation – at the April Conservative convention – attended by Anderson, Bryant, Hawkins, Ellis, Rosborough, and others – were elaborated and embellished. In place of the politics of nativism, the premier offered a decent, practical pluralism, evidenced by the government's record of tolerance and fair play to all groups – native and immigrant; French and English; Protestant, Catholic, or Jew. Gardiner spoke kindly about the fine message of tolerance delivered by a distinguished rabbi to the recent United Church conference, praised the local archbishop as 'an ideal Christian gentleman' and dismissed as fantasy claims that Catholics enjoyed privileged access to the government, that the papacy was likely to relocate to Canada, or that he himself intended to convert to Catholicism.[147] The premier insisted that whatever sectarian abuses may have crept into the educational system were minuscule and had been vigorously corrected by a government free of bias towards any social groups or religion, including the Catholic church. In a Cabinet of seven, the premier noted at Hanley, and elsewhere, only Dr Uhrich, the minister of public works and health, was Catholic. Although 20 per cent of the population were Catholic, of the fifty-three legislators, seven were Catholics, and, within the civil service, 13 per cent.[148]

The culmination of the campaign was a debate, at Lemberg, between the premier of Saskatchewan and the Klan's major hustings orator. From the day of his opening attack in the legislature in January, Gardiner had been extended – and had refused – repeated invitations to debate the Klan. As his tour wound down, however, the premier agreed to debate J.H. Hawkins, in his home constituency. The contest, before more than a thousand persons, including a contingent of heckling Klansmen, was long, raucous, and, by most accounts, won by the premier, who was convinced, at the conclusion of the debate, that his opponent had been floored. Hawkins, who spoke first, spent the better part of an hour and a half extricating himself from charges elaborated at Gardiner's earlier meetings, of huckstering, graft, endless infighting, and Tory collaboration. The remainder of his portion was filled with repetitions of homilies about patriotism, one public school, the drawing of 'lines between the races,' and the reticence of the Klan to go 'out of its way to help the Jew.'[149] As for the premier, he elaborated, once again, on legacies, lineages, and linkages; the eastern and American connections; the Yankee legacy of 'lawlessness, crime and persecution'; the Tory ties; the readiness to undermine courts and overturn government; the attempt to 'legalize begging to improve the financial standing of a few individuals at the expense of the many who are relieved of $13 apiece.'[150] The premier closed with a prediction: 'In the past in this province we have prided ourselves on living together harmoniously, and in the future we can live in exactly the same way because we shall be devoid of any of the influence of the Klan.'[151]

In furtherance of its eradication program, the Gardiner government, and its federal allies, put the courts and the immigration department to good use following the Lemberg debate. Floored in the Lemberg skating rink, Hawkins, on 20 July was deported, following a ruling and hearing – in which he was defended by J.F. Bryant – by the Immigration department, an act that confirmed to his own satisfaction the sinister Catholic bias of federal immigration officials. Nor was this all. Prominent Klan organizers R.C. Snelgrove and T.H. Pakenham were both hauled into the courts and convicted on weapons charges. Found with a revolver in a club bag, Packenham pleaded guilty to carrying a concealed weapon and was sentenced to two months in jail and fined fifty dollars.[152] Snelgrove's troubles began outside the Lemberg skating arena, on the eve of the Gardiner-Hawkins debate, where local RCMP officers discovered, concealed in a bag in a Klansman's car, a loaded revolver. According to *The Klansman*, Snelgrove had carried the gun since the previous spring, when he was threatened and chased 'by a car loaded with drunken Roman Catholics who, flourishing fire arms, threatened to break up his meeting and run him out of town.'[153] Defended by J.F. Bryant, Snelgrove produced in court a permit – issued by the chief of police of Melville and a Klansman – which the magistrate held invalid, and was sentenced to two months in jail and fined seventy-five dollars in costs.[154] Several months later, the Imperial Wizard himself appeared before the courts on charges of theft of two hundred dollars in November 1921, from the rural municipality of Herschel, where he was employed as an auditor. Bryant again appeared in defence, and won the Wizard's acquittal.[155]

With the Klan drawn, quartered, and exposed as alien bigots wedded to native Tories, Premier James Gardiner was prepared, in the autumn, to test the results of his handiwork in a by-election in the constituency of Arms River, a seat held by the Liberals since 1908 and recently vacated by Liberal incumbent George Scott, who had accepted a federal government appointment. For Gardiner and the Liberals, Arms River was a critical contest, the culmination of a campaign of denunciation of the Klan's divisive hate politics and Tory alliances – against 'a type of opposition,' Gardiner admitted to King, the Liberals had 'not necessarily been accustomed to.' 'When we have a contest there,' he wrote to a colleague, 'we want to strike a blow at the movement which has been on foot in the province stirring up religious prejudice, I think it is taking as strong a hold in Arms River as any part of the province.'[156] A historically Liberal, mixed constituency, dotted with Klaverns, Orange Lodges, and American émigrés – who constituted approximately 50 per cent of the population – Arms River provided the perfect electoral battle, and testing ground for the premier's assault of the dark forces of disorder and bigotry.

The disordered bigots, it turned out, did not fare badly in a campaign so low, ugly, and protracted that the premier thought it the toughest he had ever faced during his career in Saskatchewan politics.[157] The Ku Klux Klan did not contest the seats; it was, after all, a fraternal organization, professedly non-partisan and non-political. It did, however, play a key auxiliary role in the contest, aiding and abetting the Conservatives, who had gained considerable strength and number following a summer of intense organization. After months of demagogic agitation, the Klan had excited and heightened public emotions in Arms River, as elsewhere, on the touchy issues of immigration, education, and political immorality, issues taken up by campaigning Tories like J.F. Bryant who predicted that 'within five years or ten at the most under present political conditions, Roman Catholics will be in the majority in Saskatchewan, and the French will control the political destinies of Quebec, Saskatchewan and all of Canada';[158] by M.A. MacPherson and others, who played on the alleged links of the Bronfman liquor interests to the Liberal party;[159] and by editorialists of the new Conservative daily, the *Regina Star*, which neglected the Klan entirely and warned instead of the biological fact of the degradation of the character of the people through 'the intermixing of the nationalities' resulting from an 'indiscriminate policy of immigration.'[160] At the organizational level, the Klan was forthcoming. 'The whole constituency was organized by the Ku Klux Klan during the early months of the summer,' Gardiner informed King in a letter, 'with meetings held in every one of the towns and villages, with the exception of Holdfast, which happens to be fairly strongly Catholic.'[161] As election day neared, Klan organizers circulated among the polls, flitted in and out of Tory committee rooms, aided in bringing out the vote, and, if we are to believe Jimmy Gardiner, reminded constituents of Rome's political presence by sending a fake priest to wander the streets in several towns on election day.[162]

In the face of a virulent Tory-Klan attack, the Liberals held Arms River, by a mere fifty-three votes, a result both the opposition and government found encouraging. The 90 per cent turn-out; the shift of prominent Liberal voters to the Tories;[163] the flat response to the government's Tory-Klan linkage strategy; the easy float of the immigration, education, and political immorality issues; and the tolerance among Protestants of hate-sloganeering were promising omens to Dr Anderson, who, without ever attacking the Klan, reminded voters that it was the Liberals who granted the Klan a charter, and encouraged its growth by attacking it, before inviting Emmons back to snuff out their own creation.[164] The premier, for his part, was convinced that Arms River was the triumphant conclusion to his campaign of exposure and eradication begun in the new year. 'The only matter which has injected anything new into the political situation here,' Gardiner wrote national organizer Thomas Taylor following the by-election,

> was the attempt which was being made to build up a strong case against both the provincial and federal government on the ground that favor was being shown to foreign-speaking people and Roman Catholics in the matter of immigration and school administration. This was being fostered by Conservative organizers ... and a carefully laid plan to have in a great many centres – the actual number in the province being one hundred and four – secret organizations of the Klan for the purpose of spreading propaganda of all kinds against both the federal and provincial governments to be sprung in the open when the election might occur. We undertook a year ago to bring this campaign out into the open. We succeeded in doing so. The general opinion today is that this organization is making very little progress in the province. On the other hand, it is generally admitted that in many places it has absolutely ceased to function.[165]

The premier's prognosis of the Klan's stagnation, and decline, may have been an exercise in wishful thinking. It was not, however, entirely without foundation. Throughout the winter and spring of 1929, the Saskatchewan Klansmen continued along their merry, bigoted ways. They played at whist, gawked at crosses, Klonvocated, and nodded to the repetitions of Rondeau and the malarkey of Moloney. When a general election was announced for 6 June 1929, they traded in their invisible hoods for Tory bonnets and rushed to join Dr Anderson's ethnic and religious revolt. The Conservative leader, once again, acknowledged neither their existence nor their help. But he did reap the benefits of their agitation. Changes were afoot in Saskatchewan, in June 1929 – Conservative changes. For the first time since Saskatchewan became a province, in 1905, the Liberals were denied a majority and, following the passage of a want-of-confidence motion soon after the legislature convened in September, the premier resigned and was succeeded by Dr Anderson, who headed a Cooperative government consisting of Conservatives – the preponderant group – Progressives, and independents.[166] The causes of the Liberal defeat were many. Conservative saw-offs with the Progressives eliminated damaging three-party contests in a host of constituencies. A quarter-century of one-party Liberal domination, machine rule, and patronage politics, induced a powerful receptivity to the slogans 'Break the Machine' and 'Time for a Change.' Anxieties over power production and distribution and federal natural-resource retention added fuel to the opposition's attacks, as did several nagging scandals involving patronage, liquor, and corrupt electoral practices. Among the several issues favoured by the Tories, immigration and education bulked especially large; these were emotional issues, pregnant with stereotype, which the Klan discovered, linked up with political and economic questions, and magnified soon after the Klan's timely arrival. The Gardiner government fell victim in part to a nativist Protestant revolt feeding on the fears of displacement by alien immigrants and Catholics, who had gained, in the eyes of troubled Protestants, through unwarranted channels, unreasonable access to governments; a revolt fuelled by the status anxieties and social paranoia Klansmen had effectively exploited in similarly vulnerable constituencies throughout North America.[167]

Though the Klan had found a soft spot in Saskatchewan, it was unable to take root. In his prognosis of the Klan's imminent demise,

Jimmy Gardiner was not wrong; he was merely a trifle premature. On the eve of the Liberal defeat, Klansmen celebrated with a burning cross and declarations that the day of political judgment had arrived. There was another joyous time, in 1930, when the federal Liberals were defeated and R.B. Bennett was elected prime minister of Canada. But these were merely momentary effusions, chastened by the realization that the Klan was in organizational disarray, wracked by infighting and depleted in number. By the time the depression hit full stride, the Ku Klux Klan had shrivelled to the status of a petty sect, or a lonely P.O. box number.

At its peak, the Saskatchewan Klan was a wild brush-fire ignited by volatile xenophobic sentiments towards immigrants, Catholics, and aliens. But it was a fire contained, and quickly spent. The Tory victory, the transfer of natural resources to the province, the adoption of a restrictionist immigration policy by the federal Tories, and changes in the school laws enacted by the provincial government robbed the Klan of the key issues it sniffed and sold, just as the exercise of power by the new Conservative government ended whatever avenues of influence may have existed in opposition. For all of his set views on immigration, education, and Canadianization, Dr Anderson was a politician and an opportunist who dallied at the right time, for a limited purpose, with an organization whose impact on opinion contributed to his party's election. The Klan had served its purpose of helping turn out the Liberals, and future contacts, in light of the needs of the federal party and imperatives of governing a plural society – at a time of extreme economic distress – were out of the question. In the aftermath of the Conservative victory, J.J. Moloney, R.C. Snelgrove, J.W. Rosborough, and other prominent Klan leaders disappeared, gone to new hustings, or pursuits.[168]

Contributing to the Klan's swift demise was its economic obliviousness and awkward cultural fit. As a *Queen's Quarterly* correspondent observed, the Klan in Saskatchewan had economic beginnings – as a scheme to put dollars in the pockets of its promoters. But it developed no economic program, or sustaining philosophy, other than bigotry – the targeting of certain social and religious groups as enemies, exploiters, and strangulators of economic society. In lumping the Klan, for polemical purposes, together with other American-based agrarian protest movements, like the Non-Partisan League, Gardiner neglected an important difference. The farm movements developed discrete economic programs, reflecting class needs and interests. The Klan focused exclusively on race and religion; a monomania that, in the special circumstances of the 1929 election, sensibly contributed to political change. But more sustaining challenges faced economic groups as the depression deepened, and the Klan offered nothing more than exotic paraphernalia, tedious ritual, and emotional hate-objects.[169] According to our *Queen's Quarterly* observer, it was the 'independent, thinking, farm vote' that determined Saskatchewan elections, and appeals to race and religion could succeed only if they made 'an impression on these people.'[170] 'The pools know no race, no religion, no creed,' the observer concluded. 'Their aim, and that of their parent organization, is cooperation – between all classes of the community. Only by the closest cooperation can the pool survive. Cooperation cannot exist with a great wedge driven between neighboring farmers.'[171] Unlike the great farm protest movements, the Klan found the bulk of its converts in small towns and never succeeded 'in penetrating the heart of rural Saskatchewan.'[172]

The Klan's penetration of the Canadian political culture was equally limited. Peaceful protestations notwithstanding, the Klan brought with it a legacy, heritage, and reputation that hampered its expansion in Saskatchewan, and elsewhere in Canada. In the United States, the reborn Klan was a nativist movement feeding on the heritage of nobility and honour bequeathed by its Reconstruction predecessor. The American Klan was wreathed in southern honour and, after the First World War, national patriotism. But no profusion of charters adorned with maple leaves, wavings of the Union Jack, or renderings of 'God Save the King' could hide in Canada its Yankee origins. The Canadian Klan remained a Yankee import without the cultural resonance recalling the noble days of Reconstruction, or the home-baked apple-pie chauvinism of Babbitt America. A bootleg import that slipped in under the cultural barrier, the Klan ran smack into British tradition, institutions, and cultural idolatry. Itself an alien institution in British North America, the Klan could hardly feed on anti-alien sentiments. From the moment of their arrival, Klans-

men had to contend with reams of editorials and political pronouncements from diverse opponents, condemning the Klan's ways
as foreign, American, and inimical to the British tradition of commitment to fair play, common sense, tolerance, give and take, and
the rule of law.[173] For all of their bombast and righteousness, Canadian Klansmen remained a nervous, fidgety, non-violent lot, who
shunned tar and feathers, avoided lynching, drove cars by day instead
of horses by night, and abandoned even their soiled bed sheets in
search of an acceptance they never won.

4

Goglus

BOBOLINK. Skunk Blackbird. Ricebird. Fr – Le Goglu. *Dolichonyx oryzivorus* ... The Bobolink in spring and summer is a bird frequenting the hay and clover fields. It can be seen any summer's day perched on the surrounding fences or launching into the air on quivering wings, pouring forth its song of ecstasy. Later in the season the rollicking male doffs his parti-coloured gayness for the duller ochre and brown stripes of the female. His song is replaced by metallic clicks and with hundreds of others of this species joined together in flocks he seeks the marshes in autumn. On leaving Canada for his winter home in South America he stops for a time in the rice fields of the Carolinas and here he is hailed not as Bobolink, the merry songster, beloved for both practical and sentimental reasons, but as the plaguy 'Rice Bird' that settles upon the crops in thousands and causes decided damage. In the south he is shot and sold for food in great numbers.

P.A. Taverner, *Birds of Eastern Canada*, Memoir 104, no. 3, Biological Series (Ottawa: Department of Mines 1930), p. 157

They were, to be sure, a chummy, *Völkisch* pair – the gaunt French Canadian with the lit eyes and trim moustache; the smiling, bow-tied

Nazi emissary charged with representing his party's interests in the United States, Mexico, and Canada. Their meeting, in the autumn of 1932, in the city of Montreal, was relaxed and reassuring. Herr Kurt G.W. Ludecke was taken with Adrien Arcand, with his 'vibrant, intelligent, fine-featured' face, his 'genuine fighting spirit,' his fiery leadership of the Ordre Patriotique des Goglus, later described in the Nazi's autobiography, not inaccurately, as 'a violently anti-jewish, in the main Catholic folkic movement ... growing rapidly in French-Canada, with three publications, all very demagogic and clever.'[1] As for Arcand, he found Herr Ludecke, and his wife, Mildred, an utterly charming couple and, what is more, useful contacts with an international movement ordained, in Arcand's view, to sweep the world. 'He was greatly pleased when I gave him an autographed photograph of Hitler,' Ludecke recalled. 'We understood each other perfectly, and agreed to cooperate in every way.'[2]

Adrien Arcand's discovery of National Socialism was the culmination of a career that descended, in the waning years of the 1920s, from the humming editorial room of a large Montreal daily into the gutter of hate journalism and Fascist politics. A glib hack with a lively imagination and twisted sense of mission, Arcand admired and served, at one time or another, a variety of patriotic and eminent persons, among them Mgr Georges Gauthier, Archbishop of Montreal; Prime Minister R.B. Bennett; Mayor Camillien Houde; and Premier Maurice Duplessis. None of these gentlemen, however, captured the journalist's admiration more than Adolf Hitler, whose National Socialist cause, and violent anti-Semitism, Arcand and his followers embraced with a chilling and relentless enthusiasm.

The strange descent of Adrien Arcand into the underworld of Fascist politics followed the onset of the depression, when the former employee of the large Montreal daily *La Presse* found himself at loose ends, professionally and ideologically. Born on 3 October 1899, in the Montreal parish of L'Immaculée-Conception, the son of Narcisse Arcand of Deschambault – an organizer of the local of the carpenters and joiners' union – and Marie-Anne Mathieu of Sainte Marie de Beauce, Arcand took his primary schooling at L'Ecole Saint-Stanislaus de Montreal before entering, in 1916, the Sulpician-run Collège de Montréal.[3] Here he studied the classics; read Pascal; submitted to, and admired, the regime of discipline imposed by the Sulpicians; and briefly contemplated a career in chemical engineering, which was quickly abandoned, in 1919, in favour of journalism.

La Patrie, a Montreal daily, was the first to hire Adrien Arcand as a reporter, then the Montreal Star where he was known among colleagues 'who made their living amid the scarlet vice and downy cocaine that flaunted in dingy passages of Recorder's Court as Narcisse, because of the chaste, blossoming innocence of his prose.'[4] Narcisse soon abandoned the Star for La Presse, where he remained for almost ten years, honed his writing and editorial skills, married Yvonne Giguère of Quebec in April 1925, raised a family, pursued his interest in astronomy – as a member of La Société Astronomique de France – and, in 1923, served as one of the founders and as vice-president of La Société des Auteurs Canadiens-Français. In 1924, he was commissioned a lieutenant in the Régiment de Chateauguay of la Milice du Canada and, with his brother, Major Louis-Georges Arcand, proudly designed the regiment's official coat of arms. Five years later, he joined other ranks – the unemployed – when La Presse publisher Pamphille du Tremblay fired and blackballed him from the industry, following an unsuccessful attempt to organize a union of journalists.[5]

Banished from the big dailies, Arcand launched, in concert with Joseph Ménard, his own little weeklies. A short dumpling of a man – with ample jaws, broad neck, and inflated head similar to that of Mussolini – whom he admired – Ménard was a printer, and son of a printer, whose father's press was placed at the disposal of the maverick pair. Dr P.E. Lalanne, a friend of Ménard's and owner of a local radio and appliance shop, helped finance the venture with loans. In short order, three nasty weeklies, brimming with invective, spoofery, caricature, and patriotic fulminations, began circulating in and around Montreal: Le Patriote, a 'journal du dimanche,' printed at 987 Boulevard St. Laurent; Le Goglu, a 'journal humoristique,' heavily laced with violent caricature; and, beginning March 1930, Le Chameau in honour of the hornless, ruminant, cushion-footed quadruped, of the Bactrian type, with two humps – the one, perhaps, representing the editor, the other, the publisher.[6]

Though riddled with swipes and invective, the little weeklies of

Adrien Arcand were not lacking in direction, underlying seriousness, or effect. Quebec, after all, was wanting, and there were targets galore for the virulent pair. The twin processes of industrialization and urbanization had created large and telling strains on the province's social and economic structures. Adrien Arcand was born into a society still predominantly agricultural. Three decades later, when *Le Goglu* began chirping its nasty songs, the province's face was radically changed. The development of labour-intensive small-scale industry – clothing, textiles, shoes, furniture –protected and encouraged by the tariff, was followed by a surge of investment in large capital-intensive primary industries producing for export: forest products, pulp and paper, and mining. The new economic development of the 1920s was fuelled by increased exploitation of hydroelectric power and by a succession of Liberal regimes that welcomed foreign investors – American, Canadian, and others – with easy concessions, ample infrastructure, a lax regulatory system, disabling labour legislation, and favourable taxation. Accompanying the growth and investment surge were serious dislocations and deprivations. Levels of unemployment remained, at the best of times, higher than in neighbouring Ontario, while the development of manufacturing and wage-scale levels remained substantially lower. Power and control of industry rested with the Anglo-Canadians who monopolized jobs in managerial, executive, and technical strata of the population. Poverty, poor technical training, and illiteracy were rife among wide stratum of French-Canadian workers who, in increasing numbers, deserted the countryside and streamed into the cities – Montreal and environs primarily – where overcrowding, inferior housing, contagious diseases, high infant-mortality rates, and poor sanitary conditions awaited them.[7]

With the arrival of the depression, matters worsened substantially. Investment dried up, while external demand for the province's forestry and mineral products declined. Plummeting wheat prices slowed the shipment of grain through the ports of Montreal and Quebec City, while the western farmers' diminished demand for finished goods starved local industry.[8] By 1933, the city of Montreal boasted a 30 per cent unemployment rate with 280,000 people on direct welfare, drawing meagre benefits from a poorly developed, underfinanced relief system paralysed by overlapping jurisdictions and dependent on voluntary, charitable agencies like the St Vincent de Paul Society. 'For one-industry towns throughout Quebec,' a leading historian of the Taschereau regime wrote, 'for workers whose port-related employment was already highly seasonal, for employees in the dozens of small-clothing and other manufacturing concerns, which were marginal at the best of times, and even for employees of bigger firms, which had never paid more than subsistence wages, the impact was swift, brutal, and highly visible. For those in the construction trades, and for small merchants, professionals, and landlords with a working-class clientele, hardship was only slightly mitigated and delayed.'[9]

It was plainly a time, and place, for causes and critics, and the little weeklies of Adrien Arcand and Joseph Ménard – the Katzenjammer Kids of Quebec journalism, as they were sometimes called – joined the chorus of exposure and denunciation. From the first days of their publication, the front and back pages of their journals were rife with swipes and swats against the enemies of their province, society, and race. The trusts and combines, the St James Street barons, the paper and electrical interests, the alien exploiters of Quebec's resources, and, not least, political cliques who served foreign masters and wallowed in patronage and corruption, were relentlessly assailed. Favourite demons were the federal regime of Mackenzie King, removed from power in the federal election of 1930, and the provincial Liberal government led by L.A. Taschereau.

Not content with exposing and criticizing, Arcand and Ménard were prepared to offer prescriptions and solutions. What Quebec, and Canada, needed, Arcand surmised, was a national saviour, a great leader at the helm of the right sort of party.[10] Provincially and municipally, Arcand's first, albeit fleeting choice was the endomorphic Camillien Houde, the 'p'tit gars de Sainte-Marie,' who, in 1928, was elected mayor of Montreal and, a year later, leader of the provincial Conservative party.[11] Though a partisan Conservative, Houde was at bottom a populist who rose to eminence and office from extreme poverty and chronic bankruptcy, on the broad shoulders of the tenement unwashed. Among the oversized mayor's most ardent supporters, according to Robert Rumilly, were the Italians who appreciated his Fascist tendencies, if not his resemblance to Mussolini.[12] Following his election as Conservative party leader, Houde arranged a subsidy to the Arcand papers and received, albeit briefly, their support in his campaign of denunciation of rings, cliques, and liberal perfidies. When Camillien Houde threatened to shove his puffy fist through Taschereau's patrician top hat, Arcand and Ménard applauded and lent their support as 'Houdistes Indépendants' to his successful campaign for re-election as mayor in March 1930.[13]

A more likely candidate as saviour was the national leader of the Conservative party, Richard Bedford Bennett, whom *Le Goglu* described as 'un homme énergique, courageux, puissant ... un Chrétien à foi robuste et à principes inébranlables.'[14] Soon after his election as leader, Bennett appointed as Quebec organizer Senator Joseph Rainville, who recruited Arcand and Ménard as publicists in support of the Conservative cause. Short of support among the established press, Rainville solicited contributions from a number of professionals and businessmen, then handed over the monies – totalling eighteen thousand dollars, with more promised – as a subsidy to Arcand and Ménard, whose press and weeklies were placed at the disposal of the Tories during the summer 1930 federal election campaign.[15] Arcand worked hard for Rainville and Bennett. He plotted publicity strategy, met with the national leader, printed tens of thousands of circulars favouring the Conservative cause, and widely distributed copies of his newspapers throughout the campaign. When the Conservatives swept the country in the election of 28 July 1930, and returned twenty-four members of Parliament from the province of Quebec, Arcand rejoiced and was convinced that Canada, and Quebec, were at last entering a brave new era.

But while the Conservatives were pointed in the right direction, they did not quite satisfy Adrien Arcand's nagging yearning for the picturesque, the exotic, or the martial, the right sort of vehicle to gather and focus the released energies of Quebec's excited youth. As the depression deepened, Quebec became a fertile breeding ground for new social and political movements – and a nursery for *enfants terribles*. Adrien Arcand's own claim, on the super-patriotic far right of the political spectrum, was staked out in late November 1929, when *Le Goglu* announced the creation of an organization known as L'Ordre Patriotique des Goglus.

The new organization was as much fantasy as real, the elaborate invention of a semi-destitute journalist who dreamed of glories – national and racial – and vanquished enemies. For the duration of its life (less than five years), it remained more of a fragment than a movement. The numbers remained small; the claims, exaggerated. But, like the bobolink that served as their symbol, the Goglus were busy, noisy, and fiercely dedicated, according to Arcand, to exterminating dangerous vermin.

The structure, goals, and strategy of Arcand's pet movement were set out in successive issues of its journalistic mouthpiece, *Le Goglu*, a loud rag edited and largely written by Arcand, who invented the fictional Emile Goglu, appointed him founder and leader, and invested him with an assortment of positions, including propagandist, publisher, and editor. The result was an odd, exotic addition to the accumulating inventory of Quebec's patriotic societies. A product of Arcand's proness to fantasy, military training, and interest in Fascist Italy and Imperial Rome, the Goglu organization was elaborate, articulated, and hierarchical. At the top was the Supreme Chief. Below him was a Supreme Council, consisting of representatives from various zones, fifteen in all, covering the entire breadth of the province, country, and city. A *rmées* of Goglus congregated in zones, *légions* in counties, and *phalanges* in parishes. The *phalanges* themselves subdivided into 'cohorts de Rue ou de Rang.'[16] In all, Arcand's figment allowed for 150,000 members. The real membership, never disclosed, was likely minuscule.

For the joiners, the Goglus offered the dubious reward of queer ritual, including a mysterious numbering system, exotic passwords, and a uniform with varied stripes and colours for different ranks. In an age of shirt movements, the Goglus wore blue broadcloth, smart ties, and Basque wool berets bearing a heraldic coat of arms consisting of a maple leaf, a cross, other less precise symbols, and the slogan 'Sempir Service.' Women, or Gogluses, wore waistcoats of the same colour and cloth as the men's shirts. Les Jeunes Goglus, over the age of four, paraded in replicas of their parents' outfits.[17]

Perched at the very top of the coat of arms of L'Ordre Patriotique des Goglus, in full song with wings spread, was Adrien Arcand's favourite bird, the goglu or bobolink, 'un oiseau irréprochable qui nous charme de son chant harmonieux et auquel nous n'avons pas encore découvert de mauvaises habitudes.'[18] Native to North America and found in abundance in the fields, meadows, and forests of Quebec, the bobolink's free-spirited and pure ecstatic song, its brave defence of kin and appetite for insects and vermin, symbolized for Arcand the new awakening, the nascent idealism of youth and renewal of a race in thrall to foreign masters. 'Le Goglu est un oiseau charmant, d'agréable plumage,' Arcand wrote, 'qui affectionne particulièrement la province de Québec. Si nous avons d'aussi belles forêts, nous en sommes redevables au goglu pour une large part car il y dévore chaque année des millions et des millions d'insectes nuisibles. C'est notre plus courageux petit chasseur de vermine, infatigable au travail comme une abeille ... Il a l'instinct de race, communiquant sans cesse avec les siens par son chant mélodieux, défendant son nid, sa famille et ses petits avec une énergie féroce ... Le goglu symbolise la nouvelle génération d'une race fière et vigoureuse.'[19]

While the structure, ritual, and plumage of L'Ordre Patriotique des Goglus were unique among Quebec's growing colony of patriotic groups, its ideology and program were not, at the outset, terribly different. In editorials signed by Emile Goglu or Adrien Arcand – the same individual – in pronouncements throughout *Le Miroir* et *Le Goglu*, at public meetings in Quebec City and Montreal – at the Monument National and elsewhere – at conferences of zones or *phalanges*, old and new nationalist themes were played upon. Goglus were reminded that they formed, one and all, a society of friendship, mutual aid, and vigilance, a non-partisan patriotic organization open to all who loved their race and were prepared to defend it from foreign invasion and occupation. The Goglus heard about heritage conservation; the preservation of language, customs, and traditions; the protection of natural and historic rights; the purification of public life through education and vigilance.[20] The virtues of small business and rural life were extolled, and state-directed colonization was offered as a remedy for unemployment and urbanization. A new equilibrium was needed, according to Emile Goglu, between 'le capital financier' and 'le capital humain.' Family and church were celebrated as the core institutions of a wholesome, Christian society. Trusts were assailed as economic strangulators and, in the case of hydro-electric power production and distribution, nationalization was offered as a remedy.

The Goglus' program was neither liberal nor revolutionary. Their goals were, instead, nationalist and restorative. Like other professed patriots, Emile Goglu was obsessed with the imperatives of national survival, cultural and economic; a survival keyed to the renewal of public and economic life and secured by liberation from alien powers and institutions. Without education, vigilance, and combat against the predators stalking the forest and fields of their native land, the people's progress, and very survival, were imperilled.

In the beginning, Adrien Arcand was not entirely clear about the true identity of the enemies of the people. Though great beasts stalked the forests of Quebec, their species and shape remained, for a while, hazy and ill-defined. Arcand's dislikes seemed as legion as the noisy Goglu flitting in the forest around Lac-Saint-Jean, or the Saguenay. Among those who qualified as public enemies were press barons, American financiers, 'trustards,' Liberal and Conservative politicians of every stripe and level – municipal, provincial, and federal. 'Il faut à tout prix libérer la province de la "Bête" qui a retardé son progrès et la Bête c'est l'égoïsme, l'incurie, le pillage, la trahison, la vente du pays aux Américains, le dépeuplement des campagnes, le désastre agricole et économique.'[21] It was not too long, however, before Arcand concentrated his hates and focused on a clear and appropriate target. The one true source of his people's, and mankind's, woes, *Le Goglu* disclosed, week after week – in vicious editorials and hideous cartoons – was the Jews, who became the centrepiece of Adrien Arcand's weird astrology and the hate-objects of a lifelong obsession. Without ever shedding entirely his other baggage of diffuse resentments, Adrien Arcand seized with a vengeance on the Jews, and the 'Jewish problem,' as the key to the mystery of the enslavement of not only his own noble and suffering people, but the world.

The object of Arcand's consuming obsession was a people, or ethnic group – comprising approximately 1.5 per cent of the national population in 1931 – who, battered and victimized throughout the world, had managed to gain, in Canada and Quebec, a minor and, relatively speaking, inconsequential place, in the social, economic, and political system. Though depicted by their Quebec detractors as strangers and aliens, Jews, in tiny numbers, had arrived early. New France, by ordinance and policy, was barren of Jews, though several, including Abraham Gradis, a Bordeaux resident of Portuguese origin, naturalized in France, whose cargo ships carried merchandise between Old and New France, played an important role in the colony's economic life.[22] Jewish settlement did not really begin until the Conquest, when a trickle of Jews of British origin, including Aaron Hart – a commissary officer on the staff of General Amherst, who eventually became seigneur of Bécancour – made Quebec their home.[23] Subsequent immigration until the early 1880s was minuscule, spotty, and, for the most part, of British origin, including a number who had fled, to Britain, from persecution in Germany and Lithuania.[24] The first census of post-Confederation Canada counted 1,233 Jews in 1871, or 0.03 per cent of the population, a number exceeded even by the local blacks.

Although Canada's Jewish population, fed by European immigrants who came directly from, or via, the United States, doubled in the post-census decade, there was no substantial growth until the 1880s. The new influx was mainly from Central and Eastern Europe – especially Romania, parts of Austro-Hungary, and the section of the Russian Empire known as the Pale of Settlement, a vast territory encompassing provinces in Russia, Poland, the Ukraine, and Lithuania.[25] For the Jews of the Pale, life was hell. Civil and educational disabilities, mobility restrictions, onerous taxation, grinding poverty, and military conscription were supplemented by mob violence and pogroms, sanctioned or incited by reactionary regimes seeking scapegoats, which spread death and terror among wide sections of the Jewish population. The First World War, and its bloody aftermath in Russia, added to Jewish miseries. Hundreds of thousands died in combat during the war or from pogroms, in the Ukraine primarily, during the bitter civil war following the Bolshevik assumption of power. The upshot of the accumulating calamities was a clamour to emigrate and, to Quebec and Canada, an increased flow controlled and restricted by a variable, and somewhat exclusionist, immigration policy. From the approximately 2,500 Jews resident in Canada in

1881, the population rose, by 1911, to 74,564 – a function of substantial economic growth, a rising demand for labour, relaxed immigration policies and procedures, and an increased awareness among immigrants of economic opportunities. A decade later, in 1921, the Jewish population of Quebec stood at 47,977 and, in Canada, at 126,196, or 1.44 per cent of the population; this number, and proportion, barely altered during the next decade, as a result of the adoption of new discriminatory immigration procedures – that classified Jews as 'non-preferreds' – as well as the implementation, following the onset of the depression and rise of nativist sentiments, of a policy of rigid exclusion. In 1931, the year of Canada's seventh census and Adrien Arcand's broadcast of a Jewish plot to take over Quebec, Canada, and the world, there was a grand total of 156,606 Jews in Canada, forming 1.5 per cent of the population.[26]

The Jews of Quebec, and Canada, were, overall, moderately successful in earning a decent living and modest place in their adopted land. Occupationally, they were spread across a range of groups, with a preponderance in the urban middle class. Though pedlars and storekeepers could be found in numerous villages and towns across the country – from the Maritimes to British Columbia – the major concentration was in the larger cities, in Toronto, Winnipeg, and Montreal – Adrien Arcand's home base – where the Jews settled into a variety of occupations between the two extremes, upper and lower class, of the Canadian and Quebec economic systems. The Jewish presence, as proprietors or workers, in agriculture and in the 'submerged group of unskilled laborers,' remained tiny and substantially smaller than that of French- and English-Canadian groups. In skilled trades, Jews were employed as metal workers, printers, electricians, plumbers, cigar makers, and in numerous other vocations apart from the textile and clothing trades where, concentrated in Montreal, Toronto, and Winnipeg, they formed, in 1931, 'the largest occupational group engaged in manufacturing amongst the Jews of Canada as a whole in each of the provinces and the larger cities.'[27] Clerical workers – bookkeepers, stenographers, and office assistants – constituted 10.16 per cent of the gainfully employed over ten years of age, the third-largest occupational group among Jews in Canada.[28]

Above the ranks of the blue- and white-collar workers, the Jews of

Canada and Quebec gathered mainly in the middle. Victimized by discriminatory hiring practices in government, industry, and commerce, Jews were underrepresented among the 'salary-earning' professionals: 2.85 per cent of all gainfully employed Jews were salaried professionals, a figure 44 per cent below the national average for all ethnic groups. Fee-earning professional Jews, by contrast, totalled 2.21 per cent of the gainfully employed, compared to 0.99 per cent among persons of all origins.[29] Overall Jewish representation in the professions was, in 1931, 17 per cent below the national average.[30]

While many Jews were attracted to business, they remained, for the most part, small proprietors, distant from the summits of economic power. In rural towns and villages, they were mostly pedlars or storekeepers. In Montreal, Toronto, or Winnipeg, they were represented in light industry – especially the clothing and textile industries, which required, comparatively speaking, little start-up capital – or, in larger communities, in the wholesale and retail trades, selling groceries, fruit and vegetables, meat and poultry, new or used clothing, furniture, hardware, dry goods, confectionery, or tobacco. Attracted to small business, they none the less owned a minuscule proportion of the total number of enterprises in Canada.[31] In big business, their representation was virtually non-existent. At the onset of the depression, when a rash of anti-Semites, including Adrien Arcand, took up their poison pens against the Jewish menace, the command posts of the Canadian and Quebec economies, the economic élite, which ran the great industrial corporations, the financial houses, the banks and insurance companies, and the large retail chains were virtually devoid of Jews. 'To put it plainly,' Louis Rosenberg concluded in his survey of the place of the Jews in the Canadian economic system, 'Jewish directors form only .94% or less than 1.0% of all directors enumerated in the "Canadian Directory of Directors," and hold only .74% of all directorates listed therein. Since Jews constitute 1.5% of Canada's population it is evident that far from holding a dominating position in the control of Canada's financial, commercial and industrial structure, the participation of Jews in controlling positions is less than half of that which might be warranted in view of their percentage of the total population.'[32]

The political power of Quebec's and Canada's Jews was equally

circumscribed. While they enjoyed a substantial measure of civic freedom, the Jews remained, for the most part, a relatively weak and
submerged element in the Canadian political system. Immigrant
Jews, like other newcomers, qualified for citizenship, deliberated
upon public issues, exerted whatever meagre pressures they could
command on elected or appointed officials, supported or joined the
Conservative, Liberal, or, in small numbers, the socialist parties, and,
in variable numbers, voted in elections. In due time, a few scattered
Jewish aldermen, school trustees, or mayors appeared here and
there, as well as a tiny handful of MLAS in Ontario, Manitoba, and
Quebec, where Peter Bercovitch and Joseph Cohen were elected to
the legislature as Liberals in constituencies with large Jewish populations. It was not until 1917, when Samuel Jacobs was returned in
Cartier to the House of Commons, that the first Jew entered the
House of Commons. Until David Croll's appointment as minister of
labour, minister of municipal affairs, and minister of welfare, between 1934 and 1937, in the Ontario Liberal government of Mitchell Hepburn, no Jew had ever served in a federal or provincial government as a cabinet minister. Nor had any attained the position of
senator or deputy minister, or served as a judge or magistrate, apart
from Samuel D. Shultz, appointed assistant county court judge in
Vancouver in 1913.[33]

The meagre political representation of Jews derived, in part, from
their limited numbers, modest economic and social standing, and
restricted integration in a country defined by many of their gentile
contemporaries as Christian and binational. Refugees of pogroms
and centuries of discrimination, the Jews discovered in Canada and
Quebec, as Michael Brown concluded, only a 'Minor Land of Promise.'[34] They were able, for the most part, to earn decent livings, ed-
ucate their children – at private and public schools – and freely prac-
tise their religion. They formed, wherever they settled, congregations
and synagogues, welfare societies and fraternal orders, cultural organizations, immigrant-aid and burial societies – a matrix of parallel institutions that cared for their collective needs and fostered an
autonomy and ghettoization within the larger host community. As
the Jews banded together, so did they grow apart from their host
communities in English Canada and in Quebec where, among sig-

nificant groups of French Canadians, they were perceived as aliens and strangers, or as adjuncts of a dominant Anglo-Canadian community. Outside Quebec, Canada's Jews had won an uncertain niche somewhere near the lower end of a multi-ethnic pecking order headed by the Anglo-Saxons. Inside Quebec, they were jammed, uncomfortably, during the pre-depression decades, between the French and the English, a separation sustained by their own highly developed communal consciousness, endogenous marriage, residential segregation, a proliferation of parallel institutions, and, not least, a vibrant tradition of anti-Semitism that, in the early years of the Great Depression – among Goglus and birds of other feathers – assumed a virulent form.[35]

Like their political and spiritual kin elsewhere – in France and Germany – the Goglus of Quebec did not invent the anti-Semitism that formed the core of their credo. It was already there, when Arcand first began dreaming of shirts and drills, protocols and deportations, embedded in the culture of an insecure nationality, a product of imported and indigenous influences and circumstances. The true extent and depth of its penetration of the hearts and minds of ordinary French Canadians, of workers in Montreal, or farmers in the Gaspé, is, of course, difficult to gauge. Not a few writers and commentators on Quebec anti-Semitism have tempered their revelations – or admissions – with the observation that Jews and ordinary French Canadians, in their everyday contacts, got along rather well, and that whatever prejudice did exist was of the superficial sort and, in any event, decidedly non-violent. 'One must not perpetrate the error of considering the French-Canadian as irretrievably anti-semitic,' Israel Rabinovitch warned a meeting of the Eastern Division of the Canadian Jewish Congress. 'Those Jews who come into contact with our French-Canadian neighbors, in business or in any other walk of life, will testify to the fact that often one can most excellently harmonize with them, and particularly when one speaks their language and when one manifests an understanding of their national sensibilities.'[36] To the question 'Is the French-Canadian a Jew-Baiter?' the civil libertarian R.L. Calder responded in the negative, noting, in the pre–First World War years, 'there was not a village in Quebec where a Jew could not set up his store, with absolute security for his

person, his family, and his stock. Then, too, was the heyday of the
pedestrian peddler. Jews overran the province, offering wares for sale
or barter. They were kindly received by the French-Canadian farmer, fairly treated, fed at the family table, gratuitously lodged for the
night. There was not an instance of a solitary peddler having been
molested.'[37] Pogroms, assaults, incitements to violence, rampages by
parish peasants were clearly not the way in Quebec where, among the
washed and unwashed, a time-honoured respect – whether British or
French – for law and order prevailed.[38] Whatever anti-Semitism existed in Quebec, André Laurendeau retrospectively observed, was
not only mischievousness and erroneous but, in most cases, superficial, hardly in keeping with the sound common sense and funda-
mentally tolerant character of French Canadians. 'The vague anti-
semitism of the depression years,' Laurendeau wrote,

> was a feeling that came naturally to shopkeepers going broke who
> were furious against merchants who were smarter than they were and
> reputedly less scrupulous. It was a kind of astonishment and revulsion
> directed against foreigners whose habits were disconcerting, and who
> had the reputation of getting rich quick. It was a kind of pseudo-
> religious emotion working against the people who had sacrificed the
> Saviour, against the race who had shouted, 'May his blood fall on the
> heads of our children and our children's children.' In short it was the
> whole apparatus of anti-semitism which was popular in the western
> world ... French-Canadians had no monopoly on this prejudice, but
> they expressed it more noisily than others. I must admit its existence
> among some of us. It was older than Nazism and had no connection
> with dogmatic racism. More often than not it was a skin-deep senti-
> ment, unpleasant enough, but luckily quite harmless.[39]

Among many of the Jews congregated in and around Montreal, in
the decades preceding the Great Depression, no similar conclusions
about the benign nature of skin-deep prejudices were drawn. Jews
did business with French Canadians in Montreal, Quebec City, Trois-
Rivières, and assorted towns and villages across the province. They
traded, chatted and smiled, cohabited under the same regimes and
constitution, but otherwise remained wary, displaying a circumspec-

tion and vigilance coloured by their own historical experiences and sensibilities and by the common expression (particularly among sections of the leading classes) of opinions and attitudes – home grown and imported – antipathetic to Jews. Beyond the ritual and etiquette, the circumscribed interaction, there remained a chasm of suspicion induced and sustained, in no small part, by select spokesmen of Quebec's leading classes, who entertained, and vocalized, decades before the tirades of Adrien Arcand were heard, hoary and modern notions about the mean character of local and international Jewry.

Quebec, after all, was predominantly French and Catholic, a cultural island, or fortress, besieged on all sides by Protestant, materialist North America. It was a place suffused with insecurity and nostalgia; with fear of the modern and a yearning, among established élites, for the archaic and orderly threatened, at home and abroad, by liberals, secularists, and revolutionaries. The official guardians of fortress Quebec were religious and nationalist élites – journalists, writers, church officials, professors, teachers, and politicians – who sought guidance and solace in Rome and in the causes and values of the embattled reactionary royalist and clerical elements of modern France.[40] For Quebec's Jews, the Old World linkages – demographic and cultural – to Rome and France spelt trouble. Along with priests, religious institutions, theology, and literature came the timeworn tenets of European Catholic anti-Judaism. Old, jaded, coinage from the Middle Ages – depicting Jews as demons; uncanny, mysterious creatures; Christ killers; perpetrators of ritual murder; and usurious blood-suckers – circulated freely in religious and lay circles in nineteenth- and early twentieth-century France, and they entered Quebec, where they were embraced by elements of the clergy dominant in the social, educational, and ideological system from the early days of New France. Quebec's religious establishment had invested itself with an urgent mission: to preserve the language, culture, and racial homogeneity of the French-Canadian people. In pursuit of this goal, they embraced, throughout the nineteenth and early twentieth centuries, noble and worthy causes: the restriction of immigration of 'foreigners,' colonization of unsettled land, the purchase of anglophone-owned land by French Canadians, the return and settlement on the land of French Canadians who, for economic reasons, had emigrated abroad. And they fostered, through the media they monopolized, a relentless and profound xenophobia, a fear and suspicion of aliens among whom the uncanny, covetous, and wandering Jews, who arrived in menacing waves in the decades preceding the First World War, were pre-eminent.

The flickering anti-Semitism of pre-depression Quebec was not restricted to the purely religious spheres. It was diffused, as well, in the popular street culture; in the journalistic discourse; in fictional and travel literature; in the speeches and writing of nationalists, polemicists, and literati. Street slang absorbed the derogatory 'youpin' and 'yourtes' common among anti-Semitic Frenchmen. Novelists such as Pierre Joseph Olivier Chauveau, premier of the province from 1867 to 1873, wrote of a Jewish money lender whose sole purpose in life was to 'persecute, to condemn, to seize and to sell.'[41] Priests on pilgrimages to the Vatican, Jerusalem, and the holy shrines in Europe returned – their anti-Semitic batteries recharged – and composed books, some with wide circulation, describing Jews as 'a deicide race,'[42] venal, cunning, cowardly, and afflicted by a 'degeneracy peculiar to their race.'[43] Pulpits sometimes served as outlets for anti-Semitic utterances and directives. Curé Belanger, for example, of St Louis Parish in Montreal, spiced his sermon one Sunday in 1908 with a little advice on real estate. He urged his parishioners not to sell to 'strangers,' an admonition that led the *Jewish Times* to characterize his remarks as a 'pitiable exhibition of weakness, bigotry and cowardice.'[44] Annual meetings of the Association Catholique de la Jeunesse Canadienne-Française (ACJC) a broadly based Catholic youth organization that brought together lay and religious nationalist leaders – and lobbied furiously against Jewish and other 'alien' immigration – were filled with anti-Semitic pronouncements. At the 1908 convention at Laval University, delegates heard from the lips of L.-C. Farley, an expert on 'La Question Juive,' that Jews were 'a deicide race' who needed to be isolated and combated by a French-style anti-Semitic league.[45] Abbé Antonio Huot used the forum of a public lecture, delivered under the auspices of the Montreal chapter of the ACJC in 1913 – the year of the infamous Beiliss trial in Russia – to quote extensively from the notorious German anti-Semite August Rohling in support of his claim that Jews practised ritual murder.[46]

Quite apart from the pulpits and podiums, the press and journals of Quebec – nationalist and religious – provided a common outlet for anti-Semitic expression. There were, first of all, the little papers or journals like W.A. Grenier's *La Libre Parole* and, three years later, *La Libre Parole Illustrée*, which specialized in Jew hatred, taking their cues and titles from the publication of the notorious French anti-Semite Édouard Drumont, the author of *La France Juive* (1886), who once declared: 'As soon as you attack the Jew, you engage in hand-to-hand combat with reality, you pit yourself against your true enemy.'[47] Drumont's writings were favoured as well by a host of little journals and papers, including *La Croix, Le Nationaliste, L'Action Sociale, L'Etudiante* (the Laval University student newspaper), and, not least, *Le Pionnier*, a sheet published by L.G. Robillard, a swindler who, through a clever life-insurance scheme, operated by his 'Union Franco-Canadienne' company, filched thousands of dollars from parishioners and priests. According to the *Montreal Jewish Times*, the priests were paid 'a premium of one dollar for every parishioner who joined the Life Annuity Section, and something extra … for advocating it.'[48] Robillard's paper was so filled with vitriol – from France's anti-Semitic press – that criminal libel charges were eventually laid against him. Released on bail, he chose to flee the country, alleging, in a statement left behind, that his health required a 'milder and more congenial climate.'[49]

The climate of tolerance towards Jews was hardly improved in Quebec by the occasional utterances – home grown and imported – in the more mainstream and nationalist journals and newspapers, views that gained common currency during several widely broadcast controversies or 'affaires.' One involved, oddly enough, a British-born Italian socialist Freemason and Jew, Ernesto Nathan, who, following election to the office of mayor of Rome, offended Catholic sensibilities by criticizing the Pope for interfering in Italian political affairs.[50] The impolitic utterance invited a wave of protest in Rome and Montreal, where the city council, headed by the Irish-Canadian Mayor Guerin, protested and passed, unanimously, a vote of censure.[51] Civic bedlam followed. Jews and Protestants denounced the decision of the council as a confusion of religion and politics and an example of ultra-montane meddling in domestic Canadian affairs. The nationalist and religious establishment responded with an editorial barrage, a mass meeting, and a march of 25,000 people – advertised in *La Presse* and other papers – on the Monument National and Champ de Mars, where placards denouncing Nathan, Jews, and Freemasons were prominently displayed. Among Nathan's severest critics was Henri Bourassa, who referred to the mayor's criticism of the Pope as but a recent variation of a two-thousand-year-old battle against the Christian religion, and Omer Héroux, who wrote in *Le Devoir* that Nathan was 'hereditary hatred of the Church incarnate.'[52]

A more protracted, and bitter affair involved, not the Roman mayor, but a French captain – Alfred Dreyfus – whose arrest in 1894, on fabricated charges of selling military secrets to Germany, bitterly divided France into two hostile camps for more than a decade. The Dreyfus affair became the focal point of a struggle between liberal, democratic, republican France and reactionary, anti-Semitic nationalist and royalist elements who used the invented transgressions of the Jewish officer as foil for a broad assault on the culture and institutions of the Third Republic, manipulated and exploited, it was alleged, by Jews. In Quebec, it turned out, anti-Dreyfus sentiment was rife, as well, among nationalists and clerics sympathetic to the noble struggle of their reactionary kin in the Motherland. Among Quebec's little papers – tinted and tainted with anti-Semitism – Dreyfus's guilt was a foregone conclusion, a view shared by Montreal's large daily *La Patrie*, which assured its readers, on 3 December 1897, that Dreyfus was the pawn of a 'Jewish Syndicate' plotting to seize power in France.[53] During and following the entire affair, the writings of Drumont, France's arch anti-Semite, were widely published and distributed throughout Quebec, by the fringe press and by more respectable nationalist publications like Henri Bourassa's *Le Devoir,* which provided a useful and respectable forum for the views of Drumont; the fascist precursor Maurice Barrès; and Karl Lueger, Vienna's anti-Semitic mayor. 'The anti-semitic movement in Europe is not without an echo in this country,' the *Jewish Times* of Montreal editorialized in its first issue, on 10 December 1897. 'It is to be found daily in those newspapers which take their old world inspiration largely from those organs of opinion which are inimical to the Jewish people.'[54]

Prominent among organizations in the new world propagating opinions inimical to Jews were the more modern national formations, whose xenophobic pronouncements multiplied with the collapse, in 1929, of the economic system. The Ligue des Droits du Français, formed in 1913, became a favourite outlet for new and old nationalist ideas and nostrums among Quebec intellectual leaders, including the prominent professor, historian, priest and publicist Abbé Lionel Groulx, editor of the influential *L'Action Française* during the 1920s.[55] As self-appointed guardians of the national culture, nationalist spokesmen, writing in *L'Action Française*, exposed a host of enemies threatening the language, culture, and way of life of an old Quebec besieged by modernizing forces. Urbanism, materialism, the degradation of private and public morality, according to the nationalist spokesmen, were the products of an insidious invasion orchestrated by dangerous aliens, prominent among whom were Americans and Jews.[56] The Jewish threat was, at once, demographic, political, and cultural. Although Jewish immigration slowed dramatically during the 1920s, and halted when the depression descended, *L'Action Française* occasionally fed its readers ominous and misleading statistics on Jewish demographics. In constituencies with large populations of Jews, political practices were assailed as corrupt, although no comparisons were made with accepted practices in other constituencies.[57] In the cultural sphere, *L'Action Française* readers were warned, by writers like Harry Bernard, of the dangers of moral corruption by the 'cinéma judéo-Américain.' Since Jews had no sense of morality and were only anxious to make money, they were ready to produce any kind of film to attract the crowds. 'In their hands, the cinema became a school of corruption and revolution,' Susan Trofimenkoff wrote, summarizing Bernard's views. 'Divorce, free love, Malthusian practices (birth control), socialism, crime, deception, and scandal all found favour in Jewish films, which, according to Bernard, developed in their viewers an unhealthy imagination and a taste for excitement and luxury.'[58]

The critiques of Jews involved more than demographics, politics, and culture. 'Money-making and the financial control of the world, claimed one writer in *L'Action Française,*' wrote Trofimenkoff, 'was the aim of the Jew. *L'Action Française* made little distinction between the American Jewish film producer and the European Jewish owner of a corner grocery store in Montreal.'[59] Excluded from the command posts of trade, commerce, and industry, many French Canadians – élites and masses, nationalists and others – were prone to blame others for their economic disabilities and deprivations. For some, the Jews sufficed. While a minority, their numbers were not minuscule; there were enough around to invite notice. Hoary stigmas and stereotypes from the Middle, and later, Ages trailed, like ivy, along the greystone walls of churches and seminaries, nurtured by time-honoured traditions and institutions. Prominent in small business, their relationship with French Canadians often did not extend beyond the market. To consumers, they were petty exploiters; to small businessmen, proficient and unwelcome competitors. Aspiring professionals and 'a certain class of half-baked highbrows' resented their predilection for education and push into the professions.[60] The banks, the large corporations, the great financial houses, the large retail chains were, it is true, mostly Anglo-Canadian. But the Anglos remained a powerful and respected group with whom political and social accommodations had been worked out. Jews, as Everett Hughes pointed out, were convenient scapegoats, weak and conspicuous targets for the exploratory aggression of frustrated elements of the national community, reticent, for reasons of fear or bad conscience, about shifting the blame for their deprived condition on the powerful and respected Anglo community.[61]

It is little wonder, then, that the sporadic and muted anti-Semitism of the 1920s yielded, with the onset of the depression, to louder, more virulent varieties.[62] The crunch was on; relief lines stretched and multiplied, and the search for causes and targets assumed, among old and new nationalists – and other groups – a frantic intensity. Groulx's *L'Action Nationale,* a reborn version of *L'Action Française,* reflected the new anti-Semitic mood, and time-worn concerns about cultural survival, alien domination, economic emancipation, and the discomforting Jewish menace. Allegations of Jewish economic dictatorship and 'special privileges' – including their exemption under section 7 of the Lord's Day Act from compulsory rest – corrupt electoral practices, their internationalism and predilection for communism, their crowding into the professions, the threat of invasion through immigration – all were dealt with in the pages of *L'Action Nationale*, which served as a forum for writers like Anatole Vanier who wrote of the need to deny Jews naturalization rights, the franchise, and citizenship.[63] Among the foreign contributions to *L'Action Nationale* was an extract from a pastoral letter of Mgr Gfoeller, bishop of Linz, Austria, who traced both egoistic capitalism and revolutionary Bolshevism to 'degenerate Judaism.'[64]

Earning the applause of *L'Action Nationale* were movements and demonstrations of commercial chauvinism, youth protest, and professional exclusion – all tainted with anti-Semitism. When interns at the Nôtre Dame Hospital decided to strike in May 1934, in protest against the appointment of Dr Samuel Rabinovitch, a Jew, as one of the thirty-two residents at the hospital, a variety of nationalist organizations supported their principled stand.[65] Support for the demands of the Sunday Observance League – La Ligue du Dimanche – which opposed the Jewish 'special privilege' of exemption from application of provisions of the Lord's Day Act, derived as much from economic as religious or moral considerations, and peaked when anti-Jewish feeling in the province ran high. Jeune-Canada, a collection of radical youth from the University of Montreal, led by André Laurendeau and Pierre Dansereau, were praised by their elders when they staged, on 20 April 1937, a rally in opposition to an anti-Hitler meeting sponsored by the Montreal Jewish community and addressed by sympathetic liberals like Mayor Rinfret, Honoré Mercier, and Senator Raoul Dandurand. Several speakers warned of Jewish internationalism, affinities to communism, and unwarranted economic and political power to the detriment of French Canadians.[66] The Achat Chez Nous movement received substantial support from the clergy, nationalist journals like *L'Action Nationale* and a range of weeklies and dailies, big and small, including Montreal's *Le Devoir* and Quebec City's *L'Action Catholique* – and from a variety of professional, business, and patriotic organizations, among them the venerable Saint Jean Baptiste Society, the largest social and cultural organization in French Canada.[67] Among the alimentary concerns of *Le Restaurateur*, the official organ of L'Association des Restaurateurs de Montréal, was the Jewish presence in tobacco. It urged its readers to smoke Christian ('fumez Chrétien') by boycotting the products of Imperial Tobacco, a Jewish-owned firm.[68]

The anti-Semitism of the early 1930s in Quebec was a diffuse and troubling thing – hydra-headed, according to Israel Rabinovitch;[69] 'a cloud,' according to André Laurendeau, polluting 'the atmosphere' of the province.[70] It touched broad strata of Quebec's élites, including leading journalists like Georges Pelletier, editor of Le Devoir. Though common enough among a broad spectrum of nationalist groups of diverse persuasion, it rarely, however, assumed the proportion of an obsession, total answer, or principal guide to action. Nor was it centre-piece of the official national religious ideology – or astrology – which claimed to regulate, as Trudeau wrote, the destinies of French Canada with all 'the precision of the celestial system.'[71] The nationalist organizations, though tinged and tainted with anti-Semitism, did not, separately or together, comprise an anti-Semitic movement whose primary purpose was to combat and eradicate an alleged Jewish menace. Anti-Semitism of the other sort, the virulent, obsessive kind, the psychopathological species, which elevated the Jewish question into the key to the mystery of the world, and served as the one, true, guide to social and political action, remained, in Quebec, the property of the marginal, misshapen few; coteries of troubled men, women – and bobolinks — who, as the depression deepened, descended into the gutter of Jew-baiting and Fascist politics.

The precise source of Adrien Arcand's anti-Semitic pathology remains an elusive mystery, beyond the ken of historians – or contemporaries – unaided by the psychoanalytic couch or supporting scaffolds of biographical – or autobiographical – data.[72] The timing, however, of the public onset of an infirmity, akin, as Tolstoy wrote, 'to the lowest perversities of diseased human nature,' was more easily discernible. Hitherto taken with chasing a living, churning prose, trumpeting nationalism, impaling liberals, and conjuring Goglus, Arcand, in mid-spring 1930, discovered and embroiled himself in a fight that, in short order, launched him on a career on the far Fascist fringe of the Canadian political spectrum. What worked the journalist up into a lather of hate was the plain matter of schooling for

Jews in his beloved province of Quebec, an issue that assumed a terrible urgency among Quebec's Catholic religious and educational establishment in early spring 1930 when Premier Alexander Taschereau's provincial secretary, Athanase David, introduced into the legislature of Quebec a bill providing for the creation of a separate Jewish school commission.[73]

Offered by a besieged government as relief to an impasse between colliding factions of the Jewish and Protestant communities, and as an antidote to a recent decision of the Judicial Committee of the Privy Council invalidating sections of a basic statute underpinning and regulating established Jewish participation in the Protestant educational system, the David bill met with a determined and relentless opposition from an aroused episcopate fearful of the subversion of the entire constitutionally validated Christian education system. A Jewish school commission was, in the eyes of Cardinal Rouleau, Archbishop Gauthier, and their colleagues, quite clearly draped in a red flag; it was a dangerous sop to a cheeky, communist-prone, minority without charter or constitutional status, living on sufferance in a land not their own, as well as an invitation to other groups to assist in the replacement of the confessional with a secular educational system administered by a feared department of education. In winning concession after concession from a besieged government during the weeks and months of the David bill's gestation and passage, the episcopate employed a variety of effective strategies and weapons. A sympathetic press was enlisted and swamped the public and government with editorials. Groups like L'Association des Voyageurs de Commerce and the Montreal Chapter of the Saint Jean Baptiste Society were mobilized, joined the assault, and bombarded the government with representations. Private meetings between the premier and his education minister, and the cardinal, the archbishop and bishops, served as forums of advice and amendment. Correspondence between church officials and the premier and his education minister was released for public consumption. At a public ceremony at the Oratoire Saint-Joseph in Montreal, Mgr Gauthier read and elaborated upon his own letter to the premier, exhorting the government to withdraw the bill. Among the sympathetic Catholic and nationalist journalists mobilized, was the gaunt Adrien Arcand who, according to Robert Rumilly, joined the school fight at the behest of Mgr Gauthier.[74] 'The School Law is the most vital challenge to our race and to our national unity, the gravest issue since the British conquest,' Arcand explained to a rally of Goglus at the Monument National on 3 November 1930. 'Our survival as a national unity, our prestige and our influence hang on it.'[75]

In the school war, Adrien Arcand discovered a cause worthy of his talents as a polemicist and purveyor of hate.[76] Intermittently, during the months following introduction and passage of the David bill, the little weeklies argued the rejectionist case. They wrote and spoke of untimely concessions to a coddled minority, an alleged breach of the confederation pact, which recognized only two official minorities – the French and the English – the deception of the episcopate by venal politicians, the prospective pillaging of neutral school taxes, and the undermining of the powers of the Council of Public Instruction and integrity of the Christian confessional school system. As their attack sharpened, however, it became readily apparent that the Goglus' attentions were not limited to the thrust and mechanics of the David bill, or to the mere politics of education. What emerged was something larger, more ominous. The school issue served as mere foil and fodder for an attack – unrelenting and vicious – on Jews, local, national, and international, an assault bristling with a panoply of lies and calumnies, traditional and modern, in vogue among select contemporary sister publications, organizations, and movements in parts of continental Europe and Britain.

Being a patriotic folk movement, the Goglus were mindful of the local dimensions of the Jewish question. Every available local anti-Semitic current or issue was picked up, and magnified. Arcand and Ménard railed against the Jewish immigration and cultural threat, set up a patriotic fund to combat 'the youpins,' and supported the Ligue du Dimanche's Sunday observance campaign. The appearances of Jews – or of persons with Jewish-sounding names – before the courts, in criminal or civil actions were proudly announced. Anti-Semitic stickers were printed and distributed by the thousands. Public assistance to Jewish parallel institutions was condemned. The national history was rewritten with appropriate pernicious and demonic roles assigned to Jews like Abraham Gradis and Ezekiel Hart, as well as

Rouge benefactors, including Louis Joseph Papineau, who supported the extension of basic civic and political rights to Jews.[77] Contemporary Jewish public figures such as Montreal alderman Max Seigler, Joseph Schubert, and Bernard Schwartz (nicknamed 'Matzo-Blood'), MP S.W. Jacobs, and MLAs Peter Bercovitch and Joseph Cohen were reviled and caricatured, along with contemporary Liberals thought friendly to Jews, including Bourassa, Senator Dandurand, and Premier Taschereau, described in *Le Miroir* as 'valet des Juifs.'[78] In the economic sphere, the Achat Chez Nous movement was hailed as a national saviour, and lists of Jewish-owned businesses were published to facilitate boycotts. In scores of articles in *Le Goglu, Le Miroir*, and their successors, and at public lectures sometimes delivered under the auspices of local chapters of the Saint Jean Baptiste Society, Jewish businessmen were denounced as practitioners of fraud, theft, exploitation, and incendiarism.[79] 'Le Juif a usé ... les moyens sournois et frauduleux pour s'emparer de notre commerce,' Ménard observed. 'Les incendies ... les faillites nombreuses, les vols en pleine nuit dans leurs propre magasins par les accomplices, pour retirer les assurances sur le vol ... furent pour le Juif des armes pour ruiner le commerce honnête des autres.'[80]

In the Goglus' Manichean scheme, the Jews no longer competed with other groups as arch-fiends. Their pre-eminence was clearly established in the months and years following the quick fade of the school issue, and they became subjects of an endless stream of slander, fabrication, and invective. The derogatory epithets 'youpins' and 'pouilleux' abounded. Hideous caricatures and cartoons were featured amidst the strewn ads of chiropractors, notaries, and pharmacists, displaying gnarled, leering creatures, with horns and faces of monsters, their claws dripping with the blood of Christian children. And fairy tales abounded. Lenin, *Le Goglu*'s readers were informed, was of 'Judeo-Mongol' origin – son of a Jewish mother and mixed Mongol-Russian father – spoke a fluent Yiddish and declared the Jewish sabbath as the official day of rest in the Soviet Union.[81] In one of its many *cherchez-les-Juifs* exercises, Lady Bessborough, the wife of the governor general appointed by the 'Jew Lover' Mackenzie King on the advice of Zionist Elders, was pronounced Jewish. When the Lindbergh baby disappeared, it was concluded the rabbis had stolen him, to drain the blood for use in Jewish rituals.[82] The valet of Baron de Rothschild, *Le Patriote* readers learned in a front-page, boldly headlined story designed to scoop its world competitors, who arrived one day unannounced in America via Shanghai, was really Leon Trotsky, bent on meeting secretly in Washington's Maison Rouge with Bernard Baruch and fellow Brain Trusters to plot a communist revolution.[83]

The fanciful excursions of Quebec's 'twin racketeers of journalism'[84] reflected their arrival as accomplished Jew-baiters, keepers and purveyors of a full inventory of anti-Semitic hate figments and notions. Like its equivalents elsewhere – in continental Europe, Britain, and scattered other places – Arcand's anti-Semitism grossly inflated the importance of Jews who were, at the same time, condemned as and elevated to the role of the wire-pullers of the destiny of mankind. A small, vulnerable, minority of diverse national affiliation, religious tendency, and political persuasion, in Quebec, Canada, and elsewhere, the Jews were transformed, in Arcand's fevered brain, into an evil brotherhood plotting world domination; the conspiracy myth featured in a long line of nineteenth- and twentieth-century hate tomes, including the *Protocols of the Elders of Zion,* a classic of anti-Semitic reaction, copies of which Arcand imported by the thousands and peddled, for a few pennies a copy, in his own hate sheets. A product of the inventive genius of the Czarist secret police in Paris, the *Protocols* – a lengthy document translated into numerous languages outlining the schemes and agenda of a group of Zionist Elders to dominate the world – was exposed, in the early 1920s, as a clumsy hoax. Among true believers, however, in Germany, Poland, England, France, and a host of other countries, including Canada, its authenticity and continued usefulness as a weapon in the arsenal of political anti-Semitism remained unquestioned.[85]

Arcand's own anti-Jewish notions and figments, like the Zionist Elders' concoction he peddled, were a product of diverse elements, traditional and modern. Archaic bogeys abounded. Jews were Christ killers and children of Satan, consumed with an atavistic hatred of Christianity; a deicide race ready to spread plagues, cause famines, poison wells, and murder children in furtherance of perverse ends dictated by Talmudic injunction.[86] Coexisting with the hoary bogeys were more modern notions and precepts developed by race theorists like Gobineau and Chamberlain and adopted by nationalist reactionaries who embraced political anti-Semitism as a weapon against liberal and democratic forces, men like Maurras, Barrès, and Drumont in France, who enjoyed a certain vogue among select clerical nationalist élites in Quebec in the pre– and post–First World War years. To Arcand and his racist cohorts and predecessors, Jews were more than a people; they were a wandering Asiatic race, base and materialistic, with fixed physical and mental characteristics, consumed with lust, envy, and hatred of morally superior Christian peoples whom they regarded, following the precepts of the Talmud, as beasts.[87] And they were a race, Arcand concluded, responsible for the chaos of modernism, the corruption of the arts, the anarchy of liberal democracy, and suffering of classes victimized by a heartless capitalism. 'La Juiverie, à cause de son essence ... à cause de ses intincts destructifs, à cause de son immémorial atavisme de corruption, à cause de son sentiment exclusivement matérialiste, voilà le grand danger ...'[88]

In the Jewish menace, Arcand and the Goglus discovered a comforting magic key to the mysteries of the world, the one true source of the afflictions of modern society. 'We believe that the Jews are responsible for all the evils of the world today,' Arcand declared to an interviewer from *The Nation.* 'Through the two internationals that they control, the proletarian and the financial, they provoke economic crises and revolutions with a view to taking world power.'[89] The class struggle, trade crises, depressions, the economic injustices and disorder of liberal capitalism were products of Jewish control of international banking, finance, and industry, just as the oppressions – economic, civic, and political – of Bolshevism were the handiwork of Jewish radicals, progenitors of all modern disorder and revolution, beginning with the French, in which the Jews connived with Freemasons to overthrow the Ancien Régime. 'La Juiverie commande déjà directement à plus de la moitié du Globe,' Arcand concluded from a cherchez-les-Juifs international political survey in 1933. 'C'est la preuve tangible de l'exécution d'un vaste plan de conquête, qui s'étend sans cesse avec chaque révolution, avec chaque emprunt consenti par la banque internationale d'or.'[90]

Arcand's embrace of the conspiracy myth admitted him into some

select exotic international circles. Founder of a patriotic youth movement, Arcand shared, at the outset, with diverse nationalist compatriots, a profound concern with the defence of his homeland and
people. Like Jeune-Canada, and other groups, the Goglus fought the
good fight, addressing a range of issues certified as worthy by established nationalist élites, from immigration restriction to economic
boycotts, school autonomy, and Sunday closing. The school battle,
however, became a point of departure of the Goglus from other
nationalists who remained bound by diverse inward-looking strategies of emancipation. Unlike the great majority of nationalists, whose
anti-Semitism rarely assumed the intensity of a consistent burning
hate or a form of Manichean ordering of the universe, the Goglus
were seized by the strange and hypnotic obsession of a Jewish conspiracy to dominate not only Quebec, but the world; an obsession
that moved them to dilute and confound their patriotism with a
peculiar internationalism, which drew them to groups in diverse
countries of similar paranoid persuasion. When Arcand discovered
the true Antichrist, Quebec shrank into the local battlefield of a vast
global war between Aryan Christian civilization and international
Jewry.

The company Adrien Arcand joined was hardly illustrious. In
France, there was Monsieur René Albert Léon Gauthier, known
under an alias as Monsieur Gauthier de Leroy Lacroix, who, from the
editorial department of a Parisian journal, *Amitié Franco-Canadienne*,
deluged the French-Canadian and world press with anti-Semitic copy
and material, including copies of the *Protocols of the Elders of Zion*,
whose authenticity Monsieur Lacroix was prepared to guarantee.[91]
Exposed by Olivar Asselin's *L'Ordre* as a forger, swindler, ex-convict,
and likely recipient of Nazi propaganda funds, Lacroix had his products prominently featured in several issues of Arcand and Ménard's
Le Patriote.[92] Arcand's own productions, for that matter, were not unknown among France's leading professional anti-Semites. According
to Norman Cohn, *The Key to the Mystery* was first distributed in France,
in 1937, at meetings of the Rassemblement Anti-Juif de France, an
organization founded and led by the monocled maverick Darquier
de Pellepoix, who flogged, as well, the *Protocols* and advertised a program based upon the Third Reich's anti-Semitic legislation. It was

Darquier de Pellepoix who stated, in May 1937, that 'the Jewish question must be solved, and very urgently: either the Jews must be expelled or they must be massacred.' As commissioner general for Jewish affairs in Laval's second cabinet, Darquier de Pellepoix arranged the deportation of nine thousand French Jews.[93]

Arcand's British associates had equally sound anti-Semitic credentials. Prominent among them was Lord Sydenham of Combe, former governor of Bombay (1907–23), whose belief in the glory of the British Empire, the partnership of Bolshevism and Judaism, and the validity of the *Protocols* remained unshaken, throughout the 1920s, by fact or argument.[94] Lord Sydenham, it appears, was willing to help the good cause abroad and, according to Arcand, favoured the Goglus with financial support.

Among the organizations enjoying Sydenham's patronage was the Britons, a patriotic society founded in 1918 by Henry Hamilton Beamish, a professional international anti-Semite who formed, with Adrien Arcand, a society of mutual admiration.[95] Born in Ireland in 1874, the son of a rear-admiral and former ADC to Queen Victoria, Beamish visited Canada at the age of eighteen, then continued to Ceylon, where he eventually enlisted in the Ceylon Planters' Regiment and fought in the Boer War. Settled in South Africa during the pre–First World War years – where he developed some bizarre notions of a Jewish world conspiracy – Beamish served with the Natal Regiment of the South African Infantry during the First World War, then returned to Britain following the war, where he contested a pair of seats in 1918 – on a platform of extreme patriotism – as a discharged sailors' and soldiers' candidate. Defeated in both tries, Beamish retreated to the fringe. His first abode was with something called the Vigilance Society, which soon gave way to the more enduring Britons, an ultra-conservative patriotic 'society to protect the birth right of Britons and to eradicate alien influences from ... politics and industries.' Though small in number, the Beamish Britons became avid publishers, printers, and propagandists of anti-Semitic causes, nationally and internationally. Following a much-publicized libel suit, Beamish left Britain in the early 1920s for South Africa – and later Southern Rhodesia – where he launched a lengthy career as itinerant Jew-baiter. Both Hitler and Mussolini were favoured, in

1923, with meetings with Beamish, whose address to a Nazi meeting at the Krone Circus in January 1923 was enthusiastically received. Beamish's fraternal link with the Nazis and an international network of anti-Semitic organizations continued throughout the 1930s. He travelled, organized, and propagandized around the world – including Japan and the United States – corresponded and traded hate literature with fellow devotees, and visited Germany in 1936, where he was welcomed by Julius Streicher as a true friend of National Socialism, treated as an official guest of honour, and addressed several public meetings on the Jewish conspiracy.[96]

As founder and head of an organization dedicated to the eradication of the Jewish menace, H.H. Beamish entertained some novel thoughts and prescriptions on the Jewish question, notions he readily shared with fraternal friends, including Adrien Arcand. Pogroms, it appeared, were out since 'history ... proved that they had never produced the desired results.'[97] So, too, were sterilization and extermination, both of which lacked appeal to 'the kind-hearted English nation.' More sensible, and British, were confiscation of the money and properties Jews accumulated at the expense of British, Ayrans, and Christians, and forced segregation, along lines prescribed by white South Africans for their native population. Since the proximity of Jews might be infecting, Beamish entertained briefly Palestine, then Madagascar – an island off the east coast of Africa – as the sensible destination of shipment of Jews under a scheme of forced Zionism. Purchased from France with confiscated Jewish money, and cleared of the local native population likely to serve the greedy and domineering new settlers, Madagascar was large enough to hold the Jewish world population, estimated at fifty million, and, 'being an island, would make the problem of complete segregation a simple one.'[98]

Beamish's causes and notions were well-received, not only in Munich and Berlin, by Julius Streicher, but in Montreal, Quebec, by Adrien Arcand who maintained long and lasting links with the eccentric Rhodesian. They corresponded regularly, traded hate pamphlets and articles, swapped reports and gossip on the state of the anti-Semitic world crusade – from Bulawayo, Rhodesia, to Montreal, Quebec – met privately when Beamish toured Canada in the autumn of 1936, and shared a platform in New York City with other deranged luminaries.[99] Nuggets of Beamish's wisdom were strewn among the speeches, journals, and papers edited by Arcand, including *Le Fasciste Canadien*, which included, in the April 1938 edition, an article entitled 'Madagascar, réponse a l'idéal des Juifs,' accompanied by a sketch of the island supplied, as an acknowledgment noted, by the Britons.[100] For his part, Beamish was delighted to receive and distribute Arcand's own creations, including copies of *Le Miroir* and his anti-Semitic opus, *The Key to the Mystery*, which was pushed, with great vigour, in South Africa in both English and Afrikaans versions.[101] 'A splendid and quite unique production,' Beamish noted, 'appreciated in all quarters' and 'quite fashionable for speakers to quote ... from public platforms.'[102] Beamish, it appears, was quite taken with Arcand, whom he rated a mere notch below Der Führer himself. 'After Hitler,' the Rhodesian wrote a supporter, 'I consider Adrien Arcand the one leader who stands out far above any others I have met as he has all of the necessary flare, vim and originality which a REAL leader requires ... At the first sign of a Jew-bolshevik upheaval in Canada he is in a position to take over the Govt of the country, his Movement is remarkably well-organized: he has the right penchant for handling men and has great administrative ability, above all no personal Ego.'[103]

Lack of ego was certainly not an attribute of Arnold Spencer Leese, founder and leader of Britain's Imperial Fascist League, who cultivated fraternal links with both Beamish and Arcand. Leese, like Beamish, was a fringe eccentric with a tiny following. But he and his organization contributed handsomely to the perpetuation of the political anti-Semitism initiated in the 1920s by the Britons. While the Jews earned Arnold Leese's undivided hate, his love was portioned – among camels, the Empire, and Fascism.[104] Until early middle age, the camels ran first. Born in 1878 in Lancashire – the nephew of a baronet – to a comfortable middle-class family, Leese trained as a veterinary surgeon and worked for a few years in London's east end before departing for India and Kenya, where he practised his first love – dromedary medicine. After writing a standard textbook on camels, a copy of which he sent to George V, and serving during the First World War in France and Somaliland, with the Royal Army Veterinary Corps, Leese abandoned his khakis, and veterinary smock, for a black shirt. He joined something called British Fascists Ltd, served briefly on the Stanford Municipal Council, as a Fascist representative, then trotted off, in 1928, with a dozen or so disgruntled colleagues, to form his own organization.

Leese's Imperial Fascist League was noisy and combative. Though small in number – the organization never had more than two hundred members – they were loud in their hatred of Jews, defence of the Empire, and commitment to a racial Fascist ideology. Political democracy to the imperial Fascist was a failure. Only a new Nordic governing caste of character and service, at the head of a corporate state, could restore hierarchy, order, and the past glories of the Empire. Italy's Latin brand of Fascism was not favoured by Leese, who suspected the Jews swayed Mussolini, just as they got to Sir Oswald Mosley, whose rival organization – called 'the British Jewnion of fascists' – was filled with 'kosher Fascists.'[105] Although the imperial Fascists wore black shirts and black britches, of the Italian mode, and toyed with the fasces as a party symbol, their true model was Adolf Hitler's NSDAP. Leese swore by the *Protocols*, studied and adored *Mein Kampf*, reprinted in his *The Fascist* slander from Streicher's *Der Stürmer*, adopted the swastika – set against the Union Jack – as the party emblem, and advocated, as Hitler did, extreme measures against the Jews. Like Beamish, Arnold Leese preferred Madagascar as the Jewish homeland – or leper colony. Monies earned from confiscation of Jewish property would secure ownership of the island and buy out the natives, and a League of Aryan Nations navy would patrol surrounding waters to intercept Jewish escapees. A teetotaller with a soft heart for camels, Leese was not above contemplating harsh solutions. Good solid pogroms, involving orgies of 'Jewish window-smashing,' were helpful, though by no means a final solution.[106] 'It must be admitted that the most certain and permanent way of disposing of the Jews,' he wrote in his *The Fascist* in 1938, 'would be to exterminate them by some humane method such as the lethal chamber.'[107]

The ruminations of Leese, like the fantasies of Beamish, suited Adrien Arcand just fine. The two of them – the rabid British racial imperialist and the Quebec crypto-nationalist – were, in fact, a fine, if odd, couple, comrades in struggle against what Leese often referred to as 'the Menace.'[108] They exchanged badges, emblems, gossip, and progress reports on their shared noble cause. Copies of Leese's *The Fascist* were sent on to Arcand, who translated and reprinted select articles in *Le Miroir.* So pleased was Arcand with Leese's creations that he passed a copy of *The Fascist* to his party leader, R.B. Bennett, prime minister of Canada, for his perusal.[109] Leese also supplied Arcand with copies of the *Protocols* and reams of materials from Nazi propaganda bureaus. Arcand's *Le Chameau* was likely named after Leese's favoured animal, and the IFL constitution was admired and used as a model for Arcand's own organization.[110] When Arcand later formed his National Unity Party, Arnold Leese was made an honorary member. But the traffic was not all one way. *Le Miroir* and other Arcand publications were sent out to Leese, who was kept abreast, by Arcand, of North American Jewish machinations and updated on the exotica of the Jewish Who's Who. Leese, it seems, was so impressed with the piece *Le Miroir* did, in its 18 October 1932 edition, on the alleged Jewish Damascus Ritual Murder that he asked Arcand for his sources.[111] Whatever Arcand supplied, however, benefited him little during his widely publicized trial, on a charge of public mischief, stemming from publication and distribution of material on Jewish ritual murder.[112] Leese was convicted and served six months in prison.[113]

Joining the fringe French and British anti-Semites as the Goglus' comrades in struggle were an assortment of dispersed groups that tickled Arcand's anti-Semitic fancies. When Lord Rothermere's *Daily Mail* trumpeted a 'Hurrah for the Black Shirts' in January 1934, Arcand cheered from afar and subsequently announced himself and colleagues, in a note to his national political leader, as 'Rothermereans unaware,'[114] a designation he doubtless regretted months later when the changeful lord withdrew support from Mosley's Black Shirt movement on account of its growing anti-Semitism and support for dictatorship.[115] What Rothermere found unacceptable, however, attracted Arcand, whose warmth for the Mosleyites increased with their growing anti-Semitism and support for Hitler's New Germany. 'You proved at your life's peril,' Arcand later wrote Mosley, whom he had once designated a 'kosher Fascist,' 'Britons are no more at home in Britain and aliens rule the street.'[116]

Outside Britain, among its far-flung commonwealth dominions, in continental Europe, South America, and the United States, Arcand discovered and commiserated with a wonderful proliferation of groups 'not what can be ... termed anti-Jewish but pro-Aryans,' opposed to 'a pest which has been contaminating the whole White Race in all domains.'[117] Peculiar emanations garbed in shirts of every colour – except red – kinsmen of hate in Poland, Austria, Romania, and South America, Arcand's empire brethren assembled in formations called the National Social Christian Party of South Africa, the National Guard of Australia, the Fascist Party of Rhodesia, earned his support for 'labouring to free the White Race from its Jewish chains, to free our respective countries from the disastrous effects of Judeo-liberal internationalism.'[118] In the neighbouring United States, the emergence of anti-Semitic propagandists such as William Dudley Pelley, James B. True, Robert Edward Edmondson, and Fritz Kuhn was evidence of a growing awareness of both the gravity of the Jewish menace and the hope offered by Hitler's New Germany.[119]

While Arcand was delighted with the quaint eruptions of embryonic Fascisms in diverse countries, there was no leader or party that excited his imagination and loyalty more than Hitler and his National Socialists. The growing support for the Nazis following the 1930 election in which the NSDAP gained 6.5 million, or 37 per cent of the popular vote; the triumph of November 1932, when they received 33 per cent, or nearly 14.5 million out of 45 million votes cast; the accession of Hitler to the chancellorship in late January 1933,[120] and Concordat with the Vatican in the summer of 1933; his ruthless iron-fisted consolidation, were all wildly cheered by the smitten Arcand who filled his rags with tributes to the Nazi miracle, praising Hitler as a visionary, patriot, dedicated Christian, and mankind's, and the new Germany's, greatest hope. 'Nous saluons avec un vif enthousiasme le triomphe suprême de ce grand patriote,' Le Goglu declared upon Hitler's accession the the chancellorship, 'dont l'exemple s'impose à tous qui aiment leur patrie ... liberée des parasites, prospère et généreuse pour ses enfants.'[121]

Hitler's accession, in Arcand's view, radically changed the course of modern history. It was a massive arrest, a dramatic point of reversal of the drift of Germany and the world towards Judaeo-Bolshevik domination; a landmark in the defence, and renewal, of a besieged Aryan Christian civilization. 'Il a placé l'anti-sémitisme à la base de sa politique,' Arcand exulted, 'non pas pour le plaisir de persécuter une race particulière, mais dans le seul but de libérer ses compatriotes, de refaire une Allemagne Chrétienne, de rendre à sa race la colossale fortune que les Juifs lui avaient volée, de protéger l'idée nationale Allemande contre le poison dissolvant des doctrines juives.'[122] The uniqueness and beauty of National Socialism lay not merely in its program and ideals, but in its success – its will and way of translating race hate and violence into public policy and legislation. Hitler's persecution and disfranchisement of the Jews – the sanctioned boycotts and hooliganism; the dismissals from the public service; the removal from the professions, individual enterprises, and institutions of higher learning; the dreaded flood of violence codified in legislation preceding and including the so-called Nuremberg Laws of 1935, which legitimated racial anti-Semitism by forbidding marriage and sexual relations between Jews and non-Jews and disenfranchising 'German subject' or 'nationals' not of 'German blood' – were hailed by Arcand as examples to be emulated around the world, including Quebec.[123] 'Aucun pays ne peut être vraiment libéré et économiquement indépendant s'il n'est pas d'abord délivré de la juiverie,' Arcand wrote in an editorial titled 'Hitler et les Juifs' on the eve of Hitler's triumph:

Et ce qui s'accomplit présentement en Allemagne ... comme en Roumanie en Lithuanie, en Tchécoslovaquie, en Pologne et dans une foule d'autres pays, peut être accompli dans la province de Québec, où vivent l'immense majorité de tous les Juifs du Canada, particulièrement à Montréal. Un pays dont les activités nationales ne sont pas entre les mains des Canadiens, ... est présentement à la merci des Juifs ... La grande majorité de la population Canadienne aspire à la libération, afin que notre commerce, notre finance et notre industrie redeviennent complètement canadiens. Heureusement, la juiverie n'a pas fait ici autant de progrès qu'en Allemagne et elle n'a pas atteint le degré de puissance qu'elle détient dans certains pays européens. C'est pourquoi elle sera plus facile à repousser. Dans un pays où la situation était presque désespérée, Hitler a prouvé que la délivrance est encore facile, quand le sentiment national est bien canalisé.[124]

With Hitler leading the way, Adrien Arcand was ready to follow. During the months and years of the rise and consolidation of the Nazis in power, Arcand cultivated useful, if covert, contacts with Nazi propagandists, contacts that warmed his heart, assuaged his appetite for intrigue, and assisted in the task of channelling sentiment in Quebec in the right, anti-Semitic direction. Formerly gadflies – or bobolinks – the Goglus became, in the wake of Hitler's rise to power, cogs in a vast network of hate, centred in Nazi Germany. An important early contact was Kurt Ludecke, an old pal of Hitler's sent by the Nazi Party to North America as early as the autumn of 1930 to spread the gospel of National Socialism. Soon after arrival in Washington, Ludecke set up shop and housekeeping, flashed his credentials as official representative of the Nazi press, announced the creation of a National Socialist press service – to serve as the official news agency of the Nazi Party – wandered into the Capitol's press galleries, and buttonholed a variety of government politicians and legislators, including representatives Benton of Texas and T. MacFadden of Pennsylvania, who delivered impassioned defences of the Hitler regime.[125] Outside of Washington's corridors, Ludecke built up a network of useful contacts in the United States, in Mexico – part of his designated territory – and in Canada, where his September 1932 meeting with Arcand in Montreal opened his eyes to the pioneering effects of the *Völkisch* Goglus, resulting, as Ludecke later wrote, in an agreement 'to cooperate in every way,' including the appointment of 'several representatives to serve as contacts ... to supply ... material.'[126] Delighted with the remarkable successes of Ludecke's boss, Arcand tried, unsuccessfully, to arrange a meeting between the Nazi emissary and Prime Minister R.B. Bennett.[127] In a letter to the itinerant Nazi propagandist Major Frank Pease, who was visiting Germany, Arcand referred to Ludecke as 'a most estimable friend' and 'my good friend,' noting that Ludecke was also 'a friend of Hitler.' 'If it can help you,' Arcand offered Pease, 'you can act as correspondent of "Le Patriote" which is known [to] Hitler and which is very well appreciated by the Nazi propaganda bureau.'[128]

Arcand's contact with the Nazis did not end with Ludecke. The *Völkische Beobachter* of Munich, Streicher's *Der Stürmer*, and the *Hammer Verlag* of J. Monneche were all prominent Nazi propaganda sources that supplied Arcand with useful materials. At the centre of the Nazi propaganda network was the Fichtebund, Hamburg, and Dr Fleischauer's World Service, Erfurt, which shipped bales of propaganda around the world, including to Canada where, according to one account, more than four hundred different kinds of anti-Semitic pro-Nazi leaflets, pamphlets, and books were circulated.[129] On several occasions, *Le Goglu* reported the convening of 'important' conferences of the 'anti-semitic international,' in unnamed European cities, at which it had representation.[130] At a conference in Erfurt in 1937, organized by Dr Fleischauer's World Service, a 'lieutenant' of Arcand was reported to be in attendance.[131]

The Goglus' entry into the import business aided their cause, of exposing the Jewish Menace, in several ways. It was, first of all, a matter of economy. The availability of ready-made pre-packaged hate literature reduced the need for local invention and manufacture. Propaganda made in Germany, at Erfurt, Hamburg, or Munich – where Rolf Hoffmann's Foreign Press Service supplied Nazi Party propaganda to Adrien Arcand – or in England at the Craven Street headquarters of the Imperial Fascist League, was both a saving and a supplement, serving as fillers for the home-grown copy produced at their local hate plant. Alfred Rosenberg's misanthropic caricatures, Streicher's rogues' galleries of Jewish Bolshevik revolutionaries, hideous accounts of ritual murder, and the subversions of 'Le Juif Bela Kun [Kohn]' added breadth and tone to locally produced fairy tales and conspiracies, plots and threats so widely advertised that Samuel Jacobs, the Jewish member of Parliament for Montreal–Cartier was moved to comment, to an American colleague, that at no other time in his 'whole life' had he ever 'seen anything so virulent as the campaign which is being propagated against the Jews in the Province of Quebec.'[132] Jacob's views were shared by the *Canadian Jewish Chronicle*, which noted a peculiar syncopation; whenever Hitler sneezed, Canada's twin racketeers of journalism caught cold. 'Thus, the pest of Jew-hatred,' the *Chronicle* concluded, 'like the bubonic plague, was being brought from continent to continent, through the medium of rats.'[133]

5

Embryo Nazism

The overseas passage of the contagion of hate, which supplemented 'a form of anti-semitism ... indigenous to the temperament and
disposition of a certain local philosophy,'[1] did not go unnoticed, or
unchallenged, in Quebec or Canada. Committed to Jew-baiting, to
bracing and blending home-grown antipathies with the potent brew
of imported hates, the Goglus and their successors, heartened by the
surge of Fascism overseas and by the prejudices – or indifference –
of diverse local élites, succeeded in provoking from their target
group, the Jewish community, a powerful, defensive reaction.
'Whether it is the result of economic stress or not, we cannot tell,'
the *Canadian Jewish Chronicle* concluded on the eve of a historical
national convention, 'but the ugly monster of anti-semitism has
reared its head with more than ordinary force, and spurred on by
what is happening in Germany, a veritable mess of intrigue has arisen
everywhere, especially in the province of Quebec ... all of this has
aroused Canadian Jewry from its lethargic complacency, and we
begin to realize that there is a need for action.'[2]

The Jewish reaction took on many forms. Of primary importance
was the formation of a national umbrella organization to unify and
coordinate defensive, as well as constructive, activities among the
widely dispersed Jewish communities. The first All-Canadian Jewish
Congress, formed in 1919, had proved a short-lived affair.[3] Created
in the aftermath of the First World War, to deal with the multitude
of problems – nationally as well as internationally – faced by Jews in
the early post-war period, the new congress quickly lapsed and be-

came, as Abella and Troper noted, 'little more than a name on sta-
tionery letterhead.'[4] The impetus for the revised version, which convened for the first time in Toronto in late January 1934, and thereafter became a permanent fixture on the Canadian scene, was
provided, as the *Canadian Jewish Chronicle* observed, not by 'hysteria
or excitement' but 'the rational desire to bring together our scattered forces and unite ourselves against an insidious enemy that has
been undermining our security for many years.'[5]

The functions of the new congress varied. As with its evanescent
predecessor, much of its work was 'internal' or 'constructive,' involving, for example, aid to colonization and immigration, Jewish education, community organization, heritage conservation, and statisti-
cal economic and social research and analysis of the structure and
conditions of the Jewish community. Equally important were its activities in the areas of public education, public relations, and anti-
defamation. Spearheaded by general secretary H.M. Caiserman,
assisted by a tiny volunteer staff, the congress, together with sister
institutions and organizations – working jointly or separately – addressed the task of countering and containing the new surge of anti-
Semitic propaganda.[6] The rise of anti-Semitism, locally and internationally, was tracked in congress speeches and reports and in Jewish
community newspapers, which published statements and articles by
local leaders as well as by prominent scientists and writers including
Albert Einstein, Lion Feuchtwanger, George Bernard Shaw, and
Thomas Mann. The French- and English-Canadian press were closely
scrutinized. Innuendoes, statements, or outbursts – written or spoken, whether in Quebec or across the country – were duly collected
and passed on to local committees or national headquarters for re-
buttal or intervention. Liaisons were cultivated and material exchanged with sympathetic French-Canadian journalists such as Olivar Asselin. Church officials were encouraged and cajoled to muzzle
errant subordinates or editors of religious publications. Advertisers
were approached, often successfully, to withdraw support from *Le
Goglu* and other stridently anti-Semitic journals.[7] Papers like the
Canadian Jewish Chronicle, an English-language newspaper, and the
Keneder Odler, a Yiddish paper, both published in Montreal, countered
anti-Semitic propaganda with disclosure, argument, ridicule, and

scorn. Arcand's *Key to the Mystery* was thoroughly dissected and dismissed as hateful nonsense in a series of articles – by Professor S. Cohon, a professor of theology at Hebrew Union College, at the behest of the Canadian Jewish Congress – and published by the *Canadian Jewish Chronicle*, which printed, as well, Lucien Wolfe's learned refutation of the *Protocols*, originally written for the *Spectator*.[8] Pamphlets compiled by Caiserman on Jew-baiting in Canada, or the Fascist Network in Canada, documenting the rise and activities of Fascist or anti-Semitic groups, were published by the congress, which compiled comprehensive mailing lists of communities and 'representative citizens,' including teachers, journalists, professors, and clergy, who received copies of the more than 1.1 million pamphlets distributed by 1936.[9] Assisting in the task of disclosure and counterattack was the sister institution of the B'nai B'rith, a Jewish fraternal organization headquartered in the United States with branches across Canada, whose Canadian Anti-Defamation Committee, formed in 1920, played an important role, during the 1920s, in combating spillover propaganda from the Ford agitation in the United States, as well as the *London Morning Post*'s sensational anti-Semitic series, reproduced in several Canadian papers, alleging a Jewish-Bolshevik conspiracy to foment international revolution.[10] At the third annual convention of the Canadian Jewish Congress, it was announced that anti-defamation work would be centralized in a committee known as the Joint Public Relations Committee of the Canadian Jewish Congress on which the B'nai B'rith and the congress were accorded equal representation.[11]

The counter-attack against anti-Semitism, by the congress and related groups, was both varied and wide ranging. Sympathetic liberals such as Senator R. Dandurand, Montreal mayor Fernand Rinfret, and Honoré Mercier were joined by Bishop Farthing, the Reverend Leslie Pigeon, and a host of prominent Jewish public figures – religious and secular – to speak at a massive anti-Nazi rally in Montreal in April 1933;[12] this meeting had inspired Jeune-Canada's remarkable counter-demonstration at which standard anti-Semitic lore was repeated by radical youth leaders convinced that Jewish economic and political influence in Quebec – modest to be sure – was both powerful and dangerous, and that the problems of the Jews in Germany were less worthy of attention than the privations of the Québécois. As the Nazi vice tightened, a national boycott of German goods was organized and advertised by the congress, but was of limited effectiveness. Henri Bourassa was approached to lend his eloquence to the anti-defamation cause, and he responded with an impassioned speech in the House of Commons, asserting that 'anti-semitism on the part of a Frenchman, a Catholic, is absurd; yes, even a monstrosity.'[13] Anti-Semitic intrusions on the CBC and CKAC invited protest letters, delegations, and other interventions with management that resulted in careful monitoring of radio broadcasts. The postmaster general received letters of complaint and was approached by a joint delegation, including sympathetic Protestant clergymen, to seek ways and means of halting the distribution of hate literature through the mails. And, in 1936–7, important contacts were made and meetings arranged with Catholic church officials, in which Rabbi H.J. Stern played a key role, 'to create a better relationship with the organized Jewish Community in Canada.' 'The third meeting was at the Montefiore Club,' Caiserman later recalled, 'where a larger number were present. An important discussion took place about the Arcand movement which at that time posed a serious threat to Canadian and Jewish security ... We sensed the beginnings of a movement, of a leadership and desire to combat hatred against the Jew.'[14]

Among the key players in the anti-defamation game were the thimbleful of elected Jewish politicians in the House of Commons, and in the Quebec provincial legislature. Educated at McGill and Laval, where he obtained a law degree in 1894, Samuel W. Jacobs was first elected – as the representative for Montreal–Cartier – to Parliament in 1917, and served without interruption until his death, in 1938.[15] Head counsel in the celebrated Plamondon libel case in 1913, and an expert on public accounts and railways, Jacobs observed, during the heat of the anti-Semitic wave of the early 1930s, that the 'language used by American Jew-baiters' was 'mild to that compared to that here' and concluded that 'money required for that purpose is being supplied by Berlin.'[16] Hopeful that Quebec was 'but going through a phase of insanity (the Moon is near the earth and drives men mad),' Jacobs noted that the flood of hate literature lost 'a great deal of its effect through its virulence' and that 'we shall in due time return to normal conditions.'[17] In aid of the return to normalcy, Jacobs organized and addressed public meetings; occasionally denounced anti-Semitic utterances in Parliament;[18] encouraged people like Bourassa to speak out on the hate campaign in his home province; brokered meetings between Jewish community representatives and government officials following the return of the Liberals to power in 1935; leaned on his Liberal and Conservative colleagues on a variety of issues, especially immigration; and played a pivotal role in the revival of the Canadian Jewish Congress, which he served as president during the years 1934–8.[19]

Quebec's pair of provincial *shtadlonim* were equally active. Like Jacobs – their federal counterpart – Joseph Cohen, who sat for the St Lawrence constituency, and Peter Bercovitch, the member for St Louis, were Liberal. A lawyer by profession, Cohen served in the House as representative of the Liberal party, a multi-ethnic electoral constituency – of whom the Jews counted one-third – and the Jewish community. More senior, and effective, was Peter Bercovitch, also a lawyer, educated at the Protestant schools, McGill and the University of Montreal, who, following the provincial general election of 1916, became the first Jew to sit in the provincial House. Bercovitch was re-elected without interruption for over two decades and served until 1938, when he resigned his seat and was returned to the federal Parliament, by acclamation, as the representative for the Montreal–Cartier seat, following the death of Samuel W. Jacobs.[20] An urbane, reform Jew from the toney uptown segment of Montreal's riven Jewish community, Bercovitch was an important link between his ethnic compatriots and the governing Liberal political establishment.[21] He practised law in the prominent firm of Bercovitch and Calder, served as president of the Laurentian Insurance Company, and occupied a number of official posts in the Jewish community, among them the first presidency of the Jewish Immigrant Aid Society and executive board member of the reform Temple Emanuel. No avid hustings politician, or loud House debater, Bercovitch was a quiet-spoken, keen, analytical legislator who excelled in committee work and preferred to 'annihilate his opponents,' as the *Chronicle* observed, 'with the unimpassioned restraint of understatement.'[22]

Though Bercovitch's talents were many, there was one lacking, as the *Chronicle* observed, which cost him the cabinet position of provincial treasurer, for which he was eminently qualified – the talent 'to efface his Jewishness.'[23] Throughout his lengthy legislative career, Bercovitch keenly interested himself in issues affecting the Jewish community, downtown as well as uptown. He introduced a rent bill favouring his poor downtown constituents, maintained good working relationships with unionists and workers, took care of legislation affecting Jewish civil disabilities, and immersed himself in the protracted debates, litigation, and legislation affecting the status of Jewish schools. Both preceding and during the crisis precipitated by the David bill, Bercovitch played a pivotal role in the conflict involving the government, the divided Jewish community, and the pressing Protestant and Catholic educational interests. 'It might be said ... without any hesitation,' the *Chronicle* wrote, in an obituary, more than a decade after the resolution of the school crisis, 'that in his handling of the delicate school question during the thirties, Mr. Bercovitch stood out the best, for it was an occasion when the greatest of skill, knowledge, and delicacy was required.'[24]

While the *Chronicle* admired Peter Bercovitch's skill and diplomacy, there were other journalists ready to condemn him and his legislative co-religionist as agents of the devil, working day and night to corrupt a weak and decadent liberal regime. Bercovitch, to the Goglus and other strident anti-Semites, was anathema, one of the many pernicious instruments that had turned Louis-Alexandre Taschereau into a valet of the Jews.[25] The assault on Bercovitch began modestly enough, in the 11 April 1930 edition of *Le Goglu*, which featured a caricature of the St Louis MLA with an accompanying text alleging *à propos* of the David bill, 'Deux seuls députés juifs, lui et M. Cohen, ont obtenu en un tour de main ce qu'il a fallu à nos pères des siècles de combats pour nous gagner.'[26] By January 1932, Bercovitch was no longer the ' "Beau Brummel" of his race,' or the mere perpetrator of insidious one-sided legislation. He became, instead, a 'false prince of the filthy ghettos,' 'flotsam and jetsam of the Red Sea,' a 'fugitive from the massacres of Egypt,' and, not least, 'a leftover from the justifiable furnaces of Nebuchadnezzar'[27] – designations Adrien Arcand invented and peddled in response to a bill, introduced into the legislature of the province of Quebec, on 27 January 1932, by the MLA for St Louis, 'concerning the publication and distribution of outrageous subject matter against any religious sect, creed, class, denomination, race or nationality.'[28]

The Bercovitch group libel bill, aimed at *Le Goglu, Le Miroir,* and *Le Chameau,* was, quite simply, a product of the frustration of the Jewish community leaders and, to a limited extent, the premier himself. The Goglu torrent unleashed by the school crisis, reinforced by the ancillary hate utterances of vocal others, the curious silence of church authorities, and the influx of imported hate propaganda invited apprehension, rage, and a quick search for appropriate responses or remedies. *The Canadian Jewish Chronicle* and *Jewish Daily Eagle* heaped scorn and ridicule. Advertisers were contacted to withdraw business. The silence, or tolerance, of opinion leaders – church officials and journalists – was publicly noted and frowned upon, while the virtue, or otherwise, of ignoring the vipers, or mosquitoes, was debated by Jewish leaders intent on mobilizing opinion within their own community and among French Canadians, whose failure to resort to mob violence in response to 'hair-raising and inflammatory outbursts' indicated, according to Israel Rabinovitch, that they 'were not so hopeless as one would have us believe, nor ... such easy prey for the anti-semitic charlatans as one would have us imagine.'[29] Among the sympathetic audience of Jewish complainants was the premier himself, who considered tolerance of religious minorities a corner-stone of national pride and democratic government. A consummate juggler of competing religious and ethnic communities, who created a minor and relatively inconsequential niche for the Jews in the legislative system, Taschereau disdained the politics of hate, dismissed political anti-Semitism as unworthy of his compatriots, and condemned its appearance and use during the trying David bill debate. Camillien Houde, who briefly flirted with the Goglus during his early days as Conservative leader, was described by Taschereau, during the heat of a by-election campaign, as 'chief of a group of bobolinks, little birds that eat what they can when the horses have passed.'[30]

When Peter Bercovitch presented his group-defamation bill for the consideration of the legislature, Taschereau was sympathetic, though not strongly supportive. The end – to shut up the Goglus and other nuisances – was desirable, but the means, questionable. What Bercovitch proposed, after all, was unprecedented and, as Taschereau quickly discovered, politically dangerous. According to existing law, as Joseph Cohen informed the legislature during his subsequent debate, an aggrieved individual had redress for libel or slander. A group, however, had no similar resort. 'If one were to call me a thief or a murderer or a seducer of women, I could go to court and obtain justice,' Cohen announced, 'but if one says that all Jews are murderers, thiefs and seducers there is no redress.'[31] In presenting his bill, which was subsequently modified and reintroduced in early February, Bercovitch hoped to make the libelling of a race, religion, or national group actionable.[32] The action would be civil rather than criminal – within the jurisdiction of the province – and the proposed remedy, an injunction to halt publication of libellous materials, rather than damages, which might lay the courts open to a run of suits. 'The object of the bill under consideration,' Bercovitch informed the House, 'is merely to prevent a repeated and a systematic publication of libels, not only against Jews, but against any nationality, any religion and any race ... the law does not authorize the claiming of damages by the race or nationality that has been libeled nor is there any provision for punishment by imprisonment; it merely gives a judge of the Superior Court the power to issue an injunction to restrain the repeated publication of libel against any nationality or race – in other words, the real object of the law is to give bigotry no sanction, persecution no assistance.'[33]

Bercovitch's intentions were noble enough and he, and his St Lawrence colleague, supported by Dr Anatole Plante, whose Mercier constituency included a large Jewish vote,[34] spoke eloquently in support of a measure to protect 'the good name and reputation of the Jewish community.'[35] Bercovitch warned that the concord and good will, the 'good feeling and respect' among 'all classes and races,' that had evolved in Quebec was being undermined by 'vilifiers and slanderers' who held the 'dear and sacred' institutions and 'a respected element of the population of this province up to contempt, hatred and ridicule.' While individuals libelled had remedies under existing laws, he reminded the House, racial, national, and religious groups did not; such an absence of remedies threatened the peace and stability of a fragile body politic composed of diverse nationalities and religious groups. Citing the unfortunate example of the Weimar Reichstag, which, in 1929, suspended the immunity of its members from civil prosecution, thereby enabling court cases to proceed against several stridently anti-Semitic editors, Bercovitch closed with the assertion that 'the best authority against the contemptible lies of the Protocols of the Elders of Zion' was the Bible itself. 'One law, one statute, one judgement shall be for you, for the stranger who lives with you,' said Bercovitch, citing Exodus 12:49, 'and for all people who acknowledge the fatherhood of God and the brotherhood of man.'[36]

Joseph Cohen's supporting speech was equally impassioned. For Cohen, the House debate on the Bercovitch bill served as a forum for a wide-ranging and eloquent appeal to 'the French-Canadian people whose inherent sense of justice and fair play, whose claim for the protection of the rights of minorities has become proverbial.'[37] Cohen reviewed and dismissed, with argument, scorn, and appropriate references to the Bible and Talmud, the entire panoply of Goglus' slurs, from ritual murder to *Protocol* conspiracies, to alleged Talmudic prescriptions to malign, rob, and assault gentiles. He warned that a new and dangerous anti-Semitic campaign and spirit had been introduced into the national political life, a campaign almost invariably associated with lawlessness, brutality, injustice, and 'other sinister forces, particularly those which are corrupt, reactionary and oppressive.'[38] Fighting anti-Semitism, Cohen concluded, was not merely a job for the Jews. It was the duty of citizens 'of Gentile birth and Christian faith' as well, especially moulders of public opinion and political leaders whose predecessor, 'the immortal patriot, Louis Joseph Papineau,' had introduced, one hundred years earlier, into the legislature of Lower Canada, the bill granting Jews equality of rights. It was to secure and protect those rights, Cohen averred, that the Bercovitch bill was introduced in the legislature. 'There is no attempt to infringe on the liberty of the press,' Cohen informed the House, 'but even the press, the decent honest press cannot and should not defend the rights to publish matters such as that complained of. A distinction must be made between the liberty of the press and license to libel, malign and traduce.'[39]

Unfortunately, for Bercovitch and Cohen, the distinctions between liberty and licence and remedies – in the form of group-libel legislation limiting expression – were not lightly entertained by a press, which, with a few exceptions, avidly pursued the rabbit released by the Bercovitch bill.[40] The assault was virulent, widespread, and troubling to a premier who despised the anti-Semitic campaign and was prepared, at the outset, as Bernard Vigod noted, to 'support at least a watered-down version' of the restrictive legislation.[41] The breadth and intensity of the response, however, was disheartening. The Goglu publications predictably went beserk, waved the banner of freedom, challenged the reticence of the Jews to use existing laws, and taunted a regime prepared to 'permit the residue of Yiddish immigrants from Poland and Russia to hinder the rightful claims of an honest and upright race which does not want to submit any longer to the exploitation, thievery, perfidy, immorality, filth, corruption and bolshevik propaganda of the Sons of Judas.'[42] The mainstream press, nationalist or otherwise, of varied stripes and persuasions, had their own reasons for opposing the bill. The *Gazette*, edited by the Jew Abel Vineberg, likened the Bercovitch bill to 'a huge steam-driven crusher deployed to crush tiny kernels of fanaticism.'[43] *Le Progrès du Saguenay* saltily observed that the laws 'common to the province and satisfying to this population ought to suffice for the Jews.'[44] *L'Action Catholique* was troubled by reputational considerations and thought its native province 'a paradise of minorities,' which did not 'merit the affront of a law which would give her the appearance of being more of a persecutor than her sister provinces.'[45] A major press opponent was *Le Devoir,* whose mordant Georges Pelletier thought the bill's injunction machinery so heavy and awkward that any libel against the Jews that his rival Abel Vineberg might choose to publish would 'be consumed with the breakfast rolls before the law catches up with it.'[46] Pelletier had visions of censors, appointed by Bercovitch and Cohen, screening printing plants 'like the Kosher butcher shops whence nothing goes out which is not approved according to Talmudic prescriptions.'[47]

If Taschereau was merely testing the waters with the Bercovitch bill, he discovered them, by the end of the session, to be exceedingly hot. The task of clearing the legislative way, to oblivion, fell to the Westmount Liberal MLA R.F. Stockwell, a rival of Bercovitch's for the post of provincial secretary. Stockwell informed the House that the matter was really within federal jurisdiction, that the Jews were seeking an additional right to the ones they already had – the right to immunity from criticism – and that ignoring the hate campaign of the yellow journals was really enough.[48] When the premier rose to speak, the bill's fate was a foregone conclusion; its fate had been sealed by the raucous press campaign labelling the measure a Jewish demand for undue special privilege.[49] Taschereau was sympathetic, even apologetic, to his Jewish constituents and urged them to ignore their traducers or resort to existing laws to combat the hate campaign. He understood their sensitivity, their suffering in the face of vicious attacks. He praised the efforts of their representatives, whose standing among the citizenry remained high, and condemned the Goglu campaign as anti-national and anti-Quebec, a blot on the reputation of a province that prided itself 'on being the refuge of liberty and tolerance, of harmony among races.' But public opinion, the premier sadly concluded, was 'not ready for such a radical measure.'[50] Accordingly, in the final days of the session, the Bercovitch group-libel bill was tactfully killed, with three dissenting votes, by an amendment referring the question to a House committee, which, with its sister committees, automatically dissolved on prorogation.[51]

The death of the Bercovitch bill stifled neither the Goglus, who ignored Taschereau's appeal delivered from the floor of the House to desist, nor their Jewish opponents, who sought new ways of silencing the hate campaign. Throughout the weeks of the bill's consideration, Arcand and Ménard filled their sheets with the usual venom. When the bill failed, they cooed with delight and quickened the hate flow, which crested on the day of celebration of the centenary of Jewish emancipation in Quebec, when *Le Miroir* bedecked its front page with the wild Lindbergh kidnap and ritual-murder accusation. Jewish community leaders, for their part, commiserated briefly over the bill's demise, turned to the task of community mobilization – leading eventually to the congress resurrection – and debated options ranging from studied silence to the launching of criminal or civil actions.[52] In the midst of the debate, E. Abugov, a Jewish merchant from Lachine, Quebec – represented by the law firm of Cohen, Gameroff, and Gross – took the matter in hand and stepped forward, into the courtroom, to challenge the conventional wisdom, repeated by the premier and his colleagues during the debate on the Bercovitch bill, that sufficient remedies for libelled persons existed under the law.

The judicial hearing of the Abugov petition before Superior Court Judge Gonzalve Desaulniers, in July 1932, for an injunction restraining Joseph Ménard, publisher of *Le Miroir, Le Goglu,* and *Le Chameau,* or his agents, servants, or employers, from writing, publishing, editing, or distributing articles libellous of the Jews in general, or 'the petitioner in particular,' proceeded, as the *Chronicle* observed, 'like an apocalypse of incredibilities.'[53] The twin racketeers, by one account, comported themselves in court like characters out of Gilbert and Sullivan. The Talmud, oft-cited in Goglu publications as the source of Jewish perfidy, the Court learned, had been read by neither Arcand nor Ménard, who made a 'magnanimous exception' of the apostles when pressing their claim that all Jews were murderers.[54] Ethnographic references to Jews as misanthropists, Arabs, thieves, Mexicans, and assassins were scattered among heaps of other nonsense. 'The notes of the court's stenographer read like a medieval romance,' the *Chronicle* concluded, 'or like the autobiography of Baron Munchausen.'[55] Witness, and judge, to a circus of hate, Judge Desaulniers, a fair and decent man who pronounced the Goglu propaganda as 'anti-Christian, anti-social and anti-national,' postponed judgment until early autumn, imploring, in the meanwhile, the respondents to abandon their enterprise of hate.

The judge's pleas, like the premier's before him, were rebuffed. Back in their dingy press offices, Arcand and Ménard returned to the attack – on the judge, the courts, and the Jews.[56] Mouldy blood libels, sinister Sanhedrins, mysterious 'Kehelas,' boycott lists, the Lindbergh idiocy, world-wide directories of anti-Semitic agencies and papers, appeals for contributions to a patriotic fund to combat the 'Youpins,' filled their sheets during the weeks preceding the reconvening of the court in early September, when Judge Desaulniers delivered his verdict, a lengthy, discursive document replete with learned historical and biblical references and quotations described by the *Montreal Star* as 'remarkable' and deserving of a 'place along side the great pronouncements on British liberties and tolerance.'[57] For the defendant, Judge Desaulniers reserved nothing, in his seven-page document, but scorn and censure. Ménard and his associates were reminded that the French Canadians themselves were a feeble minority, dependent, like the Jews, on the tolerance and understanding of majorities. The judge argued, and supported with historical illustrations, that disorder and revolution followed from intolerance and persecution; that blood libel, the imputation of demonic lineage, and similar assertions were the same dangerous anti-Christian inventions employed by Drumont in France, whose campaign 'ended only in leaving France divided against herself, in weakening her moral forces and in the banishment of an innocent man to Devil's Island.'[58] Of the Jews, Judge Desaulniers had only understanding and praise. 'The Jewish race is one marvelously gifted,' the judge observed; 'they offer for our reflection the prodigious and outstanding example in history of a people surviving the empires which enslaved it.'[59]

Sympathetic as he was to Jewish circumstances and complaints, Judge Desaulniers was not, however, prepared to offer a judicial solution. Noting that the Quebec legislature had refused to place 'in the hands of the magistrature' the necessary instrument to keep 'such movements within decent limits,' he rejected the Abugov petition as beyond the bench's 'discretionary power.' Instead of a remedy, the judge offered hope – 'that the defendant will himself understand the irreparable harm that he is causing his race in the eyes of the people of this continent.'[60]

Though the Goglus remained free to pursue their hate, Jewish community leaders were not displeased with the decision of Judge Desaulniers, whose scathing denunciation of the Goglu campaign was reprinted in leading English and French dailies. For the Jews, the Desaulniers judgment was a moral, if not legal, victory and a challenge to Taschereau who, according to the *Chronicle*, was directed 'by an illustrious member of the bench to remedy this evil.'[61] Taschereau responded with a bill of modest breadth and toothless application, a measure 'of the utmost innocuousness,'[62] introduced, then quickly

withdrawn, during the 1933 session; a withdrawal occasioned by the
sudden suspension of the Goglu publications and welcomed by the
nationalist press, including *Le Devoir*, which featured the Taschereau
retreat on the front page, alongside the denunciation, by Jeune-
Canada, of French-Canadian politicians who participated in the anti-
Hitler rally organized by the Montreal Jewish community.[63]

In evading legislative containment and judicial stricture, the
Goglus won a victory of sorts. But their ugly little war with the Jews,
the Liberal government, and other individuals and groups offended by their strident hate had taken its toll. Though they wore a brave
– if vicious – face, the Goglus were, in fact, straining woefully to keep
their enterprises alive. Organizationally, their numbers were minuscule; their occasional public meetings, poorly attended. Financially,
they struggled and staggered, from week to week: '1931 has been for
us but a year of poisoning,' Arcand wrote to the prime minister,
'knocks and blows which we had resisted to this date, as well as the
effects of the general depression suffered by everybody.'[64] During the
1931 provincial election campaign, political opponents vandalized
and set fire to Ménard's printing shop, destroying his equipment.[65]
Large advertisers, approached by lobbyists, shunned their pages. A
succession of lawsuits drained their resources, resulting, on one occasion, in the conviction and imprisonment of publisher Ménard for
fifteen days.[66] Though Arcand boasted to a roving pro-Nazi propagandist that the Goglus' moral capital was increasing in 'unexpect-
ed proportion,'[67] their financial capital was diminished by 'bitter
losses,' resulting, as Samuel Jacobs happily disclosed to the founding
convention of the Canadian Jewish Congress, in a painful tour
through the bankruptcy courts and shut-down of their three papers
in the spring of 1933,[68] a closure that provided Taschereau with his
excuse to withdraw the libel legislation.[69]

The Goglus might have avoided the bankruptcy courts had their
conservative political friends, provincially and federally, been more
forthcoming. Provincially, the man 'que la Providence a visiblement
marqué pour une destinée speciale'[70] – until mid-1930 – was Conservative party leader Camillien Houde, who likely contributed financially to the Goglu paper during its formative months and enjoyed, in
return, the enthusiastic support of *Le Goglu* in his successful cam-

paign for re-election as mayor of Montreal, in April 1930. Houde shared with the Goglus a number of dislikes, among them the Taschereau government and its dangerous David bill.[71] But Houde fancied himself the mayor, and candidate, of all the people, including the Jews, and was troubled by Arcand's descent into raw Jew-baiting. Angling for the minority ethnic vote, and sensitive to accusations that Tories – who counted Saskatchewan premier J.T.M. Anderson, author of controversial restrictive minority language and educational legislation, in their ranks – were prejudiced against minorities, Houde publicly dissociated himself from and condemned the campaign, during the mayoralty contest, to 'soulever le cri de race et de religion dans un pays libre, dont les institutions doivent protéger les citoyens de toutes origines et particulièrement les minorités.'[72] The mayor's disavowal notwithstanding, the Goglus affirmed their support during the campaign, then turned on the corpulent man of destiny like a pack of mad dogs. 'Plus on étudie le Houdisme,' Le Miroir announced on 12 July 1931, 'plus il est laid et répugnant: plus on conçoit que cette organisation d'arrivistes est en somme une bête immonde.'[73] So violent was their opposition to the Conservative provincial leader during and following the 1931 provincial campaign that Israel Rabinovitch, editor of the Keneder Odler, was moved to speculate whether 'financial pearls' of the Liberal party had been somehow cast 'into the water-trough of the anti-semitic swine – the Goglu, Chameau and Miroir.'[74] 'These three fire-spouting sheets,' Rabinovitch observed, 'as soon as their love affair with Camillien Houde was over, betook themselves like shameless prostitutes to proffer their passion to the Liberal party, the party, be it said, of Sir Wilfrid Laurier, and to spill bile and gall upon the head of their former paramour – Houde.'[75]

Though Arcand and his associates fell out with a provincial Houdistes, they remained loyal supplicants of the governing federal party, which included in its Quebec wing several notables who appreciated and supported the Goglus' efforts. The prime minister himself was, it appears, not terribly receptive to Arcand's flood of requests for personal interviews, his gratuitous advice, his whining about adversity, his fulsome expressions of praise and loyalty, and, above all, his search for subsidies. Bennett did meet with the impecunious

editor following the 1930 election on at least one occasion but there
is no evidence he arranged for any substantial support for the Goglu papers during the heat of the libel wars or, indeed, that he ever
fully appreciated Arcand's view that 'the Jewish Question, then in its
infancy, did enormously for the Rightist cause in 1930' and could 'do
more and more in the future not only in politics, but for the public
affirmation of religion.'[76] It is likely, on the contrary, that Bennett,
like Houde, was less than pleased with the descent of the Goglu papers – which his party subsidized and utilized in the successful 1930
general election campaign – into raw racist politics, and it was on his
advice and unwillingness to continue financing their operation that
the papers suspended operation.[77] 'At about this date last year,' the
Conservative deputy speaker of the senate wrote to Bennett, 'I had
a short interview with you in the early morning, at your office – following which I advised Arcand and Ménard that their enterprise and
their papers had better be brought to an end – and that they should
turn a new sheet. Consequently, their three papers, their printing
establishment and their debts were liquidated; without a complaint
on their part, without an attack; – all to the contrary, because the last
issue of their papers was full of appreciation for you and your work.'[78]

Appreciation, for Adrien Arcand and his work, was not uncommon among a solid, well-placed coterie of Quebec federal Conservatives. It was the view of Leslie Bell, for example, the MP for St Antoine, that Arcand had rendered 'efficient and valuable' services to
the party during the 1930 election, and he urged Bennett to meet
with Arcand and Dr Lalanne, the Goglus' principal financial supporter.[79] Similar sympathies were entertained by Montreal MP John A.
Sullivan, who thought Arcand 'without exception the best French-
Canadian writer.'[80] Armand Lavergne, deputy speaker of the House
of Commons, was, apparently, so pleased with the reflections of *Le
Miroir* that he chose to contribute an article himself, to correct the
wrong impressions created by Judge Gonzalve Desaulniers, who, in
his judgment of the Abugov case, dismissed charges of Jewish ritual
murder as a medieval concoction. Lavergne, deemed by the *Canadian Jewish Chronicle* to be 'the sublime failure of Canadian politics, the
man who so persistently ran for office that he finally succeeded in,
tripping over the Deputy Speaker's footstool,' included, in his disser-

tation, a protestation that some of his best friends, Peter Bercovitch included, were Jews, and a taxonomy, which divided Jews into three categories – good, not so good, and very bad.[81] His main attentions, however, were directed at the matter of ritual murder – described by the *Catholic Encyclopedia* as 'one of the most notable and disastrous lies in history'[82] – which, Lavergne insisted, was a 'historical fact,' a conclusion that moved his good friend, Peter Bercovitch, to affirm, in a letter to *Le Canada*, his continued strong 'allegiance to Judaism ... notwithstanding the startling, apocalyptic revelations drawn from the Middle Ages by Mr. Lavergne.'[83]

In his flirtations with, and support for, Arcand and his papers, which he described in a letter to R.B. Bennett as 'important,'[84] Lavergne was joined by a further pair of notables – Samuel Gobeil, the MP for Compton, and, in 1935, postmaster general for Canada, and P.E. Blondin, speaker, no less, of the Senate of Canada. Gobeil was a vintage Quebecker, proud of his seventeenth-century Canadian ancestry, who produced and sold cream and butter for a living, serving as director of the Dairymen's Association of Quebec, mayor of La Patrie, and prefect of the County of Compton before winning election, after several unsuccessful tries, to the House of Commons in 1930.[85] A dedicated nationalist, Catholic, and Conservative, Gobeil was sympathetic to the Goglu enterprise, pressed Arcand's case for support with the prime minister, and, apparently, shared some of his views on the Jewish question, views expressed in a speech delivered before his electors at Lac Megantic, in the County of Compton on 17 March 1934 and reprinted in pamphlet form at Ménard's Rue St Denis plant, with a swastika enblazoned on the front cover, entitled, *La Griffe Rouge sur l'Université de Montréal* – elaborating charges made in the House of Commons that atheism and other nefarious doctrines had managed to infiltrate a university in which, a *Canadian Forum* columnist noted, 'no one was allowed to teach any subject ... unless he had been previously approved by a board of clerics.'[86] Spokesman and conscience of the wholesome, milk-fed rural counties, the pious parishes, and unsullied classical colleges, Gobeil traced the contamination of the University of Montreal to the provincial Liberal government which appointed Jews to positions of honour 'dans notre legislature canadienne-francaise et catholique';[87] to assorted unnamed professors who filled students' minds with atheism and nihilism; and to Jews, whom he described in a battery of distortions and misrepresentations drawn from Benjamin Disraeli, the Talmud, and *L'Encyclopédie Judaïque* – found in the Senate library – as dangerous, dishonest, thieving, unassimilable, hateful of Christians, red, and revolutionary.[88] Citing the presence of a smattering of Jewish students in assorted faculties, Gobeil warned that 'L'Université de Montréal est devenue l'incubatrice de l'élite juive anti-chrétienne, qui aujourd'hui se dresse contre notre propre élite dans toutes les professions.'[89]

While the speaker of the senate, the Honourable Pierre Edouard Blondin, was more circumspect than his Compton colleague, and maintained a safe public distance from Arcand and Ménard, he none the less forcefully argued their case within Conservative party circles for subsidy and support. Blondin met occasionally with Arcand,[90] and reassured the prime minister that the journalist – essentially and intensely Conservative' – deserved support, since there was in Quebec 'no Conservative paper worth mentioning' and 'no man of the size and power and moral character of Arcand.'[91] And when Adrien Arcand took a new, and promising direction, the Senate speaker was positively enthusiastic. 'Debunking had been the motto of Arcand, for the four previous years,' Blondin wrote to Bennett; 'now that he was left with nothing but his pen and his ink stand, he adopted a new motto: creating! – although penniless, he had the genius of creating an organization all to himself, and also a new publication called "Le Patriote," on a much higher plane than his former publication, and also much more powerful ... by the means of public lectures and intensive publicity, he has launched a movement which (under the name of "The Christian National Party") aims simply at the debunking of all the rot in the old parties, – which party, when the end comes, will be found to be "a regenerated Conservative party" in Quebec, which, I think we need.'[92]

The object of the speaker's excitement was a new organization formally launched by Arcand and his friends on 22 February 1934, at a public meeting at the Monument National. The time, and circumstances, it appeared, were propitious. The vibrant bobolink had become, in a few short years, a scrawny scavenger with clipped wings and ruffled feathers, feeding off the dung of hate. Programs of social restoration and revolution, both left and right, were crowding the political market-place, offering competing solutions attractive to Quebec's disoriented youth, which seemed up for grabs and likely converts to new and diverting political formulas and movements. Liberalism, it increasingly appeared, was fast declining, and the Jewish influence in society, economy, and government was incontrovertibly on the rise, an influence reflected locally in the school-law push, the group-libel legislative attempts, the consolidation of Jewish communal organizations, and the willingness of the Liberal government to placate Jewish interests. Internationally, Arcand concluded, the Jews commanded 'à plus de la moitié du globe.'[93] The surge on the extreme left was particularly menacing, an expansion noted by Quebec's fidgety clerical élites who opposed the 'atheism' and 'materialism' of the new Cooperative Commonwealth Federation, whose Regina Manifesto called for a centralized Canada based on planning and public ownership. Most compelling of all was the encouraging world-wide surge of patriotic anti-communist movement in diverse countries in the British Empire, in Europe, and in North and South America. At the centre of the coming apocalyptic World Revolution, affirming hierarchy, order, nationality, and Christianity, were Italy, whose Mussolini stood bravely alone, for a decade, against the Bolshevik hordes, and, above all, Germany, home in 1933 of a remarkable 'révolution constitutionelle.'[94] 'Le régime hitlerien constitue une nouvelle forteresse contre l'internationalisme bolchévique, un autre rampart pour la défense du Christianisme,' Arcand exulted on the eve of the Nazi accession to power. 'Bientôt le monde sera divisé en deux groupes distincts: le groupe des dictatures chrétiennes et le groupe des dictatures anti-chrétiennes, qui se disputeront la suprématie mondiale. La lutte sera terrible, mais elle sera définitive et il ne fait aucune doute que, grâce à ses chefs vigoureux, grâce à la justice de sa cause et la force de ses principes, le groupe Chrétien l'importera.'[95]

Somehow, as Quebec's deranged publicist appreciated, an organization called L'Ordre Patriotique des Goglus was not quite suited to the daunting task of terrible political combat. The invention of a dreamer, who dressed and arranged his toy combatants in quaint shirts, zones, and ranges, the Goglus had performed ably enough, during the early years of the depression, as self-appointed protectors of the traditions and interests of their race against predatory enemies. But they seemed, however, on the eve of Europe's Fascist surge, a trifle quaint, out of fashion; too parochial and ornate, meagre in number, ineffectively non-partisan, and distant from the muscular street wars or marbled corridors of political power. In an era of apocalyptic combat, debunking, as Canada's Senate speaker observed, no longer sufficed for Adrien Arcand. The times and struggle called for something bold and new, a vehicle of combat to replace an ornate order, and a formula or doctrine encapsulating the wisdom and will to power of a growing international movement. The vehicle was a political party – successor to the L'Ordre Patriotique des Goglus – known as the National Social Christian Party; the formula, quite simply, fascism.

Arcand's Canadianized Fascism, outlined in an assortment of articles in his newspapers and journals – old and new – in public addresses like 'Fascisme ou Socialisme,' delivered at the Palestre Nationale on 20 October 1933, and reprinted in pamphlet form, and in the program of his new party, was a hurried hybrid of imported nostrums and native Goglu residues. At its core was the conviction that liberal democracy, a device invented by Jews and Masons to undermine Christianity, nationality, and property, was fast exhausting itself, just as capitalism was entering into a state of acute disequilibrium and crisis, pincered between the extremes of Jewish international finance and Bolshevik revolution, also Jewish. Representative government, in Arcand's view, was no more than a shell, or smokescreen, obscuring the hidden dictatorship of money powers that presided over 'butter plate' national treasuries 'emptied from year to year by alternating politicians who grew always richer as the country became poorer and more indebted.'[96] The democratic party struggle was sham, divisive, and inconclusive, both symptom and cause of the moral and political anarchy exploited by socialist and Bolshevik revolutionaries organized in Canada in the Cooperative Commonwealth Federation and the Communist Party of Canada, prime enemies 'du nationalisme et du christianisme ... du droit de propriété et de l'autorité de la famille ... de la loi naturelle en laquelle il refuse de reconnaître l'inégalité des hommes.'[97] Neither of the two centrist parties or ideologies in Canada, or elsewhere, was willing or capable of sustaining a system in imminent danger of succumbing to Marxist revolution. The Conservatives meant well, but, in Canada, where they were known as 'Le Parti Liberal-Conservative du Canada,' they had 'subit complaisamment les vieilles lois libérales du passé' and were not, therefore, 'le parti de l'avenir.' As to liberalism, it was, like socialism, a doctrine of negation, opposed to the verities of nationalism, Christianity, family, and property. Socialism was merely an advanced form of liberalism. 'Le libéralisme, en favorisant un capitalisme corrompu et qui dévorat tout, a fait disparaître une forte proportion de la propriété individuelle; le socialisme veut faire disparaître toute propriété.'[98] Dangerous and suffocating in itself, liberalism was a shaky half-way house, fated to give way, in a polarizing political environment, to extreme forms of economic and political dictatorships. 'Le socialisme a le libéralisme pour père,' Arcand loved to repeat, quoting Pope Pious XI, 'et le bolchévisme pour héritier.'[99]

The sole political formula, and movement, capable of halting the slide from liberal democracy to communism was Fascism, a revolutionary doctrine, like its radical-left nemesis, but one committed to preserving the sacred spiritual and traditional values of nationality, Christianity, order, inequality, private property, and the family. Socialism and communism were doctrines of negation, sacrificing spiritual to material values; Fascism was a doctrine of affirmation and restoration of values and institutions eroded under regimes of liberal democracy.

The Fascism of Adrien Arcand was, overall, a disparate and muddled collection of social, economic, and political planks and notions drawn primarily from foreign European sources and models – in Germany, Italy, Britain – modified and adapted to fit, as best they could, national conditions and circumstances.[100] Socially, Arcand's Canadianized Fascism promised a Christian ethnocracy. Christian values and education would be pre-eminent in a country 'officiellement et positivement Chrétien.'[101] Non-Christian religions would be tolerated (Judaism presumably excluded) only if they did not conflict with the authority of the state, national security, and the common good. Charity would be the basis of social justice, as in Hitler's

New Germany, where religion, Arcand quoted Hitler approvingly, was 'la seule base de toute morale, de l'instinct de famille, du peuple et de l'État.'[102] National citizenship and the 'positive civil rights' that flowed from it would be restricted to members 'des deux grandes races qui forment, depuis son début, la population du Canada, et les autres membres Aryens du reste de la population qui [ont consent] à s'identifier avec les deux races-mères.'[103] 'L'étranger non-Britannique' would be treated 'comme un hôte de passage, soumis aux conditions réglementaires d'entrée au pays.' Restriction of entry, through vigorous application of quotas and, in the case of Jews, forced emigration, would maintain the racial homogeneity of Arcand's new Canada.[104]

Economically, Arcand envisaged a highly centralized and regulated corporative system. Major public utilities would be nationalized, and a powerful state-owned central bank created. Otherwise, private property would prevail. In place of the endemic class struggle of liberal capitalism, a new regime of class cooperation and national unity would prevail. 'Chaque classe accomplit sa fonction, dans l'organisme social; chaque class a ses devoirs et ses droits propres qui forment sa tradition. A la haine de classe socialiste, comme à la tyrannie de classe du capitalisme, le fascisme oppose une solidarité sociale basée sur une juste répartition des droits et des devoirs.'[105] Workers, protected by a charter of labour and schemes of profit sharing, would be enrolled in compulsory associations that jointly determined, with employer associations, problems of industrial and labour policy and administration. Agriculture would enjoy a preferred status and disproportionate representation in the new corporate parliament. 'Le fascisme considère l'agriculture,' Arcand wrote in his *Fascisme ou Socialisme*, 'la première, la plus importante et la plus vitale des industries nationales ... et lui accorde préséance, même dans la représentation parlementaire, où elle a droit à une plus grande représentation que toute autres industries.' State-sponsored schemes of colonization, settlement, irrigation and improvement, aid to cooperative organizations, would facilitate agricultural production, which was 'pour tout pays, la plus importante de toutes.'[106]

The political regime projected for Arcand's new Canada contained some novel, imported elements. Although a national citizenship would be established, Canada would remain within, and a strong supporter of, the British Empire, a commitment that distanced Arcand from his nationalist and separatist compatriots. According to Arcand, the empire was 'une union librement consentie par les pays autonomes et égaux entre eux ... le cri anti-impérialiste comme tous le cris révolutionnaires de gauche, est un cri judéo-libéral ... parce que la Juiverie cherche à disloquer toute force qui peut retarder l'avènement de son empire universel.'[107]

Voting in the fascist state would be compulsory, and party competition, based upon election in geographical constituencies, eliminated – 'the whole nation to become its own undivided party, crowned by its own state.'[108] At the base of the new corporative state would be three 'grandes confédérations' representing employers, employees, and 'les travailleurs intellectuels' (professors, artists, etc.), from which representatives would be elected to a 'Parlement industriel d'experts pratiques.' The seat of power of the state, or 'permanent government' administration, was a 'Grand Conseil National' composed of senior officials of the Corporations Economiques 'et d'autres personnes.' Opposition in Arcand's divinely ordained system of power, in which all would be 'in and with the state, none ... without or against,' would be eliminated by 'la suppression énergique' of all associations deemed subversive as well as the banning of 'des livres, journaux, publications de toutes sortes, représentations théâtrales et cinéma ... oeuvres d'art malsain etc. ... qui exercent une influence pernicieuse contre la morale, le caractère national et les traditions acceptées.'[109]

The chosen vehicle of Canadian deliverance, from the shabby partisan quarrels of liberal democracy, was the National Social Christian Party (NSCP), an exotic creature that rose, like a swastika totem, from the spent ashes of the Goglus, in early winter 1934. The NSCP's statement of rules, formal organization, and symbolic accoutrements illustrated, once again, Arcand's penchant for fantasy, toy charts, and ornate construction. Power was vested at the top in the person of Le Chef du Parti, designated by the party constitution as 'l'Autorité Suprême.'[110] Below the chief was a Grand Conseil with powers to 'former, contrôler et de diriger' party activities.[111] Other groupings proliferated. There was a Conseil Corporatif, composed of technical experts drawn from varied professions and industries whose duty it was to advise the Grand Conseil; assorted committees – including a finance committee, a propaganda committee, and political committee chosen by and responsible to the *chef*; groupements divided and subdivided into *provinciaux, comtés, municipaux, zones, quartiers*, and *sections*. All of these were part of the Organisation Régulière.There was, in addition, a paramilitary grouping 'Les Troupes de Choc,' with their own separate hierarchy, comprising, at the bottom, groups of *légionnaires* and, at the top, le Chef National des Légions, responsible to the Chef du Parti.

Membership in the Organization Régulière of the NSCP was of two sorts: *active* and *associée*. Applicants were carefully screened, and membership was restricted in La Section Française du Parti to 'tous les Canadiens-français et les aryens résidents en Canada qui veulent s'identifier comme Canadiens-français.'[112] Provision was made for a *section anglaise du parti*, for members of Canada's other founding race. Active members were expected to contribute twenty-five cents in monthly fees; to 'connaître parfaitment' the principles of the party program; to join and spread the word in other associations, including unions; to distribute the party newspaper, *Le Fasciste Canadien*, among friends, neighbours, and associates; and to enrol new members wherever possible. In addition to diffusing, propagandizing, and recruiting, members were expected to attend rallies, sometimes announced as 'conférences anti-communistes,'[113] and monthly meetings that opened with a 'Notre Père' prayer, the making of the sign of the cross, and a pledge of allegiance and loyalty to God, Canada, the King, the British North America Act, and, not least, the NSCP, its leadership, and constitution. Meetings closed with a Fascist salute and a quartet of cheers: 'Vivre Le Roi! Vive Le Canada! Vive Le Parti! Vive Arcand!' The order of cheers, it appeared, was discretionary. 'Il n'est pas toujours nécessaire,' the party's organization and rule manual allowed, 'de suivre l'ordre indiqué ci-haut.'[114]

Among the scanty rewards offered to party members was the opportunity to purchase and wear solely at party functions a uniform consisting of a marine blue shirt, without a tie, and trousers of the same, or approximate, blue hue. The sleeves of Arcand's shirted adherents were decorated, three and a half inches below the shoulder, with felt discs or badges. Armbands, below the badges, were reserved for officials, and varied according to rank and position: section secretaries wore red; zone secretaries, blue; municipal secretaries, white. Members of the propaganda committee sported a circled P below their badge, while Grand Conseil officials carried a silver stripe. The bony, flailing arms of the party leader were decorated with three silver bands.[115]

The coat of arms, and flag, of the NSCP, like the shirts of its adherents, were fetching and not devoid of Canadian content. The background was blue azure; the motto below the crest, in black letters on a white band, read SERVIAM. Wrapped around the centre circle, of white background, was a splendid wreath of green maple leaves. On top of it all, a furry, brown beaver, successor to the fled goglu, its pugnacious nose facing left and rump – trailed by a flat tail – right. Firmly planted in the centre of the white disc, on the coat of arms, as well as on the badges of the shirt sleeves of its warriors, was the key 'd'un internationalisme, qui doit répondre à l'internationalisme juif'; a large red swastika – the Aryan answer to the Star of David and symbol of the white race engaged 'dans son effort mondial pour se dégager de la domination économique et politique des Juifs.'[116]

Though the war was global, the battlefield, Arcand appreciated, was here and now, in Canada. The furry beaver; the maple leaves; the sworn allegiances to King, Empire, and the British North America Act; the use of the red, white, and blue – 'the British and French colours,' as Arcand informed a correspondent in Germany[117] – on party insignia all were statements of independence from foreign Fascist domination, protestations of autonomy that Arcand repeated in the months following the party's creation. The solidarity with Hitler was 'moral,' he later protested to a *Nation* correspondent, not financial or organizational. The party's turf was Canada, and its route to power would be by electoral, constitutional means – as in Germany. In the meanwhile, it would serve as a propaganda agency, a cadre of militants spreading the Fascist word, whose leader, and several of his lieutenants, were prepared, before the march or ride – in Pullman cars – on Ottawa, to support and work, as individuals – as convenience and conscience dictated – with candidates and parties of the right political persuasion.

The first dip into the electoral cauldron by the NSCP – or its principals – was the Montreal mayoralty election of April 1934. The NSCP's favoured candidate was Salluste Lavery, King's Council, bigot, member of the Native Sons of Canada, and fellow traveller of the Arcand movement, who, in the words of the *Canadian Jewish Chronicle*, 'was picked up out of obscurity by the steel-helmeted, swashbucklers ... goose-stepping over the province of Quebec under the grand title of Christian-Social Party.'[118] Lavery, it appears, made a decent try of it, in an election described by the *Canadian Annual Review* as 'colourful' in which 'the feelings of the masses were aroused.'[119] He inveighed against the trusts; denied allegations – by Olivar Asselin's *L'Ordre* – that German government money financed his campaign; castigated corrupt politicians; slammed the Montreal Light, Heat and Power Company and its affiliate, La Companie des Tramways; supported the municipalization of power; and, as *Le Patriote* joyfully noted, exposed 'Le danger Juif, l'esprit de domination israélite sur le peuple Canadien et tous les peuples chrétiens du monde.'[120] Lavery's major opponent proved formidable. Pierre Desrosiers, former organizer of the Fédération des Clubs Ouvriers, collected a scant few thousand votes. Supported by the provincial Liberal machine, and overwhelmingly by the Jewish voters concentrated in the *quartiers* of Laurier and St Louis, who, according to Robert Rumilly, 'votent dans la proportion de 110 pour cent!'[121] Dr Anatole Plante, the MLA for Mercier, fought a brave battle and managed to collect 37,018 votes. But he, like Lavery, was no match for the jowly, snub-nosed, wide-girthed populist – Mussolini's endomorphic double – Camillien Houde, who posed as a non-partisan moderate; denounced anti-Semitism, racism, and the trusts; played to the 'maçons, des ouvriers d'usine, des chauffeurs de taxi';[122] made large inroads into the French-Canadian and non-English, non-Jewish ethnic vote; and, when the going roughened, sent his boys in to battle the NSCP's shock troops at the Lavery meetings.[123] The campaign produced more than 150 arrests on election day, for disturbance of the peace, impersonation, etc., and an overwhelming 89,603 votes for the victorious Houde.[124] Salluste Lavery contented himself with 12,740 votes and a dollop of praise from *Le Patriote*, which concluded, in an editorial signed by Arcand and titled 'Grande Victoire Du PNSC,'[125] that an 'immense moral victory' had been won by a party 'le plus jeune de tous les partis Canadiens ... le plus vigoureux, le plus vivant, le plus prometteur.'[126]

However gratifying was the NSCP's virgin municipal venture, there seemed little interest, in succeeding months, in the prospects of contesting as a party the approaching federal election. The problem was not merely a lack of funds, modest membership, or a determination to restrict the NSCP's functions to the narrower task of education and propaganda. More likely, the reticence derived from sensible bread-and-butter considerations, and from the schisms, and schizophrenia, that bothered its founder. A compulsive worshipper of heroes, who considered Hitler and Mussolini 'deux chefs d'État qui [sont] populaires au point d'inspirer du fantisme et une foi héroïque qui va jusqu'à la mort,'[127] Arcand was not yet ready to deny R.B. Bennett a favoured place in his firmament of Fascist demigods, or to abandon the patronage opportunities offered by the federal Conservative government and party. If socialists were liberals in a hurry, then Fascists, Arcand was ready to allow, were merely hasty conservatives. 'Le fascisme est au conservatisme,' Arcand editorialized in a closing issue of *Le Goglu*, 'ce que le socialisme est au libéralisme.'[128] Though the Conservatives had not, like himself, taken the great leap, they were at least pointed in the right direction; they were solid national Christians whose leader, and Canada's prime minister, Arcand appreciated, remained the same 'grand patriote, grand chrétien ... grand coeur ... grand cerveau' he had supported in the federal campaign of 1930. Bennett, Arcand believed, or professed to believe – until the Conservative defeat in the federal election of 1935 – was a Fascist at heart, a confirmed anti-communist ready to support the Fascist principles of law and order, to jail red leaders, to halt unemployed treks, to arrange deportations, and to propose a radical new deal fostering state regulation consistent with private property, as a counter to unregulated capitalism, on the one hand, and the doctrine of class struggle and class dictatorship, on the other. 'Quand les forces rouges, et particulièrement les Juifs, appellent M. Bennett "un Mussolini," 'Arcand wrote, 'ils ne sont pas loin de la vérité, car notre premier ministre entend défendre notre régime avec la dernière énergie nationale et chrétienne, il entend progresser aussi rapide-

ment dans la voie de la droite que le groupe opposé entend progresser dans la voie de la gauche; ses déclarations publiques sur ce que
doit être notre régime social sont en parfaite harmonie avec celles
de Mussolini et d'Hitler.'[129]

There were, of course, other groups on the right that momentarily
interested Arcand as possible allies. Among the shirted hordes in
Britain, there were the men in green, supporters of the new doctrine
Social Credit whose Canadian counterpart managed to win election
in Alberta on a radical monetary program, elevate William Aberhart
to the premier's office, and field a contingent of candidates, mainly from Alberta, in the federal election of 1935. Though critical, like
Arcand, of the national and international banking establishment,
Social Credit was quickly rejected as a likely partner in revolt. The
trouble, it seems, rested with both Major Douglas, the 'Juif-Holland-
ais' who dreamed up the scheme, and the 'naif prédicant' Aberhart,
who imported it into Canada. The 'unearned increment' of Social
Credit, *Le Fasciste Canadien* discovered, was nothing but 'la plus-
value' of Karl Marx,[130] while the proposed distribution of twenty-
five dollars per month of social dividends by the state was merely
a device to corrupt and enslave the masses.[131]

More tempting, to several of Arcand's colleagues, were the opportunities offered by H.H. Stevens, who briefly enjoyed the status of
minor hero in Arcand's Fascist galaxy. Like Bennett, Stevens, who
served until 1934 as R.B. Bennett's minister of trade and commerce,
had, in Arcand's view, a Fascist temperament, which included, among
its several components, a dislike of big business – mainly retail – and
of rigged prices. When the government-appointed commission on
price spreads, headed by Stevens, attacked the great chain stores,
Arcand grew excited and described the Vancouver member of Parliament as a great patriot in search of an appropriate anti-capitalist,
anti-socialist vehicle and constituency, a search hampered only by
Stevens's unfortunate continuing irrational commitment to liberal
democracy. When Stevens broke with Bennett and launched his own
Reconstruction Party, Arcand was faced with the dilemma of choos-
ing between the prime minister and his maverick former minister of
trade and commerce. As it turned out, *Le Patriote*, published by
Ménard – with whom Arcand had a falling out – pushed the Recon-

struction Party, under whose banner Salluste Lavery was nominated and campaigned, unsuccessfully, against S.W. Jacobs in Montreal–Cartier in the general election. *Le Fasciste Canadien*, however, stoutly backed the Bennett Conservatives as the only solid, anti-communist, national and Christian party, ready to pave the way, or give way, in the near future, to the root-and-branch sort of Fascism represented by the NSCP.[132]

Arcand's support for the Conservatives was not merely a matter of ideology, conviction, or loyalty; it smacked of opportunity as well. The Conservatives, in 1935, were a desperate party, nationally and in Quebec, where, according to one account, only seven of sixty-four newspapers – and small ones at that – supported the government.[133] A monster defeat was imminent, and desperate plans were made to revive their fortunes. In Quebec, Senator J.H. Rainville was again in charge and, as in 1930, he called on the poison-pen services of Adrien Arcand who, 'although not a partisan,' as Senate speaker P.E. Blondin wrote to Bennett, remained none the less 'essentially and intensely Conservative' and ready to attack the Liberals, whom he held in 'horror' and 'more dangerous than the C.C.F. on account of its hypocritical disguise, with the same ends as the C.C.F.'[134] Financially pressed, Arcand took up the senator's offer to direct Quebec publicity for the national Conservative party and, throughout the campaign, churned out a stream of leaflets and pamphlets under the Conservative party label, focusing on the liberal, communist, and socialist threats to nation, church, and property, exemplified by their common commitment to remove section 98 from the Criminal Code of Canada. It was all to no avail. The Conservatives were virtually shut out, in Canada and Quebec, where a meagre five MPs were returned and, for Adrien Arcand, another god had failed.[135] When questioned several years later by a *Nation* correspondent about his reputedly 'friendly' relationship with Bennett, as well as the former prime minister's 'personal views on fascism,' Arcand replied: 'Yes, I knew Mr. Bennett. But we will have to give Mr. Bennett and the Conservative Party as clean a licking as anybody else.'[136]

Similar sentiments were not entertained by Arcand, or his lieutenants, for the augmented and transformed provincial conservative party – the Union Nationale – which swept to power in the provincial election of 17 August 1936. If one hero, R.B. Bennett, had fallen, another took his place – as defender of nationalism, religion, law, order, and anti-communism – in the person of Maurice Duplessis, Camillien Houde's successor as Conservative party leader, who joined with Paul Gouin's L'Action Libérale Nationale in an alliance that ended decades of liberal government. Arcand admired Duplessis's considerable political talents, his fervent nationalism, his patronage capabilities, religiosity, and abhorrence of communism; and he said so, both in his *Le Fasciste Canadien* – which pronounced, in a July 1936 edition, the Union Nationale 'libre de toute affiliation juive' and 'un mouvement de transition' towards 'L'UNITE' based on 'le racisme'[137] – and in *L'Illustration Nouvelle*, a daily newspaper whose ownership and control had shifted in the mid 1930s from Camillien Houde to Lucien Dansereau and Eugene Berthiaume of *La Presse*.[138] Short, apparently, of editorial talent of the right sort, Berthiaume – whom Duplessis appointed to a trade post in Paris – hired Adrien Arcand as editor, a post he retained during the next few years. In Arcand, Berthiaume had a trustworthy employee who faithfully supported, in numerous editorial and reportorial sallies, the fervent nationalism and anti-communism of the Duplessis regime. The Jew-baiting and overt Nazi nonsense were, apparently at the insistence of Berthiaume, left off the pages by the schizophrenic Dr Jekyll/Mr Arcand, who moonlighted and doubled as editor of *Le Fasciste Canadien* – later *Le Combat National* – and mini-führer of the NSCP;[139] a pan-Canadian party – Arcand insisted – in no way dual to the provincial Union Nationale. There was speculation, however, among Arcand's enemies, that his editorial roles – and press runs – were sometimes confused, resulting, for example, in the production and printing of the scurrilous *Key to the Mystery* pamphlet, as well as *Le Fasciste Canadien*, at the *L'Illustration Nouvelle* printing plant.[140]

Though Arcand performed conscientiously as Eugene Berthiaume's editorial henchman, he hardly neglected the duties closest to his heart as leader and chief publicist of Canada's premier Fascist party, an organization that gained a considerable notoriety – if not following – within and without the province. The years following the NSCP's creation were filled with brave boasts of expansion by its noisy leadership, promises of marches on Ottawa, a vigorous drive to recruit adherents, the cultivation of 'moral' and fraternal ties with affinal Fascist groups elsewhere, and the continued diffusion of Fascist and hate propaganda. Arcand's import-export business continued undisturbed by scruples, regimes, or courts. Local creations like '1837 and the Jew' or 'Our French Comrades Menaced by Jewish Communists,' were set alongside translations of speeches of Goering, Hitler, and Goebbels, world Fascist updates, and internal organizational reports and announcements on the pages of *Le Fasciste Canadien*, which devoted, according to one content analysis, 62.4 per cent of its space to material that was clearly anti-Semitic.[141] Away from his editorial offices, Arcand could be found at party organizational sessions, at public meetings in or outside of Montreal, or even, on one occasion at least, on platforms outside the country, shared by other Fascist notables. In late October 1937, Adrien Arcand travelled to New York City and there joined H.H. Beamish, the home-grown native Fascists Robert Edward Edmondson and William Dudley Pelley, a leading Italian-American Fascist, the German-American Bundist Fritz Kuhn, and Rudolph Markman on stage at the Hippodrome, where the audience was reminded that the Jew was 'a microbe on the body politic,' removable by 'nothing but segregation.'[142] After addressing 'a private banquet at the Harvard Club' and a meeting, also private, in 'a prominent club house,' Arcand returned inflated to Montreal where, in the December 1937 issue of *Le Fasciste Canadien*, he announced the official birth and imminent rise to power of Fascism in North America. In a statement picked up and widely broadcast in the daily press across the country, he declared a party membership of eighty thousand people, boasted of a likely electoral breakthrough, and predicted a surge in support in 1938, the year of the National Social Christian Party.[143]

6

Le Führer

Arcand's boasts and fantasies notwithstanding, the NSCP remained, during the heady days of its expansion and notoriety, a tiny sectarian organization of zealots inspired and manipulated by a shrewd, ego-maniacal, and fanatical leader with a flair for publicity and sensational journalism and a weakness for toy organizations and cheap theatrics. Without Arcand, the NSCP was nothing; with him, it was a desultory collection of marionettes, disaffected youth, unemployed labourers, frustrated clerks, and prejudiced artisans, supplemented, here and there, by occasional wayward professionals or small businessmen.

The supreme leader was not without certain talents, energy, and commitment. A tall and spare man, with closely cropped hair, Mosley moustache, dark eyes (which blazed and popped during oratorical excitement), and a 'military walk' – a legacy, perhaps, of his reserve lieutenancy in the Chateaugay Régiment – Arcand was a glib and fluent speaker, capable of inspiring the converted, and convertible. At the peak of his flights, the supreme leader – who was fluent in English and claimed a reading knowledge of Hebrew and Yiddish – did not seem, as J.B. McGeachy noted in an interview, 'too well-balanced,' an impression not likely shared by the faithful who trooped to meetings and applauded his addresses – sometimes lasting three hours – denouncing liberalism, democracy, *rouges*, *bleus*, and Jews, in a popular prose laced with colloquialisms and, on occasion, with grammatical confusions, calculated perhaps to create the proper rustic impression. 'In mass-meetings I speak like the man in the streets speaks and thinks,' Arcand – who carried on his person a nickel-plated revolver, for protection only – boasted to a *Life* reporter, 'and nor so "educated" like other politicians who do not know a thing of the language of simple people.'[1]

As the NSCP's Supreme Leader and Canada's designated future dictator, Arcand maintained a frenetic pace and iron-tight hold over his pet organization. Funded by Mr Berthiaume, *L'Illustration Nouvelle* remained, for several years, an important source of personal financial support, freeing its editor to moonlight in the Fascist underground. Under Arcand's editorship, *L'Illustration Nouvelle*'s reportorial style was sensational, its editorial policies, pro–Union Nationale. The Duplessis regime's policies were praised and supported; liberalism, communism, and socialism – provincially, nationally, and internationally – vilified; the church praised; religion affirmed; patriotic movements like Achat Chez Nous – whose motto adorned the front page of the newspaper – supported. When a Catholic institution in Hyacinthe was destroyed by fire and forty-six of its occupants burned to death, *L'Illustration* announced an unknown communist had been arrested for setting the fire; the story was quickly dismissed as without foundation by Colonel A.P. Piuze of the provincial police. However useful, gratifying, and remunerative his work with *L'Illustration Nouvelle*, the true outlets for Arcand's visions and urges were the editorial pages of his own *Le Fasciste Canadien* and the podium of the drab meeting halls of his party where, week in and week out, he organized and harangued the converted. Between harangues, and his bifurcated editorial duties, he spent time with his wife, Yvonne, and three sons – Yves-Adrien, Jean-Louis, and Pierre – at their pleasant and modest suburban home, outside Montreal. Mrs Arcand, a former stunt double in Hollywood, according to the *Toronto Daily Star*'s David Griffin, who married Adrien following a beauty contest in which she was awarded by the judge, her future husband, first prize, remained a devoted wife and zealous party worker.[2] She worried about her husband's lack of sleep, cooked and creamed the mushrooms he favoured (and grew in his garage), nodded approvingly 'he is so right' to visiting reporters, dutifully parroted his pet words and phrases and assiduously worked in the party's women's section. Her specialty was boycotts of Jewish stores on the party's banned list, whose customers were quietly approached by the ardent lady and her associates. 'It's pretty simple,' she explained to a visitor. 'You just buttonhole the customers and tell them what the Jews are doing to Canada, so they leave.' Mrs Arcand's sons – or the eldest two, at least – seemed, at the ages of ten and twelve, to be following in their parents' Fascist footsteps. Both were obedient to paternal authority and, like good young Fascists, saluted smartly. The sole family rebel was the baby, Pierre, scarcely three years old, a cheeky individualist in need of 'proper discipline,' Mrs Arcand noted, 'if he's going to make a good Fascist.' When Pierre refused to smile for a visiting *Toronto Daily Star* photographer, Adrien predicted, jocularly, 'that boy will be in concentration camps.'[3]

Though Arcand remained, for the duration of the party's life, supreme leader, there were others, at or near the top – core leaders or prominent fellow travellers – who contributed manfully to the great cause. Salluste Lavery, who retained an office at 1575 St Denis Street, kept his membership, though not his sympathies, secret and provided auxiliary legal aid to the party, and occasional embarrassments to the Union Nationale, whose candidate Dr Zenon Lasage repudiated, during the 1939 provincial election, anti-Semitic statements made by Lavery. As early as 1935, Jean Tissot carried the Fascist cause afield to Ottawa, and back again. A detective of Belgian origin employed by the Ottawa police department,[4] Tissot convinced himself, following immersion in the commercial underworld of Canada's capital, that Jewish merchants, using dishonest methods, were plotting to drive Christians out of business. With copies of *Le Patriote* in hand, he set to work, on and off duty, to organize Christian merchants into a league in order to drive the Jews out of Ottawa. Unfortunately for Tissot, several of the merchants approached were bothered, as one told the court, by 'Christian ethics' and passed the incendiary literature on to A.J. Freiman, a prominent Jewish national leader, president of the Zionist Organization of Canada and head of a large Ottawa retail firm, who was personally named in an offending article. Freiman pressed criminal charges, for defamatory libel, against Tissot, who was suspended from police duties during the course of the trial. Tissot was defended by J. Vincent, KC (assisted by

Salluste Lavery), who informed the court that Freiman was president of a secret society of Jews attempting 'to gain control of all human activities in this as in all other countries.'[5] Though Tissot was found guilty, his activities as a Fascist publicist, or as a police official, did not end with the Ottawa trial. In the 1935 federal election, he ran unsuccessfully as an 'anti-communist' candidate in the Ottawa East constituency, then moved to Rouyn, Quebec, where he became chief of police. Soon after Tissot located in Rouyn, a local anti-Semitic sheet, the *New Citizen*, began publication there. The editor was announced as a Mr Stakanovitch, possibly a blind for Tissot.[6] Tissot subsequently served as manager of the small-arms and munitions department of the provincial police, as foreman at an Alcan construction site in Shipshaw, Quebec, and as chief of police in Port Alfred, Quebec.[7]

Though Salluste Lavery and Jean Tissot, whether as party members or as fellow travellers, nobly served the Fascist publicity cause, the hard business of leadership in organizational matters fell to others – to men such as Dr Gabriel Lambert and Major J.M. Scott, Hughes Clement and J.E. Lessard, Marius Gatien and René Chabot. A masseur and naturopath, Gatien conducted the party's public-speaking course before assuming the post of 'National Director of French Propaganda.'[8] Chabot, a graduate of Gatien's course, was a former socialist employed as a steel worker in the railway-car shops; his eyes, when he spoke publicly, according to a *Life* reporter, 'had a fantastic expression like lay priests have ... in the streets.'[9] Clement was Arcand's brother-in-law, an insurance agent by profession, who served as the party secretary. The directorship of the party's intelligence service, which included, by one account, the placement of sixty to eighty housemaids in the homes of prominent politicians, fell to Lessard, a former RCMP member and employee of the provincial attorney general's department.[10]

Perhaps the most prominent of Arcand's lieutenants were a pair of portly, middle-aged gentlemen, one of whom, Dr Lambert, headed the party's Committee on Contacts; the other, Major Scott, serving as National Director of the Legions. Suave, corpulent, and bedecked with a black-ribboned pince-nez and a tie displaying a small swastika, Dr Lambert was a medical doctor, of sorts. He variously described himself as a wonder-doctor, a 'pediatrist,' or, according to

Le Fasciste Canadien, a 'Médicin Naturiste.'[11] But he was most likely a retinalist since he strongly believed in, and loudly theorized about, the retina as the window of the body – the key, as it were, to the mysteries of diseases susceptible to diagnosis by proper ophthalmological examination. Dr Lambert's ocular approach was, apparently, coolly received by the medical fraternity and by patients, and he seemed, as one journalist noted, to have a lot of free time on hand. Free time sometimes leads to study, or political activity, and Dr Lambert filled many hours between 1936 and 1938 examining 'the international Jewish question,' accompanying Adrien Arcand from meeting to meeting and contemplating – from the vantage of his office on Hutchison Street, corner of Mount Royal and St James streets, whose banks and financial houses, he believed, were run by the Bank of Canada, dominated in turn by the Bank of England, and, not surprisingly, by 'the Jew' Rothschild.[12] Though slow and obese, Lambert was an avid party worker, who, as head of the Committee of Contacts, was charged with recruiting, distributing such creations as *The Key to the Mystery* (of which, a million copies, it was rumoured, were in circulation), or forming, and dissolving, like images in the eye, dummy or phantom organizations with names like the Anti-Communist Catholic League, the Women's Anti-Communist Society, or even the Fascist Union of Anti-Communist Youth.[13] Sometimes, the doctor tired of phantoms and dummies and entered the streets, to agitate or incite. When students gathered on 22 October 1937, at city hall, near the University of Montreal, to protest a public meeting scheduled for the Mount Royal Arena to be jointly addressed by Alfred Costes, a French trade-union leader and communist deputy, and Canadian communist leader Tim Buck – a meeting quickly banned by the major on the advice of his police director – the doctor joined in the fun, mounted a makeshift podium, urged the students to march on the arena, and promised delivery of a force of two thousand Fascists to assist in the demonstration. This was too much for R.L. Calder and others in the Civil Liberties Union, who objected to the doctor's venture and took him to court, on charges he had counselled, incited, and procured 'students and other persons' to constitute 'an unlawful assembly to commit riot ... and tumultuously disturb the peace.'[14]

The widely publicized preliminary hearing and trial afforded Dr Lambert and Adrien Arcand further opportunities for theatre and propaganda. Phalanxes of blue-shirted Fascists descended on the courts, accompanied by Arcand, dressed in a plain suit – since, as the *Chronicle* observed, unlike Hitler, Quebec's mini-führer had 'his finger in certain political pies ... allegedly not sympathetic to Fascism,'[15] – and by Dr Lambert, who clicked his heels, *sieg-heiled*, and showed off his 'outlandish getup,' adorned with swastikas, which the judge thought colourful, but not dazzling. 'I'm accused of being a Fascist,' the doctor said, standing his ground. 'I am a Fascist, so I appear before the court as a Fascist.' The presiding judge, it seems, was not terribly impressed, with either the shabby theatre, or the alleged incitements, and dismissed the charges, a decision hailed by Arcand as a great victory. Arcand was less joyous, however, several months later, when Lambert and J.E. Lessard joined together in a mini-revolt and vigorously protested 'against the supreme authority being invested in any one man, contrary to the constitution of the party.'[16]

Unlike Lambert, Major Joseph Maurice Scott – a fiftyish, square-jawed, scowling Mussolini type – avoided the perilous streets and city-hall steps; kept steadfastly to the drill and meeting halls, where his minions paraded or protested; and remained, to the end, a loyal disciple and bodyguard of Adrien Arcand, whom, he confessed to a *Toronto Daily Star* correspondent, he loved and was ready to die for.[17] A burly 275-pound six-footer of mixed Scots-French background, Scott was a happy choice for the position of director of the party's legions. He was an athlete in his youth, a gymnast who toured Europe with several squads, and a participant in the 1908 and 1912 World Olympics. During the war, the major served as a recruiting officer and physical-training instructor with the 85th Battalion of the Canadian expeditionary force, then joined, and headed, the Quebec Liquor Commission's police force. When Arcand discovered and enrolled Scott – 'a simple-minded, orderly gentleman' who liked to wear a uniform – the major was earning a living selling coal, coke, oil, wood, and auto insurance, enjoying the patronage of the numerous cadets he had trained over the years.[18] Unlike Lambert, or several others of his prominent colleagues, Scott seemed untroubled by phantoms, dummies, or exotic theorems. A strict disciplinarian who hid his potbelly behind an extravagant sash and liked to play soldier and put his troops through the motions, Scott was mesmerized by Arcand, whom he thought incorruptible and beyond purchase, even by the Jews, in the United States and Montreal. (It was the Bronfmans who had offered, the major alleged, to buy the Führer out.) 'No money, no liquor, no women,' the major whispered, of his chief, to a RCMP officer, in attendance and taking notes, at a party meeting at the Lithuanian Hall, on St Catherine Street in March 1938.[19]

The troops Major Scott drilled and the minions Arcand harangued numbered in total, in mid-1938, fewer than two thousand. After four years of organization, the NSCP's true numbers, which varied over time, were hard to come by. Early defectors, in 1936, disclosed a figure of 750; later renegades cited 1,800 members. The least-reliable source, on membership, was Arcand who had a weakness for multiplication – of membership, organizations, and publications. When he founded his Goglu organization, whose membership was never revealed, there were three, not one, newspapers to trumpet the cause. Phantom organizations, such as the Women's Anti-Communist League or the Canadian Anti-Jewish Front, as well as obscure publications, whether from London, Hamburg, or Bulawayo, appeared and disappeared. The party's legions, as RCMP commissioner S.T. Wood observed to Ernest Lapointe, were 'not numbered consecutively from number one but were given meaningless higher numbers, presumably with the idea that, by so doing, an enhanced psychological affect would be created.'[20] Arcand loved to tickle journalists with loaded memberships. 'He has a military walk,' *Winnipeg Free Press* reporter J.B. McGeachy observed, 'but his gestures when talking are too jerky for the army. His English flows glibly. He is obviously a spellbinder. As he warms to a theme, his eyes pop. He is eager and informative. He told me there were 300,000 fascists in Quebec, 85,000 in Montreal. He has given other figures to other questioners ... In the figures he gave for membership he admitted that he included "sympathizers" who, for lack of funds, could not contribute the party dues of 25 cents a month.'[21]

Whatever their numbers, party enrollees were immersed in a subculture, or underworld, that energized and gave a warped meaning to their lives. After receiving membership cards – which often bore false names to mollify fears of disclosure and possible job discrimination – and paying the first instalment of dues, members were expected to learn the literature; spread the word; and recruit among family, friends, neighbours, and fellow employees.[22] Gummed swastika stickers were pasted on windows and walls of synagogues and Jewish stores. Party literature was handed out or left on streetcars, buses, and trains. 'Papers distributed this way,' a new recruit was informed by a 'monitor,' 'acted like seeds thrown into fertile soil.' A women's section was created, headed by Mrs Arcand, and smart blue outfits designed and distributed. Children of members were taught the rudiments of saluting and posing, in little blue shirts. For the ambitious, schools for speakers and writers were organized at party headquarters on St Lawrence Boulevard, and halls in St Henri, Maisonneuve, and Rosemount, and on Jean-Talon Street in the north end. Top graduates moved up the hierarchy, and the very best were given the opportunity, at mass meetings, to warm up the crowd with anti-Semitic homilies, before the mini-führer, surrounded by guards and legionnaires, arrived for the denouement. The membership fee was twenty-five cents a month; the party's prime financial source, Arcand insisted, supplemented by local voluntary contributions from sympathetic individuals and small businesses, some of which advertised on bulletin boards and party headquarters or in *Le Fasciste Canadien*. Somewhere, in a small, two-room apartment, in a poor suburb near the Vickers Ammunition Factory, a sullen impoverished tailor lived, subsisting mainly on a weekly relief of five dollars and ninety cents and an additional ten-dollar monthly rental supplement paid by the city of Montreal. Mr Goulet was the unofficial tailor of the National Social Christian Party, who sewed party shirts on a pair of sewing machines, located in a dank, lifeless room on the second floor of a building at 1896 Orleans Street, which housed, as well, a bowling alley and a bookmaker, hidden behind the door bearing the name 'Club Tricolore.' Reputedly an ex-communist who had served a brief prison sentence for one thing or another, Mr Goulet toiled and tailored for the party for four years and so revered his leader that he bestowed on him a special honour. When a *Life* photographer arrived one day at party headquarters in March 1938, to take pictures, he was driven by car, by a pair of party workers, to the little tailor's humble home. 'Here in the dark airless two-room apartment,' he later wrote, 'I took pictures of his youngest child, famous for his three names Adrien, Adolph [*sic*], Benito. The cushions and blankets of the child's bed were decorated with swastikas, on the wall a picture of the actress Dolores Del Rio and on a little table two pictures of Adolph [*sic*] Hitler, and a book "The Jewish Question" published by Henry Ford's paper, "The Dearborn Independent" ... and another book "La Politique Sociale de la Nouvelle Allemagne" (The Social Politics of New Germany) printed in French, published in Germany.'[23]

For devotees like Goulet, or Leo Jodoin, an eighteen-year-old unemployed clerk bestowed with the title 'Adjudant de la 51ème Légion de Réserve,' the party provided activity, meaning, position, and diversion in a wanting society teaming with unemployment, futility, and resentment. To the hopeless and hateful, Arcand's Fascist dream world and organization offered position, rank, stripes, insignias, friendships, and connections with a world movement magnified by a half-demented, but persuasive leader into an inexorable force. The nerve centre of the organization was the party headquarters, a collection of shabby rooms on the second floor of a worn wooden commercial building, 517 St Lawrence Boulevard, located directly across the street from the *La Presse* building. The headquarters was decorated with lavish displays of Fascist emblems and insignias: a huge red swastika centring a strip of bunting stretching from floor to ceiling; charts illustrating elaborate Jewish plans of world domination; cartoons of Jews stealing purses and other items; proclamations of the Canadian Anti-Jewish Front. A desultory library was filled with press publications such as *The Fascist* (Mosley's Sheet), *Swastika de Foc* (a Rumanian Fascist paper from Bucharest), and books titled *Le Bolchevisme, Le Plus Grand Ennemi du Monde,* or *Appel d'Adolf Hitler contre L'Ennemi Mondial.* There were several large ominous vaults around and a large desk for the leader, above which rested a portrait of King George VI, surrounded on all sides by flags bearing swastikas.

Though headquarters served as the party's nerve centre, many of its activities, in zones, wards, sections, counties, and municipalities, were dispersed and sequestered in various premises – homes, halls, vacant stores, buildings, or sections of buildings, like the ground floor of the former provincial transport office, where the St Denis County group met.[24] Rental costs, and transportation to meetings and rallies, in private automobiles mainly, were born by small business benefactors or the rank and file, one of whom – according to Arcand – a domestic, 'pledged twenty-five per cent of her twenty dollars a month salary for a year, toward rental cost at headquarters.'[25] The party printing press was located in the basement of an old store on St Lawrence Boulevard, identified in black lettering above the windows and doors, painted over in white, as the 'Club d'Aviation Canadien.' Outside of Montreal, zone, ward, section, and county groups met in homes and halls in several Laurentian towns, in St Hyacinthe, Valleyfield, and Sorel, where, for a brief while, the mayor and a pair of councillors saluted and declared their allegiance to the NSCP. When Arcand staged a rally in Sorel, mayors from three nearby towns joined him on the platform. The Sorel mayor received, from Arcand, a mirror engraved with a Fascist emblem, which he promised to display in his office.[26]

For the party élite, public meetings were opportunities to trumpet the message, attract the media, display the leaders, interest the curious, and rally the troops and legions. Meetings were held in rented premises, sometimes parish or ethnic halls, like the Parish Hall of St Alphonse d'Youville, the Danté Hall on Danté Street, the St Thomas d'Aquin on St Antoine Street, or the Salle du Café Lithuanie. Outside of Montreal, in Sorel, St Hyacinthe, or Valleyfield, the rallies – there were three in March 1938 – were sometimes advertised as 'Assemblées Publiques Fascistes' and well attended. A large Fascist rally, attended by 3,500 people, in Quebec City, was preceded by a minor invasion from Montreal, in private cars and rented trucks, of party workers who distributed 20,000 leaflets outside churches and parish halls.[27] The agenda and procedures of public meetings were tightly controlled, and attendants were treated to a lively show. Party flags and emblems highlighted the platform on which the chairman and speakers sat. Zone secretaries, or other party officials, served as chairmen and led the audience in the reading of the Lord's Prayer, in French and English, the Fascist salute, and, right arms still raised, a pledge of loyalty to a full catalogue of deities and institutions from 'Our Gracious Sovereign' and the British North America Act to the party, its programs, regulations, principles, and leaders.[28] The meetings closed with the usual collective Fascist salute and quartet of hails: 'Vive Le Roi!, Vive Le Canada!, Vive La Parti!, Vive Arcand!'

Between the opening and closing salutes and hails, audiences at public meetings and rallies of the NSCP heard a range of desultory expositions on questions of the day. There were speeches, often three or four, from established leaders or novices, including graduates of the party's public-speaking course, on corporatism, Jews and unemployment, Jews and unions, Jews and morals, and on the '*Key to the Mystery* and the Jew,' the latter accompanied by a mass reading and recitation from Arcand's patchwork bible on anti-Semitism.[29]

The culmination of it all was the leader's address, often lasting several hours, on familiar themes, inevitably greeted with thunderous applause. Before English audiences, *Maclean's* correspondent Frederick Edwards observed, Arcand was 'clever enough to tone down his more fantastically flamboyant passages.'[30] Among his own, he was less inhibited. 'In a hall crowded with listeners of his own race, he goes all out,' Edwards concluded, 'shrieking violent damnations of his opponents, with his arms flailing the air, then lowering his voice to a throaty sob as he speaks of his love for his native land, and for his own people especially. To the French, this is the zestful red meat of oratory. They love it.'[31]

No matter how violent the rhetoric, peace usually prevailed, or was secured, at Fascist meetings by the blue boys – the party legionnaires in blue shirts who attended in droves and served as guards and ushers, maintaining order, protecting the leader, and giving short shrift to the occasional heckler. The blue boys surrounded the leader when he arrived, and invigilated carefully throughout the proceedings. 'At the conclusion,' an RCMP report noted, 'all the Legionaires in the Hall, except the officers, were ordered to fall in. The orders, attention, by the right number, form fours, right turn, left turn dismissed, were given. On the order of 'Dismiss', the double lines make a right turn, make the Fascist salute and hold it to about the count of four; then everyone walks over to his respective group, to be taken to his district by private cars put at the disposal of the Legionaires and Orators.'[32]

As guardians of the party, and the embryo police corps of the coming Fascist state, the NSCP's legionnaires were the special charge of Major Scott, the national director of Legions who led his men and women in brisk training sessions involving ju-jitsu, military drills, and marching. New recruits attended two-and-a-half-hour sessions, three days a week, for six weeks, before examination, graduation, and assignment. Special sessions were held for women, who were trained in the rudiments of first aid. Uniforms were worn during the drills, held indoors in any of four rented halls, including the St Thomas d'Aquin Hall, which served as a major training centre.

The NSCP's paramilitary wing afforded its adherents an opportunity to serve the party as protectors, to tone and toughen their bodies for the coming struggle, to combat laxity, to develop habits of discipline, and play policeman or soldier in a picturesque organization infused with a surfeit of ranks, insignias, emblems, and structures.[33] Initiates collected in a variety of squads, sections, patrols, companies, and legions, and served under a major or a brigadier-general, colonel, lieutenant-colonel, captain, lieutenant, and assorted others bedecked in a variety of insignias, stripes, colours, and epaulets.[34] Though bravely outfitted, the legionnaires drilled, marched, and invigilated without weapons. Their function and purpose, as Arcand and his lieutenants repeated more than once, were to protect the party; build character, strength, and discipline; and, as a party renegade was informed, serve in an organization designated to be 'the state police when the party came to power,' by peaceful means, without weapons or violence. Though Arcand spoke loosely and bravely, here and there, about marches on Ottawa, the repeated emphasis was on the constitutional route, in Pullman cars, filled with joyous, elected, Fascists, following the decay of a system destined to fall, like a rotten apple.[35] When rumours began circulating that the Fascists were smuggling weapons from the United States, Arcand vehemently asserted that there were already enough weapons around, which the Fascists did not need and would not use. 'Even a black-jack should not be handled,' he informed a convention of legionnaires at the St Thomas d'Aquin Hall; 'what good would a black-jack do you, if the enemy uses machine guns?'[36]

While Arcand's Fascists trained without arms, behind closed doors and covered windows, their antics – and the wild pronouncements of their pyrotechnic leader – did not go unnoticed in their native province, in English Canada, or, indeed, in the United States and Britain, where Quebec's embryo Fascism attracted, during the winter and spring of 1937–8, considerable and lurid media attention. The source of the interest – and concern – was as much international as local. Mussolini's Ethiopian adventure, Franco's bloody war in Spain, the tightened Nazi vice in Germany, reverberated abroad, inviting applause and mustering among sympathetic overseas movements like the NSCP, whose leader, a publicist by profession, hailed the coming Fascist tide. Arcand was, in some respects, prudent and circumspect. He nicely separated his editorial functions; kept Jew-baiting and overt Nazi propaganda off the pages of *L'Illustration Nouvelle*; avoided the German consulate; protested a mere 'moral affinity' with Germany; and kept his shock troops away from street fighting, weaponry, and public military or paramilitary manoeuvring in contravention of the law. But he was afflicted, none the less, by a devouring exhibitionism, a penchant for low theatre and hyperbole that invited considerable attention – both gratifying and dangerous – from both national and international media. Though spare and mean, Adrien Arcand was a glutton for publicity and notoriety, renown that spread, during spring 1938, far and wide in response to the media attention his movement received.

Quebec, English Canada – even the United States and Britain – discovered, by early 1938, it appeared, that a native Fascist movement, of uncertain size but perhaps ominous significance, had sprouted, without official stricture or interference, on the benign shores of the St Lawrence. The Goglus had been a local patriotic enterprise lost in the shuffle of nationalist organizations. The NSCP – a larger grouping with a photogenic paramilitary wing, a pan-Canadian ideology, and a swastika symbolism suggesting dangerous affinities, if not organic links, with international Fascism – was perceived as consequential, and newsworthy, by an aroused press. The press run was given early momentum by the *Montreal Gazette*, which published on its front page – and elsewhere – on 31 January 1938, a series of photographs, believed to be the first taken, of Arcand's 'organization in action,' featuring saluting uniformed legionnaires, Commander Scott posing against a swastika backdrop, and a war council of leading officers; a run of pictures, with accompanying text, deemed by the *Canadian-Jewish Chronicle* 'sensational' and 'enshrouded with a reportorial display of awesomeness and respect which intimated that the reporter was overcome by his subject.'[37] The Toronto *Globe and Mail* obliged with a series of feature articles on Canada's embryonic Fascism, followed by the *Toronto Daily Star*, whose David Griffin interviewed Arcand at his suburban residence. Arcand posed with his family, in Fascist garb, for a series of photographs, subsequently featured in the *Daily Star*, and warned Griffin: 'The moment we think constitutional government has failed, that is the moment we will move.' Western Canadians were alerted by *Winnipeg Free Press* journalist J.B. McGeachy who, following his coverage of the sittings of the Rowell-Sirois Commission across Canada, visited Quebec for three weeks and wrote a series of articles, published in leading western Canadian dailies, on 'Canada's Problem Province.'[38] Among the province's problems, McGeachy concluded, was Arcand, whom McGeachy considered the 'most picturesque' of 'several Fascist spokesmen and candidates for the fuehrer's role ... exactly the sort of warped and wide-eyed individual who might – if the chance arose – stage a putsch in the Hitler manner'[39] In an article in the *Canadian Weekly* titled 'Will Quebec Turn to the Right?' spread with a large photo of Major Scott, his legionnaires, and Arcand, eyes glinting into the Fascist future, Leslie Roberts concluded that Quebec Fascism was not 'something to dismiss with a shrug of the shoulders.' Roberts had himself 'watched these human automatons in the act of assembling and demonstrating' and concluded Arcand's 'shirt-admiring organization' was 'of sizeable proportions, a majority of its adherents being drawn from the ranks of adolescents and young men of the student and office – or mill-worker classes, so far as the cities are concerned.'[40] *Maclean's* correspondent Frederick Edwards, in the first of a two-part series, was equally emphatic. 'There is a Fascist movement in Canada,' Edwards concluded. 'It exists. It is here. It is a Fact.'[41]

The same discomforting 'Fact' was discovered and broadcast in a flurry of articles in diverse English and American newspapers and journals. The *London Daily Herald* considered it 'indeed an evil day in the history of the British Empire when it has to be recorded that there exists in the Canadian Province of Quebec a Fascist party with some 80,000 members – many of them uniformed and armed,'[42] while a *New Statesman and Nation* correspondent elaborated upon the reasons for the 'steady growth' of a Fascist party in Quebec whose leader 'by a strange coincidence ... resembled Sir Oswald Mosley, while his right-hand man, Major Scott, has been photographed on more than one occasion in an attitude strongly reminiscent of Mussolini.'[43] The *New York Post* upped the Fascist count to 100,000 goosesteppers in Quebec, and speculated about military aerodrome seizures and staging grounds for aerial bombardment of New York or Washington.[44] The *New York Times* weekly magazine supplement asked pointedly, in its 9 January 1938 edition, whether Quebec was turning Fascist.[45] The *Boston Globe* wrote of parades of Fascists marching and saluting, in mid-winter apparently, down Montreal streets in blue shirts, decorated with red and white insignias, a colour combination that French Canadians found particularly attractive.[46] *The Nation*, in February 1938, featured a lengthy interview with Arcand, 'scarcely known to the public a few months ago,' whose name 'is today suddenly blazoned in the headlines.'[47] The mass-circulation pictorial magazine *Life* provided, in its 18 July 1938 edition, for the doubters, substantial multipaged visual evidence of Quebec's virile Fascism, featuring Arcand in full oratorical flight, shirted crowds saluting, classes 'in Fascist rabble rousing,' the tiny tailor Goulet sewing his shirts, Goulet's swaddled Fascist baby, and a printing press used to run off party literature.[48] 'The goal of M. Arcand's Fascist legion is an organization of 25,000 divided into eight divisions,' the *Life* correspondent observed. 'At present it totals 3,600, of whom half have no uniforms. Their known armament is 500 Smith & Wesson revolvers recently smuggled from the U.S. ... From a cloud no bigger than a man's upraised hand, militant Fascism in Canada had grown within a year to a problem menacing enough to engage the most serious minds in the Dominion.'[49]

Quebec's Fascist bogey was not merely the plaything of foreign media; within the province there was a growing concern about the easy and open strutting and mustering of the local blueshirts. The Jewish community remained, as ever, vigilant. Its press outlets heaped scorn and derision, speculating, occasionally, as did the *Chronicle,* whether Quebec's 'political ostriches' would 'keep their heads in the political sands, or ... admit that the province of Quebec is a cesspool of foreign activities, inspired by alien influences and subsidized by foreign propaganda agitators.'[50] The handful of Jewish elected officials continued their lobbying and exhortations and delivered occasional speeches on Fascist menaces – internal and external – while the Canadian Jewish Congress collected data, distributed briefs, lobbied the federal government, and expanded its program of public education and exposure.

Sharing the Jewish concern were an assortment of groups and public persons on the centre and left. Favoured targets of the Fascists, the communists, who had problems of their own, with the Duplessis government, were convinced the right extreme was not getting due attention. So, they filled their press and meetings with warnings about Fascist preparations for a civil war and pressed for a popular front against the forces of Fascism. Fred Rose, a prominent party official and unsuccessful candidate in the St Louis riding won by Peter Bercovitch in the 1936 provincial election, wrote a widely distributed pamphlet in 1938, alleging a 'wide-spread fascist network' in Canada, involving not merely the Arcand movement, but other groups, included Paul Bouchard's Autonomist group, L'Ordre de Jacques Cartier; the German Bund; native Italian Fascists; German and Italian consular officials; and factions of big business.[51] Prominent liberal Protestant clerics like the Right Reverend John Farthing, bishop of Montreal, were troubled by the Fascist paramilitary manoeuvrings. At the annual meeting of the Anglican synod of Montreal, in April 1938, Farthing denounced the anti-Semitism of the NSCP as 'neither Christian nor British' and asserted it threatened 'the very root of our liberties ... The party that will persecute and treat unjustly one section of the community today, will, when it has the power and its interests seem to demand it, extend its oppressive measures to other sections.'[52] R.L. Calder, head of the Civil Liberties Association, warned of growing threats to basic freedoms and alleged that Fascism in Quebec was being 'encouraged by bench, pulpit and council chamber,'[53] a view shared by CCF officials convinced, like M.J. Coldwell, that Fascism was 'the last defence of a decadent capitalism.' 'Two years ago,' Coldwell informed a meeting of the People's Forum in Victoria Hall, Westmount, 'I said "it can't happen here."' When I read the *Gazette* and saw those pictures of fascists in uniforms drilling under army officers, I knew that those who said it might happen here were right ... nowhere is the threat of civil liberties more apparent than in your own province of Quebec.'[54] Contributing to the consternation were prominent officials and press supporters of the provincial Liberal party. Newspapers like *L'Autorité* wrote of Fascist posturings, plots, putsches, arms smuggling, ammunition caches.[55] J.C. Harvey, editor of *Le Jour*, described the Fascists as 'gangsters, degenerate, corrupt and stupidly sectarian ... all are dangerous because they cultivate dishonest means to attain their ends: lies, hypocrisy, calumny, blackmail, intimidation.'[56] The Honourable Cléophas Bastien, a former Liberal cabinet minister, charged, in the legislature on 2 March 1938, that 'youths are being enrolled by the hundreds weekly.'[57] According to Liberal provincial leader and future premier Adélard Godbout, 'Le Fascisme est plus dangereux que le communisme chez nous, car il a de nombreux adeptes et des moyens d'actions perfectionnés. Il va falloir y mettre ordre si nous voulons garder la démocratie et le gouvernment responsable.'[58] Liberal House leader and mayor of St Hyacinthe, T.D. Bouchard, alleged there were ten Fascists for every communist in Montreal and that fascists were extremely active and paraded openly in the industrial centres of Valleyfield and St Hyacinthe.[59] At Christmas in St Hyacinthe, Bouchard noted, the local Fascists 'attended holy communion in a body in the chapel of the Christian Brothers with banners flying and swastikas on their sleeves.'[60]

Among leading elements of Quebec's nationalist, religious, and political right, there was a corresponding concern with the menace of political extremism. Their focus, however, was markedly different from that of the Liberals who acknowledged communism's evil, but warned, as well, about the Fascist threat. Among nationalists like Abbé Groulx, prelates like Cardinal Villeneuve and Mgr Gauthier, or, for that matter, Premier Maurice Duplessis and his cohorts, the overwhelming danger, clearly and presently, was from the left. The Great Satan was communism – which threatened Catholic Quebec with the subversive trinity of property expropriation, class conflict, and atheism – and vigorous measures to control and stifle the far left, whether in the form of popular demonstration, government legislation, or police harassment, were considered entirely appropriate, in order to protect a people who represented, as Armand Lavergne asserted, 'la seule sauvegarde, l'inébranlable rempart contre la ruée du socialisme bolchévique.'[61]

Though dismissed as irrelevant – or a liberal invention – by realists like Premier Duplessis, Fascism, like other forms of authoritarian politics, had its admirers in the province of Quebec where anti-democratic sentiments were common among élites, and masses, suffused with political cynicism. Schemes of corporatism – considered by *L'Action Nationale* as 'our hope and salvation' – were rampant within the church and among nationalist and religious organizations like the Saint Jean Baptiste Society and Ecole Sociale Populaire; obsessions whose main achievements, according to Denis Monière, 'were to re-enforce authoritarian politics, sabotage the work of unions and the emergence of class awareness and give some respite to a capitalist system in the midst of crisis.'[62] Paul Gouin noted among his compatriots a weakness for legendary personages like Mussolini whose regime was considered, by Cardinal Villeneuve, not sufficiently harmful to society to warrant church condemnation.[63] Abbé Groulx pined, during the mid-1930s, for a Man of Providence, mentioning, among others, Dolfuss, Salazar, and Mussolini, as supreme movers, distributors of impetus and will-power, great leaders 'that every people needs.'[64] *Le Devoir* compared Fascism to an organized police force and communism to an organized band of criminals. 'A police force may be an annoyance,' the editorialist observed, 'may even use vexatious methods where citizens are concerned, but in principle it is a force at the service of order.'[65] Canon Emile Chartier, rector of the University of Montreal, declared: 'Même si le fascisme a ses erreurs, il contient un élément de discipline, de progrès, économique, éducationnel et social.'[66] Abbé Pierre Gravel, a popular preacher and lecturer, advertised 'une révolution de droite,' while Père Philippe, OMI, praised Italy as a fine example of the reconciliation of the church and Fascism. Père Archange, OFM, and other like-minded priests were troubled, as was Arcand himself, by an excess of red plots and conspiracies of 'la Juiverie internationale.'[67] Cardinal Villeneuve himself was sometimes critical of the 'wild, lying atheistic democracy which reigns ... in almost all the states of the world,' undermined by 'masonic organizations, secret or avowed,' communists, revolutionaries, 'and the politicians in their pay,' pursuing ends leading not to 'the sovereignty of the people, but to the absolute power of backstairs financiers and their lackeys.' Following publication, in the *Montreal Gazette,* of photographs of drilling Fascist youths, Archbishop Gauthier disavowed support for the National Social Christian Party, whose program, reflecting German Nazism 'with its errors and its tendencies,' contained 'very mixed doctrines at which Catholics should look closely before subscribing.' But he wondered, in the same breath, 'if some hundreds of young people are doing physical exercise or quasi-military training, would it not be that in their view there are not being taken against the peril which threatens us the measures which should be taken ... it is ... important for us to know whether the reasoning of our young people does not contain a part of truth, and whether our weaknesses, our evasions, our undecided attitudes do not in short act to the profit of the Communists ... If it did not exist, our behavior would bring Fascism into existence.'[68] Camillien Houde was convinced that French Canadians were, at heart, through a process of Latinization, Fascists. 'We French-Canadians are Normans, not Latins,' Houde announced in early 1939, 'but we have become Latinized over a long period of years. The French-Canadians are Fascists by blood, but not by name. The Latins have always been in favour of dictators ... the French-Canadians have always been under dictators ... always followed one man.'[69]

Within the provincial political regime, headed by Maurice Duplessis, there were, likewise, persons and tendencies that aroused the suspicions and ire of liberals and the left troubled by Fascist bogies. In addition to being a political party, the Union Nationale was an Ark, which included, in its hold and on its deck, some political animals with peculiar obsessions. Dr Roy, the member for Montmorency, was prone, on occasion, to cite the *Protocols of the Elders of Zion* as a source of wisdom.[70] J.-E. Grégoire, lecturer in economics and sometime mayor of Quebec City, who eventually bolted from the Union Nationale and formed, with several colleagues, the rival Parti National, warmly recommended to the electorate, during the course of the

1936 provincial election campaign, Joseph Ménard's *Le Patriote* as sound basic reading – an effusion headlined in the *Canadian Jewish Chronicle* as 'Grégoirian Music.'[71] H.L. Auger, Duplessis's minister of colonization, who, as a former Montreal alderman, aggressively pushed resolutions supporting a total ban on Jewish immigration, outdid Grégoire in the promotion of Ménard. After his *Le Patriote* closed down in September 1936, Auger hired Ménard, who later published, with a government subsidy, a rag titled *Le Colon.*[72] During the 1936 campaign, there were references here and there, in Union Nationale campaign literature, to American and Jewish exploitation of Quebec's natural resources, the activities of an American named Graustein, mistakenly described as Jewish – a former president of the International Paper Company – figuring prominently. When Peter Bercovitch subsequently challenged, during a budget debate in the House, Union Nationale members to name one Jew prominent in Quebec resource exploitation, there was silence for the full minute allowed by the member of the St Louis division.[73]

Though Fascist sympathies and anti-Semitic notions were not uncommon within sectors of Quebec's nationalist political establishment, the premier himself seemed notably free of impractical ideological diversions. Duplessis was, first and foremost, a political realist and practical politician intent on building lasting coalitions, albeit on the right. Schemes and isms, Groulx's distant men of history striding across the historical stage, corporative systems, and racial mystiques interested the premier less than the intricate mechanics of the power game – the forging of alliances and balancing of interests necessary to preserve stable government, foster economic growth under a regime of free enterprise, and preserve national integrity and provincial autonomy in the face of powerful forces of cultural assimilation and political centralization. Of a practical bent, Duplessis did not waste time pursuing diversions or chasing chimeras. Neither racism, nor Fascism, accordingly, interested the premier except when their perceived presence impinged on the course of the real, or symbolic, power game. 'Never will I consent to win elections by raising the race cry or by arousing racial or religious fanaticism,' Duplessis informed a Union Nationale meeting before the 1936 campaign. 'The best way of preventing fanaticism and of preventing race quarrels, is to give justice to minorities.'[74] Following election, the premier was equally emphatic. 'Those who raise racial issues are the worst enemies of this Canada of ours, and of the Province of Quebec,' he informed the annual dinner of the Dominion Commercial Traveller's Association in December 1936. 'We have numerous remedies to apply – why waste our time and our energies in fighting battles that constitute a shame to those who are fighting them, no matter what is their nationality or their religion ... As long as I am Premier of Quebec, believe me, I stand for peace, harmony and cooperation between races ... In Quebec we are in favour of separation between the good and the bad, between honesty and dishonesty, but not in favour of separation based on religion or race.'[75] If racism, in whatever form, was a shameful diversion from the hard tasks of politics, a blind obscuring distinctions between the truly good and bad, Fascism was a mere smokescreen, or bogey, invented and fomented by the regime's enemies who divided the nation and, advertently and inadvertently, played into the hands of the one true common enemy. Nothing annoyed Duplessis more than the alarmist, embellished publicity in the national and international – including American – press, taken up by the local liberal opposition and press, depicting Quebec as a Fascist haven. In a March 1938 speech to the legislature, in reply to the observation of Liberal Cléophas Bastien that American newspapers were 'giving the province very bad publicity regarding the growth of fascism,' Duplessis urged the Americans 'to start cleaning up their own home before trying to dirty a house as clean as the Province of Quebec.'[76] Lynching and 'scandalous kidnapping,' the premier averred, common in the United States, could never occur in Quebec where authorities competently intervened to prevent disorder. Talk of Fascism was part of 'a clever' campaign by the communists. Quebec, the premier concluded, was 'in no danger from Fascism and never will be.'[77]

The premier, oddly enough, did not view the communists – there were a handful in Quebec – in the same benign, dismissive way, and his determination, in league with the church hierarchy, nationalists, youth groups, and accommodating municipal authorities, to control and hamper communist organization and propaganda contributed, understandably, to the regime's growing authoritarian – even incipiently Fascist – reputation. There were, first of all, the youth marches and municipal harassment lauded and encouraged by the premier and the prelates; the meeting to hear a visiting Spanish Republication delegation banned, in October 1936, by Montreal's mayor, following a demonstration of rioting students who were praised by the premier – in a speech at the feast of Christ the King in Quebec City – as patriots true to the traditions and principles of their ancestors;[78] the projected Tim Buck–Alfred Costes meeting, a year later, banned once again by the Montreal authorities following representation by militant students praised, on this occasion, by the cardinal – at the feast of Christ the King – who congratulated the municipal authorities for their 'opposition to communist elements' and elevated 'the safety of the people,' secured by militant demonstrations and municipal ordinances restricting free assembly and speech, into 'the supreme law';[79] planned demonstrations by organizations like the Friends of the Soviet Union, or Federation of the Unemployed, also banned, as communist-inspired and likely to cause a riot, by authorities, earning the praise of newspaper like *L'Action Catholique*, organ of the hierarchy, which wrote, 'at every moment we hear noisy denunciations of Fascism and of different systems which use popular force to bring order and progress to society. We admit ... to being passably indifferent between democracy and Fascism, provided that our society takes hold of itself and sees the peril which menaces our civilization.'[80]

To better combat red menaces and pink perils, win the applause of the church, frighten the opposition, stir the masses, wave the flag, carry the cross – and fill the authoritarian vacuum created by the removal, following the federal election of 1935, of the infamous section 98 from the Criminal Code of Canada – Maurice Duplessis enacted in March 1937 the so-called Padlock Law, a repressive 'act respecting communist propaganda' that severely restricted the freedoms of assembly, speech, and press by enabling the attorney general to shut down premises he thought to be used to propagate 'communism or bolshevism by any means whatsoever,' as well as punish persons who unlawfully printed, published, or distributed in the province 'any newspaper, periodical, pamphlet, circular, document or writing whatsoever propagating or tending to propagate communism or bolshevism.'[81] A theatrical blunderbuss aimed – and fired – broadly leftward by a clever, demagogic premier who professed to know nothing, and care less, about Fascism, the Padlock Law proved an effective instrument of harassment and intimidation.[82] During the first year of its application, Red Squads were loosed on unsuspecting homes and halls, literature was seized and confiscated in the thousands, residences and meeting places were padlocked and halls were withdrawn from rental, for political or educational purposes, by frightened owners, fearful of prosecution under a law described by the *Winnipeg Free Press* as 'suppression of thought with a vengeance' and 'one of the most savage assaults upon freedom which Canada has ever seen.'[83]

Though the premier's bludgeon invited, in English Canada, a virtually unanimous condemnation, official opinion in Quebec was, overall, supportive, or accepting. There were, of course, the protesters: civilian libertarians, the CCF, English trade unionists, United Church officials, McGill University students, and others. But the provincial Liberals, out of sheer opportunism, did not oppose the bill in the House; the federal Liberals rejected the option of disallowance;[84] and English newspapers, like the *Star,* contented themselves with muted references to the premier's quaint Latin ways. The church hierarchy, of course, adored – perhaps inspired – the crusade that received strong support from the nationalist, patriotic press, whose editorialists praised the premier's wisdom and determination. Among the Padlock Law's most avid supporters, was the intense, thin-mustachioed editor of *L'Illustration Nouvelle,* the Union Nationale's 'semi-official organ,' who moonlighted off hours in shabby drill and meeting halls filled with toy soldiers, unemployed clerks, and wide-eyed domestics, awaiting the coming Fascist storm. While the communists dodged Red Squads and evaded padlocks, Adrien Arcand's little army continued to grow, as Eugene Forsey wrote, 'unhindered, to say the least, by the state, praised with faint damns by the Church.[85] In the words of liberal Cléophas Bastien, Quebec's premier seemed 'to give absolution to Fascism,'[86] – a forgiveness that Adrien Arcand welcomed, in the spring of 1938, when Hitler's army stormed into Austria, and Quebec's straggling blueshirts contemplated their own Lilliputian invasion, into the neighbouring province of Ontario.

7

Shirts

Speaking in the parlance of the textile industry the 'staples' have been pretty well grabbed by the various beshirted brigades. It will now devolve upon specially-trained artists to evolve new colour schemes which might appeal to the youth of those countries who are still shirtless.

Canadian Jewish Chronicle, 27 April 1934

Though Arcand's minions succeeded in smartly positioning themselves, by the mid-1930s, on the farthest-right fringe of the Canadian political spectrum, they were not alone, in or outside Quebec, in advocating radical authoritarian or racist remedies for the ailments of liberal democracy. Emboldened by the surge of foreign Fascisms, Quebec's blueshirts sought domestic alignment with groups who shared their ideals and antipathies.

Within Quebec, the NSCP's linkage prospects remained minimal, since neither of the two groups perched, with Arcand, on the Fascist periphery proved stable, viable, or amenable to cooperation. Members of the Fédération des Clubs Ouvriers were, it is true, picturesque enough to qualify as a Fascist horde. Formed in 1929 by the unemployed agitator J.A. Chalifoux – president of local labour groups in Maisonneuve and Ahuntsic – out of a disparate collection of working-men's social clubs politicized by the depression, the fédération added flair and colour to the cluttered street agitation of the early depression years.[1] Though small in number, and loose in organization, Chalifoux's cohorts remained, for the brief few years of their political existence, brash, florid, and impudent. They dressed themselves in brown shirts and peaked caps and applauded their leader – attired, sometimes, in yellow spats, with a dinner jacket over the obligatory brown shirt – who, on their behalf, heaped praise on Hitler and Mussolini; denounced the trusts, plutocracies, and parliamentary institutions; demanded immigration restrictions; and promised 'to fight the Jews on behalf of the merchants of Montreal.'[2] When the St Hyacinthe municipal council considered a resolution supporting subsidies to local garment manufacturers – who happened to be Jewish – in order to help expand their plants and create jobs, Chalifoux's boys covered the windows of local shops with placards urging the local citizenry to oppose a measure calculated to 'Judaïser notre ville française.' St Hyacinthe, it turned out, proved as unreceptive to the brownshirts as Montreal, home of the bulk of their membership, where the fédération sponsored marches on the Hotel De Ville and other places, demonstrations at the Carré Viger, Easter Sunday parades to St Joseph's oratory, and public meetings at the Monument National. On several occasions, Chalifoux led deputations to the premier, a patrician gentleman who scolded the impudent Fascist for his unpolitical manners and empty threats and warned him to take care.[3] When Taschereau considered postponing Montreal's 1934 municipal election, which chagrined the brownshirts, Chalifoux announced that 'one hundred thousand fascists in Montreal will hold their own elections, will elect a mayor and as many aldermen as are necessary and will take over the city.'[4] The closest the brownshirts came to effecting a municipal putsch, however, was in St Jérome where, in the October 1933 elections, A. Legault, their candidate for mayor, was defeated by Dr Alfred Cherrier by fewer than three hundred votes in a stormy campaign culminating in the arrest of Chalifoux, on charges of causing a disturbance and resisting arrest, following an argument at a local restaurant.[5]

Though the brownshirts' penchant for street politics earned them some scattered press coverage and occasional official rebukes, they failed to win the support or friendship of Adrien Arcand, who viewed Chalifoux's minions as well-meaning, honest workers manipulated by a demagogic opportunistic leader. Instead of fast Fascist friends, the fédération and the NSCP quickly became bitter enemies. During the months of the fédération's rise to prominence, Arcand's mouth-pieces spared no effort or space denouncing the clubs as tools of plutocrats and discredited politicians, serving no other purpose than to divert support from his own movement, which had a 'definite program and knows where it is going.'[6] As it turned out, the fédération proved no threat at all. Within months of their loud declamations of a municipal Fascist revolution in Montreal and elsewhere, they were riven by faction and crippled by desertions – to the breadlines, Houde's populist-municipal camp, and, in some instances, the Communist party. In April 1934, a *Canadian Forum* correspondent described the 'once-threatening' Fédération des Club Ouvriers as 'petering-out, blind, and unled.'[7]

Quebec's other Fascist grouping, led by a former Rhodes Scholar, had little in common with Chalifoux's clubs except a susceptibility to quixotic illusions, a Mussolini fixation, and an intense dislike of Adrien Arcand. Chalifoux's boys lingered in shabby clubrooms or wandered the streets, in brown shirts, paid for, a correspondent facetiously observed, with NSF cheques;[8] *La Nation*'s publicists wore white collars and collected in editorial offices or on university campuses.The brownshirts were mainly unemployed workers, momentarily diverted by the theatre of Fascist street politics. *La Nation*'s Fascist proponents were intellectuals, journalists, writers, or professionals, enamoured of Latin Fascism, verbal violence, and separatist nationalism. The inspiration and leadership was provided by Paul Bouchard, a quiet-spoken, intellectual native of Quebec City who picked up a Laval BA in 1928 and a BCL from Wadham College, Oxford, where he attended from 1931 to 1934, before returning home to launch a frenetic career, from the mid-1930s to early 1940s, as a nationalist polemicist and politician.[9]

Bouchard's European tour – which included an inspiring visit to Fascist Italy – induced, or reinforced, certain predilections that were amply reflected in his *La Nation*, a Quebec City weekly staffed by Laval University people, published from February 1936 to August 1939, which included among its many contributors Jean-Louis Gagnon, a polemicist whose *Cahiers Noir* and *Vivre* served as an intellectual antechamber to Bouchard's weekly;[10] Marcel Hamel, who assumed the editorial duties in 1937; and Dostaler O'Leary, a leader of Jeune-Canada and author of a wild book on separatism. From its first issue, *La Nation* became a strident forum for views favouring separatism and Fascism. The British Empire was pronounced an oppressive, decadent system; the Canadian federal system and constitution, a vise holding fast the Québécois in a condition of slavery; parliamentary democracy, a corrupt disintegrating system masking the rules of Anglos and Jews. While anti-Semitism was hardly centre stage, it was amply present, in print, or spoken word. A 21 March 1936 *La Nation* article, for example, bemoaned the arrival in Montreal of one thousand 'youpins voleurs et anarchistes.'[11] Dr Chaim Weizmann was referred to by editor Marcel Hamel as 'un pouacre sagouin descendant de Moise et de Josué.'[12] On the eve of Canada's entry into the war, Paul Bouchard declared to a large crowd gathered in Montreal's Maisonneuve Market: 'I am resolutely, energetically, and squarely opposed to Canadian participation in the European war because I don't want thousands of young Canadians going across the seas to die to save international Jewish finance.'[13]

Being resolute and energetic was, in fact, one of the favourite prescriptions of *La Nation*, which, in its early years, criticized the proneness to excess wordiness and empty rhetoric of the Groulx nationalists. Writers like J.-L. Gagnon stressed, instead, dynamism – a virile, muscular approach to political and social action inspired by the model and mystique of Fascism of the Latin sort. While Hitler collected occasional kudos from writers like Albert Pelletier, who thought the Nazi a humble shepherd of his German flock,[14] and other Fascists, like Franco and Vikdun Quisling, earned appropriate credit, Mussolini, by far, outshone them all. 'Benito Mussolini,' Paul Bouchard wrote, 'is the greatest man of modern time and it takes a strong dose of imbecility not to see it.'[15] J.-L. Gagnon delighted in repeating Mussolini's slogan 'La guerre est à l'homme ce que la maternité est à la femme, un parachèvement de l'être,'[16] and believed *La Nation* would satisfy the basic need to unite 'en faisceaux' the hates of 'tous les hommes qui ont encore assez d'amour pour la guerre sainte et notre avenir national.'[17] Mussolini's muscular activism, his fusion of Fascist theory and political practice, his regime of state corporatism and totalitarian control, his inspired leadership and noble conquest of Ethiopia were evidence of a Latin-Imperial resurgence in the face of a declining British Empire and Western liberal democracy and the growing menace of the world communist domination. The choice, facing Quebec and the world, as *La Nation*'s inaugural issue explained it, was simple: Rome or Moscow.

In the Rome of Mussolini, Paul Bouchard discovered a Fascist utopia and appropriate mystique – a product of resurgent Latin genius – readily transplantable to Catholic Latin countries abroad in Spain, Central and South America, and to Quebec, Canada. Long in thrall to Anglo-Saxon and Jewish domination, French Canadians, by embracing the Mussolini model, could restore their self-worth and win, at last, a free French state in America, organized along Fascist lines. 'We desire a nation renovated in a state of freedom,' Bouchard wrote in *La Nation*. 'We wish the French-Canadian a new man ... conscious of the value of his French and Latin civilization ... the antithesis of what 175 years of foreign subjugation, of democratic degeneration and of parliamentary corruption have made him ... Italian corporatism will give us a sure and perfect system for the economic and social reconstruction of the nation.'[18]

Bouchard's mélange of separatism and Mussolinism may have attracted assorted stray nationalist intellectuals; it hardly served, however, as a firm basis for cooperation with Quebec's other Fascism. Bouchard's coterie and the NSCP cadres, in fact, became bitter enemies soon after *La Nation* hit the newsstands and university common rooms. Arcand may have got off the blocks first but, to the *La Nation* people, he was an adventurer, quack, and usurper; a professional anti-Semitic racketeer feeding off Nazi propaganda funds; an impressionable dupe seduced by Hitler's theatrics; a pan-Canadian enemy of Quebec nationalism; an apologist of British Imperialism and ally of western Canadian and British Imperial Fascists; an agent of something called the Intelligence Service serving the 'puissance judéo-anglaise,'[19] whose advocacy of a 'caricatural, détestable,' and 'anti-latine' Hitlerian Nazism was calculated to discredit the true Latin Fascist sort; an opportunist ready to play games with decadent corrupt politicians in the Conservative and Union Nationale parties.[20]

While Bouchard was loud in condemning Arcand's posturing, his own subsequent political career proved strangely wayward, ineffectual, and not devoid of opportunism. Fascist theory, verbal violence, and separatist ideas were one thing; political practice another. The politics of Paul Bouchard proved, in subsequent years, more educational and electoral than muscular, and Fascism took a definite back seat to nationalism.[21] Expressing, at the outset, a preference for 'movements' and disdain for 'parties,' Bouchard formed, in time for the 1936 provincial election campaign, a political formation, or *faisceau*, called Le Comité Central Autonomiste, with representatives of various youth groups – among them Jeune-Canada, which contested the election on a program of 'autonomism' and corporatism.[22] The rout of both of its candidates – Bouchard in Montreal–Ste-Marie and Hector Grenen in Montreal–Mercier – hardly discouraged Bouchard from other political ventures. His Comité Central Autonomiste became, in March 1937, the Parti Autonomiste, whose organization, in the words of its leader, was 'fortement hiérarchisée,' and composed of 'la masse des simples adhérents ... dans les Faisceaux. Ce sont les membres des Faisceaux qui formeront les cadres du Parti.'[23] An unsuccessful federal by-election campaign, by Bouchard, against Liberal J.N. Francouer in 1937, was followed by the establishment of something new again – called Le Parti Nationaliste Fédéral – a flirtation with Social Credit and a brace of further unsuccessful Bouchard candidacies: in the 1940 general election, against Ernest Lapointe, and, following Lapointe's death, in a by-election fight against Louis St Laurent. Bouchard enjoyed substantial support from a variety of nationalist groups and gained a respectable 12,700 votes to St Laurent's 16,700.[24] The St Laurent fight proved Bouchard's last. With the war raging and conscription nearing, Paul Bouchard left for Central and South America, where he remained for three years, until August 1945, when he returned to Quebec, shook the Fascist and Social Credit dust from his polished boots, and commenced a lengthy academic career, as a Latin America specialist.

While Paul Bouchard floated, and sank, his early autonomist

projects, Adrien Arcand looked afield, outside of Quebec, in search of broadening possibilities. Ontario, it appeared, offered some modest prospects. Throughout the early, and mid-1930s, the Ontario media was filled with accounts of shirts here, shirts there, shirts everywhere. Mussolini's Latin Fascism received extensive coverage in the metropolitan press. Hitler's rise and consolidation invited lurid headlines and wide reportage, by newspapers like the *Toronto Daily Star*, whose correspondent Pierre Van Paassen sent back numerous articles tracking the Nazi rise to power and ugly repression. The antics of Mosley's blackshirts often littered the front pages, while occasional issues of the *Financial Post* and *Saturday Night* featured analytical and explicatory articles on the principles, prescriptions, and progress of Italian Fascism.[25]

With entire racks of shirts on display, it is not surprising that pockets of the alienated and impressionable began collecting in drill halls and trickling into the streets in Ontario cities like Ottawa, Windsor, and Toronto, local eruptions given impetus by acute depressed conditions. Though chief beneficiary of Canada's federal arrangement, Ontario shared the awful burden of economic crisis and high unemployment. Relief lines in cities like Toronto, Windsor, and Ottawa – where almost a third of the labour force was out of work – lengthened and multiplied, and demonstrations of the unemployed, sometimes organized by communists, were met with cold official shoulders, excuses, or truncheons wielded by police under orders from professional 'Red hunters' like Brigadier-General D.C. Draper, chief of Toronto's police department.

While some of the unemployed, or employed, drifted into the tiny Communist Party – or unions organized by them – voted for the CCF, stayed Liberal, or remained apathetic or politically neutral – preferring bread to parties or labels – there were a few, in Toronto mainly, drawn to the Fascist cause, an attraction reinforced by a willingness to blame certain ethnic or racial minorities for the people's woes. Anti-Semitism, as the Jews of Toronto or Ottawa – where A.J. Freiman grappled in the courts with Jean Tissot – realized was by no means a Quebec monopoly. It abounded in Ontario, especially Toronto where, before and after the First World War, Jews were subject to widespread prejudice and discrimination fed by 'hereditary traditions, – as the *Mail and Empire* noted[26] – and by the status and economic insecurities of varied classes. Toronto the Good was, for many of its small minority of Jews, a place riddled with resentment, both loud and muted. Journals like Goldwin Smith's *The Bystander* and *The Week*, which aimed at an 'enlightened' audience, described Jews in the 1880s as usurious, exploitive, morally 'enfeebled,' and enemies of the 'Gospel of Humanity.'[27] The ethnic identity of Jews before criminal courts often invited disclosure in the press, especially in papers like the *Telegram*, which frequently indulged in anti-Semitic sallies. Jews and Bolsheviks were often equated in post-war years, and Jewish immigration defined as dangerous innundation. 'An influx of Jews puts a worm next to the kernel of every fair city where they get a hold,' the *Telegram* noted, in September 1924. 'These people have no national tradition ... They engage in the wars of no country, but flit from one to another under passports changed with shameless swiftness, following up the wind, the smell of lucre.'[28] Genteel prejudices pervaded the gentile middle and upper classes. Wealthy Jewish philanthropist Sigmund Samuel described pre–First World War Toronto the Good, a place where some were treated better than others, as 'one of the most quietly bigoted cities in Europe or America.'[29] Jews were socially ostracized, barred from private golf, tennis, country clubs, summer resorts, and professional associations. Social pressures and restrictive covenants kept them out of better gentile neighbourhoods where, in their flight from the Ward, upwardly mobile Jews were confronted by 'spite' fences.[30] Insurance companies, along with large retail department stores, trust companies, and banks, discriminated against Jews, although some hurdled, or ducked under, occupational spite fences. In the professional spheres, Jewish schoolteachers had trouble winning placement in the public-school system, and nurses and interns in hospitals. Nor were the streets of Toronto the orderly, particularly in pre-war years, devoid of assaults. 'Outside of the Ward,' Stephen Speisman wrote, 'it was not uncommon for a bearded Jew to be attacked on the street at the turn of the century and even as late as 1917. Indeed, the danger of assault was so real in some areas of the city that East European Jewish schoolboys were instructed by their parents to make themselves inconspicuous.

Jewish peddlers were especially in danger of being dragged from their wagons and pelted with stones and garbage.'[31]

For a small minority of Toronto's toughs, 'hereditary tradition,' the heightened social tensions wrought by economic crisis, and the widely broadcast histrionics of Adolf Hitler, which reinforced the image of Jews as permissible targets, provided an opportunity, in the early depression years, for provocation and street action. Hitherto free of local varieties of imitative Fascism, Toronto's Jews, during the summer of 1933, were treated to the spectacle of surly youths roaming the boardwalks of east-end beaches, displaying on their clothing hated Nazi symbols. What troubled the youths was the perceived trespass or desecration, by noisy, immigrant Jews from Toronto's Ward, during the hot summer months, of their precious lake-front territory in east-end Balmy Beach and adjoining Kew Gardens – a prime public recreational area best reserved, it was thought, for the quiet enjoyment of local gentiles.[32] The invading Jews, to the beach people, were messy interlopers who crowded the boardwalk and beach fronts, strewed garbage in the parks, hogged picnic tables, munched garlic, dressed and undressed in cars or behind shrubs, and babbled in a Yiddish so loud it disturbed the peace and quiet and threatened to lower property values. The Jews, in short, were not wanted, and needed to be told so. So, something called 'Swastika Clubs' were formed, and nickel-plated badges sold with a scarlet swastika imprinted in the middle. In the early weeks of August 1933, swastikas became quite the rage among Toronto's beach people. The clubhouse of the Balmy Beach Canoe Club was adorned with one – until an invasion of Jewish youth forced its removal – together with an accompanying 'Heil Hitler' inscription, and sweaters, bathing-suits, armbands, and occasional bare chests of defiant youths displayed them along the boardwalk, parks, and beaches, for the edification of Jewish picnickers.

Toronto's Balmy Beach swastika contagion proved no more than a brief craze; the clubs, ephemeral clusters of distracted youth intent on provoking and educating the Jews about their proper place. 'There is no membership fee, no president, or secretary-treasurer,' a Swastika Club open letter posted on the bulletin board of the Balmy Beach Canoe Club read. 'All you are asked to do is bring an emblem and wear it. Recently, as you no doubt know, conditions have become unbearable, and Beach people are gradually being forced to go elsewhere to avoid the presence of undesirables. Local No. 5 of the Swastika Club had been formed in Kew Beach, and now has a membership of forty. Commencing Monday July 31st, our members will appear on the beaches, boardwalk, and in Kew Gardens and adjacent parks, wearing a nickel-plated badge with a scarlet swastika thereon. They will simply wear the emblem. There will be no parade or demonstrations. No speeches will be made. We feel the emblem will have its desired effect. This is quite legal, and no interference can take place.'[33]

True to their word, the Swastikas – led by a Queen Street confectionery owner, Bert Ganter, and the Beach boy W.H. MacKay – abstained from noisy demonstrations, violence, or strident publications. Their sole message was the silent symbolism of the swastika, prominently displayed. The effect, however, was something other than desired. A public furore followed, which quickly placed the Swastikas on the defensive. The press headlined the contagion, and papers like the *Toronto Daily Star* condemned the demonstration. Jewish communal leaders denounced the embryonic Fascism and implored municipal politicians to intervene. Police roamed the beaches to keep order The mayor denounced the Swastika Club activities as 'un-British and un-Canadian,' suggested the clubs drop their symbolism, and proclaimed the beaches open to everyone. Jewish picnickers continued their visits by the thousands, and gangs of Jewish youths invaded the beaches and traded shoves and blows with provacateurs. When toughs in Willowvale, a working-class district miles from the beaches, adjoining the Jewish Ward, picked up on the swastika idea, shouted 'Heil, Hitler,' and waved a black sweater with a large swastika on its back – and painted another one, for good measure, on a park building – during a softball game in August between Harbord Playground, a predominantly Jewish team, and St Peters, the stage was set for a bitter fracas, which took place following a second game between the two teams, played two days later before a ready crowd of several thousand. The Pit Gang toughs were there again, screamed the obligatory 'Heil, Hitler,' unfurled the large swastika banner, and were quickly attacked by hordes of enraged Jewish youths. What fol-

lowed was a full six hours of warfare in and around Willowvale Park
– sometimes known as Christie Pits – between youthful combatants,
augmented by reinforcements on both sides from surrounding areas,
and armed with weaponry, including broom handles, baseballs,
fence pickets, stones, and lead pipes. Numerous injuries were sustained before police, who scattered crowds with billy assaults, horse
charges, and sprays of motorcycle fumes, brought a semblance of
order to the inflamed district.[34]

Toronto's swastika skirmishes were no preludes to a Fascist surge.
To the Jewish community, however, they served as a spur to vigilance,
contributing to a heightened awareness of the potential for growing
domestic anti-Semitism; a consolidation of communal organizations;
and a growth in support for the creation of a national umbrella organization, the Canadian Jewish Congress, whose Central Division,
based in Toronto, subsequently played an active role in public education and anti-defamation.[35] For the few Swastika militants and
Fascist dreamers, the yield was limited to a dose of bad publicity, torn
shirts, black eyes, bruised heads, and several desultory phantom
organizations created during and following the contagion.

Outside of the beaches, and Christie Pits, there were a few petty
eruptions. At Lake Wilcox, a sister Swastika Club appeared, and disappeared. In the beaches, schisms, secessions, and reorganizations
resulted in the creation of something called the Swastika Association
of Canada, a body formed from seceding members of the Swastika
Clubs and the Beaches Protective Association, a vigilance organization formed following the beach fights. The new organization defended 'gentile rights' but denied connections with the Nazi movement; pronounced itself 'purely Canadian'; and promised to
promote 'good fellowship,' truth, 'loyalty to King and country,' and
'a strong gentile business appeal.' In Kitchener, O.E. Becker, a German who emigrated to Canada in 1929 and lived, as he put it, 'on the
taxpayers' pocket,'[36] was excited enough by events in Toronto to get
things rolling locally. President of something called the Hindenburg
Club, whose members wore a medallion decorated with a bust of
President Hindenburg, inscribed with the words 'century of
progress,' Becker, during the heat of the Swastika skirmishes, contacted beach organizer MacKay and soon announced the formation of

a Kitchener local. 'Some people do not know what Fascism or the swastika is,' Kitchener's Hindenburg Club president announced to a *Toronto Daily Star* correspondent on the eve of a scheduled public meeting in the Woolworth building. 'We have our own Swastika Beach not fifty miles from here. It was named many years ago. Many people think Fascism is meant to kill all Jews. I personally think that we have three different kinds: orthodox, reformers and, thirdly, what all Jews call coquettes. They hate each other very much ... It is my opinion that anyone created by heaven, no matter what his colour, race, or creed, has the right to live, but he hasn't the right to live on Christians without producing. It is his duty to work ... I got away from Germany because I didn't like the rotten, Red conditions. But in Canada, I found pretty much the same thing.'[37]

Becker's announcement, which included a preview of the dress – a brown shirt, black tie, and red armband with white circle and blue swastika – invited a flurry of denunciations by Kitchener Jews, a special meeting of the Kitchener Municipal Council, and an offer from beach boy W.H. MacKay to chair the inaugural meeting, which drew mostly a crowd of hecklers and ended in farce. Becker was soon deported, after his and related Swastika projects were shunned by his ethnic compatriots at home and, apparently, abroad. A Toronto German Harmonia Club spokesman condemned 'the swastika gangs and hoodlums in Toronto and Kitchener,' professed a political neutrality, and dismissed the Kitchener Swastikas as 'out for publicity in Germany.'[38] When W.H. MacKay solicited the help of a Toronto German fraternal organization, the Steel Helmets, which met at a little restaurant on Jarvis Street, he was refused. 'After the war,' club secretary Fred Friese elaborated, 'war veterans organized as they did in this country and in England, and our ex-servicemen's body became known as the Steel Helmets. There are between twenty and thirty former members in Toronto and while we have official connection with the parent organization in Germany, we keep up the spirit of good fellowship by holding a social meeting once a month or so. We get together, play cards, hear some music, and possibly have a little dance.'[39] Though a professed member of Hitler's National Socialist Party in Canada, a second Steel Helmeter, Max Siegert, emphatically supported the secretary's denial of any links between the Swastika agitation and the Steel Helmets or, for that matter, the Nazis in Germany,[40] a disclaimer reiterated by Ernst Hanfstaengl, spokesman for Chancellor Adolf Hitler himself. When the *Toronto Daily Star* cabled Hitler during the heat of the Swastika craze, asking whether there was 'any foundation for the rumours current here that the anti-Jewish movement was allied with German Fasciste?' Hanfstaengl replied: 'absurd to say that Canadian anti-Jewish outbreaks in any way connected with the Nazi movement here. The Nazi movement is purely German and is unconnected with any other country.'[41]

Equally unconnected with foreign fascisms – or so their claimants maintain – were the several other shirt groups that appeared in Ontario during the mid-1930s. The CCF's Regina Convention, apparently, was the occasion for Chalifoux's Quebec brownshirts to announce an expansion into Toronto and other Ontario centres in September 1933.[42] According to Montreal-based English-speaking organizer E.A. King, requests from Ontario for aid in organizing branches multiplied after the formation of the CCF, whose 'speakers too frequently indulged in attacks on the church' and aimed to 'unite all the radicals in the country under one banner.' No further announcements were made, however, and the brownshirts left the field to the white- and blueshirts, who also experienced difficulty in arranging sustained marches. Something called the National State Party – whose adherents preferred white – was formed in late October 1933, with a program supporting the replacement of party government with 'competent administration,' the disenfranchisement of 'non-Ayrans,' and 'closer co-operation between Nordic nations.' The party disappeared soon after the leader and organizer, according to an RCMP report, 'was found to be insane and deported to England.'[43] From Windsor came the announcement, also in October 1933 – it was the autumn of shirts – that two thousand men, mostly ex-servicemen, had enrolled in the Blue Shirts of Canada,' whose founder and chief organizer, Louis Meconi – a Windsor notary public and postmaster – first arrived in Canada in 1911, enlisted with the 57th Battalion in 1915, and rose to sergeant before being 'transferred to the Italian army.'[44] With war combat under his belt, and all those Reds running around, Meconi, Provisional Commander James

Element, and several other veterans got the urge to dress up in blue and drill, smartly. The Blue Shirts' motto was 'at the Service of Canada and Her People,' and their uniforms – supplied, according to the *Toronto Daily Star*, 'by an influential person whose name is being withheld' – included navy blue shirts and slacks, brass buttons inscribed 'Canada,' maple-leaf collar badges, and plain caps, slated to be replaced by regular 'tin pan' steel helmets. Meconi's cadres were expected to drill and 'look smart when they are parading or making public addresses.'[45] 'We will be able to convince people that we are right without using force, 'Meconi predicted.' We stand for law and order and against illegal revolutions.'[46]

Apart from a Queen's Park meeting with Attorney General W.H. Price – to inform him of their lawful intentions – and the announcement of the transfer of headquarters to Ottawa, little was heard from the Meconi Blue Shirts in succeeding months. Taking their place, on Ontario's precarious Fascist fringe, were a pair of organizations that, characteristically, had little do do with each other. The Canadian Union of Fascists (CUF) were tiny, Mosleyan, and wore black shirts. Formed in Winnipeg in 1934, the group had branches in Woodstock, where W.F. Elsey served as Ontario chairman, and in Toronto, home of 'secretary of the Ontario command' and 'unit leader for the Ontario branch,' Charles B. Crate, a sallow twenty-one-year-old 'third generation' Canadian, described by the Toronto *Globe* on 22 October 1936 as 'Canada's No. one Fascist.'[47] He represented the CUF at conferences of an umbrella youth organization known as the Canadian Youth Council. Under the alias of Charles Brandels, Crate edited the CUF's *Thunderbolt*, a sheet whose format switched in 1937 from standard newspaper to half size, but whose content rarely varied. Liberals and leftists were defined as 'the Scum Front' and democracy dismissed as a tool of 'international Jewish finance,' which controlled both capitalist and communist systems.[48] Mosley's *Action* and other Black Shirt publications were advertised regularly, together with Arcand's *Le Fascist Canadien*. A 'Fascist Library' column touted books like Hitler's *Mein Kampf*, Goebbels's *My Part in Germany's Fight*, and Mosley's *The Greater Britain*. Free literature on 'Germany's contribution to world peace and general recovery,' was advertised as available through Hamburg's Fichtebund and other Nazi propaganda outlets.[49] Contributing to the *Thunderbolt* was a mix of foreign and domestic writers, including Dr Joseph Goebbels, whose opinion of socialism was reprinted in one issue on a full page, two columns wide; Dr R. Muir Johnstone, an eccentric Saskatchewanian who switched shirts, from white to black, and admired, understandably, William Dudley Pelley's Grayshirts;[50] and S. Alfred Jones, an elderly Brantford magistrate (former president of the Ontario Magistrates' Association), who lectured to Toronto's Empire Club and other organizations, and wrote glowingly in *Saturday Night* about the virtues of Mussolini's corporate system.[51] Among the books recommended by CUF provincial chairman W.F. Elsey as basic reading was magistrate Jones's Mussolinian tome, *Is Fascism the Answer?*[52]

However noisy Crate's *Thunderbolt* was, the Canadian Union of Fascists remained, until its demise in 1938, a tiny organization in search of a Canadian Mosley. Its meetings were small, private, and poorly attended, by a mixture, on one occasion, of 'several elderly women' and a 'few youths in black shirts.'[53] The problem, a party spokesman complained, was partly financial; the upstart rival Arcand Party made a 'big splash' because it was financed by interests ready to trade money for control.[54] And it was partly a matter of leadership: the lack of a 'gallant leader,' as Andrew Glen of Locust Hill, Ontario – a confessed Fascist sympathizer – declared, prepared to lead party and country.[55] When the honourable H.H. Stevens brought out the price-spreads inquiry, that was dynamite,' Glen said following a dismal meeting attended by thirty people in a small Howard Street hall. 'It threatened the roots of the monied interests. If we had a man like that, vested with the power of the people, we could establish our security today.'[56]

Leadership, or the perceived lack of it, was not what concerned the Canadian Nationalist Party, headed by Joseph Farr, an unemployed beverage salesman resident, in March 1938, in room twenty-five, Isabella Hotel, Sherbrooke Street. Farr's Nationalist formation was a late arrival in Ontario – sometime in 1938 – following a round of ugly infighting with a John Ross Taylor, a hate specialist with a solid middle-class background who, in 1937, distributed in Toronto thousands of copies of a pamphlet outlining the old Madagascar Jewish relocation scheme. With Taylor bumped as Arcand's man in Toronto, Farr moved to the fore. If Arcand imitated Hitler, Joseph Farr aped Arcand, or Major Scott. He *sieged* and *heiled*, dressed in a blue shirt, organized a coterie of shabby unemployed youth, invited an occasional press cameraman by to shoot his drilling legionnaires, and claimed a membership, in March 1938, of twelve thousand, an inflation that moved a Montreal newspaper to admit it was 'decidedly comforting to learn that Ontario itself has become infected and that the disease has taken a particularly strong hold upon the City of Toronto.'[57] Farr's hold upon stray bands of Toronto's lost youth was strengthened at drill sessions on Wednesday evenings, in Toronto's Temple Hall, at Queen Street West and Dovercourt Road, where recruits, dressed in blue shirts with red insignias on their shoulders, formed fours, veered left and right, stepped smartly to the command of a former British sergeant-major, and saluted, Fascist style, whenever their leader appeared in front.[58] 'You are as good as anyone in those shirts,' Farr informed his drilling boys, some of whom hid their shirts beneath their coats on the way to Temple Hall, 'and I want you to wear them proudly.'[59]

Though Joseph Farr boosted his boys, he remained, withal, a weak and ineffective leader. He refused to describe himself as anything other than 'chairman' – until the hour of national unity arrived – and his public speeches were exercises in halting confusion. A RCMP observer at a Fascist meeting addressed by Farr found his speech so 'flat,' 'disjointed,' and 'inconclusive' that his audience was left 'wondering what he was driving at.'[60] But it mattered not. He was, after all, but a foot soldier, or sergeant, in a great national movement with swelling support, he believed, not only in Quebec, where the NSCP's mini-führer held sway, but in western Canada, home to a curious collection of petty fascisms.

Like Ontario and Quebec, Canada's West was hurting badly and provided an inviting arena for protest politics, mass movements, schemes of reconstruction, and sectarian effusions. Depressed world grain prices and drought inflicted great hardships, and mass unemployment, on the export-oriented, agriculturally based, prairie provinces. In British Columbia, the collapse of world demand for its resource products, mainly in lumber and mining, created immense public suffering. The political responses varied. Manitoba's cagey

Bracken government stealthily endured. Saskatchewan's resurgent Liberals trounced the Anderson conservative-dominated Cooperative government. A populist Social Credit movement in Alberta, led by the charismatic William Aberhart, ended, in 1935, fourteen years of government by the United Farmers of Alberta. In British Columbia, a reconstituted Liberal party led by T.D. Pattullo decimated Simon Fraser Tolmie's confused Conservative administration. The West was the birthplace of the radical populism of Social Credit and radical socialism of the CCF – created in Regina in 1933 – and the haven, in Winnipeg and British Columbia mainly, of lively sections of the Communist party. It served, as well, as the incubator, or test-tube, of several squirming fascist organisms.

In British Columbia, the epithet 'Fascist' was common enough in the heated mainstream political arena, but Fascist organizations remained few and inconsequential. A young clerk in the provincial labour department in Victoria, who defected from something called the Young Citizens League, presided over a British Columbia local of the Canadian Union of Fascists, which, in 1938, claimed about thirty members – all 'very young,' an RCMP report noted, who dressed in 'black shirts occasionally,' and were inclined to meet secretly.[61] Victoria was also home to the Praetorian League of Canada (Canadian Fascisti) formed in 1928, which metamorphosed, five years later, before the approaching provincial election, into the Canadian Guard, a super-patriotic group opposing 'all revolutionary, secessionist, annexationist and anti-nationalist movements.'[62] The Canadian Guardsmen supported 'honest statesmanlike government' and 'the cooperation of Capital and Labour'; cultivated contacts with 'other anti-communist organizations around the world'; vested leadership in a directorate expressing 'the leader ideal from which all authority must pass'; owned badges consisting of a fasces superimposed on a maple leaf (later changed to a simple flaming torch); and wore grey shirts, adopted, according to one writer, 'because the Guard is in touch not only with black-shirted groups, but with the Young Crusaders,' a fascist organization in Harbin, Manchuria, whose members wore white shirts. Their leader was a Fred Patterson – thought, by local RCMP observers – to be a pseudonym – and the mailing address of their public relations committee was 101 Robson Street – 'one better,' according to our *People's Advocate* observer, 'than the local Trotskyists who chose the address of a Chinese laundry.' Counting fewer than a hundred members in March 1938, British Columbia's Guardsmen were mostly youths and young men, 'employed individuals,' according to an RCMP report, 'in receipt of fairly good salaries, residing in good homes, and of good families.'[63] While the semi-secret Guardsmen seemed sincerely interested in alerting the public to the dangers of the Red Peril and favoured the local newspapers with occasional warning letters, they remained cool to any prospective linkages with eastern Fascisms, which they rejected as 'anti-semitic' and 'too extreme.'[64] According to spokesman Patterson, the Canadian Guard 'corresponded with other Fascist leagues but was independent of them.' It was 'not Fascist in the European sense,' and 'opposed anti-semitic campaigns,' a position apparently at odds with local Fascists such as Clive S. Thomas, a tall 'clean looking,' slightly built, eighteen-year-old clerk employed by the B.C. lands department. 'A well-educated, studious and theorizing' type, who maintained a province-wide correspondence, contributed an occasional article to Berlin-based Nazi publications, and, with several colleagues, distributed Fascist literature among Victoria's Italians, and in Indian villages and logging camps of the Island interior, Thomas, and his tiny entourage, looked, in the summer of 1938, to Adrian Arcand for leadership of the domestic Fascist movement.[65]

In the neighbouring provinces of Alberta and Saskatchewan, the shirt scene – apart from the internal politics of minority ethnic communities such as the Germans – remained pretty barren. John Schio, in Saskatoon, formed an obscure local of the NSCP, while, in North Battleford, Hans Fries, a thirty-year-old sparely built Bavarian who organized for something called the National Union of Fascists, warned occasional audiences – mostly German – of the twin alien menaces of 'communism and international Jewish finance.'[66] The most prominent of the prairie Fascists was Vidora, Saskatchewan's Dr R. Muir Johnstone, a frequent contributor to the *Thunderbolt* and Canadian Union of Fascists organizer, who regarded Social Credit as 'an imperfectly expressed form of Fascism.'[67] According to Dr Johnstone, Major Douglas 'went around the world ding-donging FASCISM AND FASCISTS,' while 'his only real friends ... have been Fascists, since

only through Fascist economics could Social Credit 'be operated.'[68]
Aberhart, in Johnstone's view, had not yet evolved into a true, full
Fascist because of 'certain religious quirks,' which *Thunderbolt* editor
Charles Brandel may have had in mind when he complained that
'Abie,' who believed 'to an undue degree ... in the myth of democ-
racy,' was 'too full of the milk of human kindness to catch the near-
est way.'[69]

In Manitoba, the nearest way was caught by a dismal collection of
local activists who busied themselves, in the early 1930s, with flurries
of meetings, hate literature publication and distribution, and feud-
ing. Compared to their mordant western brethren, the Winnipeg
Fascists were a lusty and hateful lot. Perhaps it was the availability of
ready old targets that drew the basketful of unemployed youths,
paunchy ex-servicemen, security police, occupational drifters, and
prejudiced ethnics to Manitoba's version of the politics of hate. The
proportion of Jews to general population was higher in Winnipeg
than in any other city in the country, and the communists in Winnipeg's North End were a lively lot, who in the 1930s, elected a few
people to municipal and provincial office. Winnipeg's Jewish community was not only culturally rich but civicly prominent and politically involved in left as well as centre and right politics; an involvement spurred to a considerable extent by the prejudices and
discrimination endured since the early arrival of Russian-Jewish
immigrants in 1882, described in a government report as 'altogether
too desirous of depending on Government and private charity, with
a corresponding disinclination to work, except as peddlers.'[70] In subsequent generations, the Winnipeg Jewish community grew in
number, prominence, and diversity, in the face of campaigns for
immigration restriction, the limitation of employment opportunities
in retail stores and labour shops, insurance-company discrimination,
press prejudice (including an inclination to identify Jews in criminal,
especially arson, cases), and professional restrictions in institutions
like the Manitoba Medical College, which established a quota for Jewish applicants.[71] The First World War, and the subsequent general
strike – which polarized Winnipeg's political community and identified Jews with Manitoba's lively Red and Pink politics of the post-
war decade – and the depression, which heightened the frustration

of the economically depressed, intensified the local anti-Semitism entertained by diverse groups: by Anglo-Saxon nativists like Colonel J.P. Rattray, commissioner of the Manitoba Provincial Police, who complained at a Lions' Club luncheon in 1922 that 95 per cent of the major bootleggers in Manitoba were Jews, a debased people in league with the Japanese and Prussians to destroy Christian civilization;[72] and by ethnic minorities from countries, as Louis Rosenberg noted, 'in which religious and racial intolerance, and especially antisemitism' had been 'rampant for centuries.'[73] While a considerable proportion of the Canadian, and Manitoba, population of Ukrainians were, according to Rosenberg, 'free from anti-Jewish prejudice,'[74] there remained significant residues of the old anti-Semitic culture, especially among anti-Bolshevik nationalists ready to link Moscow with Jewry. More than eight hundred persons, for example, attended a public meeting of the Ukrainian Catholic Brotherhood of Manitoba, in 1936, addressed by Dr M. Mihychuck, a Douglasite Social Crediter who peddled the *Protocols* and informed his audience that 90 per cent of Soviet commissars were Jews, 'the real curse of humanity.'[75] According to Robert England, hoary stereotypes and folk-tales of Jewish perfidies, including the ritual murder of Christian children, were sometimes present among transplanted Slavs in the Canadian prairie provinces. 'The writer can never forget the gruesome details and the terror with which it was told to him by a small Ruthenian child,' England recalled in his *The Central European Immigrant in Canada*, 'the capture by the Jews of a Christian child, the fattening of the child on sweetmeats, the murder by placing her in a barrel of nails and rolling the barrel, the drinking of the blood to secure that strength to dominate Christians forever, all reminiscent of the ghastly superstition which has, since the Middle Ages, swept Russia and Eastern Europe into pogroms, and which has had the most terrible effect on the ignorance and imagination of a people whose commerce is usually done by Jews because they themselves will not undertake this service.'[76]

Fantasies – ancient and modern – about Jews were the stock-in-trade of Winnipeg's noisy band of shirt people in the early 1930s. The existence of a Fascist entity – or club – was first brought to public attention by a police raid, during the early 1930s, of a modest home on Yonge Street, the residence of an Arthur F. Hart Parker, a lean Scotsman with an old country burr, faded tan, and brown eyes, set in a face, a *Winnipeg Tribune* reporter observed, that had 'none of the appearance of the fanatic.'[77] Appearances, it turned out, deceived. An ex-employee of the Dominion Excise Branch, Narcotics Division, and several private detective agencies, Parker developed, in the depths of the depression, an animus towards Jews, and a purpose – Fascist politics. 'The Fascist Party appears very real to him,' the *Tribune* reporter noted, 'and, discussing its objects, his face lights up with a look of intensity and determination. He quotes the history of the Jewish race in some detail, going back to King Solomon in the 9th century B.C. "King Solomon planned a peaceful invasion of the Gentile nations ... but he gave the idea up. Later, however, other Jewish leaders took up the idea and the design of the serpent was drawn up. The head of the serpent represents the administrative organization, and the Jewish people are the body. At present the serpent's head contains three hundred Jews. The Jewish people themselves do not know who they are, but they rule the world! They are our natural enemies. They have been behind every depression. They control governments with unseen hands. We must drive them out of the position of power." '[78]

To better accomplish his objectives, Parker collected piles of hate pamphlets and application forms that requested information about the applicants' military qualifications, rank, and weapon competence, and, during the summer of 1933, joined up with a fellow un-employed ex–security man, who quickly rose to the dubious status of Winnipeg's own mini-führer. Born in Ilford, London, 'within sound of Bow bells,' in 1875, William Whittaker, a balding gentleman with a large nose and trim moustache, served with a British Army unit in India, and with the Punjab police as inspector, before migrating in 1907 to St Catharines, where he served with the local police force for three years. Whittaker then went west and worked at a succession of jobs – in the freight office of the Canadian National Railways, as a security policeman with the CPR, as a detective in Winnipeg's Marlboro Hotel, as a clerk in several businesses, and as caretaker of a downtown building.[79] It was the CPR in Vancouver job that cleared his head. 'From the time that I was the appointed inspector of the C.P.R.

in Vancouver,' he recalled, 'I found I was a victim of Free Masonry. I was always conscious of the Jew having too much play in Winnipeg and, studying the history of Jews, I found that there is an alliance between Jews and Free Masons. The politics of Canada are controlled by the Jews, who use the Free Masons as their tools.'[80] The joint discoveries of William Whittaker and A.F. Hart Parker resulted, during the autumn of 1933, in the formation at Winnipeg's Plymouth Hall of the Nationalist Party of Canada, an organization dedicated to combating Jewish influence, fighting 'tooth and nail' the Communist party, abolishing provincial governments, and establishing a new corporate economic system under 'one central government.' Whittaker served as party president and Parker as secretary. Heading the youth section was a tame nineteen-year-old, named John Cole. Ernest Morelli served briefly as organizer of an Italian Section. The Nationalists wore khaki shirts and brown breeches, typical western Canadian dress, Whittaker protested. Neckties were shunned since they were 'handy things to get ahold of in a scrap.'[81]

And scraps there were. During the weeks and months following the Nationalist Party's formation, Whittaker spared no effort in getting Winnipeg placed on the Fascist map. Public meetings were called, attended by curious ethnics, supporters, and hecklers. A meeting in Market Square developed in June 1934 into a full-scale battle between anti-Fascists and Fascists, nine of whom appeared bandaged, in city police court, 'their natty brown uniforms spattered with stains.' Luminaries like H.H. Beamish, who informed a noisy Winnipeg audience that wars were 'Jews' hobbies,' addressed meetings under the Nationalist Party's auspices. A widely circulated newspaper – The Canadian Nationalist – appeared filled with common gruel of hate literature, including the Protocols and ritual-murder allegations. Ukrainian, Italian, and German communities were favoured with sales pitches, and ethnic enclaves in rural Manitoba visited, including Flin Flon where a Fascist branch appeared in the summer of 1935.[82] In Winkler, District Two, Unit One of the Nationalist Party was formed, with a core membership of twenty-five Mennonites, who set up a reading-room, met regularly to discuss Fascism, practised Nazi salutes, and printed and distributed hard-core anti-Semitic literature, advocating, among other things, the disenfranchisement of Jews and their subsequent deportation to Palestine. The susceptible locals were mostly 'new world' Mennonites who settled in the Winkler district in the mid-1920s, following the departure of their 'old world' brethren to Mexico.[83] Winkler's Mennonites were both profoundly anti-communist and, according to Mayor Peter Buecker, 'anti-semitic by nature,' since they 'had suffered in Russia under Jewish officials of the Soviet State.'[84] When T.A. Crerar visited Winkler, in February 1934, under Liberal party auspices, he found several of the Mennonites on the political platform 'giving the Nazi salute to each other in quite approved style.'[85] 'I found an extra-ordinary situation,' Crerar observed at a packed Winkler meeting. 'These Mennonites, and many of them are very intelligent, are absolutely convinced that the CCF is a communist organization. That is the line that Whittaker takes. With the Russian experience in their souls, many of them honestly feel that it is necessary to have a Nazi organization in this country to fight the menace of socialism; in other words, quite frankly, the Hitler idea. They are strongly anti-semitic. They feel that Russia today is dominated by Jews so they are out against all Jews as well as the Communists.' Behind it all, Crerar discovered another Tory plot, reminiscent of that of Saskatchewan's Anderson Conservatives during the Klan rage in the late 1920s. 'The local Conservatives in Winkler are telling these people that the only thing for them to do is vote for Bennett,' he continued, 'that the Liberals are not unfriendly to the CCF and that Bennett and the Conservative Party are the ones who have fought the communists in Canada. I would not be surprised if we have in this thing another Tory scheme. You will recall the agitation they created in Saskatchewan in 1929–1930 with the Ku Klux Klan. That movement in Saskatchewan was unquestionably a Tory movement. There is a large German vote in Canada and a large Ukrainian vote that is unquestionably anti-Communist.'[86]

In furtherance of his anti-communist crusade, William Whittaker sometimes went beyond brief excursions to local enclaves in Flin Flon, Morden, or Winkler, Manitoba. Though semi-employed, in pittance-paying jobs, he somehow arranged, during the winter of 1934, several months after the formation of his Nationalist Party, a European visit, with several colleagues, to places of interest. According to RCMP commissioner J.H. MacBrien, Whittaker and Morelli, organizer of the party's 'Italian Section,' attended the first-anniversary celebration of the founding of the Third Reich in Berlin, January 1934, and there met with – among others – Julius Streicher, the violently anti-Semitic editor of *Der Stürmer*, whose February 1934 edition (No. 8) carried photographs of Whittaker and Morelli, as well as Jack Cole and Arthur F. Hart Parker.[87] Whittaker later confided he was in regular communication with Lieutenant-Colonel Ulrich Fleischauer, publisher of the notorious Nazi propaganda outlet World Service, and had been invited by 'an important Nazi ... to spend a year in that country at the expense of the Nazi Party.' En route from Berlin, Whittaker and Morelli stopped over in London, perhaps to visit and arrange hate commerce, with Arnold Leese.[88]

Whittaker's return to Winnipeg was followed by a renewed flow of hate propaganda in his *Canadian Nationalist*, and by the mobilization of his opponents. Local communists formed anti-Fascist groupings, heckled the Nationalist meetings, engaged in occasional fisticuffs, and, through aldermanic representatives like Jacob Penner, urged the provincial and federal governments to take appropriate action. Protesting local labour bodies were joined by the Trades and Labour Congress of Canada, which, at its 1937 convention, heard from its Jewish executive member David Wolfe about Nazi propaganda and anti-Semitism in Winkler and elsewhere and passed a resolution asking the prime minister and minister of justice to investigate alleged Nazi activities 'in order to expose the vicious and malignant forces operating here.'[89] Socialist MLA John Queen warned in the provincial legislature of a 'growing sentiment for dictatorship in ... Canada' and denounced the local Fascists as 'anti-semitic seditious conspirators who should be repressed.'[90] Winnipeg's Jewish community remained vigilant and sought legislative containment. When a mathematics teacher at St John's Technical High School, in Winnipeg's North End, annoyed by fractious students, declared in class that 'Hitler's methods are the best and are the only ones that can make the Jews obey,' he was greeted by a walk-out of Jewish students – who were joined by numerous gentile colleagues – a mass petition, and vigorous representations to the educational authorities. He apologized and the students returned.[91] P.P. Martens, a newsboy flogging

Whittaker's *Canadian Nationalist,* was set upon and dispossessed of his papers by a pair of Jewish schoolboys who were apprehended by a local detective, charged with robbery, and acquitted following a spirited defence by prominent lawyer and community leader M.J. Finklestein.[92] Alerted by Nazism abroad, and the Whittakers at home, Jewish community leaders played a pivotal role in the Western Jewish Conference, an umbrella organization that spoke 'for all collectively regardless of party affiliations and individual opinions and views in other fields.' The conference organized committees in every large centre in western Canada, as well as many smaller ones, and joined with similar groupings in the East in support of the new national congress dedicated, according to Finklestein, to a 'united Canadian Jewry, united together with no thought of aggression but with every intention of defense.'[93]

Defence against the politics of hate was foremost in the minds of Manitoba's several Jewish elected officials in Parliament and the provincial legislature. Federally, the ball was carried by Abraham Albert Heaps, a British Jew who arrived in Winnipeg in 1911, worked as an upholsterer in the Canadian Pacific Railway coach shop, became active in labour and social politics, barely escaped imprisonment on conspiracy charges following the Winnipeg general strike, was elected to city council as an alderman, and in 1925, entered the House of Commons, where he served continuously until defeat by Liberal C.S. Booth in 1940.[94] Throughout his tenure in Parliament – known in Winnipeg as the Age of Heaps – Heaps remained loyal to both social democratic and Jewish causes by vigorously supporting welfare and civil-liberties measures – such as unemployment insurance, old-age pensions, the liberalization of the criminal code – campaigning for open immigration and exposing, inside and outside of Parliament, dangerous incidents of hate politics. Provincially, leadership was provided by Marcus Hyman, a British immigrant lawyer, Manitoba Law School lecturer, and community activist who served as an ILP representative on the Winnipeg School Board from 1923 until 1929 before entering, in 1932, the legislature as an ILP representative, after a pair of unsuccessful tries at the mayoralty. Among Hyman's concerns, in matters affecting the Jewish community, were the antics of Whittaker, which inspired, in March 1934, the introduction into the legislature – by Marcus Hyman – of an amendment to the province's Libel Act, with the following clause: 'The repeated publication of a libel against any race or creed likely to expose persons belonging to such race or professing such creed to hatred, contempt or ridicule shall ... entitle any person belonging to such race or professing such creed to sue for damages and for an injunction to prevent the continuation and circulation of such libel or any libel of a similar character.'[95] The Hyman bill – as it was known – co-authored by Ernest Brotman, allowed action to be taken 'against any person, firm, or corporation directly or indirectly responsible for the authorship, publication and circulation of such libel.'[96] Unlike the similar measure attempted in Quebec by Peter Bercovitch, the Hyman bill received the full support of the government, including attorney general W.T. Major, the entire opposition, and the large urban dailies who congratulated the government and legislature for unanimously passing a law that remained the only legislation in Canada covering group defamation.[97] Soon after the bill's passage, a prominent Conservative Jewish lawyer, William Verner Tobias, a decorated First World War hero and former MLA, brought libel charges under the new act against Whittaker and Herman H. Neufeld, on whose Rundschau Publishing Company's premises the *Canadian Nationalist* had been printed. Mr Justice Percival Montague, of the Manitoba Court of King's Bench, granted an injunction that, apparently, did not entirely eliminate the publication and distribution of the *Canadian Nationalist* in subsequent years.[98]

The aggressive Jewish-community and Bracken-government response – together with a strong press condemnation of Winnipeg's Fascist hate campaign – was not, in the mid-depression years, the sole cause of William Whittaker's worries. In their search for an audience receptive to hate messages and Fascist prescriptions, the Nationalists found themselves in competition with other peculiar organisms promoted, in several instances, by renegades from their own organizations. In the spring of 1934, A.F. Hart Parker, the Nationalist provincial secretary, quit the party and announced the creation of something called the Fascist Party of Canada.[99] Parker's heart had changed, it seems, on the Jewish question and he used the forum of the *Western Jewish News*, which published several of his lengthy attacks on the Nationalists, to denounce Whittaker's 'pseudo-nationalism' and inability to distinguish between the 'International Jew' and 'the whole of the Jewish race, orthodox and unorthodox.'[100] Parker's new Fascist party – which barely survived its launch – emphasized patriotism, the maintenance of the laws and constitution of Canada, the merging of all provincial governments into 'one co-operative state government,' and a willingness to accept any member or supporter – regardless of race – 'as long as that person is a good loyal Canadian.'[101]

Whittaker's other Fascist rivals proved equally ephemeral. Preferring black to brown, Howard Simpkin went Mosley and formed the Canadian Union of Fascists, whose national headquarters remained, for several years, in Winnipeg, where public meetings were held, the *Thunderbolt* was distributed, and occasional stragglers enrolled.[102] More lively was the National Workers Party, a brief left-Fascist formation led by President J. McKinnon, a Nationalist defector and editor of the anti-communist *The Trumpeter* – who served as president – and a Pat McEvan, the vice president, expelled from the Communist Party several years earlier. The executive included several other Nationalist renegades who supported a program advocating universal compulsory military-service training, 'government ownership and control of printing and circulation of currency based on national value standard instead of international gold standard,' and state medicine, hospitalization, and insurance. The National Workers pronounced themselves pro-labour, anti-union, open to defecting Whittaker supporters – although they were 'going slow in taking them in because of their anti-semitic beliefs' – and pro-Mussolini and Hitler 'with some reservation.'[103] The reservation was not strong enough, however, to dissuade the executive from displaying on the wall, at their public meeting in the Canadian League for German Culture Hall, a large swastika flag, which led, quickly enough, to altercations with an organized group of hecklers in attendance, smashed windows, and hails of flying chairs, stones, and bottles.[104] Though the meeting resumed, the National Workers Party quickly faded from public view.

By 1938, Winnipeg's native Fascist field – such as it was – belonged mainly to Whittaker who, in failing health, soldiered on with a mimeograph machine, stackfuls of hate literature, and a few stray youthful adherents. Though local prospects appeared bleak, the faith remained, sustained by the warming exploits of Hitler and Mussolini abroad, the bravado of Eastern comrades, and, perhaps, by dreams of support shared by Arcand and Farr, from a pair of ethnic groups, whose kin abroad enrolled in, or were conscripted into, humming Fascist war machines.

8

Consular Fascism

Whether they love Mussolini is a question that can be answered only
by pointing out that so far they have shown no anxiety to return to
their homeland and enjoy the doubtful benefits of fascist rule. But
Mussolini loves them, and because he loves them so much he has
spared no effort to bring them under Fascist influence. Fascism is not
only made for domestic consumption, it is also an article of export.

'Mussolini's Demands in Canada,'
Memo: prepared by the Canadian Jewish Congress, 1939

When the flag was thrown in the mud, it was the Arditi who reacted
resolutely. It was the Arditi dressed in black who defended the flag in
the public places the same as they defended it in the trenches later
on, and in their assaults. We are the Arditi of new Italy ...

There will be an end to the stupid legend of the languishing
Italian mandoline player.

Royal Consul, Giuseppe Brigidi

The speaker was animated and forthright. His job, the warm, receptive audience learned, at a banquet commemorating the twelfth

anniversary of Mussolini's March on Rome, was not merely technical, involving passports, notarization, or registration, hitherto looked after by officials who were 'passive symbols of His Majesty, King of Italy.' The task was larger now, more consequential, urgent. 'Today the Italian Consuls abroad,' Luigi Petrucci, Royal Consul General of Italy in Canada, announced,

> have been, through the work of the Fascist Government, transformed into active organs of representation of the Fascist idea. They are not amorphous, anodyne, limited to the exercise of functions which, however noble, are technical; they represent the strong arm of the Fascist Government, for the full realization abroad of the great new civilization initiated by Benito Mussolini and the new regime. Before being notaries public, officials of the civil government, protectors of your private interest and channels of your relations with the Mother country, we are Fascist officials, and Fascism is dynamism, an active exaltation of Italian values, the sum of all the forces required to affirm the greatness of new Italy in the world ... I, gentlemen, and Chevalier Ambrosi, my colleague, are first of all, Fascist Consuls. We will not compromise about our Fascism, we will not descend to compromise with those who still stubbornly remain in the contrary camp.[1]

The soaring speech of Petrucci to representatives of Toronto's Italian colony was a mixed thing: a declaration of love for the new Italy and universal civilization immortalized by Benito Mussolini; of war against stubborn, misguided opponents who were 'slaves of ignorance' and 'enemies of the homeland.' It was a measure of Petrucci's, and his colleagues', success in succeeding years that the slaves and enemies of Mussolini, in Canadian cities like Toronto and Montreal, were put severely on the defensive by a powerful campaign, originating in Rome, to enlist the Italian communities in support of the new Italy and the noble cause of Fascism – a political, moral, religious, and cultural movement, Petrucci believed, that had 'returned Italy to God' and 'in the perfect reconciliation between the Papacy and Italy ... brought back the Italian people to that spiritual unity which was the foundation for the greatness of our past history.'[2]

The success – albeit limited – of Petrucci and his colleagues in building and exploiting patriotic fervour within Canada's Italian community was not entirely a product of the loud and muscular campaign orchestrated by the Rome government. The campaign took hold, during the 1930s, because it answered certain needs, which flowed from the historical experience, social conditions, and psychological state of a vulnerable immigrant community straining to retain old identities and, at the same time, win a secure place in the world. 'Psychologically, the Italian immigrant was conditioned to respond positively to Fascism even before Mussolini's regime dazzled his mind,' wrote John P. Diggins of similar developments south of the border. 'Doubtless Fascist propaganda provided the fertilizer, but American society had planted the seed.'[3]

The seed, in Canada, grew in communities which, in the late 1920s – when the consular campaign gained momentum – were neither rich, numerous, powerful, nor cohesive. In 1931 there were over 100,000 Italians in Canada, the bulk in Ontario and Quebec. The largest settlement was in Montreal with 21,300 residents.[4] Toronto counted around 15,500 at the start of the depression.[5] The remaining were scattered in the Atlantic provinces, and in western Canada – in urban centres like Winnipeg, Calgary, and Vancouver and Trail, British Columbia.

The Italians, in the major population centres of Montreal and Toronto, settled near the bottom end of the social pecking order, in discrete communities subsequently known as Little Italies. In Montreal, they settled originally in the Mont Carmel area, around the Bonaventure Station and port, eventually forming nuclei in St Henri, St Joseph, Goose Village, Mont Carmel, and Hochelaga.[6] Other settlements subsequently emerged in the north, at Mile End, Montcalm, Ville Emard, and Lachine, adjacent to industrial satellites. In Toronto, they settled around the train yards and railway stations, then spilled into the downtown ethnically polyglot St John's ward and, eventually, west to St Agnes Parish – near College and Grace – and beyond to St Clements, a parish in the Dufferin area.[7] In both cities, they were primarily labourers or tradesmen, with small businessmen and a few professionals scattered here and there. They worked as navvies and labourers on railway and tramway construction and maintenance; as tilemakers and carpenters in the hinterland and cities; as port workers, stevedores, shoemakers, barbers, fruit pedlars and petty grocers in and outside of Little Italy. And a small professional and business élite emerged from among them, a few lawyers, doctors, priests, and businessmen who earned a living as immigrant bankers, labour contractors, shipping agents, or realtors.

The Little Italies of Montreal and Toronto were ethnic enclaves where immigrant kin lived in close proximity, in modest, vibrant neighbourhoods, attended church, and socialized in a variety of community organizations. The residents of Montreal's Mont Carmel worshipped at the local church constructed in 1903, the Mile Enders and the Montcalm people at Madonna della Difesa, whose new structure was built in 1920. Toronto's churches were attended in the three parishes of Our Lady of Mont Carmel, St Agnes (later St Frances), and St Clements (later St Mary of the Angels).[8] Other communities, in Ottawa, Windsor, Sidney, and Vancouver, had their own churches. There were, in addition, a multitude of social and recreational clubs, kinship associations, and mutual-aid societies providing insurance and burial services. In the pre-war years, the Italian community in Toronto was a maze of local subethnic associations of kinsmen drawn from numerous villages and towns of Italy who maintained their local ties in the new world. The effect of the war – which heightened patriotic sentiments – the stabilization of community life, and the emergence of culturally conscious professional élites trading in group identity, was to strengthen pan-Italian community consciousness and institutions, a process enhanced and reflected in the amalgamation of mutual-aid societies and organizations like the Grand Order of the Sons of Italy, an American-based organization formed in Montreal in 1920, and in Toronto six years later,[9] and the Circolo Colombo Club, a patriotic association, active in Toronto, whose members were enamoured of law, order, family, and, as their motto proclaimed, 'God and Fatherland.'[10] Patriotic celebrations and speechifying, surges of flag-waving, a surfeit of banquets and processions – some of them commemorating events of the First World War in which Canada and Italy joined forces in the war against the Habsburgs – were endemic in the Montreal and Toronto communities whose leaders cultivated local variants of the 'nostalgic nationalism' pervasive in Little Italies across North America.[11]

The nationalism was a product of plain ethnic pride and, as Diggins noted, a 'nascent inferiority complex' traceable to low-status and difficult conditions in the minor land of promise. The Italians were, in the main, poorly paid, exploited, labourers or small-time pedlars subsisting on pittances, tradesmen earning modest livings, or petty merchants subject to the exigencies of the market. When the depression hit, they suffered woefully and sought solace in dreams of the old country. They had long been perceived, by professional nativists and others – despite the glories of classic Italian culture and usefulness of their labours – as 'undesirables' or 'non-preferreds,' as coarse illiterates given to dirty labour, tedious fruit peddling, musty organ-grinding, or criminality.[12] 'They were used to being despised as contadini (peasants) by city people, as colonies (rubes) or bestie (manual labourers) by their own upper classes,' Robert F. Harney observed. 'If they were Southerners, they were treated with contempt by Northern officials. But they had not expected to be looked down on simply as Italians.'[13] Nor did the first generation of Italian settlers expect their children to drift away from their language and traditions. There was an urgency among parents to cement generational ties and maintain family solidarity by imparting to their children – or letting others do so – the language, culture, and glories of ancient and modern Italy.

It was not surprising that, when Benito Mussolini marched on Rome and hoisted the flag, many of his Canadian kinsmen cheered and saluted. He was, after all, a national redeemer committed to ending economic and political anarchy and restoring ancient glory; a masculine, dynamic leader who commanded international attention and magnified Italy's presence on the world stage; a source of pride, as builder of a new Italy, to colonials in estranged ethnic enclaves, beset by status anxieties, identity stress, and, after 1929, by fearful economic problems. It mattered little that Benito Mussolini rejected the institutions and processes of something called liberal democracy, favouring, instead, an authoritarian corporative system. What counted was the blacksmith's son's humble origin, his dramatic rise, his commitment to care for the ordinary workers of depressed classes and regions. Politics, after all, was greeted by many of the poor immigrants with a weary scepticism, and 'democratic self-government' remained an empty phrase mouthed by Anglo-Saxon journalists and schoolteachers. What mattered more than worn political formulas was a warm nostalgia and inflated pride, which obscured, for many, distinctions between patriotism and ideology, Fatherland and Fascism. 'The triumphal passage of Italo Balbo and his squadron of hydroplanes on the way to Chicago World's Fair,' R.F. Harney observed, 'was a major event for Italo-Canadians, as important as the appearance of a great musical maestro like Caruso. Of course, at one level, the roar of huge Savoia-Marchetti seaplanes was a harbinger of Fascism's bombast and belligerence, but at another, it was a source of pride in the new Italy: industrialism, a Great Power, and yet evoking Columbus, Vespucci and the Cabots.'[14]

Reinforcing the Italo-Canadians' sentimental predilection was a tolerance, by many of their fellow Canadians, of Benito Mussolini and his new Italy. There was, indeed, among élites in Canada in the late 1920s and early 1930s, if not a Mussolini vogue, then at least an acceptance of the Italian dictator which legitimated the Italo-Canadians' own feelings. Il Duce was self-made, a risen poor boy, who subscribed to the virtues of order, discipline, and work; made peace with the church; restored Italy's pride and stature; and beat the Reds, a matter that appealed to edgy middle-class people and businessmen wary of leftist perils. Law-and-order people, journalists, academics, veterans, and occasional politicians praised the new regime led by a dynamic leader described by American John Gunther as a 'spring of steel,' a designation a trifle more flattering than his depiction of Hitler as a blob of ectoplasm. *Saturday Night* took several serious and sober looks at Italian Fascism. Defending the position the Fascism was good for Italy, a team of Knights of Columbus debaters at McGill defeated a visiting Oxford team.[15] A Canadian senator contributed funds to a church in which Mussolini adorned a fresco above the altar. A. Lowell, chief administrator of the Ontario Parole Board, thought Canadian Italians law abiding, attributable in part to the example of discipline instilled by the regime at home. Thomas O'Hagan, a Toronto journalist, referred, in a November 1928 *Globe and Mail* editorial, to Mussolini as 'Italy's saviour' and repeated his views in a *Star* interview several years later.[16] Professor James Easton Shaw, a University of Toronto language professor, in an alumni lecture in the spring of 1923, credited Mussolini, who was moved 'by great love of Italy,' with creating order out of chaos. 'To him morality is love of country,' the professor insisted, 'and he trusts in the people's patriotism as a moving power.'[17]

Effusions like Professor Shaw's were more common in Quebec, among nationalist élites taken with Il Duce's Latin grandeur. Montreal's bulbous populist mayor, Camillien Houde, admired the man and his system and successfully courted the local Italian vote. Abbé Groulx and his cohorts, the host of right nationalist youth groups and other patriotic organizations loosed in Quebec in the 1930s, and church officials high and low were often sympathetic to the Italian system, its corporate arrangements, commitment to law and order, and reconciliation between classes, a warmth secured by the Lateran Pact between Mussolini and Pope Pius XI in 1929. The Pope made his peace with Fascism, and the church in Quebec was hardly hostile to a regime that prescribed an effective antidote to Red Revolution. In and outside of Quebec, the Italian communities' flirtation with Fascism, therefore, in the early 1930s, hardly invited a hostile external response from Canadian opinion makers, centre or rightist political leaders, or the state authorities. When *fasci* first appeared and the consuls mounted their assault, there was no hostile opinion screaming sedition, or inclination by political leaders like R.B. Bennett to apply section 98 to outlaw ethnic organizations supporting, after all, the verities of religion and family, and the maintenance of law and order.[18] Nor were there any ethnic pressure groups activated – like the Jews, who paid scant attention to Mussolini until he launched his active anti-Semitic campaign in the late 1930s – to demand the legislative containment of organizations and propaganda concentrated within the tight borders of the Little Italies.

With the ethnic soil fertile – and fertilized – and the host environment congenial, ornate *fasci* and related institutions were free to sprout in Canada's Little Italies. And they did. When Italia Garibaldi, the great patriot's granddaughter, toured Canada in 1923 to promote a proposed Italian agricultural settlement scheme, she found time to organize Fascist locals in Toronto, Winnipeg, and Montreal. They soon lapsed, however, and were succeeded by new organizations, in subsequent years, in Winnipeg and Vancouver, where tiny *fasci* were formed in the mid-1920s and persisted well into the 1930s in the Ontario cities of Ottawa and Hamilton, home to small Italian communities; and, above all, in Toronto and Montreal whose communities were exposed to intense, well-financed, and effective propaganda and organization campaigns. The impetus came from Italy, whose Fascist government was determined, in the late 1920s, to cement the loyalty and mobilize active support for the Fatherland and Fascism among their ethnic compatriots abroad. The government agency charged with regulating the export of Fascism to immigrant communities was Fascists Abroad (Fasci all'Estero), an organization that operated under the direction of the ministry of foreign affairs. Headed, during the early and mid-1930s, by Piero Parini, the Fascists Abroad agency spared no effort, in Canada and elsewhere, beginning in the late 1920s, in penetrating, mobilizing, and directing local Fascist activities.

The key players in the Fascist offensive were the Italian consular officials – the vice-consuls in Toronto and, later, Vancouver, and consuls general in Ottawa and Montreal who, as consul general Petrucci informed his Toronto compatriots, served as 'active instruments of the fascist idea' and urged immigrant Italians to sacrifice their 'personal ambitions' and 'rally round' their 'Consuls and the Fascist society.'[19] During the 1920s, a host of new consulates were opened by the Italian government in various countries, pockets of resistance among traditional diplomats wiped out, and numerous new consular officers appointed and invested with propaganda and mobilization functions. The result, in Canada, was a remarkable offensive, orchestrated by notables, both imported and local, to win the loyalty and support among ethnic kin for the Fascist Fatherland.[20]

By the mid-1930s, the consular offensive was gaining full steam.[21] The small *fasci* in Hamilton, Ottawa, Winnipeg, and Vancouver were complemented by larger formations in Toronto and Montreal, where six branches were formed by 1933. Toronto's 'Fascio Principe Umberto,' by 1937, had three sections.[22] Canada's *fasci* were basically social, educational, and propaganda organizations with limited political functions. Members swore allegiance to Il Duce, vowed to 'serve the cause of the Fascist revolution,' attended public events commemorating the founding of Rome or March on Rome and other patriotic occasions, and congregated in clubrooms where, according to one account, groups 'of similar thinking immigrants' played cards, read Italian papers and literature, discussed current events in Italy, exposed themselves to heavy doses of propaganda and official news releases, and heard lectures as varied as 'The Agricultural and Economic Foundations of the Italian People,' 'The Italian Navy,' 'Communism, the International Danger,' 'Moral Hygiene,' 'The Armed Forces of Italy,' and, not least, 'Mussolini's Youth.'[23] 'Members learn rational explanations for supporting a contemporary political movement,' a student of Montreal's Italian community wrote,' with which they actually have no direct experience and which does not possess a philosophy compatible with democratic ideals. They learn of benefits to every Italian at home and abroad and come to embody their enthusiasm in the one living man, Mussolini.'[24]

Affiliates of an authoritarian political movement, centred in the person of the great leader, the local *fasci* were, understandably, hardly democratic organizations. Memberships were approved by the Roman authorities. Running each of the organizations was a political directorate composed of prominent activists – who held positions in kindred allied organizations – nominated by the General Directorate of Italians Abroad in Rome on the recommendations of the local consular official who served as honorary president and attended, and addressed, important functions.[25] The Montreal *fascio* included a core group of militants, 'The Centuria D'Onore' (The One Hundred Valiants) composed, according to an RCMP report, of 'one hundred of the most trustworthy and dependable members of the Italian Fascist community selected from the different branches of the Fascio in Montreal.' Members of the Centuria D'Onore sometimes dressed in black shirts and paraded, in military formation, at public events. 'It is reported that the general Italian community in Montreal views the Centuria D'Onore with some apprehension,' a police report read, 'due to the fact that members of this organization will allegedly report any anti-Fascist activities and even the names of those persons who are not in sympathy with Fascism – to the executive officials of the Fascio and to the Italian Consulate.'[26]

Joining the *fasci* in celebration of Il Duce's grand achievements were a host of other social, fraternal, cultural, and national-political organizations, influenced, and in some cases created and controlled by, the consular officials and local Fascists notables. The Order of the Sons of Italy, a mutual-aid society active in Montreal and Toronto, and other cities, formally independent of politics, became an arena of contest between pro- and anti-Fascist elements. The Fascists won control and the anti-Fascists seceded and formed a separate organization, the Independent Order of the Sons of Italy, later known as the Italo-Canadian Order. Toronto's Intersocial Committee, an umbrella organization of various community groups, which exercised certain educational functions, was infiltrated and manipulated by Fascist notables.[27] The Italian War Veterans Association in Toronto and Montreal succumbed to a Fascist take over, which led to bitter recriminations, secessions, and the creation, in both cities, of independent associations. *Dopolavoros* or after-work organizations, modelled after recreational clubs in Italy, which represented 'a method for mobilizing the large mass of industrial workers and keeping them conscious of a benevolent, maternalistic government,'[28] were organized in Toronto and Montreal where they served as 'parallel and collateral' institutions to the *fasci*, 'attracting that hesitating, marginal group who while afraid of jeopardizing their status by open declaration of allegiance, still want to be in the swim of a popular movement.'[29] Montreal's six *dopolavoro* branches were controlled by an executive committee, appointed by the consul, which regulated the sports, recreation, and social activities of the affiliated associations. Attached to the Montreal associations was a chaplain and medical doctor. Meetings were held in the newly constructed Casa d'Italia in some districts, or in rented premises reminiscent, according to one observer, of 'pool halls or taverns, the behaviour is so lethargic.' The Montreal *dopolavoros* participated with other organizations in a broad umbrella organization created in 1934 by Consul General Giusseppe Brigidi, who served as honorary consul. A voluntary association that counted thirty-five autonomous organizations – including the *fascio*, *dopolavoro*, Sons of Italy, and Fascist War Veterans – the Italian United Moral Front served as a central coordinating body for community affairs, as a fund-raising agency for worthy causes like the Italian Red Cross, the raising of a Cabot monument, the construction of the Casa d'Italia, and 'as a mechanism for reviving enthusiasm appropriate to the particular political movement which it supports.'[30] Twice a year, on 21 April and 28 October, the Moral Front sponsored and organized major patriotic celebrations commemorating the Birth of Rome and the March on Rome.[31]

Among the cultural institutions sponsored and controlled by consular officials and cohorts were a number of Italian language schools and youth organizations whose job it was, as Royal Consul Petrucci frankly stated to a Toronto banquet commemorating the twelfth anniversary of the March on Rome, 'not merely to teach the language, but also to do the work of Fascist Education.'[32] By the mid-1930s, there were eight Italian evening schools in Montreal, three in Toronto, and several others in places like Ottawa and Windsor. Textbooks and manuals, published in Italy by the Italian Schools Abroad or National Foundation of the Sons of Littorio, were provided free by the Italian government, together with supplies. And with the imported books and supplies came, in several instances, teachers imported from Italy, at least one of whom doubled as a consular employee. In class, the children acquired the basics. They learned Italian reading and writing skills and were introduced to the glories of the Motherland and its wise and benevolent leadership. 'All the Italian children love Mussolini the Duce,' a first-form reader, published in Rome, affirmed, 'who guides the new Italy and who ... works for the good of the Motherland. His austere expression is illuminated by sweetness when he looks at children. The Italian children know why Il Duce loves them so much. He loves them because the bambinos form the most beautiful hope of Italy and because growing up strong and diligent and good, Italy too, will grow strong, mighty and felicitous.'[33] Complementing the schools were children's and youth groups affiliated with the Italian Youth Organization Abroad.[34] The youth groups met regularly in Toronto, Montreal, and other centres; imbibed Fascist and patriotic propaganda; and occasionally gave gymnastic and choral performances before their Fascist elders – including the Montreal Royal Consul – in which, as an Italian newspaper reported, 'beautiful hymns were sung to the Motherland and to Rome' and 'truly imposing phalanges formed, by members in beautiful uniforms ... standing in line to pass in review by the Fatherland Authority.'[35] For ardent youths, summer tours to Italy were organized, jointly financed by the chosen candidates, local *fasci*, and the general directorate of the Italian Youth Organization Abroad. The 1936 summer tour was supervised by the editor of Toronto's major Italian Fascist organ *Il Bollettino* and by the superintendent of Italian schools in Canada, an employee of the Italian consul's office. A year later, seventy-nine children from Montreal, Toronto, Hamilton, Vancouver, North Bay, and Sidney, Nova Scotia, were warmly sent off by the Montreal consul general and the vice-consuls of Toronto and Ottawa, who were convinced that the youths would return two months hence 'ready to defend in this country the great Fascist and Imperial land of ours.' In Italy, the Canadian visitors, with youth from other countries, attended government-sponsored camps; toured a range of picturesque summer resorts and historic monuments including Marconi's home; took classes on the Italian language, history, literature, and geography; and were favoured with visits and pep talks by dignitaries like Piero Parini, head of Fascists Abroad. The most prominent attended, with élite youth from other countries, a special 'Mussolini Camp' at Mount Sacro near Rome, visited the capital, and saluted Il Duce.[36]

Back in Canada, homage to Il Duce was common practice at numerous community events sponsored and attended by Italy's frenetic representatives. In their campaign of mobilization, the consuls employed a variety of tactics to win support and gain influence in local organizations and the community at large. Their own status, as representatives of King Victor Emmanuel III and Il Duce, traded well among humble colonials. The privilege of diplomatic immunity was exploited to the farthest limit. Facilities and resources provided by the home government – whether supplies for local schools, subsidies to useful press editors, or salaries for consular employees like Arnoldo Michelet, who taught and diffused propaganda in a local Italian school – were important aids.[37] Helpful, as well, were local notables, some of whom had been ardent Fascists in the home country and were active in local communities before the consular assault gained momentum. In Toronto, for example, Vice-Consul Ambrosi and his successor worked closely with people like Ruggero Bocci, an ardent early Fascist – preceding the March on Rome – who arrived in Canada in 1921 and later became political secretary of Toronto's

Fascio Principe Umberto; Pasquale Fontanella, the eloquent physician, active in community affairs since his arrival in Toronto in 1927, who practised his oratory at numerous patriotic events and served as consular representative at functions Ambrosi could not attend; or Rosario Invidiata a 'Son of Strong Italy,' physician, and organizer of the *fascio* in his home town in Sicily in 1923, who was honoured at a community banquet in 1927 at which a congratulatory telegram, from the Ottawa consul general, was read, in appreciation of his 'manifest patriotic sentiments and attachments to the Duce, the renewer of the Italian conscience.'[38]

Prominent among the local notables applauding, if not assisting, the consular effort were leading clergymen whose support of the local Fascist cause was 'a direct echo,' as one writer put it, 'of the rapprochement of Church and State in Italy.'[39] Father Truffa and Father Volonte, the two Salesian priests at Toronto's St Agnes, were both solid Fascist supporters. 'When one says Italian, he also means Catholic,' Father Truffa informed his audience during a meeting, in April 1928, at which the Fascio Principe Umberto's coat of arms was blessed, 'and because Catholicism has ... assumed its place as state religion, I give my approval and augur Fascism well; Fascism, which is composed of and directed by men of an upright Catholic faith.'[40] When Fathers Truffa and Volonte's superiors contemplated, in 1934, their removal to Italy, the vice-consul, assisted by local notables, initiated a vigorous campaign to retain their services. Consul General Petrucci helped out and reminded Rome of the need, in North America, for Italian clergy dedicated to sustaining the 'Catholic and Italian spirit' in the colonies, and blocking the incursions of the Irish church.[41]

The Montreal priests Fathers Manfriani and Maltempi, at Mile End's Madonna della Difesa, and at the Italian Catholic Church of Mont Carmel, were precisely the sort of devotees Petrucci had in mind. Fathers Manfriani and Maltempi shared, with the Toronto Salesians, the view that a good Italian was 'both Catholic and Fascist'[42] and dutifully participated in important public events and ceremonies orchestrated by local Fascist notables, sometimes held at the Madonna della Difesa Church, which displayed, as *Saturday Night* correspondent John Hoare pointed out, 'a large and very splendid painting on the curved ceiling above the altar, incorporating more than a hundred figures.' 'I have seen it myself,' Hoare wrote. 'Saints and angels are there; martyrs clothed in leaves; cardinals in their brilliant robes; in the center the Pope enthroned. Among the rich and varied colours a splash of black catches the eye from the right hand side of the picture – a group of figures in black, standing. These are no other than portraits of Italy's Fascist leaders. Balbo is clearly recognizable. Some of the others I could not identify. But one black figure overshadowed all the others, overshadows all that side of the picture, dominates everything except the Pope himself. It is Mussolini on a charger.'[43]

When the Birth of Rome was commemorated in April 1936, at Mile End's Shamrock Hall, by a crowd of the faithful – including Consul General Brigidi and black-shirted *fascio* members who brought a musical band along – Fathers Manfriani and Maltempi were there, up front, solemnizing proceedings and blessing the flags of the Fascist male and female sections.[44] And they were prominent at the Madonna della Difesa Church on Sunday, 17 February 1936, a day of sacrifice, during the Ethiopian war, when the local Italian women traded in their gold, including wedding rings, and received in return rings of steel to mark their patriotic sacrifice. 'The church was filled, many more women than men were present,' Mr Bayley observed,

> many more old people than young, many more poor people than
> well-to-do. Sixteen Blackshirts marched down the aisle behind the
> flagbearers and faced the altar. Two girls dressed in Red Cross
> uniforms and four in Fascist costumes of black tan, white waist, and
> black shirt were present to assist. The priests blessed the new steel
> rings. A picture was taken of the group assembled in front of the altar
> in order that a visual reproduction might be had for the parent
> church and government. Father Manfriani, in an appeal filled with
> emotion and pleading, addressed the mothers. The ceremony, he
> told them, had been performed everywhere in Italy. This sacrifice was
> to be an expression of faith not only in the Mother Country, but also
> to their husbands. Italy was not fighting in Africa because she was
> cruel, but she was attempting to spread civilization and Christianity

among barbarous natives. Those mothers, he ended, who would stand up and give their rings at the moment, would receive first, steel wedding rings engraved 'Il 18 Novembre 1935 ... per la Patria'. The Consul's wife escorted by her husband started the mass movement. Another picture was taken to show the religious and National-political leaders before the altar. The Italian mothers surged forward hurriedly to give and to receive.[45]

Not only mothers gave and received. Publishers and editors also contributed propaganda and received subsidies. The local Italian press served as important instruments of propaganda and were looked after by consular authorities. The large New York–based daily *Il Progresso Italo-Americano* (*The Italian-American Progress*), which included material from a Toronto correspondent, was imported and distributed in Italian communities across the country. In Toronto, the Italian Publishing Company and Italian Information Bureau were set up and run by a pair of imported Fascist publicists – Tommaso Mari and Attilio Perilli – from Hamilton and New York. A prominent local Italian banker and steamship agent, whose business required consular goodwill, lent his *Il Progresso Italo-Canadese* to the cause and reproduced vice-consular speeches with appropriate praise and photos.[46] Pro-Fascist newspapers attracted advertisements from businessmen eager to maintain good relations with the consular notables and home government. The weekly *Il Bollettino Italo-Canadese* received a consular subsidy and trumpeted the cause. 'We have here a small, weekly paper,' an *Il Bollettino* report on the local *fascio*'s activities read, 'lean, we may say, but wholesome, hard and flourishing. Let us all read it and we will find the antidote against the subtle poison which the local (Canadian) press is spreading about us.' According to a Canadian Jewish Congress report on the Italian Fascist push in Canada, *Il Bollettino* was 'an interesting little newspaper and it is incredibly frank. It publishes reports, speeches, exhortations, without even blushing, and it is an information guide to what every young Fascist should know.'[47] Montreal's weekly *L'Italia*, whose office was removed, following a change of ownership, to the same building and floor as the Italian consulate, on Stanley Street, also provided useful propaganda services – without blushing – under the editorship of Camillo Veters, president of the Fascist Italian War Veterans, and his successors.[48] Beginning in 1934, an annual consular subsidy of twenty-five hundred dollars was forthcoming to support a newspaper with little advertising, sent, free of charge, to numerous clergymen and civic leaders during the Ethiopian campaign.[49] When Montreal's little pro-Fascist *Il Cittadino* stepped out of line and published an article relating to the Cabot monument deemed unacceptable by Brigidi, it was warned, in a letter from the consul, published in *L'Italia*, to 'take steps in order to avoid the future publication of articles of this kind.'[50] *Il Cittadino* was subsequently expelled from the Moral Front – organized and run by Consul Brigidi – and soon went out of business, likely because its subsidy was withdrawn.[51]

The press blitz was an important element in a campaign to mobilize patriotic sentiment. During the early and mid-depression years, consular officers and a supporting cast of local notables spread themselves around, their visits and speeches highlighted in the local press. The notables, both imported and local – men like the journalist Tommaso Mari, or the visiting American journalist P.P. Carbonelli – joined with the consuls and vice-consuls in stoking the patriotic fires and fusing, or confusing, nostalgic nationalism with political Fascism. The oratory was florid and emotional, and the occasions many 'The speeches ultimately did have a structure,' historian John E. Zucchi concluded, 'the literary equivalent of music's modified binary form (ABA – modified): sentimental gestures about the fatherland (A) followed by a summary of Italy's artistic and scientific legacy – usually covering Rome, the Renaissance, and the nineteenth century (B), with a return to other affected blurbs on the patria (modified A). Effective features included the rhetorical question ("Our Fatherland in Italy – and pronouncing that word 'Italy' are our hearts not moved; does it not strike a lively and profound chord of one's being, of one's id?") and odd metaphors ("the blood running in our veins is the purest to have been produced in Nature's laboratories").'[52]

The oratorical flights were spritely additives to a campaign of enlistment aimed at the community at large, and local associations. The consuls visited mutual-aid societies, social associations, and local kinship groups. And they, and their aligned notables, were prominent at the larger celebrations commemorating Columbus or Armistice Day, the inauguration of Italy's constitution, the March on Rome, the Birth of Rome, or the inspiring visit of Balbo's fleet. The celebration honouring the founding of Rome, at Mile End's Shamrock Hall, in April 1936, attended by a thousand people, had all of the ingredients. The stage was covered with national flags and banners of the various societies. Black shirts were worn by the faithful, and the crowd was entertained by the *fascio* band, which struck up the Fascist hymn and the Italian National Anthem at the appropriate moment when the consul general and his wife arrived on stage. Salutes followed, and renderings of 'O, Canada' and 'God Save the Queen.' Joining Brigidi on stage was a collection of dignitaries: Fathers Manfriani and Maltempi, who blessed the Fascist flag; leaders of the *fascio*; representatives of the mutual-aid societies; the special guest, P.P. Carbonelli, the New York–based correspondent of a Milan newspaper, honoured earlier at a dinner of the Montreal Italian Chamber of Commerce. Presentations were made to students of the Italian schools who demonstrated their gymnastic skills, and the flags of the local Fascist groups were blessed by Father Manfriani. The major speakers were the consul general who, according to a *L'Illustration Nouvelle* correspondent, 'had the gift of raising the enthusiasm of the crowd,' and the distinguished visiting journalist. Brigidi informed his audience that the great contemporary public work undertaken in Italy, to commemorate the anniversary of the founding of Rome, was called, appropriately, 'Ethiopia.' 'At the very moment when we celebrate here this important event which marks the creation of Roman Civilization in the world which dates back twenty-five centuries,' he rhapsodized, 'our troops are entering triumphantly at Addis Abeba [*sic*] causing the last slave empire to fall.' P.P. Carbonelli was equally eloquent in reassuring his audience that Il Duce led a regime that cared for both the general public and working-class interests. He commended 'the natural solidarity' between Italian immigrant working men and the Canadian people, urged his audience 'to continue to be good citizens' and respect 'the laws of the host country,' and closed with a reminder that Fascism taught the people to respect nation, religion, and family. The ceremo-

ny closed with the presentation of awards annually offered by the
Italian government, on the occasion of the founding of Rome, to
three local deserving working men.[53]

The endemic ceremonial binges provided fine opportunities for
the Little Italies of Torónto and Montreal to play rally round the
consul and Il Duce, to resist, in the words of Consul General Petrucci,
the 'breaking up of the Community of ours into a thousand little
colonial associations,' and create instead 'a national discipline,'
harmony and unity.[54] To strengthen the unity, the busy consuls undertook major projects of mobilization and construction, both organizational and physical. Montreal's Italian United Moral Front was
created to 'formulate general policies and lines of concerted action
whenever occasion arose.'[55] A drive to recognize John Cabot, a fif-
teenth-century Venetian explorer born in Genoa, as Canada's founder with a memorial statue inspired support and enthusiasm, and
miffed French-Canadian nationalists fearful of Jacques Cartier's
possible relegation to the status of regional explorer.[56] The Ethiopian
war evoked torrents of speechifying, proclamations of support and
solidarity, and patriotic fund-raising drives for cash and gold. Apart
from the cash contributions, more than five hundred persons, according to *Il Bollettino*, answered the call for gold in Toronto alone
by March 1936, each of them contributing at lest a ring, stickpin, or
pair of earrings.[57] Priority attention was given by consular authorities
and community notables to the construction of Casas d'Italia, which
served as centres of community activity. Montreal's, at the corner of
La Jeunesse and Jean Talon Boulevard, was built on land donated by
the city, whose mayor, Camillien Houde, was named, following disposition of the property, by King Victor Emmanuel III 'Chevalier de
la Couronne d'Italie.'[58] Toronto's was located at Dundas and Bever-
ley streets, in the heart of the city, in a converted former mansion of
the Chudleigh estate.[59] The Montreal *casa* housed an auditorium for
large public events – lectures, plays, motion pictures, meetings – a
library reading-room, and offices used by various organizations, some
of which were Fascist controlled. Toronto's housed the vice-consul's
office and, like its Montreal counterpart, served as a meeting place
of community and Fascist organizations, including the *fascio, dopolavoros*, Italian Chamber of Commerce, Italian language-school offic-

ers, War Veterans Association, and lodges of the Sons of Italy. Funding came from private donations and public benefits, including the proceeds of dances, banquets, and concerts. The consuls and the vice-consuls led the fund-raising campaigns, at the end of which, as Giusseppe Brigidi announced, 'there would be a list of those who have subscribed even one cent and, on the other hand, the list of those who, having been approached, have refused to subscribe even one cent.'[60] The names of contributors, Brigidi stated, 'would be recorded in a golden book of ... patriotism ... to be sent to Signor Mussolini in Rome, as a most sincere message of deep Italianism and active adherence to the Fascist regime.'[61]

Inscriptions, whether in golden or black books, mattered a great deal during the excited years of the consular campaign. There were many factors pushing and pulling the locals to declare their support for the home regime: the nostalgic nationalism and plain ethnic pride of an insecure immigrant community; the preparatory patriotism of the 1920s; the rise and renown on the world stage of the Mussolini regime and its acceptance – before Ethiopia – within the host Canadian community; a tolerant legal environment and willingness by Canadian élites to dismiss Fascism as an ornate internal matter within the Italian community; the prestige, energy, and acumen of the consular officials; the subsidy flow to local institutions, including press and schools; the propaganda blitz confusing national and ideological loyalties; the manipulation or co-optation of local notables seeking status and recognition, and their influence, in turn, on the 'good, honest' ordinary workers, many of them illiterate. Adherence flowed from social pressures and, in many instances, from plain fear of loss of income, citizenship status, or mobility privileges. Anti-Fascists, many of them involved in mutual-aid-association fights, were deemed anti-patriotic communists. Recalcitrants, like *Il Cittadino*, were bumped from associations like the Moral Front. Businessmen trading with the Mother Country required permits and certifications, and toed the line. Personal documents such as marriage and birth certificates and passports were obtainable only through consular officers. The names of known anti-Fascists were transmitted overseas, and travel restrictions imposed or threatened. Threats of harm to the overseas families of regime opponents were whispered, or shouted, about.[62] Relief funds, in Montreal in the early 1930s, according to one account, were diverted, in some instances, to persons of the right persuasion, a diversion that led to bitter recriminations and the subsequent replacement of Consul General Bianco by Brigidi. Anti-Fascist war veterans were threatened with loss of decorations and pensions.[63] Being anti-Fascist, in short, did not help in dealings with the consulate, home government, or local associations under consular influence. Fascist membership, by contrast, according to Consul Brigidi, was a decided asset. 'In comparison to the Fascist membership cards,' Giusseppe Brigidi informed a meeting of the local *fascio*, at which membership cards were officially distributed, 'the value of the passports, which is only a document required at the border to permit the transit, is less important. For the latter does not prove the good qualities of the bearer. When one presents himself to the Consul with a passport, he proves only that he crossed the borders regularly, but when one presents the membership card, the Consul helps him and knows that he is a gentleman. The membership card is a priceless document for everybody who changes his residency, for the Italian who goes back to Italy. From this document is ascertained that, although the bearer has lived far from his country, he has maintained such good faith in himself and such great Italianism as to deserve entire confidence. This is the individual who has well represented our Fascist Italianism in foreign countries.'[64]

Though Brigidi's sort of Fascist Italianism made significant inroads into the colonial community by the mid-1930s, there was no lack of opposition, resistance, or studied apathy to the consular campaign, which included among its enrolees a large, likely predominant, number there for social and cultural, rather than ideological, reasons. Though Bayley reported wide favourable reaction 'to the persuasions of local leaders and those who have come from Italy,'[65] he noted that supporters had 'little rational understanding of fundamental changes overseas,' and wished 'to be members of a mass movement with all its excitement, glamour, status-giving, and social satisfaction.'[66] There was, as well, significant resistance to recruitment from 'the apathetic' and 'the openly hostile,' the latter group including radical anti-Fascists – some anarchists and communists – who, in

Toronto, Montreal, and other cities, convened in occasional Mazzini Society cells or the Matteoti Club, aligned with the CCF, and published short-lived newspapers.[67] Quite apart from the small radical anti-Fascist groups, there was 'the proud commonsensical' resistance to the consular assault, not uncommon in social clubs and mutual-aid associations, some of which became bitter arenas of contest between pro-and anti-Fascists, leading, in some instances, to the creation of dual organizations. Resentment of the Fascist contagion was entertained, as well – in Toronto, at least – by displaced established notables, and older colonial associations, whose patriotism and community consciousness predated the Fascist surge.[68]

Though the consular officials, and their local adjuncts, hardly succeeded in welding the colonial communities into a solid mass, they were able, by the mid-1930s, to steal 'the thunder of patriotism' and win considerable moral and financial support through prosecution of a campaign of 'energetic tutelage.'[69] In doing so, they hoped to firm up a body of local opinion loyal to the Mussolini regime and potentially useful in time of international crisis,[70] a block capable of exerting external pressure on the host government in matters affecting the welfare of the Motherland. The consular notables were no mere community activists; they were Fascist representatives committed to polishing and firming their regime's image abroad and advancing its interests through propaganda and interventions, direct and indirect, discreet or, on occasion, indiscreet.

In pursuit of their goals, the consuls employed varied stratagems. They cultivated élite opinion, especially in Quebec, through organizations like the Circolo Universitario Italiano, which Consul Brigidi thought useful in countering the Judaeo-Masonic influence at McGill University.[71] The Institute of Italian Culture served as a forum of contact between the consular officials and Italian community leaders and élites within the francophone and anglophone communities who learned at soirées about the beauty, culture, literature, and history of Italian civilization.[72] Mr de Simone's advocacy of cultural and academic exchanges between Italy and Quebec were warmly received by representatives of the University of Montreal and L'Association Canadienne-Française pour l'Avancement des Sciences.[73] *L'Actualité Economique,* a review published by L'Ecole des Hautes Etudes Commerciales, was favoured with an article on corporatism in Italy written by Consul Brigidi who, in an address delivered under the auspices of the graduates' association of the University of Montreal, on 'the ethics of fascism and its practical application,' informed his audience that 'Fascism as a social phenomenon will give its name to the twentieth century just as Liberalism gave its own name to the last century.'[74] When Gabriele D'Annunzio died in March 1938, de Simone organized a large commemorative event for the French-Canadian élite at the Manoir des Oliviers, where eulogies were heard and D'Annunzio's poetry read.[75]

Press propaganda figured prominently in the consular drive. The loquacious Brigidi was a prolific writer and showered the local Italian papers with articles. With the Ethiopian war under way, the propaganda surge intensified. An international press bureau was set up, and local opinion leaders – politicians, clergymen, professors, heads of social and cultural organizations – were fed copy, eulogizing the Italian war effort.[76] Releases were directed, as well, at the French-Canadian press, including *La Presse, La Patrie, Le Devoir, Le Canada,* and *L'Unité,* which loosed a stream of pro-Italian articles. Among the outlets especially useful were the pair of journalists edited by Quebec's own native Fascists. Consuls Brigidi and de Simone cultivated warm relations with Paul Bouchard, whose *La Nation* received, and reproduced, piles of consular propaganda. Nor was Adrien Arcand remiss in flogging the Italian cause, with the assistance of an Italian-born journalist hired by Eugene Berthiaume – proprietor of Arcand's *L'Illustration Novelle,* during his tenure as consul in Paris. Mario Duliani had put in years of service as a journalist on the French right before arriving in Montreal, where he moved with ease in French-Canadian press circles and contributed heavily to Arcand's pro–Union Nationale *L'Illustration Nouvelle,* which, de Simone, informed his Rome superiors, 'ne cesse de manifester de la sympathie, de la compréhension et de l'objectivité à notre égard.'[77]

Nor was the press feed all. The enthusiastic Montreal consuls sometimes dabbled in local politics and were occasionally prone to impolitic gaffes. Brigidi's Fascist fervour, as Roberto Perin noted, sometimes 'l'emphêcha ... de saisir les subtilités de la politique Québécoise.'[78] When J.E. Gregoire was elected mayor of Quebec City, Brigidi was convinced the minuscule and moribund Fédération des

Clubs Ouvriers had helped him in. Warmed by Paul Bouchard's Fascist entertainment, Brigidi shipped numerous publications on corporatism to Union Nationale deputies, whom he thought sympathetic to *La Nation*'s view. The consul channelled support to Davide Ianuzzi in the Montreal municipal election of 1934 and discouraged a rival Italian candidacy, likely to split the Italian-bloc vote. The Italian United Moral Front was brought into play during the 1935 federal election in support of candidates, of either party, thought sympathetic to the Italians and their home country. A favourite of Brigidi's and his successor was Camillien Houde – an honorary Grand Master of the Order of the Sons of Italy – who enjoyed Moral Front support in the 1934 municipal election. Following the election, Houde arranged his land disposition for the construction of a Casa d'Italia. More subdued and tactful than Brigidi, whose political meddling and open flirtations with Quebec nationalists and separatists perturbed the Ottawa consul general and Rome authorities, was Brigidi's replacement, Paolo de Simone. The new consul's politics of 'non-ingérence' (non-interference) did not, however, preclude forays reminiscent of his predecessor, Brigidi. According to A.V. Spada, a prominent anti-Fascist journalist, Simone arranged, using local pro-Fascist intermediaries, a donation of five thousand dollars to Houde's unsuccessful anti-participationist campaign in the 17 January 1938 St Henri federal by-election[79] – won by the Liberal undertaker J.A. Bonnier, during which the ex-mayor announced: 'if tomorrow a conflict will break out between Italy and England, what will we people of the Province of Quebec do, we who feel united to Italy by ties of race, of culture, of religion and of blood. Can we march against Italy to which all our sympathy is turned? The answer is certainly, No.'[80]

Though critical of Brigidi's flirtation with extreme Quebec nationalists, Ottawa consul general Luigi Petrucci was himself not free of occasional impolitic utterances or naïve views. He privately welcomed the potentially destructive effects on the British Empire of the autonomist Union Nationale's victory in 1936, and was convinced that the nationalist movement in Quebec drew its major politics and agenda from Fascist Italy and Mussolini.[81] In a widely broadcast speech before Montreal's Italian Chamber of Commerce in February 1936, Petrucci set aside accepted diplomatic norms, criticized the League of Nations – of which Canada was a member – for doing 'nothing for the world' during its 'fifteen years of existence,' and expressed sorrow that Canada was considering 'applying sanctions against Italy, sanctions which are dangerous because they can bring another world war and which have destroyed the Italo-Canadian trade.'[82] Petrucci's widely broadcast speech invited a wave of condemnations by the press and politicians, including Prime Minister Mackenzie King who warned that 'if an incident of this kind should occur again, the government of the country would certainly have no option but to make immediate representation to the government of the country concerned.'[83] The flap was hardly louder, however, than what followed the Royal Consul General's widely reported remarks, on 24 February 1935, to a banquet of the Sons of Italy at the Château Laurier in Ottawa, attended by approximately two hundred persons – including Italian consular officials from Montreal and Toronto and representatives from Italian organizations in Quebec, Ontario, and the United States – in which Petrucci is reported to have said: 'I can safely say to the Canadian citizens of Italian origin that to them is reserved the great task of explaining to their fellow citizens the real meaning of the Fascism of Mussolini so that it will be much easier for the Canadian people to adapt themselves gradually to the new economic and political system which is hardly avoidable.'[84]

Quite apart from Petrucci – who subsequently regretted his remarks and claimed misrepresentation – there were other Italians, scattered here and there, not content with merely importing Fascist regime loyalties into their ethnic community.[85] They entertained, instead, the notion – advertised by Adrien Arcand and other hard-core natives – that Fascism was exportable into the larger Canadian community. This is what Louis Meconi, the Windsor First World War veteran of the Italian and Canadian armies, probably had in mind when he set his Blueshirts drilling and marching. The Blueshirt march halted quickly enough, and Meconi returned to politics within his own ethnic community in Windsor.[86] There were others, however, who in subsequent years were attracted to the notion of creating, or joining, a broad-based native Fascist movement. When Mr Whittaker formed his Nationalist Party in Winnipeg, he allowed for an Italian section – membership, if any, unknown – headed by a local Italian who seemed, for a while, disposed to flit and tinker with the Whittaker organization. Adrien Arcand's party, according to some RCMP reports, had a few Italian members, several of whom, it was reported, advocated methods that were employed 'by the first Fascists in Italy' for the 'purpose of making the Party known as something for the enemies to fear.'[87] Arcand's audiences sometimes included Italians, as well as others, and, as the *Montreal Standard* suggestively reported, the party section of St Denis County was located, in 1938, next door to the Casa d'Italia.[88]

All of this, however, amounted to little more than a tiny and inconsequential participation. By all accounts, no Italian served in an executive position in the NSCP or its successor, and whatever tiny membership existed had, by the summer of 1938, by and large deserted. The overlap was negligible for several reasons. The Arcand movement was primarily Hitlerian, and the local pro-Fascist Italians looked exclusively to Rome for guidance. The advent of the Rome-Berlin axis was, for insecure immigrants, supportive of the home regime, more a problem than an opportunity for identification with native Fascist movements susceptible to a growing war scare and financed, in the case of the Arcand party – Petrucci believed – by the German government. Far from encouraging local participation in native Fascist movements, the Rome authorities, the consuls, and pro-Fascist local notables were firmly opposed to linkages with fringe parties whose dubious, if not pariah, status threatened their search for the legitimacy and influence to press the cause of the Fascist Motherland. Contributing to Petrucci's shunning of the Arcand Party was its violent anti-Semitism which, the Royal Consul appreciated as early as 1934, was likely to provoke strong responses from the Jewish communities of Toronto and Montreal as well as Protestants and 'Franc-Maçons.'[89] 'In order to stay in our own camp,' Brigidi informed Montreal Fascists at a meeting in June 1934, in which membership cards were distributed, 'the Fascists of Montreal must be an example to Canadian citizens, so that they may see how much good Fascists can do and follow us in our ideas. To put it in commercial terms, we have to present our merchandise under the best possible label. No part should be taken in the internal politics of the country in which you live.'[90] Four years later, at a monthly meeting of Montreal's Mile End *fascio* section, the fiduciary Signor Corbo repeated the message. He asked the 'comrades to be disciplined,'

L'Italia Nuova reported, 'to rigidly observe the rules that Fascists abroad must adhere to and above all to abstain from taking part in any way in the Fascist movement in Canada.'[91]

While the Italians did, by and large, stay away from Farr, Whittaker, and Arcand – whose *L'Illustration Nouvelle*, like Paul Bouchard's *La Nation*, was used strictly for propaganda purposes – they were hardly impervious to the pressures of a shifting public opinion dictated largely by external events. *Fasci* and *dopolavoros*, the mutual-aid associations under Fascist influence, were mainly self-contained organizations independent of and distant from the mock legions and fantasy cells of Adrien Arcand. They remained ornate ethnic formations whose propaganda activities, as an RCMP report acknowledged, in November 1937, did 'not appear to apply beyond the immediate precincts' of the Little Italies.[92] Their activities were open and legal, a matter that Petrucci was quite concerned and insistent about, in his contacts with R.B. Bennett and Hugh Guthrie, the Conservative minister of justice, who, like his Liberal predecessor in the mid-depression years, was prepared to accept the Blackshirts as quaint ethnics, rather than seditious conspirators plotting, in secret organizations, the overthrow of the Canadian state.[93]

Events overseas, however, threatened ominous changes in opinion and policy. The Ethiopian war, the Spanish intervention, the Rome-Berlin axis beginning in October 1936, in which Italy played second fiddle – explained away by Mussolini as 'armed peace' – Italy's Prussianization and anti-Semitic turn, the Albanian invasion, the Anschluss and Pact of Steel of May 1939 – which gave the Nazis a free hand in Eastern Europe – dramatically shifted domestic opinion in Canada. Respected up to the mid-1930s as an Italian patriot, inspired leader, and economic innovator, Italy's dictator was metamorphosed, at the decade's end, into an inept racist and imperialist. With the axis consolidated and Fascist armies roaming across Europe, the 'Giovinezza' and 'Tarantella' no longer sold in Canada, to borrow Brigidi's terminology, 'under the best possible label.' More misguided patriots and fellow travellers than ideological militants, Canada's Fascist and pro-Fascist notables were making good time, as the guns of war boomed in distant Europe, along the bleak road to Petawawa.

9

Brethren

I left Germany in 1929 ... things were not good then in that country, but prosperous times were in evidence here. Now it is the other way around. How can we help but respect Hitler, who has done so much for our Fatherland. During years of depression he has built up the country until now there is no unemployment and wages are high.

Rudolph Boege, Toronto *Globe and Mail*, 17 April 1939

I sure like Hitler because he has done something. If every politician did as much for his country as Hitler has done, the world would be all right. I think it would be better for Canada if there was a Hitler here to put the young men to work.

Hans Schilling, *Winnipeg Free Press*, 22 July 1939

On the third anniversary of Reich Chancellor Adolf Hitler's assumption of power in Germany, a large and enthusiastic meeting was held in the hall of the Harmonia Club, on Drummond Street, in the city of Montreal.[1] It was a lively, multimedia event, filled with warm effusions directed eastward, towards a Fatherland renewed and restored by a crazed ex-corporal and his avid henchmen. There was, on that chilled Montreal winter evening, harmony plenty at the Harmonia Club; *heils* and salutes galore; solemn renderings of 'Deutschland Über Alles' and the 'Horst Wessel'; flags and swastikas gaily displayed before a large portrait of Der Führer perched under an eagle; stirring phonograph music played, augmented by a large trumpet blaring introductory fanfares; a film screened, highlighting the visit of German youth from assorted countries, including Canada, to the Fatherland, where they attended camp and marvelled, on tour, at scenic wonders, the splendours of ancient cities, and awesome military exercises.

And there was enlightenment, served up by a pair of notables. The first was Consul General Ludwig Kempff, who reminded his audience, from a small flag-draped pulpit, that Hitler's revolution had restored national dignity and discipline, ended unemployment and class hatred, and created a new, strong, Germany committed to international order and peace. The tall, dark, and fluent second speaker was Karl Gerhard, who succinctly reviewed the triumphs of the Nazi movement and, like the consul general, reiterated the regime's desire for peace. Gerhard provided the evening's most poignant moment when he delivered an emotional tribute in memory of the late storm-trooper Karl Eberhart Maikowsky, felled in the line of duty, on the eve of Hitler's accession to office. 'The song then was "ich hat einen kamaraden," ' the *Montreal Gazette* reported. ' "I had a comrade." '[2]

Karl Gerhard was well suited to eulogize a dead Nazi. He was, after all, a blood brother of the defunct Mr Maikowsky, a member and operative of an insidious movement whose tentacles extended east, into the jumble of states and nationalities flanking the Soviet Union, and west, across the ocean into the Americas. In Hitler's trans-oceanic blitz, Canada was not neglected. Among the many organizations flourishing in Canada's scattered German communities during the mid-1930s were several plainly dedicated to advancing Hitler's cause, organizations favoured and, in the case of two, led by the mysterious Mr Gerhard, described by a *Gazette* reporter, at the Harmonia Club event, as a 'representative of the German press in Canada' and 'leader of the people of German citizenship here.'[3]

The Nazi push in Canada was spearheaded by a medley of agencies who targeted vulnerable clusters of a highly variegated German community. There were, at the time of Hitler's accession to power, approximately a half million Germans in Canada, scattered in communities from coast to coast. They came from diverse cultures and countries, and varied considerably in religious and occupational composition, degree of cultural cohesion, extent of assimilation, and receptivity to the *Völkisch* messages insistently conveyed by the new Germany's propagandists. The Maritime Germans – some of whom, in Halifax and Lunenberg County, traced their origins to eighteenth-century British-sponsored settlements – remained, overall, small in number, assimilated, and unreceptive to overseas messages. Of Quebec's 10,600 Germans, over 5,000 were settled in Montreal, which contained the highest percentage in any city of Canada of German Nationals linked by citizenship, if not loyalty, to the Fatherland.[4] The use of Montreal's port by German ships and businessmen, and the location there of the offices of the German general consulate, created, for Canada's Nazis and pro-Nazis, some reasonable opportunities for intrigue and propaganda. In Ontario, the major concentration was in the southwest: in Toronto, which counted 10,000 Germans in 1931, and, above all, in and around Waterloo County, which, in 1871, accounted for 115,000 of Ontario's 158,000 Germans.[5] Included in Ontario's flourishing post-Confederation German community were descendants of American loyalist émigés and dissenting religious sectarians known as the Pennsylvania Germans, few of whom were exposed to the influences of modern German Nationalist thought.[6] The Ontario community was augmented in pre- and post-Confederation decades by renewed flows from varied places – inside and outside Germany – and developed a lively array of schools, churches, social associations, and German-language newspapers. Pre–First World War school language restrictions, however, together with the insistent effects of economic integration, social assimilation – and the surge of anti-German hysteria and repressions during the Great War, which contributed to the disappearance of the German-language press – resulted, by 1930, in a substantial decline in traditional culture and identification[7] and a corresponding chilliness to *Völkisch* calls for cultural renewal or identification with a distant Fatherland.

The western situation, with the possible exception of British Columbia, was different. British Columbia's Germans composed the
largest non–Ango-Saxon group in the province, congregated mainly
in the Okanagan and Vancouver, and included, in the pre–First
World War years, a prominent élite of businessmen and social notables, some with aristocratic pedigrees and imperial connections.[8] The
western prairie provinces had their own urban clusters, in cities like
Winnipeg, Calgary, Edmonton, and Regina. But they included, as
well, when the Nazis gained power in Germany, a substantial rural
sector, peopled by relatively recent immigrants drawn mainly from
lands outside of Germany who had been exposed, unlike Ontario's
older communities, to the ideological influences of modern German
nationalism. Catholics and Lutherans from the United States and
Central and Eastern Europe, including Poland, Romania, and parts
of the Austro-Hungarian Empire, settled, along with Mennonites
from Russia, in discrete rural blocs, communities insulated from the
assimilating effects of urban environments and exposed – perhaps
to a greater extent than the more urbanized and industrialized eastern Canadian Germans – to the hardships of economic depression.
The western rural settlers arrived in waves, beginning in the early
1870s, and, by 1931, counted 271, 352, nearly 60 per cent of a national German population of 473,544.

Though western Canada's first- and second-generation rural immigrant settlers were overwhelmingly ethnic Germans, religiously
divided, from diverse countries of origin, they were not lacking in
group consciousness or cultural identity. The proliferation of German-language schools, churches, and newspapers throughout Manitoba, Saskatchewan, and Alberta reflected and reinforced the cultural identity of the settlers, many of whom had been victimized in their
home countries in Central and Eastern Europe by oppressive national ethnic majorities. In response, they developed, and carried with
them to the farms, hamlets, and villages of Canada's prairies, the
comforting notion of a German *Volk*, rooted in tradition and language, soil and spirit, which transcended the artificial boundaries of
states and bound Germans everywhere together, a notion cultivated
and exploited, in the decades preceding Hitler's accession to office,

by a host of cultural agencies in Germany and the settlers' countries of origin.

Under Hitler, the *Völkisch* – and National Socialist – messages were beamed with increased intensity by diverse agencies to countries with German minorities, including Canada. The North German Lloyd Steamship Line, Leipzig Fair, and German State Railway offices served as clearing houses for cultural and political propaganda. Hamburg's Fichtebund served the Canadian market, along with Rolf Hoffman's Munich-based foreign press service.[9] The Berlin-based Volksbund für das Deutschtum im Ausland (VDA) – League for Germans Abroad – employed agents to collect information on Canadian Germans, subsidized local German schools with textbooks, replenished libraries with appropriate literature, and enlightened its Canadian readership about Germany and Germans abroad through its monthly *Der Volksdeutsche.* 'One can look confidently across the Atlantic Ocean to Canada,' VDA head Hans Steinacher informed an agency meeting in 1934, 'and witness there an advancing German movement, which is driven forward by inner commitment and sustained by outward support.'[10] In competition with the League for Germans Abroad was the Deutsches Auslands-Institut or German Foreign Institute (DAI), based in Stuttgart, the City of Germans Abroad. Though dedicated to serving Germans abroad through sponsorship of 'volkish-cultural activity,' the DAI, as historian Jonathan Wagner pointed out, 'would nearly always support National Socialist goals.'[11] Like its competitive VDA counterpart, the DAI collected, published, and distributed, in yearbooks, periodicals, and monographs, data on Germans abroad, including Canada, and recruited writers, like the violently anti-Semitic Russian Mennonite Dr Walter Quiring, to contribute articles to German-Canadian newspapers. Occasional DAI-funded tours to Canadian-German communities were undertaken by visiting luminaries like C.R. Henning, who concluded that Canadian Germans 'have grasped the essence of Volk unity,'[12] and Karl Götz, the schoolteacher and writer sent out to western Canada in 1936 to 'lead the distant cousins back to an appreciation of their Volk via the path of party ideology.'[13]

Complementing and assisting the agencies' cultural and political propaganda activities were several exotic organizations that, in the mid-1930s, sprouted in the Canadian-German community. When Hitler came to power, there were, in Canada, scattered here and there, German nationals who happened to belong to the Nazi Party. With the revolution at home in full swing, others joined, and a branch of NSDAP, affiliated with its foreign organization, led by E. Wilhelm Bohle, appeared in Canada, with locals, or *Ortsgruppen*, each of which contained no more than twenty to twenty-five members, formed in Montreal, Toronto, Kitchener, Winnipeg, Regina, and Edmonton.[14] Only German nationals of 'Aryan descent and free from Jewish or coloured racial taint' qualified as members, who swore 'absolute allegiance to Adolf Hitler and implicit obedience to him and the leader appointed over me by him.'[15] Successful applicants received, from Munich, a small, fifty-page booklet, on the cover of which was displayed the Third Reich's emblem, an eagle grasping a swastika. The membership booklet included a personal data sheet, photograph, pages for stamps, a foreword by Adolf Hitler, and, inside the back cover, advertisements for *Mein Kampf* and the party newspaper, the *Völkische Beobachter.*

Canada's tiny Nazi Party remained, throughout the 1930s, a tightly knit cadre organization with a membership somewhere between one hundred and two hundred persons. The membership list and meetings, at which copies of the information bulletin *Mitteilungsblatt,* published in Berlin, were read and discussed, were secret. Contacts with German consular officials or various semi-official agencies, such as the German State Railways or the North German Lloyd Steamship Line, or occasional German-owned commercial enterprises were discreetly maintained. Occasional distinguished visitors were entertained, like William Grohte – an executive member of the NSDAP's foreign section and trusted assistant of E.W. Bohle – who visited Canada in the spring of 1935. Study and public-speaking training sessions were undertaken by members who convened, as an RCMP report concluded, 'for the purpose of studying party literature and assuring each other of their undying faith in the Fuehrer and his methods.'[16] Hitler's birthday or the anniversary of the founding of the Third Reich was the occasion for party-sponsored celebrations attended by representatives from kindred organizations. About 250 people, for example, participated in the Montreal celebration of Hitler's fiftieth birthday, on 20 April 1939, an elaborate event staged at the Harmonia Club, whose walls were draped with a large Hitler portrait, a multitude of swastikas, and a single, lonely Union Jack. Musical entertainment was provided by an orchestra, which struck up a solemn march when the honoured guests entered, followed by fifteen guards of honor dressed in dark trousers, white shirts, black ties, and swastika armbands. There were salutes and 'Sieg Heils' at the NSDAP's gala event, spirited singing of the German National and Nazi anthems, a concluding dance, and a stirring address from the NSDAP Eastern District leader Dannenberg, who declared 'our Fuehrer guards everything that is of benefit to the German Empire and will destroy everything that stands in its way. The time will come when not only the German people but the world will acknowledge National Socialism as a necessary existence for the benefit of the German people.'[17]

Among the National Socialist organizations thought beneficial by men like Dannenberg to German nationals in Canada was the German Labour Front (DAF), which serviced the German workers of 'brain and fist.' A mass organization controlled by the Nazi Party, the German Labour Front – headed by Dr Robert Ley – established units abroad, including Canada, where, beginning in 1936, Ortsgruppen and Stutzpunkte were established in Montreal, Toronto, Kitchener, Waterloo, Winnipeg, Regina, Edmonton, Vancouver, Vernon, and Kelowna. The Montreal Ortsgruppe, with 165 members, and Toronto's, with 95, were the largest in the national organization – headquartered in Montreal – of approximately 500 people. The DAF was a broader, more inclusive, organization than the party.[18] Its officials were drawn from the NSDAP and members – exclusively German Nationals – conformed, according to an RCMP report, 'with the German law promulgated on September 15, 1935, ie, the so-called Aryan Law, which stipulates that in order to be regarded as an Aryan German one must be able to show that his ancestry has been free from Jewish blood for as far back as January 1, 1800.'[19] Front members enjoyed some mutual-aid benefits – including insurance, relief assistance, and discounted trips home – participated in education and public-speaking training sessions, and carried around a little thirty-two-page book with forewords by Hitler and Ley and a gearwheel – centred by a swastika – on the cover. Social and recreational affairs – parties, banquets, dances, sing-songs, and film showings – cemented relationships and organized the members' leisure time. 'Then there were the sports activities,' a RCMP report declared, 'including target shooting, a bit of drilling. The usual Nazi claptrap was much in evidence at such affairs, white shorts with Sam Browne belts and swastika armbands, German flags and Nazi salutes and heiling of Hitler, renditions of the Horst Wessel Lied and so forth.'[20] Along with the recreation and fellowship came doses of propaganda supplied free with membership, carried in journals like *Arbeitertum* – a DAF magazine – trades magazines for individual employments, and other general periodicals aimed at Germans abroad.[21]

While the Nazi Party and German Labour Front provided warm social and ideological havens for German nationals resident in Canada, they were hardly suitable vehicles for reaching the broader masses of naturalized German Canadians. Both, after all, were direct extensions of, and organizationally tied to, the controlling political institutions of a fatherland increasingly embroiled in international controversy. Marketing the new Germany to acculturated locals required a different sort of instrument, a league, or bund, with an acceptable indigenous façade. Developments below the border, in the United States, provided both impetus and a negative example. Soon after Hitler gained power, pockets of smitten German nationals in the United States – mostly recent immigrants – began collecting around a former Bavarian Seventh-Day Adventist Pastor, in a Nazi support organization known as 'Friends of the Hitler Movement' and later as 'Friends of New Germany.'[22] The leader, Heinz Spanknoebel – a war veteran and German national who lived in a 'Hitlerheim' in Detroit and wore a toothbrush moustache and brown shirt, with a swastika emblem on its sleeve – was fond of theatre and quickly interested the American authorities. Spanknoebel was eventually indicted, and fled the country, but not before his organization – which evolved into the provocative German-American Bund – responded to feelers from interested Canadians. W.B. Schwab of Winnipeg, among others, corresponded with representatives of the America's New Germany Friends and was assured by Spanknoebel's lieutenant, Hans Strauss, that Canada would be designated as 'a territory of its own' whose locals were prepared to join 'the fight for real freedom and not for so-called democracy in the hands of a few capitalists and Jews.'[23] It was not long before Canadian Friends of New Germany began organizing in Winnipeg, Toronto, Kitchener, Montreal, Waterloo, Kelowna, and Vancouver. With several of the leading American colleagues discredited, or departed, however, a quick name change was effected and something called the German League of Canada came into existence, the founders of which were a group of Waterloo residents – Ernst Kopf, Oscar Geisler, and Karl Gerhard, who, in February 1934, petitioned the secretary of state for a charter. A year later, after some jockeying and shuffling, a second petition was filed for the incorporation of a new society, the Canadian Society for German Culture, Inc. – Deutscher Bund, Canada. The petitioners in this instance were a trio of Montrealers, all of whom had served on the executive of the Montreal local chapter of the Friends of the New Germany: W.K. Hess, an accountant for a German-owned firm producing 'sensitive paper for blueprints and photographs'; Alfred Alius, a floor manager in the same company, subsequently active in the German Labour Front; and the mysterious, peripatetic, Karl Gerhard, a recent arrival in Montreal from London and Kitchener, Ontario.[24]

Of the three, Gerhard was the major player in an organization that spared no effort, until the outbreak of the war, in mobilizing support among ethnic compatriots for the New Germany of Adolf Hitler. Tall, dark, mustachioed, and affable, Gerhard was a young man when he emigrated to Canada in 1930, a mere twenty-three years of age; a product of Waldfischbach, a small town in the Palatinate; and son – or so he is reported to have claimed – of a German army general killed on the eve of the armistice.[25] At the age of sixteen, he participated in the massive resistance campaign against the French occupation of the Ruhr and, several years later, joined a small rightist party that was soon absorbed by Hitler's NSDAP. When he settled, in the spring of 1930 – with the assistance of the Lutheran Immigration Board in Montreal – in Eden, Ontario, Karl Gerhard was a card-carrying member of the Nazi Party.

In and around the fields and gardens of Eden, Ontario, the affable Gerhard worked as a labourer on tobacco farms, in Eden and

Otterville, and as a German instructor in Tillsonburg, where he sharpened his skill in English, one of the seven languages he claimed to have spoken. He volunteered as a Boy Scout leader and was resident for a while at Huron College, an affiliate of the University of Western Ontario. At Western, he worked briefly as a teaching assistant in the German department, an appointment that freed him to use, as convenience dictated, the title of 'professor' in subsequent years.

By several accounts, Karl Gerhard was both affable and flamboyant, and raised a few eyebrows among curious locals. He claimed to be a lieutenant in the German Army and made no secret of his admiration of Adolf Hitler. Portraits of Ludendorff, Hindenberg, and other German notables graced the walls of his room. He owned a Nazi uniform, wore shirts – and shorts – embroidered with swastikas, and came and went well equipped with expensive field-glasses, cameras, and, on occasion, a pair of revolvers, one of which was strapped to his leg, the other to his waist. In the fall of 1934, Gerhard moved to Montreal, where he boarded, with McGill students, at the family residence of Otto Buerger. 'In 1934 ... there came to the Buerger family to board a Carl (or Karl) Gerhardt [sic] from Germany,' Colonel E.J. Mooney informed the Department of National Defence, following receipt of a report from Ronald Taylor, who rented a room with Gerhard at the Buergers. 'His mail came addressed Dr. or Prof. etc. The Buerger family informed the students that he was Prof. of Philosophy at McGill. Gerhardt has a large suite of three rooms, dresses like Bond Street and seems to have unlimited funds. For a time the students did not bother much about Gerhardt but as time went on Gerhardt installed a large motion picture machine with sound attachments in rooms and gave parties to a large number of Germans. The students were at times distracted by clapping and speeches following movie shows ... he received a great deal of mail from all points of Canada – Vancouver to Halifax – made frequent visits to German Consul. Gerhardt was not attached to McGill in any capacity whatever. He receives at least 25 phone calls a day, is absent from the boarding house for short periods, quite often, lives very expensively.'[26]

Gerhard's absences and expenses were not unrelated to the several tasks he had undertaken as leader and unofficial ambassador of the Nazi Party in Canada. He received and distributed bundles of propaganda from the DAI and Goebbels's propaganda ministry, and supplied them, in turn, with information 'on the state of the Germans in Canada, on the cultural, political and economic development of the country, and on its (Canada's) position vis-à-vis Germany.[27] He addressed various German community groups, as well as Canadian organizations like the United Service Institute of Ottawa, whose members heard, in 1935, a glowing account, from Professor Karl Gerhard, of Hitler's defeat of German communism and the beauty of labour camps where young men lived 'a very happy and healthy life, working four to six hours a day and studying two hours.'[28] As national Bund leader, he undertook, in 1934 and 1935, promotional and organizational tours across the country. District and local groups were formed in various provinces, workshops held, leaders – regional, local, and provincial – appointed, and speeches of enlightenment about the new Germany were delivered to meetings in various places, including the farm of Herr Schuette – ten miles from the city of Regina – where, on Tuesday, 21 August 1934, local members of the Deutscher Bund, Regina, collected for a national celebration. 'It was very impressive when about ten o'clock at night the great bonfire was lit and all those present stood in a circle around the fire and sang German folk songs,' Regina's *Der Courier* reported. 'Herr Prof Karl Gerhard of Waterloo, the Dominion Leader of the Deutsche Bund in Canada, then gave a long address in which he explained the meaning of this celebration and the meaning of the youth movement in Germany stating that it called all members of the German people here in this country to unity with the German people and mentioned the homeland in several heartfelt words.'[29]

In subsequent evocations of the wonders of the Fatherland, Gerhard did not rely exclusively on distant impressions or propaganda leaflets sent through the mails by diplomatic or German shipping channels. Twice, in 1934–5 he visited Germany, met with officials of the party's foreign organization, attended rallies, and enrolled in party-run courses. 'At the Erlangen meeting,' Jonathan Wagner reported, 'Gerhard and his fellow participants were addressed by Bohle; they heard lectures from the various departmental experts; they met for discussions with A.O. officials in charge of their section of the

A.O. Finally, Gerhard's appearance at the Nazi party rally that followed closely the Erlangen assembly provided him with more ritual, ideology, and the Führer himself.'[30]

With his contacts firmed and national socialist spirit replenished, Karl Gerhard returned, in the early fall of 1935, to his dual position of leadership in Canada's Nazi party and the Bund – but not for long. Any inflated estimates he had of his role of Führer of Canada's Nazi or pro-Nazi movements were rudely shaken by a spate of struggles and intrigues. The pressure came from Consul General Ludwig Kempff, an old career diplomat who resented the attempt of Gerhard – the NSDAP's Auslands organization's man in Canada – to assert the primacy of the party over state representation in the Canadian jurisdiction. Kempff, unlike Gerhard, was concerned with the need – in conformity with the new party policy formulated in 1935 – to formally separate the party in Canada from the Bund, whose membership, Kempff maintained, should be restricted to naturalized German Canadians.[31] Kempff's antipathy to Gerhard – which inspired rigorous interventions with the home government – was shared by dissidents in Kitchener and elsewhere who accused the bogus professor of misrepresentation, self-aggrandizement, and financial mismanagement. His opponents won the day. By the end of 1936, Karl Gerhard had resigned his positions as both party and bund leader.[32]

Though Karl Gerhard lapsed into a decent obscurity – interrupted briefly during Canada's war scare in 1938 by allegations he was Hitler's führer-designate for Canada – the Bund developed into an active and noisy organization dedicated to internal cultural and educational work, and more important, to diffusing propaganda and mobilizing support, within the German and host communities, for the New Germany of Adolf Hitler. Bund members were expected, as the organization's application form indicated, to offer the hand of friendship to 'comrades ... undeservedly' in need; to work to 'improve and preserve the inheritance of our fathers'; to respect the laws and 'not to mix in the politics of the adopted land'; to maintain 'cultural connections with the fatherland, and thereby build a bridge between the old and new homeland.'[33] But they were political missionaries as well, whose duty it was, according to Gerhard, writing in a publication in Germany, 'to make comprehensible to all members of the Volk the two words national and social.'[34] Bundists were 'national comrades (German Aryans) who recognized the ideals of the New Germany,' and were ready to 'impart the ideas of our new view of life in impartial and cool explanations to our national comrades and host.' On the brown cover of the thirty-two-page membership booklet of the Deutscher Bund Canada, which contained the members' personal data, constitution, and pages for stamps, was a large maple leaf – inside the maple leaf, a swastika.[35]

Created and fashioned into a Nazi support organization, the Bund was, understandably, hierarchically organized. At the top was a national leader based in Montreal – where the headquarters was located – and an executive committee. Next in line of authority were the appointed leaders of the three main divisions: the eastern district, comprising Quebec and the Maritimes; the central district of Ontario; and the western district, including the four western provinces. There were further divisions, into subdistricts, and local groups called *Ortsgruppen* and *Stutspunkte*, with their own officials appointed, like the subdistrict leaders, from above. The organization's statutes allowed for auxiliary subgroups, sports or cultural, created 'according to necessity by the local leaders' with no constitutional status.[36]

With the organizational campaign in full swing by 1935, the Bund diffused into vulnerable crevices of the Canadian German community. There was little support in Quebec, outside of Montreal, home to one of the Bund's largest *Ortsgruppe* and seat of both the eastern district and national headquarters. Both of Gerhard's successors as national leaders – Lothar Pfau and Otto Thierbach – were Montreal residents. Ontario counted several Bund locals, with the largest in Toronto and Kitchener. Its big Bund cheese was Toronto resident Martin Kaiser, an Austrian who immigrated in 1926, was naturalized in 1931, and served as both district and subdistrict leader. Kitchener's boss, of a local that counted ninety members in 1937, was Ernst Woelfle, a loud anti-Semite and tiresome 'expert' on race and genealogy, who fled to Germany in 1938.[37]

The Bund enjoyed considerably greater support in the west, where locals were scattered across the four provinces, with the greatest concentration in Saskatchewan. British Columbia, it appeared, had a small but vibrant Nazi and pro-Nazi scene in which several Bund locals participated.[38] Locals of the Nazi party and German labour front, which drew from the small pool of German nationals employed in a newly established consular office or in shipping and related businesses, were joined by a pair of Bund locals and other organizations to produce what one author described as a 'fairly ghettoised' German community, 'a type of "Naziburg" within the city of Vancouver,'[39] whose centre was a common 'German House' on Main Street, in the core of the major area of German settlement. Outside of Vancouver, there was some support in Kelowna, where an ex–German army veteran doubled as local Bund president and DAF leader; and in Osoyoos where a prominent orchardist became district leader in 1938.[40] Alberta's diffuse community included several locals: in North Mark, Dapp, Vegreville, and Calgary and Edmonton, where Paul Abele, proprietor of the 'People's Drug Store' and president of the German-Canadian Alliance of Alberta, served as district leader. There were two locals in Manitoba, both in Winnipeg's multi-ethnic north end, led at one time or another by a Carl Schiffers and A. Brahaus, employed by the omnipresent North German Lloyd Company.[41] The Bund's largest provincial membership was in Saskatchewan, home of the largest concentration in Canada of recent German immigrants and the highest number of Germans, in relation to the general provincial population. Saskatchewan counted, at one time or another, more than 40 local groups – about 57 per cent of the total number of Bund groups in that country – totalling between 800 and 1,000 members out of a national membership that likely did not exceed 2,000,[42] Included among its leaders was a solid core of pro-Nazis, including a prominent real estate and insurance agent who headed the Leader local, served on the dominion executive, sometimes organized for the Canadian Union of Fascists, and received through the mails and distributed newspapers like Streicher's Der Stürmer, a Regina brewer, naturalized in 1934; a former member of the SS and NSDAP in Germany, who worked as a baker and bartender and headed the Bund's Saskatoon local; and a prominent activist who greeted Hitler's occupation of the Rhineland with the following declaration: 'The sun has again risen in the German Heaven. Honour and manly courage again count for something ... our duty is to make ourselves ready for that hour, to make ourselves familiar with the world of ideas of the Third Reich. Fellow countrymen of German blood, fulfil this duty and join the German Bund, Canada.'[43]

The call of the Bund's leaders was heeded by anywhere between 1,200 and 2,000 Germans across the country, drawn, as Wagner concluded from biographical samples of members, from farm, artisan, small proprietor, or other lower professional vocations.[44] Bundists tended to be young – under forty-five years of age – recent immigrants, relatively unassimilated, and badly wounded by a depressed economy, a condition that assisted in colouring the grass green in their idealized Fatherland. The majority collected in the western provinces – with the highest concentration in the rural areas of Saskatchewan – and were drawn from post-1900 settlers. In the east, they concentrated in urban centres, like Kitchener–Waterloo, Toronto, and St Catharines, also among recent immigrants. 'The Bundists youth, their status as unassimilated immigrants, their petty bourgeois values, and their relative poverty,' Wagner concluded,

go far to explain their susceptibility to radicalism in general and to National Socialism in particular. Young and unassimilated, they had no vested interest in Canadian society, and the problems of economic adjustment ordinarily faced by immigrants were compounded by the Depression. In short, Bundists were an unsatisfied, fearful, and restless lot. To such a group, the Nazi racial ideology of a Volksgemeinschaft (community of the Volk) appeared to offer security through unity in the Volk. By presenting a simplistic explanation for the economic crisis – as being due to the 'Jewish world conspiracy' – National Socialism provided the Bundists with a convenient rationale for their economic troubles. Moreover, in insisting that it was a credo for action, the Nazi movement appealed especially to the young and unsettled. Finally, the Bund's strong anti-communist emphasis catered to the social fears of a group which perceived proletarianization as an ever-present threat.'[45]

Whatever threats, or insecurities, Bundists felt were alleviated by membership in an organization whose ideology and politics were firmly embedded in a web of culture, recreation, education, and fraternity. The Bund was a social and cultural, as well as political, organization, whose members, on occasion, wore armbands decorated with swastikas. It offered some aid and relief to indigent members, sponsored winter help programs in several locations, and urged, in its strident four-year program, Canadian German employers and managers to hire local German workers. For kinsmen, and kinswomen, in need of fellowship, ethnic affirmation, and cultural enrichment, it offered pleasant opportunities.[46] Bund locals held regular meetings, at least twice a month, at which business was transacted. In between there were sports events, picnics, Christmas celebrations, discussion groups, lectures, and film screenings often held in homes, or headquarters like the one in Winnipeg, on William Avenue, which a *Winnipeg Free Press* journalist found 'clean as a whistle' and decorated with 'two Nazi flags with red fields, white circles and black swastikas' and a picture of Adolf Hitler 'looking fierce and mystical all at once.'[47] Bund libraries in places like Edmonton, Winnipeg, and Deer Creek, Saskatchewan, were well stocked with books, periodicals, and newspapers. Children of Bundists were enrolled in schools and youth groups and, during summer, sent off to camps in Marquette, Manitoba, or Maple, Ontario. Bund women formed their own affiliates in places like Regina, where the president of the local auxiliary – who visited Germany in 1934 and attended, in Erfurt, a conference of the Nazi party's foreign organization – entertained a succession of prominent visiting German journalists and officials.

While the Bund complemented, or competed with other German associations in larger communities, in remote, rural areas, it sometimes became the hub and centre of community activity. In the midst of the wild bush and hard terrain around Loon River, 186 miles north of Saskatoon, there settled, in 1929, a group of twenty families, mainly from Thuringia, in East Germany. Life was hard for the Loon River Germans, most of whom had been artisans and merchants in the old country. Devoid of agricultural experience, the pioneer homesteaders faced cruel conditions of drought, freezing winters, remoteness, and collapsed prices during the depression. Lonely homesteaders stuck in a chilled corner of the remote North, they suffered woefully and found solace in the local Bund, which linked

them to fellow Germans at home and abroad and provided enlightenment, through meetings and readings, about the machinations of
Canada's 'Jewish dominated government' and beauties of Hitler's
New Germany.[48] By 1939, the machinations, the suffering, their
neighbours' hostilities, and Hitler's call became overwhelming and
the Loon River Bundists returned to Germany, hoping to settle together there in a rural area in the eastern lands. Home, instead,
became Weimar, whose Fritz Saubel armament factory provided the
economic – and spiritual – sustenance absent in rural, arcadian Saskatchewan.[49]

Exposure, in Canada, to the beauties and bounties of the New
Germany was hardly limited to the naïve and vulnerable homesteaders of Loon Lake. The Bund leaders' offers of culture and fellowship
did not come unadorned. Ostensibly a social and cultural organization, duly registered under the laws of Canada, the Bund, in reality,
was an agency of enlightenment invested with a high mission, as Karl
Gerhard informed his Nazi superiors, of making 'comprehensible to
all members of the Volk the two words national and social.'[50] Culture,
nostalgia, and entertainment were served up, in large dollops, at
Bund events. The main offering, however, was something else: plate-
fuls of propaganda directed at both members and the larger German
community.

With the New Germany's propaganda machines humming at full
speed, there were piles of enlightenment around, and Bundists
gorged on it. They heard lectures about Hitler's genius, Horst
Wessel's life and death, putsch martyrs, the Fatherland's great economic and cultural awakening. The mysteries of race and genealogy, Bolshevism and Judaism, were unravelled in numerous lectures
and study sessions by men like Ernst Woelfle, the Kitchener–Waterloo Bund leader who reminded the German that he was 'soldierly,
heroic, idealistic and sociable,' while the Jew was 'unsoldierly, cowardly, materialistic and parasitic.[51] 'We carry the sign of day, the swastika, the symbol of the sun,' Woelfle concluded, 'while the Jew bears
the star, the sign of night.'[52]

Lectures by the likes of Woelfle were only one source of propaganda. Bundists were exposed to Nazi-produced propaganda films, like
Riefenstahl's *Triumph des Willens*, made available by consular officials,

or by itinerant propagandists like Franz Straubinger, a smooth-talking Bavarian who emigrated to Canada in 1929, at the age of twenty-four, and quickly immersed himself in the arts, including theatre, and cultural organization. A Nazi-party member, Straubinger visited Germany in 1934, where he cultivated contacts with various propaganda agencies, including Rolf Hoffman's foreign press office in Munich. Back in Canada, Straubinger busied himself with journalism and cultural and political organization in Saskatchewan and Ontario – where he served as president and secretary of the United German League of Ontario – and with the distribution and screening of films to Bundists and others. According to a RCMP report, Straubinger was a man with

> many irons in the fire. By profession he is a painter, but does not seem to have spent much time at that. He busied himself with collecting Canadian newspaper clippings about Germany and sending them to the German authorities. He gathered information on Jewish activities in Canada and forwarded reports to Munich. He was correspondent for the *Deutsche Zeitung*; he was a member of the DAF and he was an official of the Deutsche Arbeitsgemeinschaft of Ontario. Straubinger's main interest, however, lay in exhibiting German films. He imported sixteen mm films ... furnished his own movie camera and was his own operator. He travelled extensively up and down central and western Canada giving performances in German communities before well attended audiences [*sic*]. As to the films, they were of a variety, ranging from comedy to pure Nazi propaganda, but they were generally well received by the audiences, and often with enthusiasm.[53]

Equally warmly received were the celebrations commemorating important national socialist events and the youth camps and schools designed to 'form and influence' the minds of the young and generate 'respect and love for German culture.'[54] Hitler's birthday on 20 April, his assumption of the chancellorship on 20 January, and the Day of National Labour, 1 May, were occasions across the country for Bundists, alone or jointly with others, to *heil* and *sieg*, wave swastika flags, sing the 'Horst Wessel,' and, not least, hear speeches from notables describing the miracle of New Germany. Summer camps in Manitoba were rustic havens for Bund youth to learn about the wonders of woodcraft, the joys of greenery, and virtues of the Fatherland. 'Naturally, being German in spirit, we are National Socialists,' Ontario Bund leader Martin Kaiser explained to a Toronto journalist who appeared one day, as an uninvited guest, at the Waldfest Deutscher Bund camp, in a remote valley near Maple, 'but that doesn't mean we are less good Canadians. We are much better Canadians than the Reds. The Reds have their own camps, so why shouldn't we? All summer the camp has been giving children of German parents an outing, and at the same time instilling into them the ideals of the fatherland and the German language.'[55]

Schools sponsored by the Bund, separately or jointly with other organizations, and attended by students after hours, or on weekends, had a similar propaganda intent. German language, literature, and history were purveyed, together with enlightenment on the New Germany. According to the Bund's four-year plan, 'all parents who belong to the Deutscher Bund are obliged to send their children to German schools in order that the children be taught the German language and history,' and 'care should be taken that the teaching staff in the German schools are composed of National Socialists.'[56] Books and learning materials often came from Germany, via the consular authorities, who, in Winnipeg, sponsored a Christmas party for children and donated prizes for an essay contest.[57] In Ontario, the Deutsche Arbeitsgemeinschaft Ontario, which included the Bund and was run by Straubinger, suffused the curriculum of its sponsored German schools with fairy tales, past and present – Grimm and grim. 'In its description of the post-war period,' Wagner summarized the contents of an eighth-grade history course,'the course denounced the "forced peace of Versailles" and condemned "the slavery which international capitalists" imposed on Germany. Then ensued a consideration of the "fortunate destruction" of the Weimar Republic by the national socialist revolution. This in turn was followed by lessons describing not only Hitler, but his devoted followers, such as Horst Wessel, and Hermann Goering. The accomplishments of national socialism received elaborate attention, with lessons on Hitler's "saving of the economy" and his "restoration of the peasantry". The course ended with a detailed celebration of the Führer's restoring of the Saar, remilitarizing the Rhineland and returning Austria to the Reich.'[58] Whether similar snippets of enlightenment ever entered the curriculum of the Kissman rural school, west of Moosehorn, Manitoba, is unclear, but Bundists must surely have been pleased with some of the extracurricular activities there, during the 1938 Yuletide season, among students who collected 'two kazoos, aluminum pot lids, rattles, bells, tin cans,' and, apparently, a Jew's harp and formed 'a better rhythm band than they had in Moosehorn,' according to a local schoolteacher. In an area where, according to *Winnipeg Tribune* reporter Francis Stevens, Hitler was 'a hero to a large part of the German population,' band members wore swastika armbands, displayed a swastika banner, and called themselves 'Hitler's Melodiems.'[59] 'It was my own idea entirely and all in a spirit of good fun,' Miss Mildred Storsley, the Kissman teacher explained. 'I'm not a Nazi at all and I conduct my school in a proper Canadian way.'[60]

Among the Bundists' favourite propaganda outlets were the German Days or Tags sponsored by broad-based associations and coordinating committees in various provinces and held on weekends during the summer months.[61] Bundists were permeators, political activists concerned with selling the virtues of the Fatherland not only to their rank and file, but to the German community at large, through general propaganda, boring into existing organizations, creating new ones if necessary, and jointly sponsoring events amenable to pro-Nazi manipulation. The Deutsche Arbeitsgemeinschaft for Alberta was run by the pro-Nazi pharmacist Paul Abele and, later, by the Edmonton Bundist Otto Tangermann.[62] In Saskatchewan, the umbrella organization, the Deutsche Arbeitsgemeinschaft Saskatchewan (German Coordinating Committee of Saskatchewan) – on which the Bund had representation – was organized in 1934 by a prominent pro-Nazi Bundist. Manitoba's Deutsch-Kanadischen Bund von Manitoba included Bund representation and was subject to its influence. The United German Association of Quebec, formed in 1935, was headed by Lothar Pfau, who doubled as national and provincial leader of the Bund.[63] The German Alliance of Ontario was organized and headed by the Nazi Party member Franz Straubinger.[64] All of these organizations played major roles in the sponsorship and organization of the German Days, which served as important forums of cultural affirmation and, after 1933, political propaganda, within the Canadian German community.

Canada's German Days, during the 'dirty thirties,' were cheerful and lively affairs, chock full of clean fun. They provided entertainment and fellowship for thousands of participants in Saskatchewan, Alberta, and Manitoba, and later Ontario and Quebec, who, once a year, converged, sometimes via bad roads, from hundreds of kilometres away, 'primarily in order to have a reunion with countrymen from the old country, but also in order to experience the new feeling of community with so many other Germans.'[65] German Days included banquets and picnics in stadiums, pavilions, and parks, sunshine frolics on lawns and fields, film screenings, and Punch and Judy shows for tots, folk dancing and folk singing by quaint costumed ethnics, athletic contests and award ceremonies, exhibitions of arts and crafts 'made in the long winter months by German Canadians, often with great artistic skill.'[66] They provided opportunities to firm contacts and cement support for prominent politicians – municipal, provincial, and federal – who attended as guests, including Dr J.M. Uhrich, Saskatchewan's minister of health, and, in Ontario, W.D. Euler, the federal minister of trade and commerce (1935–40), who, at a pair of German Days in 1935 and 1937, in Kitchener, brought greetings from the prime minister, spoke glowingly of the promise of peaceful relations between Britain and Germany, condemned the Versailles Treaty, praised Canada's trade agreement (concluded in 1936) with Germany, denounced, according to the *Deutsche Zeitung*, alleged attempts made by 'a certain segment of the Canadian Press to poison public opinion and to stir up a racial hatred'[67] against Germans or German Canadians, and supported the passage of legislation banning the publication of hate literature.[68]

Few, if any, German Days passed without passionate affirmations of the Canadian Germans' culture and educational heritage and rights – sometimes expressed in resolutions – and, after 1933, the date of the beginning of the affairs' politicization, displays of warmth and affection for the New Germany.[69] German Days, and the resolutions passed by them, as historian Lehmann pointed out, gave 'an excellent picture' of both the 'cultural life and political aspirations of the German ethnic group.'[70] They alerted 'the German element' to the rights and duties arising from its cultural heritage, reminded governments 'by impressive demonstrations of the legitimate demands of the German ethnic group for the restoration of German language instruction in the public schools of school districts with a German majority,' refuted, 'with information and by protests in Canada, the dissemination of false and biased information about the German fatherland,' informed 'Canadian public opinion about the great foreign political questions affecting the German people,' and encouraged the adoption by fellow Canadians of 'an understanding tolerant attitude towards Germany.'[71]

It was the latter political and educational purposes of German Days that most interested the Bundists who permeated the coordinating and organization committees throughout the mid and late 1930s and, with their allies, succeeded in injecting pro-Nazi propaganda and symbolism into the proceedings of what had hitherto been primarily cultural events. Swastika flags and the 'Horst Wessel,' became as common ingredients at the numerous German Days during the mid-1930s as beer and bratwurst. With the resolutions and entertainment came an abundance of speeches from visiting dignitaries, including the pro-Nazi journalist Colin Ross who assured Saskatchewan's German Day participants in 1933 that Hitler was 'among the greatest men in history';[72] Carl Schiffers, Manitoba's Bund leader, who exulted in the unity, law, and order bestowed on Germany by the genius of Hitler;[73] and Wilhelm Rodde, the German consul in Winnipeg, whose concluding remarks in defence of the Fatherland brought the bulk of his audience of 5,000 to a standing salute at Winnipeg's River Park. 'In the thought of the united German people' Rodde thundered, 'we greet our fatherland by rising and saying, Greater Germany, its people and its leader, Adolf Hitler, Sieg Heil.'[74]

On, and between, German Days, the Bund relied on the friendly assistance of agencies and organizations based in and directed from the Fatherland. The tiny Nazi Party in Canada, an affiliate of the foreign organization in Germany, remained, it is true, formally separate from the Bund, serving, with the DAF, as the major social and political home of national socialists in Canada who retained their German citizenship, a separation that satisfied the policy preferences of the foreign-office section of the government and reinforced the Bund's claim to pure Canadian-German status. Yet the separation was never quite complete, and the RCMP, at least, remained convinced to the end that the Bund was 'an auxiliary' or 'extension' of the NSDAP, receiving 'its direction and guidance from the latter.'[75] Nazi locals in Canada co-sponsored events with the Bund, sent activists to Bund events as 'guests,' and, in several notable instances, shared prominent members well after Karl Gerhard had left the scene. The Bund's Kitchener–Waterloo leader Ernst Woelfle retained his party membership,[76] as did Bernhard Bott, the Bund's most prominent and militant national leader since the departure of Gerhard.[77]

Of considerable assistance to Bundists in spreading enlightenment were the several cultural and propaganda agencies based in the Fatherland. The Bund newspaper, whose editor was a paid agent of the VDA, carried ads of Hamburg's Fichtebund and copy from various agencies, including the Nazi Party's Munich-based foreign press office. Bund libraries and other propaganda distribution centres, like Montreal's German Book Exchange, were filled with books, pamphlets, periodicals, and newspapers supplied free from the Fatherland. According to one account, Stuttgart's Society for Germans Abroad supplied more than 8,000 books for schools and church libraries in Canada.[78] Slide projectors and other visual materials from Goebbels's propaganda ministry found their way, via the consular offices, into Bund and public meetings. For electronic buffs, the German shortwave radio provided warm updates on events in the Fatherland.[79]

Keeping Bundists and others abreast and inspired, it appears, was one of the several functions of Canada's German consular officials, who lent important, and sometimes blatant, ancillary support to the pro-Nazi propaganda. The consuls were a mixed bunch. Montreal consul Henry Eckner was a career diplomat who, according to a RCMP assessment, 'confined himself to his proper duties,' apart from a 'few pro-Nazi speeches at German gatherings.'[80] Vancouver's vice-consul, Wilhelm Herbert Mahler, a naturalized British subject of German birth, kept a low profile and, in the RCMP's view, did 'not seem to have amounted to much.'[81] Toronto's Karl Gustav Kropp, a Canadian resident for many years before being appointed consul, addressed meetings here and there, led an NSDAP local, and was considered 'fairly active' in support of the Nazi cause.[82] The consul general in Ottawa, from 1937 to 1939, Dr Erich Windels, 'confined himself strictly to diplomatic matters,' according to the RCMP, except for a brief lapse in January 1939, when he loudly demanded the banning from Canada of the Russian motion picture *Professor Mamlock*, which depicted Nazi persecution of a Jewish scientist.[83] Windels's predecessor, Dr Ludwig Kempff, who served as consul general between 1921 and 1937 – the year of his death – was more consequential. A lawyer by training, and a career diplomat and zealous bureaucrat, Kempff saw the light in 1933 and became a loyal servant of the New Germany. He supported the Bund's formation, addressed several of its meetings, defended Hitler at public meetings commemorating events back home, and, in 1933 at least, managed to pass on to a new convert, Adrien Arcand, propaganda literature.[84] But Kempff remained, withall, a keen civil servant and foreign-office loyalist who had reservations about party meddling, the consequences abroad of the Fatherland's anti-Semitic campaign, disruptions in older associations – like the Harmonia Club – caused by National Socialist loyalists, or the jurisdictional aggression of party zealots like Gerhard.

Ludwig Kempff's reticence was hardly shared by the zealous pair of consuls, based in Winnipeg, who looked after affairs in Canada's western region. A bombastic former SS man, member of Ribbentropp's Bureau, and intimate of the party's foreign organization head E.W. Bohle, Wilhelm Rodde earned a special distinction, during his year and a half service as consul in Winnipeg: he was, according to a RCMP assessment, 'the most undiplomatic diplomat on the Canadian scene.'[85] A coarse fanatic who became titular head of the Nazi Party in Canada, and moved its headquarters to Winnipeg, Rodde 'ranged up and down the Western Canada bullying, badgering, shouting and gesticulating in an effort to ram Nazism down the throats of his countrymen' and, perhaps, raise the morale of kinsmen who, he insisted at a Winnipeg gathering, were 'necessarily mentally depressed through ... systematic defamation of their homeland.'[86] Contributing to Rodde's own depressed – or manic – state was Winnipeg's Archbishop Sinnott, whose assertions, during a Christmas

sermon, that Germans celebrated a 'Christmas without Christ' invited a heated consular response;[87] and the Jews, whose exclusion from
Winnipeg's Waspish Winter Club Rodde enthusiastically applauded.
'The more Jews that come here,' he wrote a colleague, 'the more
they [Canadians] will understand us. I only hope that Canada receives a good supply of these mongrels.'[88] In the meanwhile, Rodde
contented himself with haranguing rallies, commemorative events,
and German Days, penning missives to the Bund newspaper and,
apparently, as a prescription for depression, promoting a 'strength
through joy' bathing beach on the Red River, near Winnipeg.[89]

A tad more couth than Rodde was Heinrich Seelheim who served
as consul in Winnipeg from 1930 to 1937. Like Ludwig Kempff, Seelheim was a doctor – of geography – and a career diplomat who shifted into high Nazi gear following Hitler's victory. 'Tallish, heavy-set,
well-muscled ... swarthy, alert of movement, and incessant of ges-
ture,' according to *Vancouver Sun* journalist Pat Terry, Seelheim
thought the National Socialist movement a 'spiritual thing,' a sort of
'crystallized idealistic patriotism.'[90] An animated convert who painted glowing pictures of Hitler's Germany that a credulous local journalist found 'difficult to disbelieve,'[91] Seelheim lent a considerable
consular effort to the National Socialist propaganda cause. He harangued public rallies; attended and spoke at Bund meetings;
dropped in at Winnipeg's Bundheim; reminded audiences at German Days that 'Herr Hitler is the German Nation, and the German
Nation is Herr Hitler';[92] placed recruitment ads for Hitler's army in
German newspapers; socialized with pro-Nazi activists; distributed
literature to libraries; arranged a League of Germans Abroad subsidy
of 1,000 German songbooks and readers for the school program of
the German Alliance of Saskatchewan;[93] donated consular prizes for
children's essay contests; and, overall, meddled so thoroughly that
the *Winnipeg Tribune* was moved to characterize the local Winnipeg
Nazi situation as 'a pretty kettle of totalitarian fish.'[94] Contributing
to Seelheim's renown was his unabashed anti-Semitism, which he
practised, on occasion, before organizations like Winnipeg's Wom-
en's Conservative Club, an assembly of 'strongly moralistic English
Canadian women' who were enlightened one day by the consul
about 'Jewish flesh merchants' in Berlin and South America.[95] Dur-

ing his visit to Vancouver in March 1935 to attend the goodwill port call of the German battle cruiser *Karlsruhe*, Seelheim set aside a few hours for reporters at the Devonshire where, in a 'straight black chair, upright as a ram rod,' he spoke about Hitler, modern Germany, and the Jews. His Jewish excursion which included references to Jewish control of vice and the professions, began with a rhetorical question: 'You ask of the Jews? There are Jews who work side by side with Hitler. Can you imagine if a Jew should go to Hitler with constructive suggestions, that Hitler would merely turn away?'[96]

While Seelheim spared no effort, until his relocation to Yokohama in 1937, in addressing, before varied audiences, the issues of the day, he understood, like his colleagues, that consular harangues, buttonholing, and meddling, while helpful, were not quite enough to sell the Fatherland's virtues to the locals of Minnedosa, Vegreville, or Vibank. Something more was needed to firm up support – a reliable, locally based press. It was this realization that moved Heinrich Seelheim in 1934–5 to join with a local Bund activist in an enterprise calculated to speed the flow of enlightenment to the local Germans.

There was, to be sure, before the appearance of the first issue of *Deutsche Zeitung für Canada*, no lack of appreciation of Hitler, and his new Germany, in Canada's German-language press.[97] With the exception of the Muenster, Saskatchewan, *St. Peters Bote* – a tiny (1,200 circulation) ultramontane and anti-Nazi rural weekly founded by Benedictine Catholics – and Regina's larger (12,000 circulation) liberal Catholic *Der Courier*, which held the National Socialist movement 'at arm's length,' Canada's German-language press, limited exclusively to western Canada, was, by and large, sympathetic to the New Germany. Winnipeg's non-sectarian *Nordwestern* weekly, Canada's oldest German newspaper, with a circulation of 13,000, was an early believer, and editorialized, in 1933, about a New Germany, 'under the strong hand of a far-sighted government' entering upon 'a victorious resurrection.' Several years later, it was still applauding the exploits of 'Greater Germany' and its 'great leader.' Western Canada's three Mennonite newspapers – *Mennonitische Rundschau*, Saskatchewan's *Der Bote*, and the *Steinbach Post* – were similarly positively inclined. Edited by Hans Neufeld, a post–First World War immigrant, the *Mennonitische Rundschau* reflected the anti-communist, *Völkisch*, and, in many instances, pro-Nazi sentiments of its readers whose identification with German culture, according to Mennonite historian Frank H. Epp, 'began in Prussia and continued in Russia, where it reached its zenith after the unpleasant experiences of the hate campaign against everything German and the liquidation decrees after the outbreak of World War I.'[98] The *Steinbach Post* owned since 1924 by a pair of post-communist revolution immigrants, and *Der Bote*, whose subscribers were almost exclusively recent Russian immigrants, shared, in varying degrees, the *Mennonitische Rundschau's* affinities towards German culture, the *Volk*, and, to a lesser extent, the National Socialist resurrection, and antipathies towards communists and, not uncommonly, Jews. Along with the *Nordwestern*, they heaped occasional praise on Hitler, as a 'master born out of the Volk'; lauded the Nazi resurrection; published reports, features, letters, and editorials praising the New Germany; and reprinted copy from Goebbels's Propaganda Ministry, Hoffman's foreign press office, and other agencies. Nor did they neglect the local scene. Advertisements of Bund meetings, announcements and reports of public events like German Days and National Socialist celebrations, even occasional appeals from Heinrich Seelheim for volunteer recruits for Hitler's army, were prominently displayed in the local papers.[99]

While the established German-language weeklies helped, they were not, to consular meddlers or militant Bundists, ideal vehicles of enlightenment. Something more reliable was needed – a press outlet funded, covertly, from abroad, or by local agents of the home government, and directed by a skilled propagandist with impeccable ideological credentials. Heinrich Seelheim and the Bundists found their man, in Regina, in the editorial offices of the widely circulated liberal Catholic *Der Courier*. A short, thin, dark, energetic Bavarian – with a faint resemblance to Joseph Goebbels – Bernhard Bott assumed *Der Courier's* editorial post soon after his immigration, in November 1923, from Germany, where he had studied two years at the local university, served for five with the Ninth Bavarian Infantry, edited a Catholic newspaper, and supported a Catholic Centre Party.[100] A chronic busybody who became a naturalized Canadian in 1929, Bott lent his considerable skills, throughout the 1920s and early 1930s, to the good cause of 'reviving the German-Canadian movement,' which, according to Heinz Lehmann, 'had completely collapsed under the consequences of the World War.'[101] He assisted the Catholic organizations; revived, in 1928, the dormant pre–First World War German-Canadian Alliance of Saskatchewan; and organized German-Canadian central committees in Regina and Saskatoon, which sponsored the German Day celebrations in Saskatchewan, beginning in 1930. Under Bott's leadership, the umbrella United German Association of Saskatchewan was formed in 1934. 'Saskatchewan Germandom is awake,' Bott later boasted, 'and ready for its great cause.'[102]

Bernhard Bott's own readiness was enhanced by a cordial relationship with Heinrich Seelheim, cemented during the many social and cultural events they jointly attended, and by two subsidized trips back home to the New Germany, in 1933 and 1934, where he immersed himself in 'the spirit and essence of the national socialist movement,'[103] picked up an award for patriotic services,[104] attended a large party rally in Nuremburg, and developed contacts with several newspapers and agencies, including the League for Germans Abroad, whose agent in Canada he subsequently became.[105] Bott's German stay was followed by a visit to several European countries, including England, where he made the acquaintance of Oswald Mosley.[106]

Bott's embrace of the great cause doubtless pleased Regina's Bundists who heard, firsthand, from the peripatetic editor, at several well-attended meetings, of the wonders of National Socialism. *Der Courier*'s publisher, however, took a dimmer view, akin, perhaps, to those held by Jewish community leaders who monitored Bott's writings and travels and strongly protested his editorial endorsement, among other things, of Consul Seelheim's stated view that 'not a single Jew has been killed in Germany and most of the so called molestations were either deliberate exaggerations or direct lies.'[107] The protests and the publishers' dim view had their effects and, while in Germany, Bott was relieved of his duties as *Der Courier* editor. His return home to Regina, as representative of several German newspapers and magazines, proved brief.[108] In early January 1935, Bernhard Bott bid Saskatchewan Germandom adieu, and moved to Winnipeg, to take up the position of manager of the German-Canadian Press Service.[109]

The press service languished, but something new appeared, six months after Bott's migration to Winnipeg: the *Deutsche Zeitung für Canada*, a brazen weekly with editorial offices on Winnipeg's Mountain Avenue, which served, until its demise in August 1939, as the Bund's mouthpiece and as the major German-language propaganda outlet in Canada. The *Deutsche Zeitung* was published by something called the Gutenberg Publishing Company, incorporated under the laws of the province of Manitoba, which included, as major shareholders, both Bernhard Bott and Heinrich Seelheim, who, in the first issue, on 6 June 1935, welcomed the appearance of 'an independent German newspaper which is not affiliated to any Canadian political party.'[110] Among the other shareholders were a pair of clerks from the Montreal and Winnipeg consulates; the German vice-consul in Vancouver, H.W. Mahler; and several Bund notables from Manitoba and elsewhere. The company's executive committee included C.P. Franke, manager of the Winnipeg offices of the North German Lloyd Steamship Lines; Otto Gruenbichler, a Bund leader and vice-president of the German-Canadian League of Manitoba, and Hugo Carstens, honorary president of the League, former imperial consul for western Canada, and part owner of the *Nordwestern*.[111] The *Deutsche Zeitung*'s printing was done by the Rundschau Publishing House, owned by Herman H. Neufeld, the publisher of the *Mennonitische Rundschau* and printer of William Whittaker's hate sheet, *Canadian Nationalist*. Neufeld and his company were named, along with Whittaker, in the Tobias hate libel suit in the fall of 1934.[112]

With the *Deutsche Zeitung* in business, the consular meddlers, the 'German-Canadian movement,' and Bernhard Bott at last had a vehicle, with a circulation of approximately 6,000, fitted to promote the great cause.[113] The *Zeitung* became the official organ of the Bund, whose four-year plan specified that it must be read and studied by all Bund members. But it was more than that. 'This newspaper ostensibly appeared as the official organ of the Deutscher Bund and regularly featured Bund activities,' a RCMP assessment read,

> but its scope was much wider. It covered political events in the home country and DAF activities in Canada. It gave prominent space to Hitler's expansion program: the absorption of Sudentenland and the anschluss of Austria; it stressed the achievements of the German

nation and its leaders; it appealed for contributions to German causes such as Winterhilfe; it urged the return of the former German colonies; it appealed to German nationals in Canada to join the DAF; it carried advertisements for *Mein Kampf*, lectures on German poets and statesmen, speeches by Nazi leaders and numerous Jew baiting ... and anti-British articles; in short, its five year career was thoroughly anti-British, anti-semitic and anti-democratic. At the same time, however, it protested against all insinuations that it was anything but an organ devoted to the legitimate and lawful interest of new Canadians of German descent.[114]

Leading the protest against insinuations was Bernhard Bott, sometimes referred to as Canada's Heinlein, who became, in the decade's waning years, the 'real spirit behind the Bund.'[115] While other leaders came and went, at the local and national levels, Bernhard Bott soldiered on, without flinching or deviating. He served as the Bund's western district leader and *Deutsche Zeitung* editor, as VDA agent, as avid promoter of German school language and winter help programs, and as featured guest speaker at German Days and other major events across the country. And he never relented in his exposure of the conspiracy of 'malicious lies and propaganda' levelled by Jews and others at both the 'German-Canadian movement' and Hitler's New Germany. For his meritorious service to the Third Reich, Bott was awarded in 1937 a silver plaque from Stuttgart's Foreign Institute.[116]

While Bott's stridency increased with Hitler's aggressions, the Bund's following and impact – such as it was – correspondingly declined. The Bund's toe-hold was precarious to begin with. Its membership likely never exceeded 2,000, and the *Deutsche Zeitung*'s circulation peaked at around 6,000.[117] Its school program in places like Ontario, as Wagner concluded, enjoyed limited success,[118] while German Days in the West, during the peak years 1936–7, drew 15,000 to 18,000 people, out of a total population of 275,000.[119]

In their efforts to enlighten German Canadians, the Bundists and other pro-Nazi elements faced serious obstacles: the hostilities of 'stout German democrats'; the mistrust and resistance of established older associations and élites; the indifference of assimilated kin; the anxieties of immigrants eager to prove their Canadianism. While German Days were fine opportunities for propaganda, and reasonably well attended, they were hardly sufficient, as the Nazi Ernst Woelfle observed, to convince participants, who 'for the remaining 364 days' appeared 'indifferent or even engaged in politically counter-productive activities.'[120]

If inertia, indifference, or hostility plagued the pro-Nazis in the mid-1930s – when Canada's tolerance of Germany constituted an exploitable asset – then Hitler's advancing war machine, at the decade's end, severely compounded their problems. Attendance at German Days and other public events declined, the Bund membership languished, and the fight of anti-Nazi elements in both established clubs and the newly organized like the German-Canadian League increased.[121] The 'withering political cross-fire' faced, in earlier years, by German Canadians yielded to uniform anti-Nazi volleys and the hopes of Bundists of creating a 'national socialist front of all Germans in Canada,' were shattered beyond repair.[122]

Nor were there any real prospects of building a Fascist front beyond the confines of the German community, with native Fascist groups whose notoriety and penchant for fantastic political and economic restructuring little interested the insecure, ethnocentric Bundists obsessed with the green fields and peaceful intentions of the Fatherland and with protecting German-Canadian culture. Canada's pro-Nazi Germans and native Fascists coexisted, by and large, in separate, insular social and political worlds. Arcand and Bott, Whittaker and Gerhard, winked, peddled their hates – and love of Germany – and mostly kept a safe distance from one another. There were, it is true, covert sympathies and marginal overlaps: a few German members in Arcand's NSCP, petty flirtations by a few Saskatchewan pro-Nazis with Arcand's party and the Canadian Union of Fascists, and, in the case of the Winkler Mennonites, a fleeting encounter with William Whittaker's Canadian Nationalist Party.[123] But beyond these incidental adhesions, separate Fascist solitudes prevailed, a condition that pleased the German consular officials who rejected meddling and fiddling with native Fascists as counterproductive and threatening to their task of selling Hitler's peaceful intentions, and trade with the Fatherland, to Canadian élites.[124] No prominent pro-

Nazi German leader made his way into the NSCP, and Bund members took their beer with their own. The Bund's meetings, German Days, German school programs, the DAF, consular wisdom, and, not least, Hitler's glories were featured in the *Deutsche Zeitung;* the dreams and schemes of Arcand and Whittaker were ignored by a paper whose 'established policy,' as a RCMP report read, was 'to refuse publication, even paid advertisements, of any matter relating to the Canadian fascist movements.'[125]

10

The Reckoning

Though Canada's ethnic Fascists by and large stayed clear of Adrien Arcand, there was no lack of effort on his part, in the decade's declining years, to broaden and jump-start a movement mired in a swamp of hackneyed hate. Like his idol in Europe, Arcand, during the spring and summer of 1938, was thinking big, East and West. Eastern prospects enlivened momentarily with the arrival of a pair of disgruntled Maritime local leaders – Daniel O'Keefe in New Brunswick and William McDuff in Nova Scotia – while, in Ontario and Manitoba, the local chieftains, Farr and Whittaker, announced their readiness in early March to fuse with Arcand, at an undetermined future date, into a national political party for the purpose of 'attaining political power by ... regular and lawful means,' and establishing a 'corporatist Canadian state with a corporate parliament.'[1]

With his Manitoba and Ontario colleagues on board, Arcand busied himself with rousing the faithful at a flurry of meetings in Quebec and in Ontario where, at one event in early June 1938, several surprise guests stirred up enough interest to warm his publicist heart. 'Preceded by some street scuffling, in which police quelled counter demonstrators described as Trotskyites,' a *Canadian Jewish Chronicle* account read, 'the meeting was half finished when it was startled by the tramp of martial feet. In came the young soldiers in full uniform except for one who wore a bright red sweater. They marched down the aisle, raised their arms in the Fascist salute and sat down, three sergeants, a corporal, one private and an indistinguishable in a red sweater.'[2] Fresh from a regimental drill, Arcand's newest apparent recruits were members of the Royal Canadian Artillery, whose front-row presence and salute invited widespread comment and indignation from the big dailies, a mild rebuke from Colonel O.S. Hollinrake, Officer Commanding, Royal Canadian Artillery – who thought it in 'bad taste' for his men to attend political meetings in uniform – a promise from national defence minister Ian MacKenzie to 'very carefully' investigate the 'whole situation,' and, from the *Canadian Jewish Chronicle*, the observation 'that a trusted servant like a soldier cannot serve King George and Adolf Hitler at the same time.'[3]

Dual service seemed, in fact, very much on Adrien Arcand's mind during the launching of Canada's newest political party, the National Unity Party, in Toronto and Kingston in early July 1938. From the beginning, the event took on the appearance of a comic Fascist opera. When Arcand announced Kingston as the designated convention locale, he was greeted by a chorus of local protest and a warning from the mayor, H.A. Stewart, and council that public meeting halls and parade permits would not be forthcoming. So, the Fascists bypassed Kingston, for the moment, and travelled to Toronto, where they set up headquarters at the shabby Isabella Hotel on 1 July and convened in the hall of a Ukrainian nationalist organization on Queen Street. With the basics concluded, the delegates returned, surreptitiously, the next day to Kingston, reconvened in a private room at the LaSalle Hotel – a block from police headquarters – and there affixed their collective signatures to a document announcing the birth of something called the National Unity Party (NUP), with Adrien Arcand as national leader and J.C. Farr as national organizer. The party motto was 'Canada for Canadians,' and its emblem, in place of the swastika, a flaming torch set off against a white background, surrounded by maple leaves, topped with the inevitable beaver and underlined by the motto 'Serviam.' The party program included the usual references to corporatism, class cooperation, the abolition of parties, and 'the official recognition and defense of christianity.' A message of loyalty 'to King and Country' was sent off to the governor general of Canada.[4]

With the National Unity Party officially launched in Kingston – as

Arcand promised it would be – the flitting Fascists, the press in pursuit, returned to Toronto to conclude proceedings. Deliberations of committees on Propaganda, Legions, and other matters were followed by a renewed assembly at the Ukrainian hall where delegates heard from a pair of visiting American hate dignitaries – George Detherage of West Virginia and Robert Edward Edmondson of New York – who spoke on the Jewish question in the United States and Roosevelt's capitulation to the Jews. The convention concluded with a public rally, attended by about 1,500 persons, at Massey Hall, on the evening of 4 July. The stage decorations were something new: a large plaque displaying a beaver, maple leaves, and flaming torch; banners reading 'God Save Our King' and 'Canada for Canadians'; a Union Jack draped across the speakers' table. But the message was stale stuff, delivered by a succession of dreary speakers, including Arcand whose 'violent denunciation of the Jews' was punctuated, a RCMP report read, with 'loud and enthusiastic cheering.'[5]

No similar responses were heard outside the assembly of the faithful. While the Fascists convened in Massey Hall, a pair of outdoor protest meetings nearby drew sizeable crowds, until broken up by police. At Maple Leaf Gardens, ten thousand people attended a meeting of the Canadian League for Peace and Democracy, which heard first-hand from former U.S. ambassador William E. Dodd about the Hitler regime.[6] During the days and weeks following, the assault on the NUP continued: by journalists writing about rancid wine in new bottles; by politicians and military men like Colonel George A. Drew and Major G.M.R. Dingle, national president of the Canadian Corps Association, who protested the adoption of the flaming torch (symbol of the Corps) by 'subversive isms' that stole 'names and labels as a camouflage.'[7] Among the claims of sham and thievery were those advanced by a long-standing student of the Arcand movement. ' "Shinui Hashem" is an ancient Hebrew custom,' the *Canadian Jewish Chronicle* editorialized; 'when a person is dangerously ill, a new name is given to him by which it is hoped that a fresh spirit will be infused into him. Little suspecting the Hebraic origin of this practice, Fuehrer Arcand did the same thing when he scrapped the National Christian Social Party [*sic*], in name and dubbed the new child, The National Unity Party of Canada. This in itself bespeaks the shoddiness and instability of his movement, because if the old party were as strong as it was represented to be, why should Hitler's agent have gone to the trouble of labour pains and a new name?'[8]

The *Chronicle*'s assessment was on the mark. In succeeding months, Arcand's National Unity Party proved neither national nor united. The Maritime leaders returned to empty meeting halls. In the West, fragmentation and stagnation prevailed. British Columbia's 'national councillor,' C.S. Thomas, was able to muster a mere handful and soon pursued other interests. Alberta remained as moribund as ever, while the pair of Saskatchewan councillors, John Schio and William Sketcher, spent more time fighting each other than recruiting members. In Winnipeg, as the *Tribune* observed, the party consisted 'mainly of one man and a multi-graphing machine. The three tailors of Tooley Street were far better qualified to speak for the people of England than the Nationalist Party is to speak for Winnipeg.'[9] Hospitalized by a stroke, William Whittaker was unable to attend the Toronto convention. He died soon after, but not before voicing his misgivings about Arcand's Quebec-centred leadership, misgivings shared by the Ontario nationalists who took to infighting in the months following the party's birth. Arcand's leadership, differences between Protestants and Catholics, Social Credit raids on membership, Farr's weakness and mishandling of funds, a successful, much-publicized, libel suit brought against a leading party member by the editor of the scandal sheet *The National Tattler* – which exposed the party's entrails to public view – pushed the party into a quick oblivion. When Arcand boasted that three hundred legionnaires would be brought to Toronto to keep order at a much-publicized Massey Hall meeting, nobody believed him. And they were right. Fewer than thirty legionnaires participated at the gathering that drew a sparse crowd and little publicity.

With national unity, among fellow Fascists, in shambles, Arcand withdrew to his own turf, where he maintained his usual, frantic pace. *Le Fasciste Canadien* was reborn as *Le Combat National* whose sparse pages were devoted to the leader's speeches and arguments favouring Canadian neutrality. *L'Illustration Nouvelle* remained infected, as ever, with a 'strange benevolence to the Third Reich.'[10] Public rallies in Montreal, Quebec City, and elsewhere drew modest crowds and large boasts from the NUP's neo-autonomist leader – the future Gauleiter of Laurentia, according to a German shortwave radio broadcast[11] – who informed a St James market audience of his commitment to 'obtain autonomy from ... cruel oppressors,' as Hitler had done for the Sudeten Germans. When residents in and around St Agathe in the Laurentians – where Montrealers, including Jews, spent summer vacations – discovered, in the summer of 1939, a Jewish problem in their rustic midst and cheered the exhortations of the local canon J.B. Charland and Reverend J.B. Bazinet to resist 'the invasion of the Jews' and preserve St Agathe as a 'French Canadian Village,' Laurentia's Gauleiter-designate was overcome with pride and joy, called a few meetings in surrounding areas, and was the likely supplier of anti-Semitic posters that flooded the district.[12]

The St Agathe eruption provided momentary cheer for Adrien Arcand. It was hardly, however, a bracing tonic for a movement exposed to financial and morale problems, dissension, membership leakage, and insistent external pressures. Financially, the NUP was in a desperate state. Income declined with membership, district headquarters were abandoned, meetings shifted to shabbier, low-rent premises. At several meetings in Quebec City and elsewhere, police reinforcements were needed to protect the Fascists whose legionnaires proved incapable of coping with hostile demonstrators. Quarrels with J.E. Lessard and Dr Gabriel Lambert, who announced a party membership of 1,800 – Arcand's extravagant claims notwithstanding – were publicly aired.[13] Radio access to the CBC and other stations was eliminated, and the daily press instituted a virtual boycott of NUP meetings and speeches. Nor did strictures from respected official circles aid the cause. Prominant church officials like Archbishop Gauthier condemned the Fascist doctrines subscribed to by the Arcand movement as peculiar, dangerous, and anti-Catholic,[14] and Hitler, as a 'persecuting and sacrilegious potentate,'[15] in unison with Pope Pius XI, who, in his encyclical 'No abbiasmo bisogno,' condemned the 'entire monopolizing' of 'youth, from the earliest infancy to adult age, for the full advantage of a party, of a regime, on the basis of an idolatry which, explicitly resolves itself into a true and genuine ideology, in complete conflict with the natural rights of the family as with the supernatural rights of the church.'[16]

If Premier Maurice Duplessis had earlier given the Fascists absolution – or at least exemption from laws akin to the Padlock Law – as liberal critics claimed he did, then, by the fall of 1938, he seemed ready to repent. In an interview with a reporter of Montreal's *Keneder Odler*, at the Mount Royal Hotel in October 1938, Duplessis stated that Arcand 'never was, is not, and never will be my spokesman, and is in no way connected with me personally, or with my party ... Mr. Arcand is the leader of the Fascist Party, who is not only not supporting me, but is my open enemy. The Party he has created is my sworn enemy and fights the Union Nationale Party. I am not, however, worried about him, as Fascism has no appeal to French Canadians. Mr. Arcand is a fanatic who sees visions, and is not to be taken seriously by anybody. Furthermore, I may add for myself that I am a good Catholic, but I am no better Catholic than the Pope, and the Pope has recently openly declared war on Fascism, and anti-semitism and that is my personal aim.'[17] To underline his commitment, the premier recruited a very special government candidate for the approaching by-election in the St Louis Division, created by the resignation of Peter Bercovitch, to contest the federal Cartier seat vacated by the death of Samuel Jacobs. Duplessis's choice – who won the election – was Louis Fitch, a Rumanian-born, McGill and Sorbonne-educated prominent Jewish lawyer and communal leader who, in his eloquent maiden speech seconding the motion to adopt the speech from the throne, reminded the House that the 'conscience of a government may be measured by the treatment of its minorities.'[18] If Arcand, and other Fascists loose in Montreal, thought Fitch would settle into a tame House Jew, they were rudely awakened by his detailed, factual speech, in April 1939, which, as the *Canadian Jewish Chronicle* noted, 'pulled no punches, called spades spades and ... for effect found it necessary neither to guild the lily nor to barb the cactus.'[19] The subject of the speech was Fascism in Quebec, and in it Fitch named names, addresses, and telephone numbers; listed statistics and organizations; cited Montreal-Berlin correspondence; acknowledged the honour of hosting in his own riding 'in a dirty basement' at 517 St Lawrence Boulevard the NUP's general headquarters; and, for good measure, succinctly defined Fascism as a system 'which defends nonsense by violence.' Among Fitch's interested audience was the premier who, on the speech's conclusion, declared to the House that there was 'no room in this country for the type of Nazism and Fascism as it is understood in Germany and Italy,' a statement that moved the *Chronicle* to express its hope 'that Mr. Duplessis' qualificative appeared in his statement, not as a countenancing of Fascism "as it is understood in Quebec," but rather a mere oratorical tag-end, a sort of Ciceronian tail piece.'[20]

A tailpiece – flaked, rusted, and trailing meagre exhaust from Hitler and Mussolini's war machines – was, in fact, all that remained by the summer of 1939 of a Canadian Fascism condemned by events overseas to a certain oblivion. Had Hitler and Mussolini stayed home, their Canadian mouth – and tail – pieces would likely have remained free to strut, salute, and convene in musty meeting halls. But the European dictators were restless, and the holiday – legal and political – enjoyed by their support groups and imitators in Canada came, in the final years of the decade, to an abrupt conclusion. Until Hitler's arc of conquest jolted local opinion, Canada's native, and ethnic, Fascists had a pretty smooth run of it. There were no hostile press campaigns, no large public clamours for repression, no padlocks – in or outside of Quebec – no entertainment of repression by governments, provincial or federal. There were, of course, the cranks and special pleaders; CCFers who pointed accusing fingers and published noisy exposés; the Trades and Labor Congress of Canada which, in late 1937, asked the Department of Justice to probe Nazi or Fascist 'blocs' in Canada. The Communist Party filled its *Clarion* with exposés and sent placarded demonstrators to Fascist meetings. The Canadian Jewish Congress monitored Fascist activities, published and distributed exposés, and intervened with opinion leaders and politicians. Assisting the congress was a vibrant Jewish press that maintained a constant watch, along with elected representatives like S.W. Jacobs, A.A. Heaps, Peter Bercovitch – and Louis Fitch – who alerted governments and public opinion to domestic and foreign Fascist activities.

Although the noisy minorities had long sounded the alarm, there

was no real public contemplation of a domestic Fascist threat until
the spring and summer of 1938, a discovery encouraged by Arcand's
gluttonous publicity urge and, more important, by Hitler's menacing conquests abroad. The media, East and West, played a critical
role in shaping the new opinion. The *Globe and Mail,* in November
and December 1938, sent journalist Ken McTaggert to Kitchener and
published a series of articles about the progress of Nazism among
Germans there, and elsewhere. The *Toronto Daily Star* featured Arcand, and warned, as well, about Nazi inroads among German Canadians. Apart from dramatizing the native mini-führer, the *Montreal
Gazette* reported as early as December 1937 about German designs on
Anticosti, a heavily wooded, forty-mile-long island located at the
mouth of the St Lawrence, owned by the Consolidated Paper Corporation, and teeming with timber and minerals.[21] That interest invited six months of fervid front-page reporting and speculation in the
major metropolitan press across the country. In the West, the scare
alert was sounded by the *Winnipeg Tribune* and the *Free Press,* which,
as early as September 1937, reported the 'pervasive regimentation'
of the local German community by Nazi propagandists.[22] The pronouncements and activities of the German consular officials, Seelheim and Rodde, drew front-page coverage and editorial censure.
When the *Tribune* discovered consular links to the *Deutsche Zeitung* –
a newspaper it persistently rebuked editorially – a series of exposés
were run, documenting the paper's ownership structure and propaganda functions. Contributing to the scare cause were major periodicals, like *Maclean's,* which featured two articles on Arcand in
March 1938;[23] *Saturday Night,* which published several articles on the
Arcand movement and the Nazis' 'growing interest in Canada';[24] and
Canadian Magazine whose Willson Woodside quoted Nazi publicist
Colin Ross's assertion, in his *Between USA and the Pole* –'the current
Nazi handbook on Canada'[25] – that it was questionable whether 'nations suffering under unbearable population pressure will forever
tolerate that a few million should hold a whole continent to them-
selves because they happened to get there first.'[26]

With the press drums beating loudly, it was not surprising that
interest groups and individuals across the country started agitating.
Elected officials received floods of letters from concerned individuals

urging public vigilance and official enquiries. The Canadian Corps, Canadian Legion, Daughters of England, and other patriotic associations protested Nazi propaganda efforts. Numerous local and provincial veterans' associations convened, petitioned, and, in the case of the men of St Walburg, Saskatchewan, burned a mock effigy of Hitler, to the accompaniment of 'God Save the King.'[27] An umbrella anti-Fascist committee was formed, in June 1939, in Saskatoon, headed by Louis Rosenberg and representing twenty-nine associations.[28] Canadian Legionnaires and veterans' groups in Regina and Winnipeg demanded the closure of the *Deutsche Zeitung*, while Calgary veterans formed a vigilance committee and forced the cancellation of the showing, by the local Bund, of a pair of German films.[29] An anti-Nazi speech to the Canadian Legion's annual Vimy celebration in Saskatoon, in early April 1939, by Saskatoon Alderman W.B. Caswell brought enthusiastic local applause from his patriotic audience, and a death threat – with an enclosed 22-calibre bullet – from an incensed local Nazi who described the local population as 'a motley, illiterate group of bohunks.'[30]

While the groups convened and petitioned, the opposition politicians in Parliament voiced their own concerns and passed on the message to the government. CCF national leader J.S. Woodsworth brought questions about the training and drilling of Major Scott's minions, and the *Deutsche Zeitung*'s Nazi patronage, to the government's attention. As early as February 1938, M.J. Coldwell charged that 'Fascist cells' were 'established the length and breadth of the land.'[31] Agnes Macphail, the Grey–Bruce member of parliament, alleged, on 13 May 1939, that 'people ... from totalitarian states' and certain 'so called Canadians' were spreading Nazi propaganda in virtually every city and province in Canada.[32] A.A. Heaps wondered out loud about sabotage, arms shipments, subversive organizations, and the dual loyalties of some German Canadians.[33] But the biggest splash was made by R.B. Bennett, the bombastic leader of the Conservative party, whose full throat – if not iron heel – was brought to bear on the Nazi threat. In late May 1938, Bennett, in a series of sensational Commons speeches widely broadcast on the front pages of the daily press, dramatized Anticosti, asked questions about the arrival on the island of 'eminent military and naval experts' with 'very close and intimate associations with the German government,' and alleged paid Nazi agents were directing local organizations and spreading propaganda in an attempt 'to weld Canada's five hundred thousand Germans into a solid Nazi bloc.' To add urgency, and mystery, to the matter, Bennett threw in the name of Karl Gerhard – long absent from the local Nazi scene – as a possible paid personal emissary of Hitler's, whose naturalization, the Conservative leader suggested, should be revoked.[34]

If Karl Gerhard's person, if not reputation, had disappeared from the local Nazi scene, many of his comrades remained, and were the subject of increasing scrutiny by a government whose disengagement from Europe and commitment to appeasement were increasingly threatened by Hitler's inexorable expansion. The RCMP had a long-standing interest in subversives and subversion, real or apprehended, left and right. The Communist Party was closely monitored by the force whose Special Branch, formed in the aftermath of the First World War, planted spies, dispatched agents, collected data, compiled dossiers, and informed government officials about the membership, organization, logistics – and subversive potential – of the Comintern's local affiliate. While the Fascists, ethnic and native, hardly received an equivalent long-standing attention, they were not ignored, in the late 1930s, when a growing public awareness focused government attention on rightist threats, internal and external.[35] Prime Minister Mackenzie King and his senior ministers loathed the prospect of engagement in a European war, with its attendant costs in lives, economic resources, political dislocation, sectional disunity, and restriction of individual liberties. The government preferred to give its full attention to fighting – or appearing to fight – the economic depression, placating Quebec, and mollifying dissident western provinces. League sanctions, the enforcement of collective security, dangerous engagements with friendly European powers against Nazi and Fascist threats discomforted the prime minister, who thought Hitler, until events in 1939 dictated otherwise, a well-meaning peasant with mystical inclinations – like his own – harbouring grievances traceable to the Versailles Treaty and capable of being appeased by timely concessions. 'As late as August, 1939,' wrote historian Robert H. Keyserlinck,'King and his External Affairs advisors remained convinced that war could be avoided only if the British and French would back down from their ill-conceived guaranty of Poland and grant Hitler his claims to German-speaking, Nazi-governed Danzig. King received permission in mid-August, 1939, from Chamberlain to send Hitler a personal message offering his good offices to conciliate between Hitler, the mystical man of the masses so like himself, and the degenerate top-hatted and upper-class British and French leaders, who were unable to understand Hitler as he was. King put his idea to Hitler through King's only diplomatic friend in Ottawa, the German Consul-General Erich Windels, who later transmitted back to King Hitler's private if somewhat general response.'[36]

By early September 1939, Danzig was history and Hitler in Poland. Britain and France declared war and, in Canada, Mackenzie King joined the battle on Britain's side on 10 September. But, before doing so, the prime minister, in close consultation with his justice minister, tidied up some pressing domestic matters, which, throughout 1938 and 1939, had drawn the full attention of officers, agents, and informers of the RCMP who filed reports to headquarters staff and fattened files on suspected subversives, left and right. The recommendations of the Force's commissioner, submitted to the minister of justice in late August – with war imminent – were Draconian. The commissioner, 'in view of the imminent peril of war,' wanted a full clean-up; the arrest and internment – should war be declared – of leading Italian and German Fascists and Nazis 'considered dangerous'; the outlawing, by order-in-council under the War Measures Act, of their organizations, including the Bund, the German Labour Front, the *fasci*, and *dopolavoro*; the suppression of Italian and German pro-Fascist newspapers; and, for good measure, the outlawing and banning of communist and affiliated organizations and suppression of their newspapers.[37]

While Ernest Lapointe wanted action, he was not yet prepared to go the whole RCMP way. So, a meeting was arranged between a representative of the Department of Justice – J.F. MacNeill – and Norman A. Robertson, from External Affairs, who came to the conclusion that the commissioner's plan would involve a good deal of 'bitter-interracial resentment and the prospect of endless labour troubles throughout the industrial and mining areas, as well as the alienation and support of large numbers of persons who, if properly handled, could be led to support any efforts the government proposed in connection with the war effort rather than to oppose them.' The committee recommended that the police 'should concentrate on the plans for the immediate arrest of persons suspected of treasonable activity, and that they would be ill-advised to destroy organizations about which they knew a great deal and with whose personnel they were familiar, as it would drive such persons underground and greatly increase police problems in this country in time of war.'[38] When an interdepartmental advisory internment committee – consisting of MacNeill, Robertson, the RCMP's E.W. Bavin, with Sergeant John Leopold assisting – was struck in late August to look into 'the whole subject of restriction and detention orders and the measures which should be taken to suppress subversives activities,' it was directed to exclude the communists 'at that time,' go easy on other organizations unless suppressive action 'was absolutely necessary,' and concentrate on plans 'for the immediate arrest of persons suspected of treasonable activities.'[39]

With its latitude limited, the King government's interdepartmental advisory internment committee – chaired by Robertson – sat for three days, beginning 1 September 1939, examined files, drew up lists, and recommended action. Communists and native Fascists were, for the moment, excluded from consideration. A list of 'dangerous persons' of Italian nationality – based upon an examination of RCMP dossiers – was drawn up, but the police were 'enjoined ... not to take any precipitate actions against Italian suspects that might conceivably prejudice the position of Italy as a possible neutral.'[40] The Germans earned the committee's full attention. A list of 'dangerous persons' was compiled from four classes or groups whose arrest and detention was recommended: the NSDAP in Canada, whose members – all German nationals – had undertaken, in the committee's view, 'to obey implicitly and without question the orders of their Fuehrer and his representatives'; the Deutsche Arbeitsfront, a dangerous agency, like the NSDAP, capable of 'sabotage and seditious activities' during wartime; a select group of Germans not known to be members of either the NSDAP or the DAF who, 'from their political and social associations' or 'business and industrial connections,' were deemed dangerous; Deutscher Bund leaders, approximately sixty in number, all naturalized Canadians of German birth who 'had so identified themselves with Nazi propaganda activities' that they could no longer be regarded as 'loyal citizens of Canada.'[41]

With the committee's recommendation and list in hand, the government moved swiftly to administer a first 'salutary shock.' The Defence of Canadian Regulations, based upon the report of a Committee on Emergency Legislation, appointed in 1938, were proclaimed on 3 September, under the authority of the War Measures Act of 1927. Included among its provisions was the 'admittedly drastic' Regulation 21, which enabled the government, for reasons of 'public safety or safety of the state,' to order that persons 'be detained in such place and under such conditions as the Minister from time to time determines, and that while detained by virtue of an order under the Regulation, said person shall be deemed to be in legal custody.'[42] Armed with this, and other legal bludgeons, the RCMP arrested, on 4 June, 325 Germans and German-Canadian 'dangerous persons,' including 35 NSDAP members, almost 200 DAF members, and approximately 60 Bundists, including Bernhard Bott and Franz Straubinger, and sent them off to a pair of old forestry stations, converted into internment camps, in Kananaskis, Alberta, and Petawawa, Ontario.[43]

Had Hitler – and Mussolini – rested content, following the invasion of Poland, further 'salutary shocks' might have been deemed unnecessary by the authorities to remind Canada's errant ethnics, and others, of their patriotic duties. Following the war scare of the summer and fall of 1939, there was a decent interval – of several months – allowed to Adrien Arcand and Joseph Farr to cancel public meetings, suspend publications, and hibernate; to ethnic societies to maintain discreet silences and reiterate loyalties. Hitler's spring 1940 offensive changed all this. The Nazi thrust into Norway, Denmark, Holland, Belgium, and finally, France – abetted by sinister local agents – excited opinion in Canada and induced a pervasive fifth-column scare, especially pronounced in Ontario and British Columbia. The press, including papers like the *Winnipeg Tribune* – which ran a fifth-column series – featured it.[44] Numerous veterans

organizations, such as the Canadian Legion, Canadian Corps Association, the Army and Navy Veterans associations, and others, called
for increased internments and the formation of home defence forces. Municipal councillors in cities, towns, and villages; businessmen
in boards of trade and chambers of commerce; members of numerous service clubs demanded greater vigilance and suppression, in
league with prominent politicians, including the leader of the opposition in Ottawa and the Ontario government's Attorney General
G.D. Conant, who demanded the suspension of all due process of law
in the apprehension of 'enemy aliens, subversive elements and persons dangerous to the safety of the state.'[45] Conant's boss, Premier
Mitchell Hepburn, warned of an invasion of Nazi agents from the
United States.

The King government listened, and got the message. All British
subjects of German and Italian background naturalized after 1929
– and, later, 1922 – were ordered to register with the Registrar of
Enemy Aliens.[46] A broad range of societies and groups, right and left,
were declared to be illegal under Regulation 39C of the Defence of
Canada Regulations. Communists were apprehended and detained,
while new rounds of arrests of German Canadians were undertaken
until, by the end of 1940, the number totalled around 600.[47] When
Mussolini declared war on Britain and France on 10 June, the RCMP's
Italian 'dangerous person' list was activated and, in a sweeping operation across the country, scores of Italian Canadians – many of
them only peripherally associated with Fascist-controlled or -influ-
enced organizations, whose membership lists had made their way via
informers into RCMP files – were arrested and interned.[48] On 12 June
six Italian associations were added to the government's banned list,
including the *fasci*, the *dopolavoro*, the Italian War Veterans Association, and the Italian United Moral Front.[49]

With the ethnics dispatched, all that remained were the native
hibernators, Adrien Arcand and his musty men who, throughout the
winter and spring of 1940, laid low, convened surreptitiously, studied maps and press reports, and dreamt of a corporatist Laurentia,
without Jews, united in a customs union, as a German shortwave-
radio broadcast stated, with Nazi Europe – and led by an unbalanced,
angular gauleiter, with a pencil moustache.[50] But the dreaming end-

ed in late May, when teams of RCMP officers descended, in a series of twenty raids, on homes and offices of known Fascists and carted off eight truckloads of documents, including membership lists, propaganda literature, internal organizational documents, and correspondence with local and foreign Fascists, some of which subsequently appeared, for public consumption, on the front pages of the Montreal and Toronto dailies.[51] A week later, in pre-dawn raids, the arrests came under Section 39 and 39A of the Defence of Canada Regulations: of Joseph C. Farr and John Lorimer, in Ontario, and nine leaders in Quebec, including Maurice Scott, National Director of Legions; Hughes Clement, Provincial Adjutant of Legions; Henri Arcand, National Director of of Transport; and Marius Gatien, National Director of Propaganda.[52] The Führer and party treasurer, Dr Noel Decarie, were seized, among the bobolinks, at Arcand's summer home in Nominingue, one hundred miles north of Montreal, in the Laurentian Mountains.[53]

The courts gave the Fascists short shrift. After perusing documents submitted by the Crown at a preliminary hearing, Judge Rodolphe DeSerres concluded that a conspiracy against the state existed, adjourned proceedings, and passed on a report, and exhibits, to Quebec's attorney general, who, in turn, referred the matter – of national importance, under federal jurisdiction – to the minister of justice. 'The Attorney-General of Quebec,' Lapointe informed the House, 'has sent me a report, accompanied by certain exhibits which showed clearly that these people had communication and intelligence with enemies – Germany, Italy and elsewhere. Accordingly, I have issued an order directing the internment of these persons for the duration of the war.'[54] Criminal proceedings, Lapointe added, were in abeyance.[55]

And so was Adrien Arcand, who languished, with other internees deemed dangerous persons, for the duration of the war at Petawawa and, later, Fredericton. Canada's interned were a mixed group, which included, among others: Communists, 96 in number by March 1941, who won early release; 'innocuous enemy aliens' of Italian origin who somehow made it onto RCMP lists;[56] prominent and petty officials of pro-Fascist support groups; Montreal's ex-mayor who opposed the National Registration Act; and staunch keepers of the faith who – at Kananaskas – christened the daily assembly area 'Adolf Hitler Place,' and named the camp's two main streets after Hermann Goering and Joseph Goebbels.[57] Perhaps the truest of the interned believers was Adrien Arcand who, following release on 3 July 1945, returned to a humble cottage at Lanoraie, north of Montreal, where he painted a bit, listened to classical music on his old gramophone, adored the crucifix next to his bed, did some translating, reverted to pamphleteering and politics, and maintained, until his death in 1967, an unshakeable belief that Satan's Siamese twins, the Jews and Communists, were subverting the world.[58]

Notes

CHAPTER 1: *Northern Knights*

1 P.M. Richards, 'How the Ku Klux Klan Came to Canada,' *Saturday Night*, 26 June 1926
2 Ibid.
3 David M. Chalmers, *Hooded Americanism* (Garden City, NY: Doubleday 1965), 279
4 Ibid., 13. There was no reason for it to spread to the northern states or, for that matter, to Canada where tiny black communities existed in British Columbia, Ontario, and Nova Scotia. Robin W. Winks speculates that there might have been a few Ku Klux Klan members in Canada but provides no evidence: Robin W. Winks, *The Blacks in Canada: A History* (Montreal and Kingston: McGill-Queen's University Press 1971), 320.
5 Chalmers, 9
6 Ibid., 16
7 Ibid., 9. J.M. Mecklin, *The Klu Klux Klan: A Study of the American Mind* (New York: Russell and Russell 1963), 64–5
8 Mecklin, 64
9 Ibid., 78
10 Chalmers, 20
11 Ibid., 21. Chalmers concludes that 'the Ku Klux Klan was a law-and-order movement because it was directed at the restoration of the proper order.'

12 Ibid., 10
13 Ibid., 19. Mecklin (225–6) notes the similarity of the Klan to other secret resistance organizations: 'The Old Ku Klux Klan of Reconstruction days, organized to resist the tyranny of carpet-bag rule, the Vehmgerichte of Westphalia that arose in the Middle Ages to check the anarchy threatened by the dissolution of the strong government of Charlemagne, the carbonarii of Naples who sought to throw off the yoke of Napoleon, the Mafia of southern Italy organized to resist the police and protect the smugglers, the Clan-na-Gael, an Irish secret society organized to resist English tyranny and perpetuated to some extent in the lawless Molly Maguires of the Pennsylvania coal mines, all these are illustrations of the militant oath-bound secret society which makes use of secrecy to carry out policies of vital interest to society as a whole.'
14 Chalmers, 10. For a variety of reasons, it enjoyed scant support in the large cities and the tidewater, coastal, delta, and black-belt areas.
15 Chalmers, 29; J. Higham, *Strangers in the Land* (New York: Atheneum 1963), 286–7
16 Higham, 264–99. André Siegfried, in his *America Comes of Age*, trans. H.H. Hemming and D. Hemming (New York: Harcourt Brace 1926), 130, wrote: 'The Ku Klux Klan is an extreme form of Protestant nationalism; in fact we must almost consider it a fever, as otherwise we are apt to exaggerate it during the crisis and belittle it when the temperature has fallen again.'
17 Chalmers, 28
18 Ibid., 30
19 Higham, 288
20 Chalmers, 32
21 Frederick Lewis Allen, *Only Yesterday* (New York and London: Harper and Brothers 1931), 66
22 Of good and honest men, Siegfried (134) wrote: 'In French politics "good citizens" has a Bonaparte odour, and "honest men" are those on the side of order who can be relied upon to strike hard when necessary. In French history there are many examples of dissentious appeals and coups d'etat, which have relied on the "good" and the "honest." In this sense, the members of the Klan are "honest men"

for they are ready to take the law into their own hands should the government seem inadequate.'

23 Allen, 65
24 Siegfried, 134
25 Higham, 294–5
26 Ibid., 294
27 In Texas, where Hiram Evans, a local dentist, replaced Colonel Simmons as Imperial Wizard, the Klan elected a senator and almost took the governorship. The Oklahoma Klan successfully pressed the impeachment of a hostile governor while the Arkansas organization was 'so politically powerful that it held its own primaries to decide which brother to support in the regular democratic ones' (Chalmers, 3). The Colorado Klan helped elect two senators and swept the state. In Oregon, the Klan helped defeat the governor and controlled enough of the legislature to outlaw public support for parochial schools. The Klan bulked large politically in Indiana, Ohio, and several others of the forty-five states in which it operated.
28 Siegfried, 140; Chalmers, 4
29 Siegfried, 136
30 Ibid., 112
31 Chalmers, 113
32 Although the Klan was a predominantly small-town phenomenon, concentrated in areas inhabited by old-stock Protestant Americans, it made substantial inroads into such cities as Denver, Dallas, Portland, and Des Moines. According to Chalmers (114), 'The explanation for the Klan's urban strength is probably to be found in the degree to which the rapidly expanding cities were being fed by the native American stock from the country's small towns and rural areas. The average American city dweller in the 1920s was far from cosmopolitan, and the chances were that he was no more than one generation away from either the farm or the immigrant ship.'
33 Siegfried, 136
34 Julian Sher, *White Hoods, Canada's Ku Klux Klan* (Vancouver: New Star 1983), 24
35 Ibid., quoting from the *Montreal Star*, 4 October 1921
36 *La Presse*, 28 November 1922, as cited in Sher, 25; Tom M. Henson, 'Ku Klux Klan in Western Canada,' *Alberta History* 25 (1977): 2

37 P.M. Richards, 'Claims of the Ku Klux Klan,' *Saturday Night*, 17 July 1926, and 'Ku Klux Klan Diminishes in Canada,' *Saturday Night*, 16 October 1926

38 Ibid.

39 Rev. A. McCaffrey to W.L. Mackenzie King, King Papers, MG 26, J-1, Vol. 77, Public Archives of Canada

40 Oscar Wilson to the Editor, *Welland Tribune-Telegraph* (undated), enclosed in A. McCaffrey to W.L. Mackenzie King, King Papers, MG 26, J-1, Vol. 77

41 Sher, 26, quoting *The Spectator*, 24 March 1923

42 *Toronto Daily Star*, 15 September 1923, as quoted in Sher, 26

43 Sher, 27

44 *New York Times*, 17 February 1925

45 Richards, 'How the Ku Klux Klan Came to Canada'

46 K.T. Jackson, *The Ku Klux Klan in the City 1915–1930* (New York: Oxford University Press 1967), 181

47 Ibid., 61, 176; A.S. Rice, *The Ku Klux Klan in American Politics* (Washington, DC: Public Affairs Press 1962), 42

48 Richards, 'How the Ku Klux Klan Came to Canada.' Cowan stayed briefly in Klan politics, while Fowler pushed out Hawkins, who later founded the rival 'Ku Klux Klan of the British Empire' whose regalia included a Union Jack on the right breast. Hawkins soon resigned from the new organization and returned to the United States.

49 *Regina Morning Leader*, 20 February 1925. Lewis Fowler had served as editor of the *American Standard*.

50 Robin W. Winks, *The Blacks in Canada*, 321, 325

51 Siegfried, 139. Of the Catholic Church's designs on America, the *American Standard* had this to say in its 1 October 1925 edition: 'We again take the occasion to attack the sinister purposes and persistant efforts of the Roman Catholic hierarchy to foist upon us the belief that Christopher Columbus was the discoverer of America and through this fraudulent representation to lay claim to inherent rights which belong solely to Nordic Christian peoples, through the discovery of this continent by Leif Ericson.' Ibid., 138

52 *Toronto Globe*, 18 August 1924

53 According to Colonel W.E. Clifford, one of the local commissioners,

'the local authorities were doing their best to stop the proposal and plan sending a delegation to wait on the provincial secretary to see what can be done about the matter.'

54 *Toronto Daily Star*, 12 September 1925. There were six other crosses burned in the Belleville area in the previous weeks.

55 'Klan Bigotry Crops Up in Belleville,' *Saturday Night*, 30 October 1926, 2

56 Richards, 'Claims of the Ku Klux Klan'

57 Ibid.

58 Toronto *Globe*, 30 March 1930

59 Ibid.

60 Winks, 324

61 A.D. Monk, 'Knights of the Nightshirt,' *Canadian Magazine*, October 1926

62 *Regina Morning Leader*, 19 February 1925

63 Ibid.

64 Winks, 324

65 *Canadian Forum*, April 1930, 233

66 Henson, 2

67 Ibid.

68 *The Worker*, 9 May 1924, quoted in Sher, 25

69 *Regina Morning Leader*, 17 and 18 October 1928; James H. Gray, *The Roar of the Twenties* (Toronto: Macmillan 1975), 289–92

70 *Regina Morning Leader*, 17 October 1928

71 Gray, 290

72 *Regina Morning Leader*, 17 October 1928

73 T.H. McLeod and Ian McLeod, *Tommy Douglas: The Road to Jerusalem* (Edmonton: Hurtig 1987), 62–8

74 *Victoria Daily Times*, 28 November 1922, and Sher, 31

75 *Victoria Daily Times*, 30 November 1922

76 Ibid.

77 Henson, 3

78 Jackson, 196

79 Ibid., 204. Chalmers, 88–9. According to Chalmers (85), 'Oregon was opened up to the Klan by a combination of inherited anti-Catholicism, isolation, the wartime tradition of suspicion and inquisitiveness, Prohibition, management-labour conflict and

superior salesmanship.' There were, in addition, demographic factors. The bulk of Oregonians, who were 97 per cent 'Caucasian' in the 1920s and 85 per cent native-born, arrived from the Mississippi Valley and, before that, from New England. 'They brought with them a suspicion of Rome,' according to Chalmers, 'which remained undiluted in the parochial small-town life of Oregon's valleys and broken, hilly, coastal plain.'

80 Jackson, 89
81 Chalmers, 217
82 Jackson, 194
83 Chalmers, 217
84 Ibid.
85 *Vancouver Sun*, 3 March 1955; *Victoria Daily Times*, 11 November 1925, 9
86 *Victoria Daily Times*, 11 November 1925
87 E. Starkins, *Who Killed Janet Smith?* (Toronto: Macmillan 1984), 24; and Sher, 36
88 *Victoria Daily Times*, 11 November 1925
89 Starkins, 91
90 Ibid., 92
91 Sher, 35
92 Resolution passed by Vancouver Klan No. 1, in February 1922, as quoted in Sher, 35
93 *Victoria Daily Times*, 30 November 1922, 9. This was the policy enunciated by A.W. Manson when the Klan first appeared in 1922.
94 *Vancouver Sun*, 12 November 1925
95 Ibid. Browne repeated the common view among socialist and labour politicians that the Klan was an actual, or potential, instrument of repression of American capitalist regimes: 'This movement appeals to the decaying American civilization as something that it should take over and use in the government of its country. The Klan is founded on invisible government. We have sufficient invisible government in British Columbia and elsewhere in the British Empire without it.'
96 Ibid. Manson's jugular Canadianism was carried a bit far when he stated that, if the organization were being promoted by Canadians, he would have 'no fear of it doing harm,' but as it appeared to be

of American origin, he had 'grave doubts about it.'

97 *Victoria Daily Times*, 25 November 1925

98 Ibid., 16 November 1925

99 Powell later returned to Shreveport, where he spent several years promoting an organization known as the 'Supreme Order of Destiny.' *The Bisector* 3/12 (December 1927): 2

100 Howard Palmer, *Patterns of Prejudice* (Toronto: McClelland and Stewart 1982), 37, quoting a prominent Conservative from Lethbridge. The Department of Immigration, whose restrictive policies were encouraged by Alberta élites, was very successful in limiting black immigration into the prairies. There were 98 blacks on the prairies in 1901; in 1911, after a huge general immigration influx, the number was 1,524. Pierre Berton, *The Promised Land: Settling the West, 1896–1914* (Toronto: McClelland and Stewart 1984), 186

101 Palmer, 1–60, 103

102 *Calgary Herald*, 13 April 1923, 18

103 *Toronto Globe*, 18 October 1926, as cited in Paul A. Banfield, 'The Ku Klux Klan in Alberta, 1929–1933,' BA essay, Department of History, University of Alberta, 1982, 10

104 Ibid.

105 Palmer, 103

106 Ibid., 105

107 R.J.A. Huel, 'J.J. Moloney: How the West Was Saved from Rome, Quebec and the Liberals,' in J.E. Foster, ed., *The Developing West* (Edmonton: University of Alberta Press 1983), 229

108 J.J. Moloney, *Rome in Canada* (n.p.: Columbia Protestant Publications n.d.), foreword

109 Moloney's views on Catholic domination, and diverse other subjects, are outline in his *Rome in Canada*. Moloney maintained that the French Catholic Quebec block in Canada used its influence, before the 1930 resolution, to withhold natural resources and Crown lands from the western provinces in order to force 'acceptable' separate school and language guarantees: Huel, 222

110 Palmer, 102, 110

111 Moloney, 156; Palmer, 106–7

112 Moloney, 157

113 Ibid., 124

114 Ibid., 159–61. According to Moloney, the seven Klaverns organized in Edmonton were 'headed by shriners.'
115 *The Liberator,* November 1931
116 J.H. Hurley to W.L. Mackenzie King, 12 November 1931, King Papers, M.G. 26, J-1, Vol. 186
117 Henson, 5
118 Ibid.
119 Ibid.
120 David B. Mullin, a farmer and former Edmonton Klan member, did later assume the portfolio of minister of agriculture in the Aberhart Social Credit government.
121 Palmer, 106
122 Allan Seager, 'A History of the Mine Workers' Union of Canada, 1925–1936,' MA thesis, McGill University, 1977, 151–4
123 Huel, 232–5
124 Ibid., 234
125 Ibid., 238
126 Ibid.

CHAPTER 2: *The Sasklan*

1 *Regina Morning Leader,* 8 May 1928
2 Ibid.
3 On the Indiana Klan, see K.T. Jackson, *The Ku Klux Klan in the City, 1915–1939* (New York: Oxford University Press 1967), 144–60, and David M. Chalmers, *Hooded Americanism* (Garden City, NY: Doubleday 1965), 162–74. Stephenson was sent to prison, on a charge of second-degree murder, following the suicide death of a woman, Madge Oberholtzer, whom he had raped.
4 *Regina Morning Leader,* 23 May 1927
5 Ibid.
6 Ibid.
7 William Calderwood, 'The Rise and Fall of the Klu Klux Klan in Saskatchewan,' MA thesis, University of Saskatchewan, 1968, 34, from the J.G. Gardiner Papers, 12411–504, Public Archives of Saskatchewan

8 Ibid., 37, from Gardiner Papers, 12411–97
9 Robert Moon, *This Is Saskatchewan* (Toronto: Ryerson Press 1953), 41
10 Ibid.
11 *Regina Morning Leader*, 8 May 1928
12 Ibid.
13 Rabbi Ferdinand M. Isserman, 'The Klan in Saskatchewan,' *Canadian Jewish Review* 34 (15 June 1928): 7
14 *Saskatoon Phoenix*, 11 May 1928; *Regina Morning Leader*, 11 May 1928; James H. Gray, *The Roar of the Twenties* (Toronto: Macmillan 1975), 268
15 According to Emmons, Moose Jaw's Dennis restaurant was a 'Klan restaurant' and all the stock was 'held by Klansmen.' *Saskatoon Daily Star*, 11 May 1928
16 Quoted in Isserman, 7
17 Moon, 42–7; Gray, 267–72
18 *Regina Morning Leader*, 23 May 1927
19 Gray, 271
20 Moon, 46
21 Ibid., 47. According to C.H. Higginbotham, Moose Jaw Klansmen acted as 'secret vigilantes on a block to block basis to spy on the morals of their neighbors, mostly on the basis of who is sleeping with whom': C.H. Higginbotham, *Off the Record: The CCF in Saskatchewan* (Toronto: McClelland and Stewart 1968), 32. Not all businessmen, it seems, were pleased with the results of the Klan's River Street clean-up campaign. As Higginbotham noted (28), 'they complained that the sale of fur coats and expensive dresses had dropped to zero. Virtue was fine, of course, but the River Street girls had been good spenders.'
22 Ibid., 29; Moon, 45–6; Gray, 267–9
23 Higginbotham, 29
24 Gray, 269. The Klan enjoyed some considerable success in Moose Jaw municipal politics. Three of the five successful aldermanic candidates in the municipal election of December 1927 were Klan nominees. The Klan contributed a member to city council in 1928 and, in 1929, a Klansman was elected mayor (Calderwood, 262). James W. Brennan, 'A Political History of Saskatchewan, 1905–1929,' PhD thesis, Department of History, University of Alberta, 1976, 705

25 *Regina Morning Leader,* 31 January 1928
26 *Saskatoon Phoenix,* 10 May 1928
27 Toronto was notified of four hundred Klan members in the province, whereas in Moose Jaw alone, fees had been collected from fourteen hundred. Statement of Imperial Wizard J.W. Rosborough, *Saskatoon Star-Phoenix,* 10 May 1929
28 *Saskatoon Phoenix,* 10 May 1928
29 *Regina Morning Leader,* 3 July 1928
30 *Moose Jaw Evening Times,* 28 October 1927, as cited in Calderwood, 51
31 *Regina Morning Leader,* 3 July 1928
32 *Saskatoon Phoenix,* 3 July 1928
33 Jackson, 181; Chalmers, 301; *Regina Morning Leader,* 3 July 1928
34 *Saskatoon Star,* 5 July 1928, as quoted in Calderwood, 54
35 Higginbotham, 31
36 Ibid.
37 An informative discussion of the Victorian roots of anti-Catholicism in British North American can be found in J.R. Miller, 'Anti-Catholic Thought in Victorian Canada,' *Canadian Historical Review,* 65/4 (1985): 474–94
38 J.J. Moloney, *Rome in Canada* (n.p.: Columbia Protestant Publications n.d.) 130
39 Ibid., 136
40 Ibid, 137
41 Ibid.
42 Ibid., 141
43 Ibid.
44 Ibid., 144; R.J.A. Huel, 'J.J. Moloney: How the West Was Saved from Rome, Quebec and the Liberals,' in J.E. Foster, ed., *The Developing West* (Edmonton: University of Alberta Press 1983), 244
45 Moloney, 146
46 Ibid., 20. As a loyal Canadian and Empire patriot, Moloney relocated the original Klan from Pulaski to Scotland. 'Ku for Dog,' he wrote (78), 'Klux, which is a syncopation for crux, meaning cross – etc. An organization which had its origin in the land of Scotland in the days of the Covenanters, who called their loyal followers to worship by means of the fiery cross.'

47 Huel, 228
48 Moloney, 23
49 Ibid., 22
50 Ibid.
51 Ibid., 23
52 Huel, 224–9
53 Ibid., 224
54 The incidents are recorded in the Huel article and in Moloney's autobiography.
55 Huel, 227
56 *Saskatoon Star*, 25 January 1928, as quoted in Calderwood, 90
57 Statement of Imperial Wizard J.W. Rosborough, *Saskatoon Phoenix*, 10 May 1928
58 'Canadian Province Turns to the Klan,' *New York Times*, 8 July 1928, Section 3, 7
59 *Regina Morning Leader*, 28 October 1929
60 Ibid.
61 Statement of Imperial Wizard J.W. Rosborough, *Saskatoon Phoenix*, 10 May 1928. Rosborough did flirt with the idea of regalia and corresponded with a Little Rock, Arkansas, organization known as the American Crusader Limited, which manufactured and distributed Klan regalia. According to M.J. Coldwell, a Regina city alderman at the time, hoods and robes did appear at Klan meetings in Regina's city hall: Gray, 275. According to Gray (ibid.), 'without the paraphernalia that went with it, the Klan induced as much terror as a Rotary Club. It was this kind of crazy excuse for a Ku Klux Klan that Scott and Emmons thought they could promote in Saskatchewan. Yet promote it they did.'
62 J.F. Bryant to R.B. Bennett, 2 June 1928, R.B. Bennett Papers, Public Archives of Canada 25117–18
63 *Yorkton Enterprise*, 13 March 1928, as quoted in Calderwood, 93
64 Ibid.
65 Calderwood, 82–110
66 Affidavit declared before W.H. McEwan, dated 17 May 1928, *Regina Morning Leader*, 31 May 1928
67 Ibid.
68 Ibid.

69 Ibid.
70 Brennan, 698; Calderwood, 146
71 An Observer, 'The Ku Klux Klan in Saskatchewan,' *Queen's Quarterly* Autumn 1928: 592

CHAPTER 3: *Glory Days*

1 *Regina Morning Leader,* 11 May 1928
2 William Calderwood, 'The Rise and Fall of the Ku Klux Klan in Saskatchewan,' MA thesis, University of Saskatchewan, 1968, 144
3 Ibid., 144–5
4 Ibid., 50
5 Ibid., 142
6 Ibid., 138
7 Ibid., 141
8 Ibid., 182
9 James W. Brennan, 'A Political History of Saskatchewan, 1905–1929,' PhD thesis, Department of History, University of Alberta, 1976, 704; Calderwood, 189
10 Hinds and Surman were elected in 1930 president and secretary, respectively, of the Baptist Convention of Saskatchewan: Calderwood, 185.
11 Calderwood, 181, as quoted in Gardiner Papers, 12848
12 See Calderwood, 170–2.
13 *The Klansman* (April 1930)
14 Copies of *The Klansman* are available in the Rt Hon. John George Diefenbaker Papers, MG 26, M, Series 11, Pre-1940, Vol. 14, 'Ku Klux Klan' File 1928–36, Public Archives of Canada.
15 *The Klansman* (April 1930)
16 Ibid.
17 Ibid.
18 Ibid. (November 1928). Other journals favoured by Klansmen were Moloney's *The Freedman, The Sentinel,* and *The Beacon,* a Vancouver publication edited by the Reverend Duncan McDougall.
19 André Siegfried, *America Comes of Age,* trans. H.H. Hemming and D.

Hemming (New York: Harcourt Brace 1926), 134–5. Louis Budenz's characterization of the Indiana Klan's constituency was not far different: 'literate but ignorant, Anglo-Saxon but decadent, colourless in imagination and vocabulary but given much to the tinseled pomp of fraternal organizations – these worthy brethren of the Tennessee anti-evolutionists were merely awaiting the whispered message of the Klan.' 'There's Mud on Indiana's White Robes,' *The Nation*, 27 July 1927

20 James H. Gray, *The Roar of the Twenties* (Toronto: Macmillan 1975), 277

21 J.F. Bryant to R.B. Bennett, 2 June 1928, R.B. Bennett Papers, Public Archives of Canada, 25117–18

22 David Smith, *Prairie Liberalism: The Liberal Party in Saskatchewan, 1905–71* (Toronto: University of Toronto Press 1975), 144

23 Patrick Kyba, 'The Saskatchewan General Election of 1929,' MA thesis, University of Saskatchewan, Saskatoon, 1964, 24

24 Robert England, *The Central European Immigrant in Calgary* (Toronto: Macmillan 1929), 6. Citing the *Canada Yearbook* (1926, 148), England noted (5–7) that, in 1924, in Saskatchewan, 'children born to foreign-born mothers out-numbered children born to Canadian-born mothers.'

25 Ibid., 10

26 Ibid.

27 J.G. Gardiner to W.L. Mackenzie King, 15 December 1928, King Papers, Public Archives of Canada, MG 26, J-1, Vol. 152, 129782

28 *Saskatoon Star*, 11 June 1927, as quoted in Brennan, 685

29 Brennan, 682–3

30 According to T.C. Davis, Bishop Lloyd's Association was 'a sort of half brother to the K.K.K.' T.C. Davis to W.L. Mackenzie King, 29 May 1928, King Papers, MG 26, J-1, Vol. 151, 129024

31 In pursuit of this latter goal, he was severely wounded at the Battle of Cut Knife while serving with the University Company of the Queen's Own of Toronto, in the North West Rebellion of 1885. Stints with the Rothesay School for Boys, in New Brunswick, Emmanuel College in Saskatoon, and the ill-fated Barr colony of Saskatchewan – which he led and served – as chaplain were fol-

lowed by his election as bishop of Saskatchewan in 1922. *Pioneers and Prominent People of Saskatchewan* (Toronto: Ryerson Press 1924), 42

32 T.C. Davis to W.L. Mackenzie King, 1 June 1928, King Papers, MG 26, J-1, Vol. 151

33 *Regina Star,* 29 May 1929, as quoted in Calderwood, 187. The bishop, it appears, was no bosom friend of the Jews. 'When the Jews form one half of one percent of the population, and own 16 out of 46 [liquor] export houses,' he announced during the 1920 liquor export campaign, 'it is time they were given to understand that since they have been received in this country and have been given rights enjoyed by other white men, they must not defile the country by engaging in disreputable pursuits': *Calgary Herald,* 8 October 1920, as quoted in James Gray, *Booze* (Toronto: Macmillan 1972), 183.

34 *Canadian Annual Review,* 162–3. Lloyd's argument in favour of maintaining a preponderant proportion of British immigrants was, apparently, bought by the Social Service Council of the Church of England, which passed a resolution in September 1928 urging 'the regulation of new comers to Canada in such a way that at no time would the number of non-preferred continentals bare a greater ratio to the British-Born than 50%.' According to Robert England (36), the declining proportion of British immigrants to Canada in the 1920s was attributable not to a lack of effort by the federal government, the railway and steamship companies, and various religious and patriotic societies promoting immigration, but derived, instead, from the better employment and welfare conditions in Britain where the employed were 'reasonably well-cared for' and were not 'easily persuaded' that Canada offered better opportunities.

35 C.J. Houston and W.J. Smythe, *The Sash Canada Wore: A Historical Geography of the Orange Order in Canada* (Toronto: University of Toronto Press 1980), 64–5

36 Calderwood, 173

37 Houston and Smythe, 128

38 J.F. Bryant to R.B. Bennett, 2 June 1928, Bennett Papers, 25118

39 As quoted in R.S. Pennefather, *The Orange and the Black* (Toronto: Orange and Black Publications, 1984), 14

40 Ibid.
41 An example of the intensity of Orange political participation was
provided in the election of 1917, when the Kitchener Loyal Orange
Lodge No. 267, Prince Albert, sent all Liberal and Conservative
candidates a questionnaire containing, among others, the following
questions: 'Are you prepared to resist any special privileges being
granted to any section of the population of Saskatchewan either on
account of race or religion? Are you opposed to all bilingual
teachings in the schools of the Province and in favour of placing
the French language on the same footing as other foreign languages? Are you in favour of a law providing that all School Trustees
must be able to read and write in the English language?' Introduc-
ing the questionnaire was a bold statement of Orange principles –
'One School, One Language, One Flag.' Private papers of W.F.A.
Turgeon, General Files, 1909–21, as quoted in Calderwood
42 23 August 1927, King Papers, MG 26, J-1, Vol. 143, 121723
43 Pennefather, 42–3. Pennefather noted that Orangemen were avid
joiners of British and Protestant associations like the Masonic
Order, service clubs, churches, and political organizations.
44 See Keith A. McLeod, 'Politics, Schools and the French Language,
1881–1931,' in Norman Ward and Duff Spafford, eds., *Politics in
Saskatchewan* (Don Mills: Longmans, Canada 1968), for an exposition of the language and schools issues preceding the depression
period.
45 *Canadian Annual Review of Public Affairs* (Toronto 1905), 242
46 R.J.A. Huel, 'La Survivance in Saskatchewan: Schools, Politics, and
the Nativist Crusade for Cultural Conformity,' PhD thesis, University of Lethbridge, 1975, 121, quoting the *Orange Sentinel*, 30 June 1927
47 *Regina Morning Leader*, 7 June 1928
48 *Orange Sentinel*, 2 December 1926, as cited in Calderwood, 4
49 Huel, 121
50 *Regina Morning Leader*, 5 June 1928. According to *Queen's Quarterly's*
'Observer,' the opponents of French 'domination' of Catholic
schools included some English-speaking Catholics: 'There is a
feeling among English-speaking Catholics that the hierarchy is too
French in its outlook; that the priesthood is influenced as much by
considerations of language as of faith and that there might well be

common ground between Orangemen and Irish Catholics against
the increasing domination of Quebec': 'The Ku Klux Klan of
Saskatchewan,' *Queen's Quarterly,* Autumn 1928, 598.

51 *Saskatoon Phoenix,* 4 June 1928
52 *Young Journal,* 1 March 1928, in Calderwood, 193
53 Calderwood, 194
54 Ibid., 196
55 Ibid., 190
56 J.W. Grant, 'The Church in the Canadian Era,' *A History of the
Christian Church in Canada,* Vol. 3 (Toronto: McGraw-Hill Ryerson
1972), 123
57 *Saskatoon Phoenix,* 4 June 1928
58 Ibid. According to Reverend H.D. Ranns, the Saskatoon Presbyter-
ies anti-Klan overture failed because 'a large body of ministers and
laymen, certainly not because they supported the Klan but in the
desire for harmony, wished to shelve the matter': *Regina Morning
Leader,* 4 June 1928.
59 Ibid. The Presbytery of Assiniboia, located in the southwest corner
of the province, was a hotbed of Klan support. According to
Calderwood (97), seven local ministers in 1926–7 were Klansmen,
several of whom sat on influential committees. The policy pronouncements of its social committee, which included three Klansmen, reflected the usual concern with moral, as opposed to progressive social questions: the combating of bootlegging and
gambling and Sabbath Day enforcement.
60 Rabbi Ferdinand M. Isserman, 'The Klan in Saskatchewan,' *Canadian Jewish Review* 34 (15 June 1928)
61 Ibid.
62 An Observer, 596
63 Huel, 150–1
64 MacLeod, 143
65 Huel, 149–50
66 C.B. Sissons, *Church and State in Canadian Education* (Toronto:
Ryerson Press 1959), 294–5
67 MacLeod, 143
68 Huel, 153
69 Ibid., 152. By law, a primary course in French could not be taught

beyond the first grade in public schools, nor could French be used as a language of instruction beyond grade one or a child's first year in school.

70 Huel, 152

71 *Saskatoon Phoenix*, 5 June 1928. According to Premier Gardiner, it was government policy to advise the trustees to remove the crucifixes upon complaint: 'Neither the wearing of religious garb, nor the display of emblems was contrary to the law.'

72 J.F. Bryant to R.B. Bennett, 2 June 1928, Bennett Papers, 25118; Huel, 153; Irene H. McEwan, 'Religious and Racial Influences on a Senate Appointment, 1931,' *Saskatchewan History* 25/1: 23

73 Huel, 153

74 S.P. Rondeau, *The Gravelbourg School Situation and Its Effect upon School Administration in the Province* (Woodrow, Sask.: n.p. n.d.), 8, as cited in Huel, 125

75 The offensive passage in the reader frequently cited by Rondeau described the conversion of a Protestant family to Catholicism following a visit to a Catholic church where a burning lamp signified the presence of Christ behind a 'little golden door.' The reader, widely used in Ontario and elsewhere, was delisted following complaints in 1926, but continued in use – with the offensive passages deleted – until a substitute was found. *Saskatoon Phoenix*, 5 June 1928

76 George Weir, *The Separate School Question in Canada* (Toronto: Ryerson Press 1934), 17. Unlike in Ontario, the Catholic in Saskatchewan was required by law to support a Roman Catholic separate school if he resided in a district where one was established. 'To the ardent Orangeman,' Weir concluded (157), 'the implications of the Saskatchewan separate school law in the matter of school support remained little less than coercion or ecclesiastical tyranny.'

77 J.H. Archer, *Saskatchewan: A History* (Saskatoon: Western Producer Prairie Books 1980), 193

78 Memo, W.C. Barrie, 1 June 1926, King Papers, MG-26, J-1, Vol. 150, 128105

79 J.G. Gardiner to W.L. Mackenzie King, 23 August 1927, King Papers, MG 26, J-1, Vol. 143

80 *Regina Morning Leader,* 31 January 1928
81 Ibid.
82 Ibid.
83 Ibid.
84 Ibid.
85 Ibid.
86 J.F.C. Wright, *Saskatchewan: The History of a Province* (Toronto: McClelland and Stewart 1955), 179
87 W.L. Mackenzie King to J.G. Gardiner, 30 August 1927, King Papers, MG 26, J-1, Vol. 1433
88 *Regina Morning Leader,* 31 January 1928
89 W. Calderwood, 'The Decline of the Progressive Party in Saskatchewan, 1925–1930,' *Saskatchewan History* 31/3 (Autumn 1968) 90
90 Ibid.
91 *Regina Morning Leader,* 31 January 1928
92 Gardiner responded to Whatley's question with: 'Just give me some time. You will be quite illuminated when I get through.' He then proceeded to elaborate on Klan and opposition matters without being explicit, or factual, regarding Klan-Progressive ties.
93 *Regina Morning Leader,* 1 February 1928
94 Calderwood, 'The Decline of the Progressive Party,' 97
95 Progressive MP John Evans spoke at a Klan rally in Saskatoon. Calderwood, *The Rise and Fall of the Ku Klux Klan,* 223–4, quoting Gardiner Papers, 125081 and 12411–510
96 *Manitoba Free Press,* 24 May 1928; Calderwood, 'The Decline of the Progressive Party,' 93–4
97 *Western Producer,* 23 February 1928
98 Smith, 133
99 *Manitoba Free Press,* 24 May 1928
100 A.G. Mackinnon to R.B. Bennett, 28 March 1928, Bennett Papers, 25005
101 *Manitoba Free Press,* 23 May 1928, and E.C. Gregory to R.B. Bennett, 26 June 1928, Bennett Papers, 25154–7
102 W.D. Cowan to R.B. Bennett, 16 January 1928, Bennett Papers, 24885, as quoted in Calderwood, *The Rise and Fall of the Ku Klux Klan,* 116
103 Ibid.

104 J.F. Bryant to R.B. Bennett, 2 June 1928, Bennett Papers, 25117
105 J.F. Bryant to R.B. Bennett, 31 May, 1928, Bennett Papers, 25113
106 Francis B. Reilly to R.B. Bennett, 14 April 1928, Bennett Papers, 25025–26
107 Biography of J.T. M. Anderson, clipping file, Public Archives of Saskatchewan; *Regina Daily Post*, 7 September 1929. Born in Fairbank, Ontario, in 1878, Anderson attended high school in Toronto before taking BA, MA, and LLB degrees at the University of Manitoba. He later returned to the University of Toronto and picked up a doctoral degree in pedagogy in 1917–18. Anderson taught school in Ontario and Manitoba, in the Icelandic settlement of Gimli, before immigrating in 1908 to Saskatchewan, where he taught in Melville and Grenville before pursuing his career in educational administration.
108 Anderson's views on immigration, Canadianization, and education were outlined in his *The Education of New Canadians* (Toronto: J.W. Dent 1918).
109 *The Reporter*, 23 February 1929
110 Affidavit of H.F. Emmons, 17 May 1928, in *Saskatoon Phoenix*, 31 May 1928
111 Ibid.
112 Ibid.
113 Testimony of H.F. Emmons, *Regina Morning Leader*, 8 May 1928. The Conservative leader, it seems, was not free of association with other prominent Klansmen. According to M.J. Coldwell, Anderson one day introduced him to a 'man called Hawkins' in Regina's Kitchener Hotel. Transcript of interview with M.J. Coldwell, June 1963, as cited in Calderwood, *The Rise and Fall of the Ku Klux Klan*, 215
114 Patrick Doherty to R.B. Bennett, 21 April 1928, Bennett Papers, 25035
115 J.F. Bryant to R.B. Bennett, 16 March 1928, Bennett Papers, 24954. Bryant's estimate of the Klan's large representation and activity was corroborated by others, including MacPherson, who wrote Bennett 'that undoubtedly a large number of Klansmen were delegates.' M.A. MacPherson to R.B. Bennett, 16 March 1928, Bennett Papers, 24996
116 J.F. Bryant to R.B. Bennett, 16 March 1928, Bennett Papers, 24952. Negotiations with the Progressives, spearheaded by several promi-

nent Conservatives, on cooperative electoral arrangements were
undertaken before the convention and continued thereafter.
Brennan, 714–15

117 Brennan, 717
118 J.F. Bryant to R.B. Bennett, 16 March 1928, Bennett Papers, 24951
119 J.H. Hearn to R.B. Bennett, 28 March 1928, Bennett Papers, 24988
120 According to J.F. Bryant, MacMillan was convinced that the culprit
was the Nomination Committee secretary Fred Somerville, who
dictated the list of nominees from a pencil memorandum to Prince
Albert delegate John Diefenbaker, charged with typing and distributing the list to the convention (J.F. Bryant to R.B. Bennett, 11
April 1928, Bennett Papers, 25014). Somerville later denied
altering the list, insisting 'that if any change had taken place it was
in the typewriting.' Diefenbaker's contacts, if any, with the Klan
have long been the subject of speculation among political opponents and observers. During the 1929 provincial election campaign
in the Prince Albert constituency, C.S. Davis, the younger brother
of incumbent T.C. Davis, and Mackenzie King's local lieutenant,
alleged that Diefenbaker, the Conservative candidate, was close to
the Klan and would be answerable to it if elected: G.W.D. Abrams,
Prince Albert: The First Century, 1866–1966 (Saskatoon: Modern Press
1966), 278. Davis claimed knowledge of the existence of the Prince
Albert Klan's membership list and announced: 'it is only necessary
to go to Mr. Diefenbaker's committee rooms then you will find the
heads among them there.' Religious and educational issues bulked
large in the Prince Albert contest, as elsewhere, and Diefenbaker
was defeated by a few hundred votes. In Prince Albert city, Diefenbaker received a large majority in the predominantly Protestant
east end just as Davis was overwhelming supported in the Catholic-
dominated west end. Rumours that Diefenbaker flirted with the
Klan surfaced as late as the 1956 National Conservative leadership
convention. 'In 1956 the Hon. Earl Rowe's group from Toronto
decided to prevent me from becoming leader of the Conservative
Party,' Diefenbaker wrote in his memoirs, 'by charging that I had
been a Ku Klux Klan member. This allegation was completely
disproved when a provincial Cabinet Minister, an outstanding
Liberal and a man of recognized integrity, the Hon. Hubert

Staynes, who had a complete list of the Klan membership, denied
categorically that my name was on that list. He further stated that it
was clear that I had never been a member of that organization': J.G.
Diefenbaker, *One Canada: Memoirs of the Rt. Hon. John G. Diefenbaker,
the Crusading Years, 1895–1956* (Toronto: Macmillan 1975), 151.
When Premier Gardiner spoke to a Loreburn audience in support
of Liberal candidate Thomas Waugh, during the October 1928
Arms River by-election campaign, Diefenbaker, an ardent Tory
worker and former candidate, was given the platform and prefaced
questions addressed to the premier – on political corruption and
sectarian influence in the public-school system – with a disavowal of
membership in the Klan: *Regina Morning Leader,* 22 October 1928.
In his memoirs, Diefenbaker claimed (150) he met 'Klan leader, J.J.
Moloney, only once and then for a period of not more than five or
ten minutes,' when Moloney sought his legal advice on Klan
financial matters relating to the Emmons swindle. Diefenbaker
considered his defeat in the 1929 provincial election fortuitous
since he would likely have served as attorney general in the Anderson government, which subsequently legislated against French-
language use and sectarian influence in the public-school system.
Though Diefenbaker disagreed with measures barring nuns in
habits from teaching in public schools, he later wondered whether
he would have had the courage to resign over the issue. 'I think my
normal reaction would have been, after my labours in three
elections, "Why should I resign?" That would have been my destruction. I would have been irredeemably associated in the public mind
with the religious and racial bigotry of the period': ibid., 151.
Diefenbaker's first reported case as a young lawyer, it may be noted,
involved an appeal against the conviction of two French-Canadian
school trustees near Domremy, a French-speaking area south of
Prince Albert, who were found guilty by a Wakaw Justice of the
Peace of permitting the use of French as a language of instruction
beyond the first grade. The appeal was won, and Diefenbaker's fees
were paid from a subscription organized by L'Association
Catholique Franco-Canadienne de la Saskatchewan: ibid., 121.
Diefenbaker, like other Conservatives, blamed the Liberals for the
Klan's expansion. 'If left alone,' he concluded, 'it might have

disappeared as quickly as it had emerged. Unfortunately for
everyone, Gardiner began in 1928 to use it as a political straw man.
He launched a series of political attacks on it in the Provincial
Legislature, bringing the K.K.K. out of its obscurity, giving its leaders
the appearance of political martyrs, and making it a recognizable
centre of opposition to his government and its policies': ibid., 150.
Gardiner's use of the Klan to tar the Conservatives was not dissimi-
lar, according to Diefenbaker, to tactics employed by Mackenzie
King's federal Liberals who 'deliberately stirred up racial strife in
the 1921 federal campaign in Prince Albert by claiming the Conservatives supported the removal of the right to vote of all naturalized Canadians' and, in 1925, by quoting 'the unjust and callous
statements of three Ontario Conservatives of minor importance'
who claimed King ran 'in a riding among the Doukhobors, up near
the North Pole where they don't know how to mark their ballots':
ibid., 149. References to King's preference for 'garlic-smelling'
continentals over native-born Canadians in his old riding of North
York were also widely broadcast.
121 J.A. Hearn to R.B. Bennett, 28 March 1928, Bennett Papers, 24988
122 E.C. Gregory to R.B. Bennett, 28 June 1928, Bennett Papers, 25155
123 Patrick Doherty to R.B. Bennett, 21 April 1928, Bennett Papers,
25035–8
124 R.B. Bennett to A.G. MacKinnon, 3 April 1928, Bennett Papers, 25077
125 R.B. Bennett to J.T. M. Anderson, 17 April 1928, Bennett Papers,
25624
126 Diefenbaker, 150
127 Letter to the editor, James F. Bryant, 8 May 1928, in *Regina Morning
Leader,* 10 May 1928
128 C.H. Higginbotham, *Off the Record: The CCF in Saskatchewan* (Toronto: McClelland and Stewart 1968), 29
129 Letter to the Editor, J.F. Bryant, *Regina Morning Leader,* 10 May 1928
130 *Saskatoon Morning Herald,* 7 May 1928
131 *Saskatoon Star,* 11 May 1928
132 *Regina Morning Leader,* 8 May 1928. Emmons later complained that
he returned home to the United States after Snelgrove and others
threatened to 'bring in the United States lot and start Knight-riders
[*sic*] known as the Black Robes ... and they were going to build up

an organization and march down the streets of Regina and there would be blood shed.'

133 *Saskatoon Star,* 11 May 1928

134 28 May 1928

135 *Regina Morning Leader,* 31 May 1928

136 Ibid.

137 W.M. Kipp, 'Canadian Province Turns to the Klan,' 8 July 1928, section 3, p. 7. Kipp thought the Saskatchewan Klan lacked 'the robes and goods and the militancy of its southern brethren' but bristled with 'Kleagles and Wizards and above all with well-paid organizers.'

138 *Regina Morning Leader,* 11 May 1928

139 J.F. Bryant to R.B. Bennett, 31 May 1928, Bennett Papers, 25113

140 R.B. Bennett to J.T.M. Anderson, 20 June 1928, Bennett Papers, 25130

141 J.G. Gardiner to S. Moyer, 10 May 1928, Gardiner Papers, 12197, cited in Brennan, 726–7

142 J.G. Gardiner to T.F. Waugh, 15 May 1928, Gardiner Papers, 12209, cited in Brennan, 727

143 Andrew Haydon to W.L. Mackenzie King, 7 December 1928, King Papers, MG 26, J-1, Vol. 152, 130058–9

144 Memo of W.C. Barrie, 1 June 1928, King Papers, 128105–6; James G. Gardiner to W.L. Mackenzie King, 7 June 1928, King Papers, MG 26, J-1, Vol. 152, 129769; Calderwood, *The Rise and Fall of the Ku Klux Klan,* 211, noted a number of prominent Liberals in the Klan, including J.A. Wilson, the MLA for Rosetown.

145 J.G. Gardiner to W.L. Mackenzie King, 7 June 1928, King Papers, MG 26, J-1, Vol. 152, 129770

146 *Saskatoon Phoenix,* 2 June 1928

147 On the matter of the archbishop's influence, Gardiner stated: 'We do everything he tells us, for he never tells us to do anything': *Saskatoon Phoenix,* 22 June 1928.

148 Ibid., 2 and 22 June 1928, for reports on the Gardiner speeches at Hanley and Dysart

149 *Regina Morning Leader,* 3 July 1928

150 Ibid.

151 Ibid.

152 *Regina Post*, 3 July 1928
153 *The Klansman*, November 1928
154 *Regina Morning Leader*, 25 July 1928
155 *Winnipeg Tribune*, 19 November 1928; *Regina Morning Leader*, 21 November 1928; *Saskatoon Phoenix*, 21 November 1928
156 J.G. Gardiner to J.F. Johnson, 18 June 1928, Gardiner Papers, 8810, as cited in G. Unger, 'James G. Gardiner: The Premier as a Pragmatic Politician,' MA thesis, University of Saskatchewan, Saskatoon, 1967, 109
157 J.G. Gardiner to C.A. Dunning, 29 October 1928, Gardiner Papers, 8837–8, as cited in Unger, 112
158 *Regina Star*, 10, 12, 16 October 1928, cited in Brennan, 739
159 Key players in the provincial and national liquor trade, the Bronfmans had long been the target of an assortment of purists, politicians, and envious competitors. The royal commission investigating the administration of the Department of Customs and Excise in 1927–8 heard allegations from officials against Harry Bronfman of attempted bribery and tampering with witnesses and recommended in an interim report, early in 1928, that Bronfman be prosecuted. The wide currency given to the charges, and the reluctance of the provincial and federal Liberal governments to prosecute, provided ample fuel for Tories, Klansmen, and others to repeat old claims that the Liberals were beholden to Bronfman and feared damaging revelations in court. Soon after its election, the Anderson government brought Harry Bronfman back to Regina to face charges. He was acquitted: Peter Newman, *The Bronfman Dynasty* (Toronto: McClelland and Stewart 1978), 115–21. Contributing to Bronfman's troubles was a minor current of anti-Semitism prevalent among, though not restricted to, purists like George Exton Lloyd who commented, as early as the 1921 plebiscite on the liquor question, on the prominence of Jews in the liquor trade and warned them not to 'defile the country by engaging in disreputable pursuits': ibid., 118; Gray, *The Roar of the Twenties*, 287. Prominent Saskatchewan Klansmen, like their colleagues elsewhere, maligned the Jews but devoted their prime attention to 'non-preferred immigrants' and Catholics. J.J. Moloney's world conspiracy was Catholic, rather than Jewish, and the sectarian education and

immigration issues favoured by the Klan targeted the Catholics as the prime villains. Demographic factors doubtless contributed to this preference. The Jews in Saskatchewan, unlike the Catholics, comprised a minuscule segment of the population and were hardly prominent, civically, economically, or politically.

160 *Regina Star*, 19 October 1928, as quoted in Brennan, 739

161 J.G. Gardiner to W.L. Mackenzie King, 29 October 1928, King Papers, MG 26, J-1, Vol. 152, 129218

162 Calderwood, *The Rise and Fall of the Ku Klux Klan*, 159

163 According to a prominent Liberalist strategist, 'a great many Protestant Liberals voted straight against the Government and the German vote, which in that riding is strongly Lutheran, voted Tory for the first time in the history of this settlement': Andrew Haydon to W.L. Mackenzie King, 7 December 1928, King Papers, MG 26, J-1, Vol. 152, 130058.

164 *Regina Morning Leader*, 19 and 24 October 1928. There is no evidence that the Gardiner government ever granted the Klan a charter.

165 J.G. Gardiner to Thomas Taylor, 17 December 1928, King Papers, MG 26, J-1, Vol. 152, 129778. To C.A. Dunning, Gardiner noted that the Arms River campaign was the bitterest he had ever fought and 'had the effect of bringing out every attack which the opposition could possibly make against us ... I do not see how they can effectively make use of the propaganda in any general election': J.G. Gardiner to C.A. Dunning, 29 October 1928, Gardiner Papers, 8837–8, as quoted in Unger, 112.

166 See Patrick Kyba, 'Ballots and Burning Crosses – The Election of 1929,' in Norman Ward and Duff Spafford, eds., *Politics in Saskatchewan* (Toronto: Longman's 1962), 120. The 6 June results were: Liberals 26, Conservatives 24, Progressives 5, Independents 6. Two more Liberals were returned in deferred elections.

167 According to Kyba, the Liberal defeat was secured by the desertion of Protestants, Anglo-Saxons and Scandinavians, to the anti-government forces, with the Catholic and immigrant bases of Liberal support remaining intact. Liberal support and representation was maintained in the southwest border region, the north, and southeast area adjoining the Manitoba border – areas with a high concentration of Catholic and Central European immigrant voters.

The Tories, conversely, drew their support from predominantly Protestant and Anglo-Saxon or Scandinavian areas. While past elections in Saskatchewan had not been free of ethnic and religious strife, the 1929 contest was unique in the extent to which emotional non-economic issues predominated. The ethnic and religious differences became, in the late 1920s, pivotal rather than auxiliary, reflective of a weakening of the social concord hitherto sustained by the harsh conditions of a frontier province and the early subordination of new immigrants in existing structures. Gardiner himself traced the Liberal defeat to 'the application of racial and religious prejudice to the political situation ... fostered through a discussion of individual school difficulties, based upon the separate school law in this province, the activities of the Immigration Department at Ottawa and the fact that the Liberal party gains a considerable part of its support from the Province of Quebec and the Province of Saskatchewan:': J.G. Gardiner to W.R. Motherwell, 15 June 1929, Gardiner Papers, 9576–8, as quoted in Unger, 118.

168 The Anderson regime held power for one term and was decimated in the provincial general election of 1934, in which the Gardiner Liberals won 60 seats, and an overwhelming majority. The Conservatives failed to return a single member. Contributing to the Liberal landslide was the severe economic depression, which drove many Protestant liberals back into the Liberal party, as well as the wholesale alienation of the Catholic vote from the Conservative party – a legacy of both the polarized 1929 election, as well as the legislative and political performance of the Anderson government, which included a healthy representation of Orangemen, among them the premier, who took the post of minister of education; J.F. Bryant, appointed public works minister; and F.D. Munroe, minister of public health. See G.J. Hoffman, 'The Saskatchewan Provincial Election of 1934: Its Political, Economic and Social Background, MA thesis, Department of History, University of Saskatchewan, 1973. The Conservatives' perceived anti-Catholicism prevented them from exploiting the reticent support of Irish and Scottish Catholics – a growing constituency relative to the French – among whom the Liberal party's defence of French-language rights had not always been warmly received. Catholic opposition – French and non-

French – to the Anderson government was fortified by the absence of Catholic representation in the party caucus and government, by the Orange affiliations of government notables – including the premier – and by legislation relating to language and religious educational issues. In 1930, the Anderson government passed a bill restricting the teaching of French as a subject to no more than one hour per day, prohibiting the use of French as a language of instruction at all levels in the public-school system, and ensuring that 'English shall be the sole language of instruction at all schools, and no language other than English shall be taught during school hours': Weir, 113. Further changes in the school law required that school meetings be conducted in the English language; all trustees must be able to read, write, and conduct school meetings in the English language; and 'no emblem of any religious faith, order, sect, society or association shall be displayed in or on any school premises during school hours, nor shall any person teach or be permitted to teach in any school while wearing the garb of any religious faith': ibid., 115–17, 202–3. Like Anderson's earlier reputed flirtation with the Klan, the French-language and denomi- national legislation distressed R.B. Bennett, who had earlier counselled 'the greatest moderation ... in dealing with our Roman Catholic friends': R.B. Bennett to J.F. Bryant, 13 May 1929, Bennett Papers, 25255, as cited in McEwan, 19. Soon after the prime minister learned of the details of Anderson's French-language legislation, his personal secretary cabled Regina that the proposed changes would probably result in the downfall of the federal Conservative administration, 'will divide the country and do more to wreck Canadian unity at this time than any other single thing that has happened for many years': A.W. Miriam to M.A. MacPher- son, 5 March 1931, Bennett Papers, 351714, as cited in McEwan, 31. To minimize the damage, Bennett, in 1931, appointed a French- Canadian Catholic from Ponteix in the Gravelbourg area, Arthur Marcotte, to fill the Senate seat vacated by the late senator Ben Prince, a designation that disappointed the premier and his colleagues and invited loud protest from the Loyal Orange Associa- tion and the remnant Ku Klux Klan: ibid., 32.

169 By 'expressing the sentiments of the community' through 'outlaw

methods,' Siegfried concluded, the Klan was 'Fascist in inspiration':
Siegfried, 134.

170 An Observer, 601
171 Ibid.
172 Ibid.
173 According to the *Literary Digest*, 3 February 1923, Canada's easy
rejection of the Klan stemmed from uniquely Canadian conditions
and historical development quite apart from British cultural
inheritances. Quoting a Toronto *Globe* editorial, the *Digest* author
noted that racial and religious differences were tolerated and
accommodated in Canada as early as the post-Conquest years. No
real attempt was made to assimilate the French, and the subsequent
adoption of a federal state and flexible system of government
secured national unity without forced integration: 'The student of
… history reads a great deal about racial and religious questions,
but always as a problem of statemanship, not a matter to be settled
by mob violence … and political leaders received a certain training
in toleration and goodwill as essential to national unity, and the
people were educated along the same lines … to a people having
such traditions, so crude a device as the Ku Klux Klan would seem
like sticking a lever into a delicate piece of machinery.'

CHAPTER 4: *Goglus*

1 K.G.W. Ludecke, *I Knew Hitler* (London: National Book Association
and Jarrold's 1938), 482
2 Ibid., 483
3 Biographical details of Arcand's early career are drawn from Lita-
Rose Betcherman, *The Swastika and the Maple Leaf* (Toronto: Fitzhenry and Whiteside 1975), 5–6; David Rome, *Clouds in the Thirties:
On Anti-Semitism in Canada, 1929–1939*, Vol. 1 (Montreal: Canadian
Jewish Congress 1977), 84–5; Réal Caux, 'Le Parti National Social
Chrétien,' thesis essay, Department of Political Science, Laval
University, 1958, 20; *Biographies Canadiennes-Françaises* (Montreal
1931).
4 *Montreal Gazette*, 2 December 1937
5 Betcherman, 5

6 *Le Goglu* was published from 8 August 1929 to 10 March 1933.

7 For a summary of socio-economic changes and conditions see Andrée Lévesque, *Virage à Gauche Interdit: Les Communistes, les Socialistes, et leurs Ennemis au Québec* (Montreal: Les Editions du Boréal Express 1984), 9–39; Pierre Trudeau, 'The Province of Quebec at the Time of the Strike,' in Pierre Trudeau, ed., *The Asbestos Strike* (Toronto: James, Lewis and Samuel 1974), 1–6.

8 Bernard L. Vigod, *Quebec before Duplessis: The Political Career of Louis-Alexandre Taschereau* (Montreal and Kingston: McGill-Queen's University Press 1986), 164

9 Ibid.

10 *Le Goglu*, 30 May 1930

11 Kathleen Jenkins, *Montreal: Island City of the Saint Lawrence* (New York: Doubleday 1966), 477

12 Robert Rumilly, *Histoire de Montréal*, Vol. 4 (Montreal: Fides 1975) 159

13 Ibid., 140

14 'An energetic, courageous, powerful man ... a Christian with strong faith and unshakeable principles': 12 June 1931

15 A. Arcand to R.B. Bennett, 22 May 1930, Bennett Papers, Public Archives of Canada, 303526; A. Arcand and J. Ménard to R.B. Bennett, 14 January 1931, Bennett Papers, 402075; and Betcherman, 9, 10

16 See Rollande Montsion, 'Les Grands Thèmes du Mouvement National Social Chrétien et d'Adrien Arcand vus par les Principaux Journaux Fascistes au Canada Français, 1929–1938,' MA thesis, University of Ottawa, 1975, 19.

17 *Le Goglu*, 16 May 1930, 1 April 1932

18 'A bird beyond reproach that charms us with its harmonious song and whose bad habits we have yet to discover': ibid., 22 July 1932

19 'The bobolink is a charming bird with pleasant feathers, who is particularly fond of the province of Quebec. If we have such beautiful forests, we can be grateful to the bobolink to a great extent for each year it gobbles up millions and millions of noxious insects. It is our most courageous little hunter of vermin, a tireless worker, like the bee ... It has a racial instinct, communicating incessantly with its own with its melodious song, protecting its nest, its family, and its young with a ferocious energy ... The bobolink symbolizes

the new generation of a proud and vigorous race': ibid., 26 December 1930.

20 See, for example, Le *Goglu*, 6 December 1929.

21 'It is imperative to free the province from "the Beast" that slowed down its progress, and the Beast is egoism, carelessness, looting, treason, the selling of the country to the Americans, rural depopulation, agricultural and economic disaster': ibid, 31 January 1930.

22 Louis Rosenberg, *Canada's Jews: A Social and Economic Study of the Jews in Canada* (Montreal: Bureau of Social and Economic Research, Canadian Jewish Congress, 1939), 9

23 Ibid.

24 Bernard L. Vigod, *The Jews in Canada* (Ottawa: Canadian Historical Association 1984), 4

25 Ibid., 5

26 Pierre Anctil, *Le Rendezvous Manqué: Les Juifs de Montréal face au Québec de l'entre-deux-guerres* (Quebec: Institut Québécois de Recherche sur la culture 1988), 39

27 Rosenberg, 175

28 Ibid., 158

29 Ibid., 190

30 Ibid.

31 Ibid., 183

32 Ibid., 214

33 The first Jew to be elected to a legislative assembly was Ezekiel Hart, whose father, Aaron Hart, settled in Three Rivers, and became a substantial businessman, following the conquest of New France by the British, whose forces he served as a provisioner. Ezekiel Hart's election to the Lower Canada Legislative Assembly in 1807 became the focal point of a struggle between the English and French, resulting in the passage of a resolution by the Assembly denying him a seat following his insistence on taking the oath of office on the Hebrew Bible, with his head covered, in the traditional Jewish way: Michael Brown, *Jew or Juif: Jews, French Canadians, and Anglo-Canadians, 1759–1914* (Philadelphia, New York, Jerusalem: Jewish Publication Society 1986), 196. Hart was subsequently re-elected and again denied a seat. He later declined renomination. In June 1832, his stand was vindicated by the passage of legislation granting

Jews political and civic equality. It was in British Columbia, decades later, that the first Jew, Henry Nathan, sat in a legislative assembly. When British Columbia joined Canada in 1871, Nathan was elected to the House of Commons, where he represented Victoria until 1874. His seat in the provincial legislature was filled by another Jew, Selim Franklin. Other Jewish MLAs and MPs included S. Hart Green (first elected in 1910) and Marcus Hyman in Manitoba, Peter Bercovitch and Joseph Cohen in Quebec, and David Croll and J.J. Glass in Ontario. Federal Jewish representatives include Samuel Jacobs,MP for Montreal–Cartier in Quebec, Samuel Factor from Toronto, and Abraham Heaps from Winnipeg.

34 Brown, 251

35 While Quebec's Jews formed a separate and distinct group, their gravitation was towards the English. For the most part, they learned and spoke English, and valued the English cultural and political tradition. Assimilation, however, was out of the question, and there was minimal integration into the anglo community. Michael Brown sensibly concluded (211–50), in his study of the interplay of the Jewish, English, and French communities, that the Jews formed a 'third solitude.'

36 Israel Rabinovitch, 'Anti-Semitism in Quebec,' paper read before the Canadian Jewish Congress, Eastern Division, 22 October 1933, reprinted in the *Canadian Jewish Chronicle*, 10 November 1933, 5

37 R.L. Calder, 'Is the French-Canadian a Jew-Baiter?' *Canadian Jewish Yearbook, 1939–1940*, 153

38 One should not overstate the non-violent case. There were, here and there, during the decades preceding the depression, acts of hooliganism resulting in property damage: Brown, 147. These were, however, isolated and exceptional events.

39 André Laurendeau, *Witness for Quebec*, essays selected and translated by Philip Stratford (Toronto: Macmillan 1973), 72

40 'In this other, reactionary France,' Michael Brown noted (149), 'French Canadians might legitimately seek their roots. And of this France, which looked to the past with nostalgia, anti-semitism was an integral part. Jews, who owed their freedom in Canada as in France to the destruction of the ancien regime, were ready symbols of the new order. In French Canada, where their numbers grew

steadily in the nineteenth century, they served increasingly as a symbol of the threat to French Canadian homogeneity. For the fanatics, for the paranoids, for anyone seeking a scapegoat for the ills of urbanization, industrialization and other trials of the twentieth century, Jews provided a convenient candidate. Their symbolic value was enhanced by their identification as the traditional Antichrist allegedly responsible for many of the Church's setbacks.' Louis Rosenberg noted (300) that, 'while a majority group may sometimes act magnanimously towards a small minority, a minority group of considerable size is often too much concerned with extending its rights and privileges to be generous in recognizing the rights of other minorities.'

41 Brown, 134
42 Ibid., 139
43 Ibid.
44 3 November 1908, as quoted in W.D.K. Kernaghan, 'Freedom of Religion in the Province of Quebec, with Particular Reference to the Jews, Jehovah's Witnesses and Church-State Relations, 1930–1960,' PhD thesis, Duke University, 1966, 32
45 Brown, 146
46 Neither of these gentlemen, however, outdid J. Edouard Plamondon, a Quebec City notary and journalist who, on 30 March 1910, delivered an address titled 'Le Juif' at the Cercle Charest, in the Saint Roch district of Quebec City, under the auspices of L'Association Catholique de la Jeunesse Canadienne-Française. The substance of the Plamondon speech was a malicious attack on all Jews who were designated as enemies 'without exception, in Quebec or elsewhere, by their faith and their acts ... of the Catholic faith, the life, honor and property of christians' in which the blood ritual, invented Talmudic apologetics for usury, theft, murder, and incendiarism – in order to collect insurance – and the desecration of the Lord's Day all figured prominently. Plamondon's speech was apparently well received by René Leduc, manager of La Société de Publication de la Libre Parole, who published and distributed the address in pamphlet form throughout Quebec City; and by local toughs who molested and stoned local Jewish residents and shattered windows in private homes and the local synagogue during

religious services. Two local Jews, Benzion Ortenberg and Louis
Lazarovitz, responded with a civil suit for defamation in the Quebec
Superior Court, against Plamondon and Leduc, which received
continent-wide publicity. The original lower-court decision, which
dismissed the plaintiff's action, was based on the supposition that
there could be no defamation if no particular person was named.
The appeal court noted, however, that the Quebec City Jewish
community numbered only seventy-five families. The plaintiff,
therefore, as a member of the 'restricted collectivity of the Jews of
Quebec' was entitled to bring an action of defamation against the
lecturer, 'the Jews of Quebec being sufficiently designated as the
object of the lecturer's attack.' Of Plamondon's claim of blood
ritual, Canon Scott testified at the trial: 'I have to say this. It gave
me a nice feeling. I am an archeologist and I like old-fashioned
things, and I find more old-fashioned things in Quebec than I do
anywhere else. This old-fashioned idea died out in the Middle Ages.
I think it is a terrible thing to revive these old charges': S.W. Jacobs,
'The Quebec-Jewish Libel Case,' address delivered before the
Superior Court of Quebec, 23 May 1913, Montreal, 1913, 20–1, as
quoted in Kernaghan, 53. The Plamondon case is discussed in
Anctil, *Le Rendezvous Manqué*, 267–70; Bernard Figler, *Samuel Jacobs,
Member of Parliament* (Gardenvale, PQ: Harpell's Press Cooperative
1970), 23–7; and Kernaghan, 52–9.

47 As quoted in Ernst Nolte, *Three Faces of Fascism* (New York: Holt
Rinehart and Winston 1966), 50
48 28 February 1902, as quoted in Figler, 9
49 Ibid., 8
50 The Nathan affair is ably outlined in Brown, 140–5.
51 Ibid., 140
52 Ibid., 141
53 Ibid., 136. *La Patrie* and *La Presse*, whose editor, Jules Heilbronner,
was Jewish, usually dealt with Jewish matters fairly. The English-
language press was predominantly pro-Dreyfus. Dreyfus was finally
acquitted, and vindicated, in 1906, twelve years after the initial
charges were laid.
54 As quoted in Figler, 5. Samuel Jacobs and his friend Lyon Cohen
launched the English-language paper whose first editor, curiously

enough, was an Irishman, Captain Carroll Ryan, who had worked previously for the *Montreal Witness*. The anti-Semitic stream in Quebec was fed, as well, by the arrival of a number of anti-Dreyfusard priests from France following the acquittal: Brown, 135.

55 The Ligue changed its name to the Ligue d'Action Française in 1918. In 1927, following the pope's condemnation of the French movement, it became Ligue d'Action Canadienne-française. Groulx joined the group in 1917 and was influential in broadening its approach from mainly linguistic and commercial concerns 'to advocating a general renaissance of all aspects of French-Canadian life': Susan Mann Trofimenkoff, *Action Française: French-Canadian Nationalism in the Twenties* (Toronto: University of Toronto Press 1975), 13. Their journal *L'Action Française* commenced publication in 1917. Though its personnel roots, and concerns, were French Canadian, the Ligue was influenced and inspired by the reactionary clerical, monarchical, French *Action Française*. Among the major influences on Groulx and several of his colleagues, was Charles Maurras, founder of the French *Action Française*, fascist precursor, and author of the famous conspiratorial doctrine of the 'Quatre états confédérés': Juifs, Protestants, Franco-Maçons, and Métèques (Jews, Protestants, Free Masons, Aliens), which, according to E. Nolte, divided France into two groups 'and denied one of them the right to call itself French': Nolte, 68. Sharing Groulx's admiration for Maurras was the youthful Jean Drapeau, who thought the Frenchman had 'a great mind.' His work, according to Drapeau, 'was marvellously written, with very powerful reasoning ... his ideas were true for any political regime': Brian McKenna and S. Purcell, *Drapeau* (Toronto: Clarke Irwin 1980), 35. In an October 1940 editorial in *Le Quartier Latin*, Drapeau scathingly denounced the 'disloyal competition' facing French-Canadian business. 'What good has it done us to open wide our door to refugees of the Russian revolution? How have these "poor unfortunates" who had to flee before the guns of revolution, showed us their gratitude? By none other than transforming the main business artery of our city ... into a filthy carnival where rotten meat sits ... beside stale crusts of bread, and where the sidewalks too often serve as garbage pails for decomposing fruit and vegetables; by bestowing on our metro-

polis repulsive neighborhoods we cannot pass through without our stomachs turning ... finally by ruining French-Canadian business by disloyal competition, based on immoral if not openly dishonest tactics': ibid., 37.

56 It needs be born in mind that anti-Semitism, while not uncommon in nationalist intellectual circles in the pre-depression and depression decades, was by no means universal. Leading dailies like *La Presse* and *La Patrie* usually dealt with Jewish matters fairly: Brown, 137. Journalists like J.C. Harvey and Olivar Asselin and liberal publications like *Le Jour*, *Le Canada*, and *L'Autorité* vigorously condemned anti-Semitism: Michael Oliver, 'The Social and Political Ideas of French Canadian Nationalists, 1930–1945,' unpublished PhD thesis, McGill University, 1956, 281–2. Nor should the existence of anti-Semitism in the French-Canadian community imply an absence of like sentiments in Anglo-Quebec. According to R.L. Calder (155), the Jews' undoing 'would not be wholly displeasing to the English-speaking Canadians. They harbour a deal of anti-semitism, more cleverly dissembled.' On discrimination against Jews at McGill University during the 1920s and 1930s, see Anctil, 59–104.

57 Kernaghan, 46

58 Trofimenkoff, 77. Israel Rabinovitch wrote the following trenchant analysis of the source and nature of nationalist vigilance: 'The French-Canadian, proudly vaunting a pioneer genealogy, amongst whom are found ancestry who "vanquished this land with sword and cross," lives in continual fear lest he loses his national identity before the steady and strengthening onslaughts of English influences in their own province. Quebec is still the home of everything Gaellic [*sic*] in Canada and the walls of this home are buttressed by all manner of national, patriotic and religious constructions, erected to ward off the foe of assimilation and to preserve the soul of the French-Canadian in its absolute integrity. Too impetuous, however, are the streams of life, which go their turbulent way, regardless of all the patriotic and religious dams constructed so as to prevent the mingling of the stream of French with that of the English life; the bulwarks often break; the dams crumble, and the loyal guardians of French-Canadian nationalism find themselves continually pointing with alarm and viewing with fear the prospect

of national inundation. It is in the nature of professional custodians, however, to exaggerate the real danger, and to make a mountain out of a molehill, so as to keep the French-Canadian populace in unremitting concern for himself and his national identity. He must constantly stand on guard for the protection of his language; he must be on the qui vive for the safeguarding of his national traditions; he must be ever vigilant for the preservation of his national traditions; he must not forsake either his political or economic positions. For if for a moment the French-Canadian will forget his interest and allow his national "boneé" to degenerate ... then will he be deprived of the last vestige of national and economic personality. Others will become the rulers and he, a slave in his native land. Such are the "whispers of death" that circulate daily in the press, through the radio, and at all patriotic assemblies': Israel Rabinovitch, 'Anti-Semitism in Quebec,' paper read before the Canadian Jewish Congress, Eastern Division, 22 October 1933, *Canadian Jewish Chronicle*, 10 November 1933, 5. R.L. Calder described the national custodians as college-bred, 'trained by a system devised to teach them not how to think, but what to think.' To this indoctrination 'they have added the curse of easy rhetoric.' The custodians or leaders, according to Calder, were locked out of 'positions of command' in finance, trade, and industry – a lock-out traceable to 'their own educators, and to those who controlled them.' Rather than blame themselves, or their controllers, they chose the easier path of shifting the blame. 'How easy it is,' Calder asserts, 'as a tactical side step, to hint, if not assert, that there is a conspiracy of the other races to prevent the French-Canadian from coming into his own – a conspiracy hatched and promoted by that shadowy figure, the "international financier" – the Jew of course.' See Calder, 153–5. Calder's assertion that the professional anti-Semitism of the 1930s and earlier decades was 'born of a few arrivistes, and some visionaries who ... impregnated a limited ... ephemeral class,' suggests why it was less evident in the neo-nationalist and independentist politics of the post–Second World War decades. The new class of managers and technocrats was neither limited nor ephemeral, and its status anxieties were less extreme or easily diverted and confounded by fruitless mystiques like anti-

Semitism. Contributing factors were the new secularism, the effect of the horror of the holocaust on public opinion, and the emergence of new liberal tendencies within the church.

59 Trofimenkoff, 79
60 Rabinovitch, 6
61 Everett C. Hughes, *French Canada in Transition* (Chicago: Phoenix Books, University of Chicago Press 1943), 212–19. Of the mix of Christian anti-Judaism and economic anti-Semitism, Rabinovitch (5) noted: 'the average French-Canadian professional man is naturally inclined to leave celestial matters to theologians; but when the Jew appears and opens a store or office in direct competition with his – then the aforementioned businessman can no longer remain unconcerned. Then, indeed, the religious cry, as much as it can contribute to the destruction of a competitor, can properly be mixed with one's business.' According to Louis Rosenberg (302), 'the French-Canadian ... who has attended the high schools and Catholic colleges of Quebec, with their emphasis on classical philosophy and literature, faces life in the larger cities of Quebec where the majority of the population is French and Catholic, but the large department stores and business offices conduct the major portion of their business in English. He falls an easy prey to demagogues ... who paint a rosy picture of the economic and political future of a Canada in which all immigration is prohibited and the choicest of white collar jobs in all the country are preserved for him. Unaware that there are thousands of Canadians of English, Jewish and other origins who find the struggle of life just as difficult as he does, his resentment is aroused by the story that is dinned into his ears that the choice things in life are monopolized by non-French and non-Catholic elements while he is relegated to the position of a hewer of wood and drawer of water, and is sometimes inclined to accept the Jew as the convenient scapegoat upon whose head his resentment is to be poured, ignorant of the fact that the great financial institutions, department stores, public utilities and business offices give even fewer opportunities for employment to Jewish fellow citizens than to his own relatives.'

A bit hard on his countrymen, Henri Bourassa, in May 1935, suggested the different economic and social behaviour of Jewish

and French-Canadian small businessmen contributed to the
development of anti-Semitic attitudes. The Jewish storekeepers,
Bourassa noted, worked hard and enlisted their family's help in
building their businesses. Their French-Canadian counterparts
quickly pretended they were self-made men and wished their son to
be 'a gentleman' and daughter a lady. Both, it was hoped, would
marry into rich families: *Canadian Jewish Chronicle*, 24 May 1935.

Denis Monière insists that the anti-Semitism in Quebec during
the 1930s was not 'cultural atavism,' or an 'inseparable expression'
of the French-Canadian mentality. Instead, it was merely a particular form of xenophobia, an ideological reflex in response to the
socio-economic effects of colonialism. 'Fearing their own extinc-
tion,' Monière concluded, 'they sought assurances, not by going
after the real cause of their situation, but by attacking groups that
were weaker than themselves.' Relatively successful economically,
the Jew's material advancement was resented by the French-
Canadian 'urban petty-bourgeoisie': Denis Monière, *Ideologies in
Quebec* (Toronto: University of Toronto Press 1981), 218.

62 According to Michael Oliver (282), anti-Semitism was not a very
active ingredient in the 1920s, in L'Action Française's nationalism,
but 'latent hostility' to the Jewish minority in Quebec was evident.
Kernaghan noted that, 'beginning around 1930, the mild form of
anti-semitism manifested in earlier years by the nationalist movement was given enormous impetus by the severe economic crisis,' a
view shared by Robert Rumilly: R. Rumilly, 'L'Affaire des Écoles
Juives,' *Revue d'Histoire de l'Amérique Française*, June 1956: 240.

63 Betcherman, 33. As early as 1923 Vanier had called for a Canadian,
Eduard Drumont, to disclose the Jewish presence in commerce,
industry, finance, politics, and the professions: Trofimenkoff, 79.

64 As quoted in Oliver, 284

65 Anctil, 132–8; Kernaghan, 101–2; and H.M. Caisserman, 'Anti-
Semitism (Canada),' *Universal Jewish Encyclopedia*, 1939: 388. Notre
Dame protesters were joined by striking interns from four other
hospitals. Dr Rabinovitch finally resigned his position, and the
striking students were eventually reinstated after signing an apology.

66 The several speeches at the meeting were eventually published as a
sixty-seven-page pamphlet entitled *Politiciens et Juifs*, which was well-

received by *L'Action Nationale* and other nationalist journals: Kernaghan, 82. 'I was one of the speakers at that meeting,' Laurendeau later wrote (278), 'and I spoke a great deal about politicians and just a little about Jews. But it was still too much. For our speeches were dreadful. One of us went so far as to proclaim: "You can't tramp on the tail of that bich Jewry in Germany without hearing it yap in Canada."

'Forgive them, Lord, they know not what they do. And, really, we didn't know. The speeches of twenty year old youths reflect ideas that are current in their milieu. And the ideas that were floating around then weren't always very lucid or beautiful.

'But that's exactly the frightening part. Take my four friends, the speakers that night. They were nice guys, all of them. None, as far as I know, has turned bandit or Jew-baiter. They were sincere and ardent. 'At the very time Hitler was getting ready to kill 6,000,000 Jews, they could speak very sincerely about "alleged persecution" and "so-called persecution" in Germany, which they contrasted to the bad treatment, "very real – by contrast," which French-Canadians were subject to here. I can still see myself and hear myself braying with the best of them at that meeting.'

67 Kernaghan, 85. Though the message of Achat Chez Nous was positive and prescriptive, its effect, albeit limited, and direction were against Jewish small businesses.

68 As cited in Kernaghan, 87

69 Rabinovitch, 5

70 Laurendeau, 278

71 Trudeau, 7

72 Arcand never did write an autobiography and little is known of his family background. Born and raised in Montreal, he obviously had some early contact and familiarity with Jews, as well as with Anglo-Canadians against whom he never developed an animus. His religious education and immersion in nationalist politics afforded him a good opportunity to be influenced by traditional, Christian anti-Judaism. How, as opposed to when, these sentiments developed into an overriding hate and commitment to professional Jew-baiting is not easily explicable.

73 See Anctil, 165–217; David Rome, *On the Jewish School Question in*

Montreal 1903–1931 (Montreal: Canadian Jewish Congress, National Archives 1975); Rumilly, 'L'Affaire des Écoles Juives'; Vigod *Quebec before Duplessis,* 156–61.

74 According to Rumilly ('L'Affaire des Écoles Juives,' 230), Mgr Gauthier 'Engage un jeune journaliste, Adrien Arcand, collaborateur ... de Joseph Ménard à combattre le bill – ce qui lance Adrien Arcand dans l'anti-sémitisme' [hired a young journalist, Adrien Arcand, a collaborator ... of Joseph Ménard, to fight the bill – which launched Adrien Arcand into anti-Semitism]. Montsion (32) and Caux (30) note that no anti-Semitic articles attributable to Arcand preceded his treatment of the school question.

75 Rome, *On the Jewish School Question in Montreal,* 126

76 Rumilly noted that 'un vent d'anti-semitisme' blew in the province during the David affair, which Arcand and Ménard contributed to.

77 *Canadian Jewish Chronicle,* 8 July 1932

78 6 November 1932. 'Since Jews only seek parliamentry favour when a country is corrupt,' Arcand wrote, 'there had to be extensive decadence in Quebec before they could come to demand recognition as an official minority by means of the David Bill. The province must be sufficiently dominated by money, dance, jazz, cinema, fashion, literature and Jewish prestige before Jews would dare demand what they never saw fit to demand in any other country in the world': quoted in Rome, *On the Jewish School Question in Montreal,* 123.

79 The 7 December 1933 edition of *Le Patriote,* for example, published a lecture of Ménard's, violently attacking Jewish business, delivered under the auspices of a local chapter of the Saint Jean Baptiste Society. A local priest presided. Publications published and edited jointly, or separately, by Arcand and Ménard included *Le Patriote,* which first appeared in May 1933; *Le Fasciste Canadien,* 1935–8; and *Le Combat National.* Arcand and Ménard split in late 1935. *Le Patriote* continued under Ménard's direction until October 1936, while Arcand busied himself thereafter with *L'Illustration Nouvelle,* considered the semi-official organ of the Union Nationale party, as well as *Le Fasciste Canadien* and, briefly, *Le Combat National.*

80 'The Jew has used sneaky and fraudulent means to get hold of our commerce. The fires ... the numerous bankruptcies, the robberies in the middle of the night in their own stores by accomplices to

collect theft insurance have been for the Jews weapons to ruin the honest commerce of others': *Le Patriot*, 7 December 1933. Sometimes, according to *Le Goglu*, the Jews used gentile flunkies to undermine legitimate established business in Quebec. When J.J. Harpell conducted a campaign against the Sun Life Insurance Company, he was accused of being in the pay of American Jewish competitors.

81 *Le Patriote*, 5 October 1933

82 *Canadian Jewish Chronicle*, 2 June 1933. The Lindbergh revelation was accompanied by a gory cartoon depicting a bearded, horned creature slitting the throat of a Christian child. The article and cartoon coincided with the centennial celebration of the emancipation of the Jews. *Canadian Jewish Chronicle*, 8 July 1932

83 David Martin, 'Adrien Arcand, Fascist – An Interview,' *The Nation*, 26 February 1938, 241

84 *Canadian Jewish Chronicle*, 8 July 1932

85 An excellent exposition of the history of the *Protocols* can be found in Norman Cohn, *Warrant for Genocide* (New York: Harper and Row 1966).

86 For a summary of his views, see *Fascisme ou Socialisme* (Montreal: édité 'Le Patriote' 1933), 22–67, and the series by Professor S. Cohon, 'Mystery and the Key – Ancient Falsehoods in Modern Guise Meet Scholarly Refutation,' *Canadian Jewish Chronicle*, 4, 11, 18, 25 February and 4, 11, 18 March 1938.

87 Arcand, *Fascisme ou Socialisme*, 28

88 'Jewry, because of its nature ... because of its distructive instincts, because of its immemorial atavistic corruption, because of its exclusively materialistic sentiments, there is the great danger': ibid., 34

89 Martin, 241. Arcand's views on the Jewish questions, as expressed in *The Key to the Mystery*, published under the imprint of the Research Committee of the Montreal Women's Communist League, were summarized by Professor Cohon: 'Lies and half lies are placed side by side of distorted facts. The present publication presents an assortment of passages from works of fiction, pathological ravings of anti-semitic paranoiacs and victims of persecution complexes, fraudulent fabrications, defamations by renegades and ravings by drunkards.'

90 'Jewry already directly controls more than half the globe. This is tangible proof of the execution of a vast plan of conquest, which ceaselessly expands with each revolution, with each loan consented to by the international gold bank': Arcand, *Fascisme ou Socialism* 35. Included in Arcand's bizarre catalogue of powerful political notables were Mustapha Kemal, 'Un Juif Originaire de Salonique,' and 'Le Général Cohen.' The reference is to Morris 'Two Gun' Cohen, a former bodyguard to Sun Yat-Sen who played a limited, if shadowy role in Chinese nationalist politics. Cohen, it turn out, was 'le maître de la Chine Soviétique.' Bismark, according to Arcand, was merely a half Jew. *Le Patriote*, 5 October 1933

91 *Canadian Jewish Chronicle*, 23 March 1934

92 Ibid.

93 Cohn, 243–6

94 Gisela C. Lebzelter, *Political Anti-Semitism in England, 1918–1939* (London: Macmillan 1978), 26, 64–6

95 Ibid., 49–67

96 Beamish claimed he taught Hitler and was consulted 'often' by the Nazis on the Jews who, quite apart from the French and Russian revolutions, were behind the conquest of England as well as the Cromwellian Revolution: *Winnipeg Tribune*, 24 October 1936. In his opus *The Jew's Who's Who* Beamish claimed, from study of the *Protocols*, and other documents in the British Museum, that the Jews offered Cromwell £500,000 to buy St Paul's Cathedral, which they hoped to convert into a synagogue. After settling in southern Rhodesia, Beamish served briefly, in 1938–9, as a member of Parliament, before internment, from 1940 to 1943, as a fascist sympathizer, following his opposition to the 'Kosher War.' Beamish died in 1948. During Beamish's prolonged absences from England, the *Britons* were presided over by Dr John H. Clarke, a student of homeopathy and chief consulting physician at the London Homeopathic Hospital. George P. Mudge, lecturer at the London Medical School, and an early member of the Eugenics Society, was the *Britons'* accredited race expert. It was Mudge's view that every Briton owed 'a debt of honour to England, to his race and to the dead, to replenish the race.' Marriage to a Jewess or any other 'oriental' woman was 'an act of treachery': Lebzelter, 56.

97 Ibid., 61, quoting *The Hidden Hand*, May 1921, 4

98 Ibid., 62. Palestine was eventually rejected because of its strategic location and occupation by Arabs who might be roused by 'a race of people who for countless ages have consistently stirred up trouble, revolution and anarchy amongst any nation with which they have come in contact.'

99 Beamish toured Canada in October/November 1936, and spent ten days in Montreal where he was introduced to a number of fascist locals: *Le Fasciste Canadien*, December 1937.

100 When asked by a correspondent of the *Nation* his solution to the Jewish problem, Arcand offered Beamish's prescription: 'The Jews? We will ship them off to Madagascar. The French and Polish Governments have investigated the island and according to their report it is capable of sustaining 110,000,000 people. We will not give it to them for nothing, of course; we will make them pay for it. Rothchild personally can pay $1,000,000. I have nothing against the Jews as long as they leave us alone. I would like to see them all together and happy. Palestine would be alright, but it is too small.' When pressed whether he could be 'put ... down as a Zionist,' Arcand replied he was 'the greatest Zionist in the World': Martin, 244.

101 Cohn, 232

102 H.H. Beamish to Adrien Arcand, 20 September 1937, RCMP Security Service Records, Canadian Security Intelligence Service, 1454–5

103 H.H. Beamish to Schepers, RCMP Security Service Records, 1501–2; also *Montreal Gazette*, 20 June 1940

104 The material on Leese and his organization is drawn from Lebzelder, 68–85, and Colin Cross, *The Fascists in Britain* (London: Barrie and Rockliff 1961), 60–5.

105 In 1931, Leese announced 'with deep regret' that Mussolini had fallen under Jewish influence. Italy's subsequent invasion of Abyssinia was denounced by Leese as 'a Jewish plot': Cross, 64, 140.

106 Lebzelter, 80

107 Cross, quoting *The Fascist*, February 1935

108 A. Leese to A. Arcand, 1 May 1934, RCMP Security Service Records, 1472

109 A. Arcand to R.B. Bennett, 10 September 1932, Bennett Papers

110 A.S. Leese to A. Arcand, 31 March 1939, RCMP Security Service Records, 1467

111 A.S. Leese to A. Arcand, 27 May 1934, RCMP Security Service Records, 1473

112 Leese mused about his trials, tribulations, and Jewish ritual murder in *My Irrelevant Defense: Meditations Inside Goal and Out, on Jewish Ritual Murder*, a volume that found its way to Arcand's shelves.

113 Cross, 156, and Lebzelter, 68. The Imperial Fascist League was disbanded and its headquarters closed at the outbreak of the Second World War. Leese was subsequently arrested and detained under defence regulations until 1944. Following release, he took up his old anti-Semitic ways and was subsequently designated by a failing H.H. Beamish as his anti-Semitic heir. Colin Jordan eventually assumed the dubious mantle: Lebzelter, 82.

114 Memo, A. Arcand to R.B. Bennett, Undated, Bennett Papers, 402136

115 Rothermere's *Daily Mail*, with a circulation of three million, was once described by Lord Salisbury as 'written by office boys for office boys': *Ottawa Morning Journal*, 16 January 1934. Lebzelter, 93. Rothermere apparently warned Mosley that anti-Semitism served as blinkers for politicians, preventing them from 'seeing nothing but Jews': Cross, 102.

116 *Regina Leader Post*, 20 June 1940

117 'Declaration of the Parti National Social Chrétien du Canada,' 10 February 1936, in *M.J. Finkelstein Scrapbook*, 1936–8, Roll 2, Public Archives of Manitoba

118 Ibid., for a good, albeit brief, survey of the anti-Semitic International, see Cohn, 232–50.

119 According to Norman Cohn (232–50), there were by 1939 some 120 American groups and agencies disseminating pro-Nazi anti-Semitic propaganda, the vast majority tiny and insignificant. The three largest 'purely American' agencies were Father Charles E. Coughlin's the National Union for Social Justice and the Christian Front, and the Winrod and Pelley organizations. Father Coughlin was a late convert to the cause, and it was not until 1938 that he discovered the corporate state, Jewish world conspiracy, and the virtues of Nazism. A Kansas Protestant fundamentalist, Winrod formed his Defenders of the Christian Faith in 1925 to combat modernism in religion. He turned to anti-Semitism and pro-Nazism

in the early 1930s and built a substantial following among the small-town and rural poor in Bible Belt states like Texas, Missouri, and Kansas. Winrod's rabid anti-Catholicism inhibited any enthusiasm Arcand may have had for his fascist ideology. The Silver Shirts peaked briefly in 1933–4, when they counted fifteen thousand members, and collapsed following Pelley's indictment and conviction on stock fraud charges.

120 Lucy S. Dawidowicz, *The War against the Jews, 1933–1945* (New York: Seth Press 1986), 42–8

121 'We greet with keen enthusiasm the supreme triumph of this great patriot, whose example commands the attention of all those who love their country ... freed of parasites, prosperous and generous for its children': *Le Goglu*, 10 March 1933. See also *Le Miroir*, 12 June 1932, 9 November 1932, 5 February 1933, 22 January 1933; *Le Patriote*, 23 November 1933.

122 'He put anti-Semitism at the foundation of his politics, not for the pleasure of persecuting a particular race but for the sole purpose of freeing his fellow countrymen, of rebuilding a Christian Germany, of giving back to his race the colossal fortune that the Jews had stolen from it, of protecting the German national idea against the corrosive poison of Jewish doctrines': *Le Miroir*, 12 June 1932.

123 Dawidowicz, 63

124 'No country can be truly free and economically independent if it is not first liberated from the Jews. And what is being done in Germany ... as in Romania, Lithuania, Czechoslovakia, Poland, and in countless other countries, can be done in Quebec, where the great majority of Canadian Jews live, particularly in Montreal. A country whose national activities are not in the Canadians' hands ... is at present at the mercy of the Jews ... The great majority of the Canadian people aspire to deliverance so that our commerce, our finances, and our industry become Canadian again. Fortunately, Jewry has not progressed here as far as in Germany and has not reached the level of power it has in certain European countries. That's why it will be easier to repulse. In a country where the situation is almost desperate, Hitler proved that deliverance is still easy when the national sentiment is well channelled': *Le Miroir*, 12 June 1932.

326 Notes to pages 123–5

125 Ludecke, 482–3 and Ludwig Lore, 'Nazi Politics in America,' *Canadian Jewish Chronicle*, 15 December 1933
126 Ludecke, 483
127 Betcherman, 28
128 A. Arcand to Major Frank Pease, 28 September 1933, *Report on Anti-Semitism*, Box: Group Relations, Jewish Canadian Collection, Jewish Public Library, Montreal. Ludecke quickly passed out of favour with Hitler, was imprisoned briefly, and later made his way to the United States.
129 *Report on Anti-Semitism*, Box: Group Relations, Jewish Canadian Collection, Canadian Jewish Public Library of Montreal, 4
130 See, for example, *Le Goglu*, 12 August 1932, announcing 'Le premier Congrès Mondial des Chefs Anti-Semites a eu lieu, cette semaine, dans une ville de l'Europe Centrale. L'Ordre Patriotique des Goglus était officiellement représenté, le même que plusieurs organisations de différents pays.'
131 Memo (unsigned) to H.H. Beamish, 13 October 1937, RCMP Security Service Records, 1451–2
132 S.W. Jacobs to Dr Harry Friedenwald, S.W. Jacobs Papers, MG 27, III, C3, Vol. 7, Public Archives of Canada
133 8 July 1932. *The Canadian Jewish Chronicle* was fully aware of the melding of home-grown and imported anti-Semitism. 'In the province of Quebec,' an editorial stated, 'we find a form of anti-semitism which seems to be indigenous to the temperament and disposition of a certain local philosophy. This in itself is disturbing. Add to this the nefarious network which stretches from the other side of the Atlantic and penetrates into every corner of the Dominion, and we begin to see the enormity of the ogre before us': *Canadian Jewish Chronicle*, 19 March 1937.

CHAPTER 5: *Embryo Nazism*

1 *Canadian Jewish Chronicle*, 19 March 1937
2 Ibid., 26 January 1934
3 *Canadian Jewish Congress – Fifty Years of Service, 1919–1969*, 28–9

4 Irving Abella and Harold Troper, *None Is Too Many* (New York: Random House 1982), 10

5 *Canadian Jewish Chronicle*, 16 July 1934

6 The congress's general secretary was H.M. Caiserman, a former director of the Zionist Organisation of Canada who had been active in Jewish community affairs for over a quarter of a century. In its anti-defamation, relief, immigration, and other work, the congress worked in conjunction with the American-Jewish Committee, the American-Jewish Congress, the Board of Deputies of England and South Africa, and B'nai B'rith. *Jewish Post*, 23 January 1936

7 According to Caiserman, eighteen young men were employed across Canada to collect data on the conditions of Canadian Jewry. A clipping bureau, which perused 103 newspapers, was established, together with sixty-four anti-defamation committees scattered across the country.

8 See *Canadian Jewish Chronicle*, 4 February 1938 to 18 March 1938, and 9 November 1934

9 *Jewish Post*, 23 January 1936, in *M.J. Finkelstein Scrapbook, 1936–1938*, Roll 2, Public Archives of Manitoba

10 The Canadian anti-defamation committee supplied the western Canadian press, and civic leaders, with articles refuting the *Protocols* nonsense.

11 *Canadian Jewish Chronicle*, 5 June 1936. While the congress and B'nai B'rith were busy in the field of public education and anti-defamation, they were not necessarily powerful or effective. Nor did unity always prevail. According to Abella and Troper (14), 'any notion of a Jewish Community that was well-financed, well-organized and united in a common cause during the crucial years immediately preceding the war is a fiction. Divisions and fractiousness festered, and whatever national organization there was, was weak.'

12 *Canadian Jewish Chronicle*, 14 April 1933

13 Ibid.

14 Bernard Figler and David Rome, *Hannaniah Meir Caiserman: A Biography* (Montreal: Northern Printing 1962), 249

15 *Canadian Jewish Chronicle*, 26 August 1938

16 S.W. Jacobs, to Dr Harry Friedenwald, 26 December 1933, S.W. Jacobs Papers, MG 27, III, C3, Vol. 7, Public Archives of Canada

17 Ibid.

18 Bernard Figler, *Samuel Jacobs: Member of Parliament* (Gardenvale, PQ: Harpell's Press Cooperative 1959), 185

19 Jacobs was one of several *shtadlonim* – intermediaries between the Jewish community and power centres – in Parliament. Serving with them during the early years of the King administration were A.A. Heaps, from Winnipeg, and Samuel Factor, Toronto: Abella and Troper, 14. The influence of the *shtadlonim* was variable, depending on the issue, but overall – given their tiny number and absence from the Cabinet – minimal.

20 Bercovitch was returned in the 1940 election and died in 1943. For biographical material on Bercovitch, see *Canadian Jewish Chronicle*, 1 January 1943, 6, and *Montreal Gazette*, 5 October 1938. While their vote in the St Louis division, at the time of Bercovitch's first election, was larger than in any other constituency, the Jews did not form a majority.

21 On the distinction between the well-established uptown Jews and their downtown compatriots – new, working-class immigrants – see Erna Paris, *Jews: An Account of their Experience in Canada* (Toronto: Macmillan 1980), 42–8; Jack Jedwad, 'Uniting Uptowners and Downtowners: The Jewish Electorate in Quebec Provincial Politics, 1927–1939,' *Canadian Ethnic Studies* 18/2 (1986) 9; Pierre Anctil, *Le Rendezvous Manqué: Les Juifs de Montréal face au Québec de l'entre-deux-guerres* (Quebec: Institut Québécois de Recherche sur la culture 1988), 183.

22 *Canadian Jewish Chronicle*, 1 January 1943

23 Ibid.

24 Ibid.

25 See *Le Miroir*, 1932

26 'Two Jewish MLAs alone, he and M. Cohen, have instantly gained what it took our fathers centuries of battles to win for us': *Le Goglu*, 11 April 1930

27 *Le Miroir*, 31 January 1932, as cited in Lita-Rose Betcherman, *The Swastika and the Maple Leaf* (Toronto: Fitzhenry and Whiteside 1975), 14

28 Ibid.

29 *Canadian Jewish Chronicle*, 10 November 1933

30 B.L. Vigod, *Quebec before Duplessis: The Political Career of Louis Alexandre Taschereau* (Montreal and Kingston: McGill-Queen's University Press 1986), 163

31 *Canadian Jewish Chronicle,* 26 February 1932

32 In the revised bill, only the libel of race, religion, and nationality was covered. References to class, sect, and other groups were dropped. There were also procedural alterations. See Betcherman, 16.

33 *Canadian Jewish Chronicle,* 19 February 1932

34 *Canadian Annual Review,* 1932, 174

35 *Canadian Jewish Chronicle,* 26 February 1932

36 Ibid., 19 February 1932

37 Ibid., 26 February 1932

38 Ibid.

39 Ibid.

40 *Le Devoir,* 13 February 1932, as cited in Betcherman, 16

41 Vigod, 160

42 Betcherman, 16, quoting *Le Miroir,* 31 January 1932

43 Betcherman, 15

44 Ibid., 16, quoting *Le Devoir,* 6 February 1932

45 Ibid., quoting *Le Devoir,* 3 February 1932

46 Ibid., 15

47 Ibid., quoting *Le Devoir,* 18 February 1932

48 Ibid., 17

49 Vigod, 160

50 *Le Soleil,* 19 February 1932, as quoted in Vigod, 160

51 *Canadian Annual Review,* 1932, 174

52 'One does not argue with a barking dog,' the *Chronicle* (26 February 1932) observed, 'or a quarrelsome drunkard.'

53 On the Abugov case, see *Canadian Jewish Chronicle,* 15 July and 16 September 1932. A few days after presentation of the petition for an injunction, Abugov instituted an action for damages, claiming five hundred dollars. In all, Abugov and his lawyers included in their petition fifty allegations that the respondent had 'caused to be written, published and printed in his journals calumnious, lying, horrible, outrageous, and libelous articles, illustrations, cartoons and slogans, against the Jews in general, with the object of hurting

their good reputation in general and your petitioner in particular, by holding up the Jewish race and your petitioner to hatred, ridicule and contempt.'

54 *Canadian Jewish Chronicle*, 22 July 1932
55 Ibid.
56 Ibid., 16 September 1935
57 As quoted in *Canadian Jewish Chronicle*, 16 September 1932
58 Ibid., 16 September 1932; *Montreal Gazette*, 14 September 1932
59 Ibid.
60 Ibid.
61 *Canadian Jewish Chronicle*, 16 September 1932
62 Ibid., 2 June 1933
63 Vigod, 279. The *Canadian Forum* cited Taschereau's proposed Defamatory Libel Act as one of several examples of why Quebec was rapidly becoming 'a center of Fascist infection and of the blackest kind of reaction.' That the bill was contemplated as a weapon against Fascist hate literature was apparently of little consequence to the *Forum*. See 'A Focus of Fascism,' 153/3 (June 1933): 323.
64 A. Arcand to R.B. Bennett, 2 January 1932, R.B. Bennett Papers, 402106, Public Archives of Canada
65 R. Rumilly, *Histoire de Montréal*, Vol. IV (Montreal: Fides 1974), 136
66 *Le Devoir*, 31 May 1933
67 A. Arcand to Major Frank Pease, 28 September 1933, 'Canadian Nationalist Party and National Social Christian Party,' File-Anti-Semitism, Box – Group Relations, Jewish Canadian Collection, Jewish Public Library of Montreal
68 *Canadian Jewish Chronicle*, 2 February 1934. 'We have one paper in Quebec worse in its attitude to Jews than any in Germany,' Jacobs reported. 'It must be subsidized, for prior to its present campaign against the Jews, it was dragged through the bankruptcy courts. No decent firm would advertise in such columns.'
69 Vigod, 160. A new mouthpiece of the Arcand movement, *Le Patriote*, began publication on 4 May 1933: Betcherman, 36
70 *Le Goglu*, 17 January 1930
71 A propos of the school issue, Houde commented to the legislature: 'If the Jews don't like it, they can get out.' As quoted from *L'Action Catholique*, 19 November 1930, in D. Rome, *Clouds in the Thirties: On*

Anti-Semitism in Canada, 1929–1939, Section 1 (Montreal: Canadian Jewish Congress 1977), 68

72 'Raise the rallying call of race and religion in a free country whose institutions must protect citizens of all origins, and minorities in particular': *Le Goglu*, 25 April 1930. 'Lorsque j'ai été élu maire de Montréal, il y a deux ans,' Houde continued. 'J'ai déclaré que j'étais le représentant de tous et que je ne désirais pas voir soulever de questions de race sous mon régime ... Je ne veux pas plus de rôle de M. Anderson de la Saskatchewan que celui de M. Norris du Manitoba' [When I was elected mayor of Montreal, two years ago, I declared that I was the representative of everyone and that I did not wish to see questions of race raised under my regime ... I do not want the role of Mr Anderson of Saskatchewan or that of Mr Norris of Manitoba]. Though Houde denounced anti-Semitism, he enjoyed little support among Jewish voters in either the 1930 or the succeeding election of 1932, in which he was defeated by Liberal Fernand Rinfret. According to Robert Rumilly (159), Houde was a favourite of the Italian community: 'L'élément Juif l'abomine,' Rumilly wrote, 'mais l'élément Italien, lui devinant des tendances fascistes, le soutient d'instinct' [The Jewish element abhors him, but the Italian element, sensing in him Fascist tendencies, supports him instinctively]. Rumilly was convinced the Italians accepted Houde 'comme une sorte de Mussolini Candien' in the mayoralty campaign of 1934. Years later, Houde called attention to the broad sympathies, among Italians and French Canadians, for Fascism in Quebec. *Winnipeg Tribune*, 22 April 1939

73 'The more one studies Houdism, the more [it appears] ugly and repugnant: the more one realizes that this organization of *arrivistes* is, in short, a vile beast': *Le Miroir*, 12 July 1931.

74 *Canadian Jewish Chronicle*, 10 November 1933

75 Ibid. In the 12 August 1932 edition of *Le Goglu*, Emile Goglu editorialized: 'Nous n'aimons pas le régime Taschereau, mais il est encore mille fois mieux que ce que le régime Houde-Bray a pu faire' [We do not like the Taschereau government but it is a thousand times better than the Houde-Bray government in terms of what it has been able to accomplish].

76 A. Arcand to R.B. Bennett, 8 March 1934, Bennett Papers, 345014–15

77 With reference to *Le Miroir*, E.D. Morgan, a Montreal Conservative lawyer, wrote R.B. Bennett: 'This paper was to a great extent sponsored some months ago by Mr. Rainville, and at his request I gave him One Hundred Dollars for the owner, and many other friends did the same': E.D. Morgan to R.B. Bennett, 26 May 1930, Bennett Papers, 303537.

78 P.E. Blondin to R.B. Bennett, undated, Bennett Papers, 299279–80. The Tories remained chronically short of press support in Quebec. In 1933, only seven of sixty-four newspapers, according to one account, supported the Conservatives: Marc La Terreur, *Les Tribulations des Conservateurs au Québec: de R.B. Bennett à Diefenbaker* (Quebec: Les Presses de l'Université Laval 1977), 71.

79 Betcherman, 25

80 Ibid.

81 *Canadian Jewish Chronicle*, 29 July 1932 and 7 October 1932

82 See Abraham M. Klein, 'The Holy See versus Armand Lavergne,' *Canadian Jewish Chronicle*, 12 August 1932. Lavergne asserted: 'There have been ritual murders in the Middle Ages, and perhaps since': *Canadian Jewish Chronicle*, 7 October 1932.

83 Letter of Peter Bercovitch to the Editor, *Le Canada*, 29 September 1932, reprinted in *Canadian Jewish Chronicle*, 7 October 1932

84 Quoted in Betcherman, 25

85 *Canadian Who's Who, 1958–1960*, 423

86 J.E. Keith, 'The Fascist Province,' *Canadian Forum*, April 1934, 252

87 S. Gobeil, *La Griffe Rouge sur L'Université de Montréal* (Montreal: Editions du Patriote n.d.), 17

88 Ibid., 12, 18, 19

89 'The University of Montreal has become the incubator of the anti-Christian Jewish élite, which rises today against our own élite in all professions': ibid., 19. For a full discussion of l'affaire Gobeil, see Anctil, 119–31.

90 Albert Miller, 'Canada's Fifth Column,' *Contemporary Jewish Record*, July–August 1940, 389

91 P.E. Blondin to R.B. Bennett, undated, Bennett Papers, 299279–80

92 Ibid. Blondin had represented Champlain in the House of Commons from 1908 to 1917. He served as minister of inland revenue

in 1914–15, secretary of state in 1915–17, and postmaster general in
1917 and again in 1920–1. He was appointed in 1918 to the Senate
and served as Senate speaker from 1930 to 1935.
93 A. Arcand, *Fascisme ou Socialisme* (Montreal: 'Le Patriote' 1933), 34
94 *Le Miroir,* 3 February 1933
95 'The Hitlerian regime constitutes a new fortress against Bolshevik
internationalism, another bulwark for the defence of Christianity.
The world will soon be divided into two distinct groups: the group
of Christian dictatorships and the group of anti-Christian dictatorships, who will dispute for world supremacy. The struggle will be
terrible, but it will be decisive, and there is no doubt that, thanks to
its vigorous leaders, thanks to the justice of its causes and strength
of its principles, the Christian group will prevail': ibid.
96 A. Arcand, 'Does Canada Need Fascism?' *Country Guide,* July 1938,
11
97 'Of nationalism and Christianism ... the right of property and
family authority ... of natural law in which it refuses to acknowledge
the inequality of men': Arcand, *Fascisme ou Socialisme,* 42
98 'The Liberal-Conservative Party of Canada obligingly submitted to
the old liberal laws of the past,' and was not, therefore, 'the party of
the future.' 'Liberalism, by favouring a corrupt capitalism that
devoured everything, made a large portion of individual property
disappear; socialism wants to make all property disappear': ibid., 43.
99 'Socialism has liberalism for a father and bolshevism for an heir':
ibid., 38.
100 'La question Juive, avec ses multiples aspectes et ses conséquences
dans tous les domaines, est ... basique est fondamentale dans tout
project de restauration nationale et politique.' Ibid., 35
101 *Program, Parti National Social-Chrétien* (Montreal: 'Le Patriote,'
February 1934)
102 'The sole basis of morality, family instinct, the people, and the
state': Arcand, *Fascisme ou Socialisme,* 147
103 'The two great races that have made up Canada's population since
the beginning, and the other Aryan members of the population
who agreed to identify with the two founding races': *Program, Parti
National Social Chrétien,* 16
104 'Non-British foreigners [would be treated as] as a temporary guest

subject to the statutory conditions of entry into the country': ibid. Madagascar remained, for years, Arcand's preferred place for the shipment and settlement of Jews. See, for example, David Martin, 'Adrien Arcand, Fascist – An Interview,' *The Nation*, 26 February 1938, 244, in which Arcand described himself as 'the greatest Zionist in the world,' after suggesting that Jews should be shipped to Madagascar, where they would be 'all together and happy.'

105 'Each class fulfils its function in the social organism; each class has its rights and duties, which define its tradition. To socialist class hatred, as well as to class tyranny inherent in capitalism, fascism opposes a social solidarity that is based upon a just distribution of rights and duties': Arcand, *Fascisme ou Socialisme*, 49.

106 'Fascism considers agriculture [to be] the first, the most important and vital, of all national industries ... and grants it pre-eminence, even in parliamentary representation, where it is entitled to a larger representation than all other industries': *Program, Parti National Social Chrétien*, 49.

107 'A union freely consented to by autonomous and equal countries ... the anti-imperialism cry, like all the revolutionary cries of the left, is a Judeo-liberal cry ... because Jewry seeks to break up every force that can slow down the advent of its universal empire': ibid., 19.

108 Arcand, 'Does Canada Need Fascism?' 11

109 Books, newspapers, publications of all sorts, theatrical representations and cinema ... works of a corrupting art, etc. ... which have a pernicious influence on morality, the national character, and accepted traditions': ibid., 44. The state, in Arcand's view, would be a 'bon père de famille, veillant jalousement au respect des droits ... de ses enfants': *Program, Parti National Social Chrétien*, 49.

110 *Organization et Réglements du Parti National Social Chrétien du Canada*, 1934, 73

111 Ibid., 74

112 'All the French Canadians and Aryans resident in Canada wish to identify themselves as French Canadian': ibid., 79.

113 Ibid., 83

114 Ibid., 88

115 Ibid., 81–2

116 'An internationalism that must respond to Jewish internationalism':

'in its world-wide effort to free itself from economic and political domination by the Jews': ibid., 6

117 A. Arcand to Major Frank Pease, 28 September 1932, 'Canadian Nationalist Party and Social Christian Party,' File – Anti-Semitism, Box – Group Relations, Jewish Canadian Collection, Jewish Public Library, Montreal

118 *Canadian Jewish Chronicle*, 6 April 1934, 1

119 *Canadian Annual Review*, 1934, 205. According to *Le Patriote*, Lavery enjoyed the endorsation and backing of an assortment of 'patriotic' organizations besides the PNSC: La Ligue du Dimanche, the Saint Jean Baptiste Society, the Commercial Travellers' Association, Jeune-Canada, Groulx's Association Canadienne de la Jeunesse Catholique, various Catholic labour unions, and remnants of a rival fascist group, the Fédération des Clubs Ouvrièrs: *Le Patriote*, 5 April 1934, cited in Betcherman, 39.

120 'The Jewish danger ... the Jewish spirit of domination over the Canadian people and all the Christian peoples of the world': *Le Patriote*, 15 March 1935

121 Rumilly, 204

122 Ibid., 205

123 Hortel la Roque, *Camillien Houde, le p'tit gars de Ste-Marie* (Montreal: Les Éditions de l'Homme 1961), 74

124 *Canadian Annual Review*, 1934, 205

125 12 April 1934

126 'The youngest of all the Canadian parties ... the most vigorous, the most spirited, the most promising': ibid. It should not be concluded that the great bulk of the vote for Lavery was pro-fascist or anti-Semitic. As the *Canadian Jewish Chronicle* (13 April 1934) noted, Lavery had so many panaceas for society's ills, it was 'possible many voted because of factors other than the Jewish question.'

127 'Two heads of state that [are] popular to the point of inspiring fanaticism and a heroic faith until death': *Le Patriote*, 16 November 1933.

128 'Fascism is to conservatism what socialism is to liberalism': *Le Goglu*, 10 March 1933.

129 'Great patriot, great Christian ... great heart, great mind'; 'When the red forces, and Jews in particular, call Mr Bennett "a Mussolini,"

they are not far from the truth, for our prime minister intends to defend our regime with the utmost national and Christian energy; he intends to move on the path of the right as fast as the opposite group intends to move on the path of the left. His public declarations on what our social regime ought to be are in perfect harmony with those of Mussolini and Hitler': ibid. Soon after his appointment, by the Grand Council, as leader of the National Social Christian Party, Arcand urgently requested an interview with Bennett in order 'to give to the Prime Minister an official copy of the N.S.C.P.'s Program' before it was made public and 'to give to the Prime Minister a clear explanation of the Party's policies and aims, and of the procedure it will follow in the future': A. Arcand to A.W. Merriam, 19 January 1934, Bennett Papers, MG26, Vol. 618.

130 *Le Fasciste Canadien*, May 1937
131 Ibid. Social Credit's linkage, in 1939, with A.W. Herridge's *New Democracy* was condemned by Arcand who, in the post-war years, made political overtures to several Socred MPs: *L'Illustration Nouvelle*, 10 August 1939 and Betcherman, 43.
132 Arcand and Ménard's association, according to *L'Illustration Nouvelle*, 24 January 1935, ended in late autumn 1934. *Le Patriote* continued publication, under Ménard's direction, until 22 October 1936.
133 Le Terreur, 71
134 P.E. Blondin to R.B. Bennett, Bennett Papers, 299279–80
135 Upon discovering, from *Le Canada*, that Arcand had been hired by the Conservatives as provincial publicity director during the national federal campaign, the *Canadian Jewish Chronicle* (11 October 1935) commented: 'It goes without saying that there are more French-Canadian voters to be flirted with than there are Jewish voters, but the Conservative Party has yet to answer why Tim Buck must be labeled a Jew in order to get Mr. Bennett back again into the saddle.'
136 Martin, 242
137 *Le Fasciste Canadien* 2/2 (July 1936)
138 *Canadian Jewish Chronicle*, 28 October 1938
139 *Confidential Report Re: French Fascism (made by an investigator of 'Life')*, New York, 16–20 March 1938. Sent by H.A.R. Gagnon to RCMP

Commissioner, 1 June 1939. File reference, National Unity Party –
Montreal, RCMP Security Service Records

140 John Hoare, 'Swastika over Quebec: Party Record,' *Saturday Night*,
23 September 1939
141 René Durocher, 'Le Fasciste Canadien, 1935–1938,' in Fernand
Dumond, Jean Hamelin, J.P. Montminy, eds., *Idéologies au Canada
Français, 1930–1939* (Quebec: Les Presses de l'Université Laval
1978), 267
142 'The Greatest War in History Now On!' – extract of speeches
delivered in New York on 30 and 31 October and 1 November by
H.H. Beamish, R.E. Edmondson, and Adrien Arcand. Adrien
Arcand Box, Canadian Jewish Congress Archives, 7
143 Betcherman, 97

CHAPTER 6: *Le Führer*

1 *Confidential Report Re: French Fascism ...*, 2. Arcand's grammatical
confusions were noted by *Saturday Night* correspondent John Hoare
in his 'Swastika over Quebec: Arcand Meeting,' *Saturday Night*, 9
September 1939.
2 *Toronto Daily Star*, 10 February 1938
3 Ibid.
4 *Canadian Jewish Chronicle*, 5 July 1935
5 Ibid., 28 June 1935
6 Ibid., 4 February 1938
7 See Fred Rose, *Hitler's Fifth Column in Quebec* (Toronto: Progress
Publishers 1943), 39.
8 *Confidential Report Re: French Fascism ...*, 4
9 Ibid.
10 Ibid., 4–6
11 Ibid., 5, and Frederick Edwards, 'Fascism in Canada,' *Maclean's*, 15
April 1938
12 *Canadian Jewish Chronicle*, 17 September 1937
13 Ibid., 1 October 1937
14 *Winnipeg Tribune*, 29 October 1937, and Eugene Forsey, 'Quebec on
the Road to Fascism,' *Canadian Forum*, 17 (December 1937): 298

15 24 December 1937

16 *Winnipeg Tribune,* 20 May 1938

17 *Toronto Daily Star,* 10 February 1938

18 *Confidential Report Re: French Fascism ...,* 4

19 File Reference – National Social Christian Party, RCMP Division C, Quebec Detachment, Montreal, 18 March 1938, RCMP Security Service Records

20 S.T. Wood to Rt Hon. Ernest Lapointe, 12 May 1939, 028–029 RCMP Security Service Records

21 J.B. McGeachy, 'Fascism in Canada – Joke or Menace?' *Regina Leader Post,* 15 June 1938

22 'I belonged to Arcand's party,' *Montreal Standard Magazine,* 10

23 *Confidential Report Re: French Fascism ...,* 5

24 Report of H.A.R. Gagnon, 12 May 1939, File Reference Re: National Unity Party, RCMP Security Service Records

25 Fredrick Edwards, 'Fascism in Canada,' *Maclean's,* 15 April 1938, 12

26 Lita-Rose Betcherman, *The Swastika and the Maple Leaf* (Toronto: Fitzhenry and Whiteside 1975), 110

27 Report of H.A.R. Gagnon to Commissioner, RCMP Security Service Records, 23 May 1939, File – National Unity Party – Montreal, RCMP Security Service Records

28 Edwards, 11

29 Report of J.A. Vanslandes, CST, forwarded to Commissioner, RCMP by F.J. Mead, Commander 'C' Division, 23 March 1938, File Reference – National Social Christian Party, 1542–6, RCMP Security Service Records

30 Edwards, 11

31 Ibid.

32 Report forwarded to Commissioner, RCMP, by F.J. Mead, Commander 'C' Division, 10 May 1938, File Reference – National Social Christian Party, RCMP Security Service Records, 1567–8

33 In a speech delivered to the Junior Board of Trade of Ottawa on 11 May 1938, Paul Gouin noted 'the wearing of a uniform and a fascination with ceremonial' as evidence of 'traces of the fascist methods of publicity,' among a tiny minority in the province. Henri Saint-Denis, 'Fascism in Quebec: A False Alarm,' *Revue de l'Université d'Ottawa,* January 1939: 5. A *Le Jour* journalist wrote (5 February

1938) the following of the PNSC's postering: 'they ... put on their shirts and decorated their arms with a cabalistic sign. They have walked with the goose step, they have raised their arms in the air with excellent discipline, and immediately run to the photographer, "see there, how pretty," they said. "Snapshottez nous ca ..." ': as quoted in W. Bovey, *The French-Canadians Today* (Toronto: Dent and Sons 1938), 306.

34 According to the *Montreal Gazette* (3 January 1938), a goal of eight divisions – 8,000 men each – had been set for the province.

35 Bovey, 306

36 Report on meeting, H.A.R. Gagnon, Commander 'C' Division, to Commissioner RCMP, 27 May 1939, File Reference – National Unity Party – Montreal, RCMP Security Service Records

37 *Canadian Jewish Chronicle,* 4 February 1938

38 *Victoria Daily Times,* 14 July 1938

39 Ibid.

40 *The Canadian Magazine,* April 1938,

41 Edwards, 10

42 *London Daily Herald,* 4 December 1937. The *Daily Herald* went on to say: 'This party, reports show, is using all the demagogic tricks which brought Hitler to power in Germany. Only the people of Quebec Province themselves can resist this attempt to introduce an altogether alien ideology into the free political atmosphere of Canada. Public opinion all over the Empire will back them up in any such resistance.'

43 A Canadian Correspondent, 'Fascism in Quebec,' *New Statesman and Nation,* 27 August 1938, 304. The correspondent concluded with the following observation: 'Valentine Williams in the *World of Action* records that when he was in Munich in 1920 he was advised to see a harum-scarum agitator called Adolf Hitler; he called, found him out, and did not have time to wait for an appointment. In that same year Mussolini was an Italian journalist whom Lloyd George was too busy to see. Always provided that he dissociates himself from any taint of Nazi-ism, Adrien Arcand may yet have an important place in Canadian history.'

44 Leslie Roberts, 'Will Quebec Turn to the Right?' *The Canadian Magazine,* April 1938, 8

45 R. Rumilly, *Maurice Duplessis et Son Temps* (Montreal: Fides 1978), 406

46 R. Rumilly, *Histoire de Montréal*, Vol. IV (Montreal: Fides 1974), 269

47 David Martin, 'Adrien Arcand, Fascist – An Interview,' *The Nation*, 26 February 1938, 241. Martin closed his article with a quote from Hubert Desaulniers, the CCF provincial secretary, who sat next to Arcand in school: 'People thought that Hitler was crazy, too, but he took power in spite of, or perhaps rather just because of, that.'

48 *Life Magazine*, 18 July 1938, Vol. V, No. 3

49 Ibid.

50 *Canadian Jewish Chronicle*, 4 February 1938. Upon hearing from *L'Authorité* charges that Arcand's fascist marionettes had built up a munitions cache smuggled from the United States, the *Chronicle* wrote (29 April 1938): 'Nobody is so naive as to believe that they hold frequent meetings for the purpose of reading the bible or holding hands. Arcand's organization, small or large as it may be, is built on a type of aggressiveness which has assumed an ugly character, and the military aspect he has given his followers very well lends itself to arms, munitions, and all the accoutrements of physical strife.'

51 Fred Rose, *Fascism over Canada: An Exposé* (Toronto: New Era Publishers 1938)

52 *Canadian Jewish Chronicle*, 29 April 1938

53 Quoted in Betcherman, 97

54 *Montreal Gazette*, 7 February 1938

55 *Canadian Jewish Chronicle*, 29 April 1938

56 As quoted in Betcherman, 98

57 Roberts, 9

58 'Fascism is more dangerous than communism here because it has numerous followers and proven means of action. It will be necessary to control it if we want to keep democracy and the government responsible': *Le Fasciste Canadien*, December 1937.

59 Rumilly, *Histoire de Montréal*, Vol. IV, 269, and Roberts, 9. If we are to believe Camillien Houde, Bouchard understated the case. 'When I have used the word Fascist,' Houde declared, during the spring of 1939, 'there has been a general hue and cry because I have dared to think about and speak the truth. I have been taken up by the

quarter of the population of Montreal who are against fascism and the three-quarters who have fascist sympathies': *Winnipeg Tribune*, 22 April 1939.

60 As quoted in Roberts, 9

61 'The only safeguard, the unshakeable bulwark against the on-slaught of Bolshevik communism': Andrée Lévesque, *Virage à Gauche Interdit; Les Communistes, Les Socialistes et Leurs Ennemis au Québec, 1929–1939* (Montreal: Boréal Express 1984), 121

62 Denis Monière, *Ideologies in Quebec* (Toronto: University of Toronto Press 1981), 219. It should be noted that there existed diverse forms of 'corporative orders' and systems, the Italian fascist scheme being only one. Christian-Social forms of corporatism pre-dated Mussolinian fascism, which wedded corporate organization to a system of state totalitarianism in which all social organisms and individual preferences were subordinated to the state, a system summarized in Mussolini's formula: 'everything in the state, everything for the state, nothing outside or above the state, nothing against the state.' Luigi Sturzo, 'Corporatism: Christian-Social and Fascist,' *Catholic World*, July 1937, Vol. 145: 7. The two papal encyclicals advocating corporatism as an alternative to anarchism, liberalism, and socialism – Leo XIII Rerum Novarum and Pious XI Quadragesimo Anno – set limits on state intervention. Quebec's corporate schemes, based upon considerations of various models, including those in Austria, Portugal, and Italy, had a nationalist component; for people like Esdras Minville, who elaborated a scheme for Le Comité de Défense Economique of the Saint Jean Baptiste Society, corporatism was a system of repatriation, as well as social and economic cooperation.

63 W.D.K. Kernaghan, 'Freedom of Religion in the Province of Quebec, with Particular Reference to the Jews, Jehovah's Witnesses and Church-State Relations, 1930–1960, Phd thesis, Duke University, 1966, 270. Laurendeau wrote in 1938 that despite its flaws and doctrinal errors 'le fascisme Mussolinian est un régime beaucoup moins inhumain que le communisme.'

64 Quoted in P.E. Trudeau, ed., *The Asbestos Strike* (Toronto: James, Lewis and Samuel 1974), 16, from Lionel Groulx, 'Langue et Survivance,' *L'Action Nationale*, Vol. IV, September 1934, 61–2

65 As quoted in *Canadian Jewish Chronicle,* 7 May 1937
66 'Even if fascism has its errors, it contains an element of discipline, of economic, educational, and social progress': quoted in Lévesque, 128.
67 Ibid.
68 Quoted in Eugene Forsey, 'Under the Padlock.' *Canadian Forum,* 18 (May 1938): 43
69 Quoted in *Canadian Jewish Chronicle,* 10 February 1939
70 *Canadian Jewish Chronicle,* 26 November 1937
71 Ibid., 24 July 1936
72 Betcherman, 86
73 *Canadian Jewish Chronicle,* 23 October 1936
74 Ibid., 21 August, 1936
75 Ibid., 25 December 1936. Duplessis, it appeared, suffered a serious lapse, on the Jewish question, in November 1943 when he quoted before an audience in Ste Claire, Quebec, from a copy of a letter purportedly written by a mysterious H.L. Roscovitz – of Quebec Local No. 6, Montreal, of the non-existent 'International Zionist Brotherhood' – to a Rabbi J. Schwartz, in which financial aid, to Liberal candidates for the House of Commons, would be advanced to win support for a 'Government Plan to establish on the farms of the province of Quebec one hundred thousand Jewish refugees from Central Europe': *Canadian Jewish Chronicle,* 12 November 1943. A clumsy fabrication, the letter raised a storm within the Jewish community and earned Duplessis the following rebuke from the *Chronicle* in an editorial titled 'Protocols of Zion: Duplessis Edition': 'The apocalyptic revelation of Ste. Clair may now join the dubious company of the Reichstag Fire, the Parnell letters, the Protocols of Zion, and other fabrications maliciously concocted for political purposes ... Today, the public figure produces a forgery for the express purpose of setting the French-Canadian population against the Jewish-Canadian. Tomorrow ... there might be another letter produced out of his magician's hat, this time to show that the British Imperial Brotherhood Local 13 intends to transfer all of Lancashire to the district of Abitibi': *Canadian Jewish Chronicle,* 12 November 1943. Except for this lapse, Duplessis was free of public utterances that might be construed as anti-Semitic. He could not

resist, however, an occasional jocular taunt of his Jewish legislative colleagues. According to Conrad Black: 'The worst defeat anyone can remember Duplessis sustaining in Assembly repartee occurred in his first term as Premier. The amiable Joe Cohen was speaking to an unattentive House when Duplessis, apparently somewhat in his cups, loudly interjected that the legislature need not bother listening to the only Jew in the room. Cohen shot back, pointing to the crucifix that Duplessis had placed above the Speaker's chair: "No there are two of us." Jean Martineau witnessed this and says that he never knew Duplessis to suffer such a put-down before or after': *Duplessis* (Toronto: McClelland and Stewart 1977), 671

76 *Vancouver Daily Province*, 3 March 1938
77 Ibid.
78 'Quebec Fascists Show Their Hand,' *Canadian Forum*, December 1936, Vol. 15–16: 8
79 'To defend ourselves against subversive doctrines,' the cardinal stated, 'against spiritual poisoning, against the overthrow of the foundations of civilization, against the dynamite which would blow up our religious family and social traditions, if that is not the law, let that law be made; if not, we shall exercise the law and right of nature. "The safety of the people is the supreme law" ... Under pretext of respecting a morbid democracy, people wave at us the spectre of an illusory Fascism, and meanwhile the enemies gain a foothold and make a mockery of our juridical scruples.' As quoted in Eugene Forsey, 'Quebec on the Road to Fascism,' *Canadian Forum*, December 1937, 300
80 Ibid.
81 *Winnipeg Free Press*, 27 March 1937
82 Eugene Forsey, 'Under the Padlock,' *Canadian Forum*, May 1938, 43
83 *Winnipeg Free Press*, 27 March 1937, and Forsey, 'Under the Padlock,' 41–2
84 According to Wilfrid Bovey, the real danger in Quebec, in 1938, was 'not communism but fascism,' and any attempt to thwart Duplessis's anti-communist drive by the federal government would encourage Fascist support to the danger level. 'The present outcry against the "Padlock Law" is without any doubt giving the fascists and potential fascists a good deal of moral encouragement, although as

long as the protest here are made by students and theorists they will
not get very far. There would be great and immediate danger if any
effort were made by the Federal Government to force Quebec to
any different course from that now being followed. I have no doubt
whatever that a disallowance of the Padlock Act ... would result in
the immediate conversion of very large groups of already organized
such as the Jeunesse Ouvrière Catholique and the Jeunesse Agricole Catholique, to the fascist point of view ... and the liquidation
of any communism in Quebec by other than lawful means.' Wilfrid
Bovey to W.L.M. King, 2 March 1938, King Papers, MG 26, J-1, Vol.
246. King replied that Bovey's point of view 'accorded completely'
with his own, and those of his colleagues: W.L.M. King to W. Bovey,
3 March 1938, King Papers, MG 26, J-1, Vol. 246.
85 Eugene Forsey, 'Under the Padlock,' 43
86 Roberts, 9

CHAPTER 7: *Shirts*

1 For brief descriptions of the Fédération des Clubs Ouvriers, see
  Andrée Lévesque, *Virage à Gauche Interdit: Les Communistes, Les
  Socialistes, et Leurs Ennemis au Québec* (Montreal: Boréal Express
  1984), 265, and Lita-Rose Betcherman, *The Swastika and the Maple
  Leaf* (Toronto: Fitzhenry and Whiteside 1975), 36.
2 *Canadian Jewish Chronicle*, 28 July 1933
3 Ibid., 6 October 1933, 19 January 1934
4 *Ottawa Morning Journal*, 13 January 1934
5 Ibid., 7 October 1933
6 Betcherman, 36, quoting *Le Patriote*, 31 August 1933
7 J.E. Keith, 'The Fascist Province,' *Canadian Forum* 14/163 (April
  1934): 251. According to *New Frontier* political correspondent Peter
  Quinn, Chalifoux was soon 'reduced to the status of recruiting
  sergeant for Montreal's Mayor Camillien Houde': 'Meet Quebec's
  Fascists!' *New Frontier*, September 1936, 5.
8 *Vancouver Sun*, 22 March 1934
9 See Kieran Simpson, ed., *Canadian Who's Who, 1987*, Vol. 22
  (Toronto: University of Toronto Press 1988), 149.

10 André J. Bélanger, *L'Apolitisme des Idéologies Québécoises: Le Grand Tournant de 1934–1936* (Quebec: Les Presses de l'Université Laval 1974), 335. Gagnon had a falling out with Bouchard and left in December 1936. Pierre Chaloult was the first editor.

11 *La Nation*, 1/6 (21 March 1936): 1, as quoted in Bélanger, 339

12 'Filthy, slovenly descendent of Moses and Joshua': quoted in *Canadian Jewish Chronicle*, 27 July 1936

13 Conrad Black, *Duplessis* (Toronto: McClelland and Stewart 1977), 202, quoting *Le Devoir*, 5 September 1939

14 Michael Oliver, 'The Social and Political Ideas of French-Canadian Nationalists, 1920–1945,' PhD thesis, McGill University, 1956, 208, quoting Pelletier's 'Le Caporal Hitler,' *La Nation*, Vol. 1, 11 June 1936

15 Quoted in J.B. McGeachy, 'Canada's Problem Province, IV,' *Victoria Daily Times*, 14 July 1938.

16 'War is to a man what motherhood is to a woman: the ultimate fulfilment of being': Bélanger, 325.

17 'All men who still have enough love for holy war and our national future': ibid., 335; Oliver, 211

18 McGeachy, 3

19 Bélanger, 351, quoting *La Nation*, Vol. 1, 22 October 1936, 1

20 *La Nation's* views on Arcand and the NSCP are outlined in several articles and editorials by Bouchard and others, including the NSCP renegade Edouard Bourassa. See, for example, Paul Bouchard, 'Adrien Arcand, Rastaquouère et Cabotin,' *La Nation*, Vol. 1, 22 October 1936, and Edouard Bourassa, 'Adrien Arcand; Un Nazi au Pays des siffleux,' *La Nation*, Vol. 2, 18 March 1937.

21 According to Michael Oliver (20), following the departure of Pierre Chaloult and J.L. Gagnon, *La Nation* lost most of its 'Fascisme de gauche,' and became 'an opportunist vehicle of the extreme right.'

22 Oliver, 214

23 'Strongly heirarchical'; 'the mass of ordinary members in "les Faisceaux." It is the members of the Faisceaux who will form the cadres of the parties': ibid., 215.

24 Black, 251

25 See, for example, J.C. Reade, 'Is Canada Fated to Go Fascist?' *Saturday Night*, 21 October 1933; Willson Woodside, 'The Fascist

Movement in Great Britain,' *Saturday Night*, 12 August 1933; B.K. Sandwell, 'Fascism or Socialism? – Or Something Better?' *Saturday Night*, 2 February 1935; C. Stollery, 'Fascism and Corporate State – Phase in Warfare of Classes,' *Financial Post*, 17 March 1934; S. Alfred Jones, 'How Fascism Solves the Labour Problem,' *Saturday Night*, 12 May 1934.

26 18 October, 1913, as cited in Stephen A. Speisman, *The Jews of Toronto: A History to 1937* (Toronto: McClelland and Stewart 1979), 122

27 Michael Brown, *Jew or Juif: Jews, French Canadians, and Anglo-Canadians, 1759–1914* (Philadelphia, New York: Jewish Publication Society 1986), 231

28 22 September 1924, as quoted in Speisman, 321

29 Sigmund Samuel, *In Return* (Toronto: 1963), 125, quoted in Brown, 230

30 Speisman, 122

31 Ibid., 121

32 The Swastika Clubs and Christie Pits riots are discussed in Betcherman, 45–60; C.H. Levitt and William Shaffir, *The Riot at Christie Pits* (Toronto: Lester and Orpen Dennys 1987); C.H. Levitt and W. Shaffir, 'The Christie Pits Riot: A Case Study in the Dynamics of Ethnic Violence, Toronto, August 10, 1933,' *Canadian Jewish Historical Society Journal* 9/1 (Spring 1985): 2–30.

33 *Toronto Daily Star*, 2 August 1933

34 Accounts of the Christie Pits riot can be found in *Toronto Daily Star*, 17–19 August 1933

35 In April 1933, an organization known as the League for the Defense of Jewish Rights was formed in Toronto, headed by Rabbi Samuel Sacks and Shmuel Meir Shapiro, editor of the *Hebrew Journal*, which, together with the Western Jewish Congress Committee in Winnipeg and Montreal's Pro-Congress Committee, pressed the revival of the Canadian Jewish Congress: Speisman, 331.

36 *Toronto Daily Star*, 14 August 1933

37 Ibid.

38 Ibid., 19 August 1933

39 Ibid., 16 August 1933

40 Ibid.

41 Ibid., 11 August 1933
42 *Ottawa Morning Citizen*, 25 October 1933
43 R.W. Irvine, Division O, Detachment, Toronto, to Commissioner, RCMP, 12 March 1935. Memo re: Canadian Union of Fascists, 002, RCMP Security Service Records
44 *Toronto Daily Star*, 5 October 1933
45 Ibid.
46 Ibid.
47 22 October 1936
48 Toronto *Globe and Mail*, 8 December 1937
49 Ibid.
50 Betcherman, 79
51 Ibid., 83; S.A. Jones, 'How Fascism Solves the Labour Problem,' *Saturday Night*, 12 May 1934
52 *Toronto Mail and Empire*, 21 October 1936
53 *Toronto Daily Star*, 4 July 1938
54 Ibid.
55 Ibid.
56 Ibid.
57 Quoted in the *Canadian Jewish Chronicle*, 18 March 1938
58 Toronto *Globe and Mail*, 14 July 1938
59 Ibid.
60 Report of M. Black, Division C, RCMP, Detachment, Toronto, 5 July 1938, File Reference: National Unity Party – Mass meeting held in Massey Hall, Toronto, 4 July 1938, RCMP Security Service Records
61 Report of J.S.D. Brandon to officer commanding, E. Division, RCMP, Re: Canadian Guard of B.C., File reference: D.D.D. 15 March 1938, 3543, RCMP Security Service Records
62 Harold Griffin, 'Fascism – Can It Happen Here?' *People's Advocate*, 30 April 1937
63 Report of J.K. Barnes, Division E., Detachment, Vancouver, Re: Canadian Guard of B.C., 16 March 1938, 3544–5, RCMP Security Service Records
64 *Vancouver Daily Province*, 4 July 1938
65 Ibid.
66 *Winnipeg Free Press*, 3 May 1938
67 Quoted in H.J. Schultz, 'Portrait of a Premier: William Aberhart,'

Canadian Historical Review 45 (1964): 202
68 Quoted in ibid.
69 Ibid.
70 Henry Trachtenberg, 'The Winnipeg Jewish Community in the
   Inter-war Period, 1919–1939: Anti-semitism and Politics,' *Canadian
   Jewish Historical Society Journal,* Spring 1980, 48
71 Ibid., 48–51
72 Ibid., 50
73 Louis Rosenberg, 'Anti-Semitism in Western Canada,' paper read
   before the Canadian Jewish Congress, Toronto, 1934, 3; Box –
   Group Relations – Anti-semitism in Canada, Jewish Public Library,
   Montreal
74 Louis Rosenberg, 'Canada's Jews: A Social and Economic Study of
   the Jews in Canada,' Bureau of Social and Economic Research,
   Canadian Jewish Congress, 1939, 31
75 Trachtenberg, 51
76 Robert England, *The Central European Immigrant in Canada* (Toronto: Macmillan 1929), 92
77 *Winnipeg Tribune,* 16 May 1933
78 Ibid.
79 *Winnipeg Tribune,* 26 October 1938
80 Ibid., 4 March 1938. Whittaker had no difficulty classifying physical
   differences between racial types. 'Ayrans,' he informed a *Winnipeg
   Tribune* correspondent, 'have certain characteristics. Their complexion is more the pink and white type. They have kind of oval
   faces and are more or less blond. Their hair is never black or kinky.
   Nordics, Swedes, Norwegians and Danes are among the best types
   and I would include the French and some Armenians but not the
   Turks or Persians as a nation.'
81 *Winnipeg Tribune,* 4 March 1938
82 *Winnipeg Free Press,* 5 August 1935
83 T.A. Crerar to Norman P. Lambert, 16 February 1934, King Papers,
   MG 26, J-1, Vol. 199, 170123–6, PAC
84 Ibid.
85 Ibid.
86 Ibid.
87 J.H. MacBrien to O.D. Skelton, 11 September 1936, Ref. D945-1-P4,

D945-3-F3 MG30, E163, Vol. 12, file 124, Norman A. Robertson Papers, PAC

88 On the internationalism of Whittaker's Nationalists, the *Canadian Jewish Chronicle* commented: 'It is ... quite obvious that a long chain extends from Streicher's loathsome paper in Nuremberg to Winnipeg ... One of the charges against the Jew is his internationalism, but in making their allegations, the anti-semites have forgotten to cover up their own international organization with its almost incredible ramifications in every part of the world': *Canadian Jewish Chronicle*, 7 December 1934.

89 *Winnipeg Tribune*, 20 September 1937

90 Betcherman, 68

91 *Canadian Jewish Chronicle*, 12 November 1937

92 *Winnipeg Free Press*, 2 March 1934

93 *The Jewish Post*, 21 September 1933

94 Trachtenberg, 57–9

95 *Canadian Jewish Chronicle*, 13 April 1934

96 Ibid.

97 On the Hyman bill, see 'The Anti-race Bill in Manitoba,' *Canadian Jewish Chronicle*, 13 April 1934, Trachtenberg, 52; Betcherman, 71. The attorney general, it might be noted, received strong support from the Jewish community in the 1936 general election.

98 Rosenberg, *Canada's Jews ...*, 303

99 *Winnipeg Tribune*, 22 April 1934

100 Ibid., 7 June 1934

101 Ibid., 2 April 1934

102 Betcherman, 76–8

103 *Winnipeg Tribune*, 24 October 1936

104 *Winnipeg Free Press*, 24 October 1936

CHAPTER 8: *Consular Fascism*

1 Address of Consul-General of Italy to Colonial Banquet in Toronto, *Il Bollettino Italo-Canadese*, 6 November 1933, MG30, E163, Vol. 12, File 124, Norman A. Robertson Papers, PAC

2 Ibid.

3 John P. Diggins, *Mussolini and Fascism: The View from America* (Princeton, NJ: Princeton University Press 1972), 78

4 C.M. Bayley, 'The Social Structure of the Italian and Ukranian Immigrant Communities in Montreal, 1935–37,' MA thesis, McGill University, 1939, 11

5 John E. Zucchi, *Italians in Toronto: The Development of a National Identity, 1875–1935* (Montreal and Kingston: McGill-Queen's University Press 1988), 44

6 Bayley, 13

7 R.F. Harney, 'Toronto's Little Italy, 1885–1945,' in R.F. Harney and J. Vincenza Scarpaci, eds., *Little Italies in North America* (Toronto: Multiculturalism Society of Ontario 1981), 51

8 Ibid.

9 J.A. Ciccocelli, 'The Innocuous Enemy Alien: Italians in Canada during World War II,' MA thesis, University of Western Ontario, 1977, 13

10 John E. Zucchi, 'The Emergence of Fascism among Italian Immigrants in Toronto 1928–1935,' unpublished paper, 5

11 Ibid., 4; and Diggins, 80

12 In describing Canada's mosaic, Goldwin Smith wrote: 'There are scatterings of other races, the last arrivals being the Italian with his grinding organ and, we hope, without his knife': quoted in R.F. Harney, 'The Italian Community in Toronto,' in J.L. Elliott, ed., *Two Nations, Many Cultures*, 2nd ed. (Toronto: Prentice Hall 1983), 345.

13 R.F. Harney, 'Italians in Canada,' Occasional Papers on Ethnic and Immigration Studies (Toronto: The Multicultural History Society of Ontario 1978), 27

14 Ibid., 30. Bruno Ramirez notes that, 'for an immigrant population in which two out of three adult persons had left Italy before the advent of fascism, in which an overwhelming proportion had little or no formal education, and whose image of the Italy they had left was one of oppression and political exclusion, the transformations that fascism advertised could not but be perceived as signs of progress. For many of those Italians, then, fascism was seen less as a political ideology and form of government, and more as synonymous with a renewed "italianita"': Bruno Ramirez, 'Ethnicity on Trial: The Italians of Montreal and the Second World War,' in

Norman Hillmer et al, eds., *On Guard for Thee: War, Ethnicity and the Canadian State, 1939–45* (Ottawa: Ministry of Supply and Services 1988), 77

15 Harney, 'Toronto's Little Italy,' 57
16 Zucchi, *Italians in Toronto*, 170
17 Zucchi, 'The Emergence of Fascism ...,' 5, 6
18 Zucchi, 'Italians in Toronto,' 170. According to A.V. Spada, *The Italians in Canada* (Ottawa: Riviera Publishers 1969), 127, R.B. Bennett's minister of justice, the Hon. Hugh Guthrie, 'flatly refused a delegation of Italian anti-fascists who urged him to ... prohibit any fascist organization in Canada. His argument was that the Italian government was a friendly government and that the Italians in Canada were justified in wearing black shirts and marching in military formation on public streets.'
19 Address of Consul-General of Italy to Colonial Banquet, *Il Bollettino*, 6 November 1933, MG30, E163, Vol. 12, File 124, Norman A. Robertson Papers
20 The major focus of this chapter will be on the cities of Montreal and Toronto where the largest Italian communities existed. Fascist and pro-Fascist activities of varying intensity and extent were present in other centres of Italian settlement in Canada: in Hamilton, Ottawa, and Windsor, as well as assorted smaller centres like Brantford, Guelph, and Welland in Ontario; in Sydney, Nova Scotia; in the major western Canadian centres of Winnipeg, Calgary, Vancouver, and Trail.
21 The Ottawa lead was taken by Luigi Petrucci, who succeeded Rogeri di Villanova as consul general and was later replaced by A. Rossi Longhi. Count Massimo Zanotti Bianco looked after consular affairs in Montreal until his replacement by the activist Giuseppe Brigidi, in 1933. Brigidi, in turn, gave way to Paolo de Simone. Based in Toronto, beginning 1929, was Cavaliere Giovanni Battista Ambrosi, a disabled war veteran from Italy, who served as the first Italian vice-consul. He was succeeded by Cavaliere Giorgio Tiberi and Prince Guido Colonna: Robert Perin, *Conflits d'Identité et d'Allégeance: La Propagande du Consulat Italien à Montréal dans les années 1930*, Migrations et communautés culturelles, Questions de Culture 2 (Quebec: Institut Québécois de Recherche sur la culture

1982), 82; Zucchi, *Italians in Toronto,* 169; Luigi G. Pennachio, 'The Development of Fascism among Toronto's Italians, 1929–1939,' unpublished paper, 8, 23.

22 The Fascists were a cadre rather than mass organization.

23 *The Organization and Activities of the Italian Fascist Party in Canada,* 30 November 1937, 22, RCMP Security Service Records, Canadian Security Intelligence Service; Bayley, 180–4. Membership in the fascio required consular approval, was vetted in Rome, and, according to Mr Brigidi, served as 'a breviary and a certificate of Citizenship of Italianity and of Fascism': 'The Solemn Distribution of Membership Cards to the Fascists of Montreal,' *L'Italia,* 19/25 (23 June 1934): 3. Translated by M.H.A., RCMP Headquarters. RCMP Security Service Records. The oath taken by *fascio* members read as follows: 'In the name of God and Italy I swear to execute the orders of Il Duce, to serve with all my strength, and if necessary with my blood, the cause of the Fascist revolution.'

24 See Bayley, 184.

25 *The Organization and Activities of the Italian Fascist Party in Canada,* 11–12, 33, RCMP Security Service Records

26 Ibid., 17. According to Tommaso Mari, editor of Toronto's Fascist *Il Bollettino,* there were, in the spring of 1936, seven hundred Fascists in Toronto and about one thousand in Montreal. The Canadian total was three thousand, with half in Ontario: *Toronto Daily Star,* 6 March 1936. Several years later, in 1940, Gerald Fauteux, the federal justice department's examining officer of interned Italians, concluded that approximately 3,500 of the Italian population were Fascists. The Montreal total was 800. Montreal's *dopolavoro* counted two thousand members, while two thousand children were connected with Fascist youth organizations: *General and Confidential Report of the Examining Officer of Interned Italians in Bordeaux Jail,* Gerald Fauteux, 5 September 1940. MG30, E163, Vol. 14, File 156, Norman A. Robertson Papers.

27 Zucchi, 'The Emergence of Fascism ...,' 24–5

28 Bayley, 184

29 Ibid., 185. An RCMP report found the *dopolavoro* to be 'a parallel and collateral institution to the Fascio ... if they do not want to join the Fascist movement and blackshirts, they must become Fascists in the

plain-shirt "After Work Institution." The only difference between the Fascio and the "After Work Institution" lies in the fact that members can wear different shirts': F.J. Mead, *Memorandum on Fascism in Canada.* Commander 'C' Division, to Commissioner, RCMP, 15 February 1937, RCMP Security Service Records.

30 General and Confidential Report of Examining Officer re: Interned Italians, 5 September 1940, MG30, E163, Vol. 14, File 156, Norman A. Robertson Papers, 8; Bayley, 191

31 Bayley, 191

32 Address of Royal Consul-General to Colonial Banquet, *Il Bollettino*, 6 November 1936, in MG130, E163, File 124, Vol. 12, Norman A. Robertson Papers; *The Organization and Activities of the Italian Fascist Party in Canada*, 24

33 Extract from a first-form reader in Appendix 2, summary of contents of Italian textbooks used in Fascist schools in Canada, in *The Organization and Activities of the Italian Fascist Party in Canada*

34 *The Organization and Activities ...*, 26

35 Translation from *L'Italia Nuova* 33/125 (18 June 1938): 13, in RCMP Security Service Records

36 Ibid., 28

37 Zucchi, *Italians in Toronto*, 182

38 Quoted in Zucchi, 'The Emergence of Fascism ...,' 11

39 Bayley, 161

40 Quoted in Zucchi, 'The Emergence of Fascism ...,' 13

41 Ibid., 14

42 Bayley, 180

43 John Hoare, 'Swastika over Quebec; Party Record,' *Saturday Night*, 23 September 1939, 3

44 *L'Illustration Nouvelle*, 4 May 1936, in Bayley, 191–2

45 'Italian Field Notes,' Bayley, 101

46 Zucchi, 'The Emergence of Fascism ...,' 19

47 Canadian Jewish Congress, Toronto, Memorandum re: *Mussolini's Demands in Canada*, enclosure in H.A.R. Gagnon to Commissioner RCMP, 31 January 1939, RCMP Security Service Records

48 Following the ownership change in 1937, *L'Italia* was divided into Italian and French sections named *L'Italia Nuova* and *Le Canada Latin*, respectively: Perin, 100

49 Zucchi, 'The Emergence of Fascism ...,' 40; *Survey of Italian Fascism in Canada*, 2 September 1937, enclosure in F.J. Mead to Commissioner, RCMP, 10 September 1937, RCMP Security Services Records

50 *The Organization and Activities of the Italian Fascist Party in Canada*, 32

51 Ibid.

52 Zucchi, 'The Emergence of Fascism ...,' 22, quoting from speeches reported in *Il Progresso Italo-Americano*, 4 December 1930 and 26 May 1932

53 *L'Illustration Nouvelle*, 4 May 1936, cited in Bayley, 191–3

54 Address of Consul-General to Colonial Banquet, *Il Bollettino*, 6 November 1933

55 Bayley, 190

56 Perin, 88–9

57 *Toronto Daily Star*, 6 March 1936

58 Perin, 92

59 Harney, 'Toronto's Little Italy, 1885–1945,' 58

60 *L'Italia*, 12 May 1934, as translated in *The Organization and Activities of the Italian Fascist Part in Canada*, 20

61 Ibid., 20–1. According to Spada (127), 'some of the expenses for the construction' of Casas d'Italia 'were covered by contributions from the Italian government at the time and by the conferring of decorations on those who donated a relevant amount of money. Also, small contributions of money and man-hours in the construction of the Casas were solicited from the general public.'

62 Zucchi, 'The Emergence of Fascism ...,' 33

63 *Memorandum on Italian Fascism in Canada*, 2, 3, in Report of F.J. Mead to Commissioner, RCMP, 15 February 1937, RCMP Security Service Records

64 'Survey of Italian Fascism in Canada,' 2 September 1937, 14, enclosed in letter of F.J. Mead to Commissioner, RCMP, 10 September 1937, RCMP Security Service Records

65 Bayley, 194

66 Ibid.,

67 Harney, *Toronto's Little Italy*, 57; Angelo Principe, 'The Italo-Canadian Anti-Fascist Press in Toronto, 1922–40,' *Polyphony*, Fall/Winter 1985: 7

68 Zucchi, 'The Emergence of Fascism ...,' 34–5

69 Harney, *Toronto's Little Italy*, 55
70 Consul-General's Address at Colonial Banquet, *Il Bollettino*, 6 November 1933, RCMP Security Service Records
71 Perin, 86
72 Ibid., 95
73 Ibid.
74 *Montreal Gazette*, 15 March 1935
75 Perin, 95
76 Ibid., 93
77 Quoted in Perin, 94
78 Ibid., 92
79 N.A. Robertson to Superintendent E.W. Bavin, Intelligence Section, RCMP, Ottawa, 9 August 1940, MG30, E163, Vol. 13, File 153, Norman A. Robertson Papers
80 Quoted in F.J. Mead to Commissioner, RCMP, 20 January 1938, RCMP Security Service Records
81 Perin, 94
82 *Ottawa Journal*, 4 March 1936
83 Ibid.
84 *The Organization and Activities of the Italian Fascist Party in Canada*, 9, 42. Petrucci later claimed he had no intention of interfering in Canadian affairs.
85 Mr Petrucci's belief in the exportability of Fascism and its utility as a remedy for the economic ills of North America was evident earlier, during a speech delivered at a colonial banquet in Toronto in November 1933, in which he stated: 'the Fascist state has preceded events, instituting that "corporative state" towards which the interest of foreigners is crystallizing.' Translated from *Il Bollettino*, 6 November 1933, in MG30, E163, Vol. 12, File 124, Norman A. Robertson Papers
86 *Toronto Daily Clarion*, 29 June 1938
87 R.R. Tait, Superintendent, 'C' Division, to Commissioner RCMP, 15 October 1938 re: National Party Unity – Montreal, P.Q., RCMP Security Service Records
88 'Italian Fascism in Montreal,' *Montreal Standard*, 24 June 1939
89 Perin, 97
90 *L'Italia*, 19/25 (23 June 1934): 3

91 *L'Italia Nuova*, 23/20 (14 May 1938): 3, in RCMP Security Service Records

92 *The Organization and Activities of the Italian Fascist Party in Canada ...*, 41. The same report, however, observed (42), 'with a sharpening of the class struggle in Canada ... it is possible (and indeed probable) that the movement may assume a wider political significance.'

93 Had they been secret and conspiratorial, however – according to an Italian-Canadian observer – it would not really have mattered. 'Every Italian secret society is an open book to anyone who wants to find out about it,' our observer noted. 'When the Italians want some real intelligence work done, they hire an Englishman or a German to do it. The Italians themselves are too voluble, too free to discuss their secrets. As spies, we are simply lousy': *Globe and Mail*, 15 June 1940.

CHAPTER 9: *Brethren*

1 *Montreal Gazette*, 31 January 1936

2 Ibid.

3 Ibid.

4 Jonathan F. Wagner, *Brothers Beyond the Sea: National Socialism in Canada* (Waterloo: Wilfrid Laurier Press 1981), 4

5 Ibid., 3–4; K.M. McLaughlin, *The Germans in Canada* (Ottawa: Canadian Historical Association 1985), 9

6 Wagner, 11

7 Ibid., 3–4

8 McLaughlin, 11–12

9 Wagner, 61–2

10 Quoted in Wagner, 28

11 Ibid., 45

12 Ibid., 27

13 Quoted in Wagner, 47

14 *The Nazi Party in Canada*, RCMP, Special Branch, Ottawa, February 1947, 2, RCMP Security Service Records, Canadian Security Intelligence Service

15 Ibid., 7; *The Auslands Organization of the National Sozialistische*

Deutsche Arbeiter Partei in Canada, RCMP Report, 15 February 1938, RG13 C1, Vol. 165, File 6, 6, Department of Justice, Public Archives of Canada

16 *The Nazi Party in Canada,* 7
17 Report covering Hitler's Fiftieth Birthday Celebration sponsored by the 'NSDAP' on 20 April 1939 in the Harmonia Club, Drummond Street, Montreal, RG 13 C1, Vol. 165, File 6, Department of Justice
18 *The Auslands Organization ...,* 12
19 Ibid., 13
20 Ibid.
21 *The Nazi Party in Canada,* 9–15
22 Joachim Remak, 'Friends of the New Germany: The Bund and German-American Relations,' *Journal of Modern History* 29 (1957): 38; *Canadian Jewish Chronicle,* 28 April 1933, 13
23 Hans Strauss to W.B. Schwab, undated, enclosed in letter of M.J. Finkelstein to S.W. Jacobs, 11 August 1933, MG27, III, C3, Vol. 7–8, S.W. Jacobs Papers, Public Archives of Canada
24 A. Lamothe to Commissioner, RCMP, 15 May 1939, Division File 212-587 re: Canadian Society for German Culture, Inc., RG13 C1, Vol. 94, File 2, Department of Justice
25 The data on Gerhardt are drawn from John Offenbeck, 'The Nazi Movement and German Canadians,' MA thesis, University of Western Ontario, 1970, 57–8; Wagner, 79–80; A.W. Hone to R.B. Bennett, 2 June 1938, 523838–9, R.B. Bennett Papers, Public Archives of Canada.
26 Report of Colonel E.J. Mooney – late Colonel Commanding, N.B. Mounted Brigade, 29 June 1939, RG24 Vol. 2496, File 965, Vol. 28, Public Archives of Canada
27 Wagner, 59–60
28 *Ottawa Citizen,* 26 March 1935
29 *Der Courier,* 29 August 1934, as translated in file 37, *Der Courier* articles, 1934, DA-1 Box 2, Canadian Jewish Congress Archives
30 Wagner, 59. The AO was the Auslandsorganization der NSDAP – the branch of the Nazi Party in charge of members abroad.
31 Ibid., 34–5
32 Ibid., 81; Offenbeck, 66
33 *The Auslands Organization ...,* 14

34 Quoted by Wagner, 67
35 *The Nazi Party in Canada,* 21
36 *The Auslands Organization* ..., Appendix D; Wagner, 67; Offenbeck, 63–4
37 Gottlieb Leibbrandt, *Little Paradise: The Saga of the German Canadians of Waterloo County, Ontario, 1800–1975* (Kitchener: Allprint Co. 1980), 267
38 Heinz Lehmann, *The German-Canadians, 1750–1937* (St John's: Jesperson Press 1986), 279
39 Offenbeck, 79
40 *The Auslands Organization* ..., 18; Offenbeck 80
41 *The Auslands Organization* ..., 24; Memo of N.A. Robertson to Ernest Lapointe, 3 September 1929. Appendix IV, RG13, C1, Vol. 965, Reel 5, Department of Justice
42 Wagner, 69; J.F. Wagner, 'The Deutscher Bund Canada in Saskatchewan,' *Saskatchewan History* 31/2 (Spring 1978): 42. Estimates of the National Bund membership varied between the one thousand members mentioned in the *Auslands Organization* ... (17) and J.F. Wagner's two thousand.
43 Quoted in Offenbeck, 73
44 Wagner, *Brothers beyond the Sea,* 68–72
45 Ibid., 72
46 Lehmann, 280
47 *Winnipeg Free Press,* 18 January 1939
48 J.F. Wagner, 'Heim ins Reich: The Story of Loon River's Nazis,' *Saskatchewan History* 29/2 (Spring 1976): 47
49 Ibid., 48–9, and *Winnipeg Free Press,* 22 July 1939
50 Quoted in Wagner, *Brothers beyond the Sea,* 67
51 Quoted in Offenbeck, 88
52 Wagner, *Brothers beyond the Sea,* 73
53 *The Nazi Party in Canada.* Background material on Straubinger is also available in Wagner, *Brothers beyond the Sea,* 86–8.
54 *Deutsche Zeitung für Canada,* 8 June 1938
55 *Toronto Daily Star,* 28 August 1939
56 Ibid.
57 *Winnipeg Tribune,* 15 June 1940
58 J.F. Wagner, *Brothers beyond the Sea,* 93

59 *Winnipeg Tribune,* 24 January 1939
60 Ibid.
61 Lehmann, 281
62 Ibid., 278; Wagner, *Brothers beyond the Sea,* 101
63 Offenbeck, 89
64 Leibbrandt, 263
65 Quoted is Gerhard P. Bassler, 'Heinz Lehmann and German-Canadian History,' Introduction to Lehmann, xxxii
66 Lehmann, 281
67 Cited in Leibbrandt, 265
68 Ibid.
69 Lehmann, 281
70 Ibid.
71 Ibid., 281–2
72 Wagner, *Brothers beyond the Sea,* 97
73 Ibid.
74 *Winnipeg Free Press,* 12 July 1938
75 *The Auslands Organization ...,* 15–16
76 Leibbrandt, 267
77 Wagner, *Brothers beyond the Sea,* 82
78 Frank Epp, *Mennonite Exodus* (Altona: D.W. Friesen and Sons 1962), 322
79 *The Nazi Party in Canada,* 52
80 Ibid., 50
81 Ibid., 51
82 Ibid., 50
83 Ibid.
84 Wagner, *Brothers beyond the Sea,* 33
85 *The Nazi Party in Canada,* 51
86 *Winnipeg Free Press,* 30 January 1939
87 Ibid., 7 January 1939
88 Quoted in Wagner, *Brothers beyond the Sea,* 43
89 Ibid.
90 *Vancouver Sun,* 11 March 1935
91 Ibid.
92 Quoted in Offenbeck, 106
93 Ibid., 60

94 Quoted in Offenbeck, 85
95 J.F. Wagner, *Brothers beyond the Sea,* 38
96 *Vancouver Sun,* 11 March 1935
97 See Lehmann, 288–93; Watson Kirkconnell, *Canada, Europe and Hitler* (Toronto: Oxford University Press 1939), 118–36; Frank H. Epp, 'An Analysis of Germanism and National Socialism in the Immigrant Newspapers of a Canadian Minority Group, the Mennonites in the 1930s,' PhD thesis, University of Minnesota, 1965; J.F. Wagner, 'Transferred Crisis: German Volkish Thought among Russian Mennonite Immigrants to Western Canada,' Canadian Review of Studies in Nationalism 1 (1974): 202–20; Wagner, *Brothers beyond the Sea,* 102–17.
98 Epp, *Mennonite Exodus,* 321
99 Frank H. Epp, *Mennonites of Canada 1920–1940* (Toronto: Macmillan of Canada, 1982), 554. While the papers were, overall, sympathetic to the New Germany, they were by no means uniformly so, or devoid of critical assessments. Mennonite opinion, according to Kirkconnell (133), was, to a degree, 'in turmoil.' Identification with the Third Reich, as opposed to identification with German culture or race, according to Epp, was 'vocalized by a minority of Mennonites,' though a 'loud and influential one.' Mennonite political action was inhibited by their adherence to a doctrine of non-resistance.
100 *The Nazi Party in Canada,* 40–1; *The Auslands Organization ...,* 23–4; Offenbeck, 65–70; Wagner, *Brothers beyond the Sea,* 82–5
101 Lehmann, 289
102 *Deutsche Zeitung,* 3 July 1935, quoted in Offenbeck, 68
103 Quoted in Wagner, *Brothers beyond the Sea,* 83
104 L. Rosenberg to S.M. Selchen, 3 January 1935 in File: Anti-defamation material, 1934–1937, No. 42, Box – DA1 Canadian Jewish Congress Archives, Montreal
105 Offenbeck, 70
106 Ibid.
107 *Der Courier,* 5 April 1933, quoted in Offenbeck 69
108 *Regina Leader Post,* 2 January 1935
109 Ibid.
110 *Winnipeg Tribune,* 13 January 1939

111 Ibid., 11 January 1939, 20 June 1940; Offenbeck, 70–1; *The Nazi Party in Canada*, 37–40

112 *Winnipeg Tribune*, 12 January 1939. Neufeld was allowed to withdraw from the case after submitting a written apology to the plaintiff and a promise never to repeat any action complained of. Early in 1939, following heated disclosures in the *Winnipeg Tribune*, arrangements were made for the transfer of the *Deutsch Zeitung*'s printing to the new plant of the Gutenberg Publishing Company. As evidence that he was no 'Jew hater,' Neufeld claimed his firm printed, among fifteen papers, two 'Jewish missionary papers': *Winnipeg Tribune*, 14 January 1939

113 Toronto *Globe and Mail*, 27 November 1937

114 *The Nazi Party in Canada*, 36

115 Offenbeck, 112

116 *The Nazi Party in Canada*, 40

117 *Winnipeg Tribune*, 13 January 1939

118 Wagner, *Brothers beyond the Sea*, 94

119 Ibid., 102

120 *Deutsche Zeitung*, 8 April 1939, quoted in Leibbrandt, 266

121 The German-Canadian League summed up the struggle as follows: 'There are in Canada 500,000 people of German origin. The membership of Nazi organizations is approximately 2,000 and that of the anti-Nazi league about 1,500. Nearly 80,000 belong to German clubs, 300,000 are affiliated with German churches. Thus we have the following situation: 1,500 struggle against 2,000 for the domination of a half million Germans.' The league organizers admitted it was 'a hard task to organize Germans into anti-Nazi organizations because some had relatives in Germany, other wanted to go back as visitors, and again other did not want to oppose any German government': German Canadian League, *German-Canadians versus Nazis,* undated pamphlet, Montreal Division.

122 Leibbrandt, 266

123 Report of F.J. Mead to Commissioner, RCMP, 2 May 1938, re: National Social Christian Party, RCMP Security Service Records

124 Wagner, *Brothers beyond the Sea*, 77

125 C.D. LaNauze to Commissioner, RCMP, Ottawa, 27 May 1939, re: Deutsche Zeitung für Kanada, RCMP Security Service Records

CHAPTER 10: *The Reckoning*

1 *Winnipeg Tribune*, 4 March 1938
2 17 June 1938
3 *Canadian Jewish Chronicle*, 17 June 1938
4 *Montreal Gazette*, 3 July 1938
5 Report of M. Black, 7 July 1938, re: National Unity Party – Mass meeting held in Massey Hall, Toronto, 4 July 1938, RCMP Security Service Records, Canadian Security Intelligence Service
6 *Time*, 18 July 1938, 19
7 *Toronto Daily Star*, 4 July 1938; Toronto *Globe and Mail*, 2 August 1938
8 *Canadian Jewish Chronicle*, 8 July 1938
9 *Winnipeg Tribune*, 3 March 1938
10 Quoted in Lita-Rose Betcherman, *The Swastika and the Maple Leaf* (Toronto: Fitzhenry and Whiteside 1975), 144
11 *Canadian Jewish Chronicle*, 5 July 1940
12 Ibid., 4 August 1939; *Montreal Gazette*, 3 and 4 August 1939
13 *Montreal Gazette*, 25 March 1938
14 *Canadian Jewish Chronicle*, 5 July 1940
15 Quoted in the Toronto *Globe and Mail*, 5 June 1940
16 *Winnipeg Free Press*, 22 April 1939
17 *Canadian Jewish Chronicle*, 28 October 1938. In response to a question describing *L'Illustration Nouvelle* as his newspaper, Duplessis stated that it was 'not my paper, nor the paper of the Government.' Arcand, he insisted, was hired as editor only because the owners – Eugene Berthiaume of *La Presse* and Lucien Dansereau – 'had much difficulty in getting a decent editor' because 'no responsible person would take the position.'
18 *Canadian Jewish Chronicle*, 20 January 1939
19 Ibid., 5 May 1939
20 Ibid.
21 'The Canadian Island Nazis Tried to Grab,' *Saturday Night* 67/2 (8 March 1952): 8
22 The *Tribune* urged the government, on 10 June 1938, to invoke section 99 of the Criminal Code against 'shirted parties' in Canada. Section 99 read: 'The Governor-in-Council is authorized from time to time to prohibit assemblies without lawful authority, of persons for the purpose of training or drilling themselves or of being

trained and drilled to the use of arms, or for the purpose of practising military exercises, movements or evolution, and to prohibit persons when assembled for any other purpose from so training or drilling themselves or being trained or drilled.'

23 Frederick Edwards, 'Fascism in Canada,' *Maclean's*, 15 April and 1 May 1938

24 See, for example, Willson Woodside, 'Nazi Germany's Growing Interest in Canada,' *Saturday Night*, 27 August 1938.

25 Vol. 90, No. 4 (October 1938)

26 Ibid., 26

27 *Winnipeg Free Press*, 24 June 1939

28 *Saskatoon Star-Phoenix*, 22 June 1939

29 *Toronto Daily Star*, 14 April 1939

30 Ibid.

31 *Montreal Star*, 7 February 1938

32 Jonathan F. Wagner, *Brothers beyond the Sea: National Socialism in Canada* (Waterloo: Wilfrid Laurier Press 1981), 124

33 John Offenbeck, 'The Nazi Movement and German Canadians,' MA thesis, University of Western Ontario, 1970, 151–2

34 Toronto *Globe and Mail*, 26 and 27 May 1938; *Newsweek*, 6 June 1938, 17; Offenbeck, 41–2; Wagner, *Brothers beyond the Sea*, 123–4. The German government was interested in Anticosti for resource supply, if not strategic reasons, and negotiations were under way between a Dutch-German company and the owner – the Consolidated Paper Corporation – for its purchase. A team of German 'technicians' visited the island in December 1937. The 'Anticosti scare' and the subsequent assertion of the Canadian government's interest – strategic and economic – destroyed any prospect of the island's sale. According to Willson Woodside (2), Gerhardt applied for, and obtained, Canadian citizenship in November 1937, and thereafter severed his ties with Nazi organizations in Canada.

35 According to C.W. Harvison, *The Horsemen* (Toronto: McClelland & Stewart 1986), 86, the RCMP recognized, as early as 1936, that 'budding Nazi, Fascist and Canadian Fascist groups' posed an even greater and more imminent threat than the communists. 'To meet this problem,' according to Harvison, 'special branch sections across Canada were increased; administrative and coordinating staffs at headquarters were strengthened; contacts and liaisons were

established with intelligence agencies in the United Kingdom and the United States; training courses were set up in Canada; and selected members were sent abroad for specialized training.

'By 1938, the Force had successfully penetrated the Nazi, Fascist, and Canadian Fascist parties to the point where officials, memberships and many of their plans were known. Copies of instructions and planning programs were reaching the Special Branches almost as quickly as they were being readied by the leaders of the espionage and subversive groups. Indeed, in many instances, the Special Branch was aware of the plans of the Fascists and Nazis before detailed instructions had been drawn up by their leaders.'

36 Robert H. Keyserlinck, 'The Canadian Government's Attitude towards Germans and German-Canadians in World War II,' *Canadian Ethnic Studies* 16/1 (1984): 19
37 J.F. MacNeill, Memorandum: For the Prime Minister's Office re: Internal Security – measures taken on Outbreak of War, 2 December 1939, 1–3, King Papers, MG26, J-1, Vol. 273; Robert H. Keyserlinck, 'Agents within the Gates: The Search for Nazi Subversives in Canada during World War II,' *Canadian Historical Review* 66/2 (June 1985): 225
38 MacNeill, 5
39 Ibid.
40 N.A. Robertson, 'Plans for the Detention of Enemy aliens and Certain Naturalized Canadians in the event of War,' 7 September 1939, 4 RG25, G1, Vol. 164, File 855-D
41 Memo: N.A. Robertson to the Honourable Ernest Lapointe, 3 September 1939, RG13, C1, Vol. 965, Reel 5, Department of Justice, Public Archives of Canada
42 MacNeill, 11
43 Keyserlinck, 229
44 See *Winnipeg Tribune*, 17, 22, 24, 26, 27 June 1940
45 W.J. Turnbull, Memorandum for the Prime Minister: Re: The Fifth Column Agitation, King Papers, MG 26, J-4, Vol. 372, File 393, 27 May 1940, 1
46 Keyserlinck, ' "Agents within the Gates," ' 235; J. Ciccocelli, 'The Innocuous Enemy Alien: Italians in Canadian during World War II,' MA thesis, University of Western Ontario, 1977, 48

47 Keyserlinck, ' "Agents within the Gates," ' 234. By the summer of 1941, the number of Germans and German Canadians arrested reached 786, of whom 143 had already been released. The number of arrests eventually reached 840, virtually one-tenth of the 8,500 German and Austrian enemy aliens detained in the First World War: Wagner, 134.

48 Ciccocelli, 56–60. According to Ciccocelli (62–3), names 'had been provided to the authorities by employees of the Italian Consulate and high ranking members of the Italian-Canadian Associations, who, for either monetary reward or promises of immunity from reprisals, singled out those individuals which they felt harbored affinities for the Mussolini regime.' By March 1941, 558 Italians had been interned.

49 P.C. 2527, 12 June 1940 in King Papers, MG 26, J-4, Vol. 372, File 39-3

50 *Canadian Jewish Chronicle*, 5 July 1940

51 See, for example, *Montreal Star, Montreal Gazette*, 19 and 20 June 1940

52 *Montreal Star*, 5 June 1940; *New York Times*, 31 May 1940. Section 39 and 39-A made it an offence 'for any person or persons to spread reports or make statements designed or likely to cause disaffection to His Majesty or to interfere in any way with the success of His Majesty's forces or to prejudice their security or training or to prejudice the safety of the state or prosecution of the war.'

53 *New York Times*, 31 May 1940

54 *Montreal Gazette*, 22 June 1940

55 Ibid.

56 Ciccocelli, 177

57 Wagner, 138

58 *Newsweek*, 24 November 1947, 44; *Time*, 8 December 1947; *Montreal Gazette*, 22 and 24 February 1947; W.E. Greening, 'Adrien Arcand Rides Again,' *The Canadian Jewish Forum* 13/4 (Summer 1955): 207–12. Arcand's post-war political group was known as *L'Unité Nationale.* Arcand contested the 1949 federal election in the riding of Richelieu–Verchères and picked up 5,590 votes; four years later, in a second unsuccessful attempt in the rural Berthier–Maskinogé–Delanaudière constituency, he picked up more than seven thousand votes.

Index

DATE DUE
